MAINSTREAMING HANDICAPPED CHILDREN: Outcomes, Controversies, and New Directions

MAINSTREAMING HANDICAPPED CHILDREN: Outcomes, Controversies, and New Directions

88-1019

Edited By

C. JULIUS MEISEL
University of Delaware

LEA LAWRENCE ERLBAUM ASSOCIATES, PUBLISHERS
1986 Hillsdale, New Jersey London

Lawrence Erlbaum Associates, Inc., Publishers
365 Broadway
Hillsdale, New Jersey 07642

Library of Congress Cataloging in Publication Data
Main entry under title:

Mainstreaming handicapped children.

Rev. proceedings of a symposium held at the University of Delaware, Apr. 6–7, 1984.
Bibliography: p.
Includes index.
1. Handicapped children—Education—United States—Congresses. 2. Mainstreaming in education—United States—Congresses. I. Meisel, C. Julius.
LC4031.M283 1985 371.9′046′0973 85-1553
ISBN 0-89859-582-7

Printed in the United States of America
10 9 8 7 6 5 4 3 2

Contents

Contributors

Dr. John Bak
Center for Human Services
University of Massachusetts
Boston, MA 02125

Dr. Jay Gottlieb
New York University
School of Education
1032 Shimkin Hall, Washington Square
New York, NY 10003

Dr. Barbara Gottlieb
Educational Development
Herbert H. Lehman College
Bronx, NY 10468

Dr. Frank Gresham
Department of Psychology
Louisiana State University
Baton Rouge, LA 70803

Dr. Michael Guralnick
The Nisonger Center
Ohio State University
1580 Cannon Drive
Columbus, OH 43210

Dr. Nancy Hall
Department of Psychology
Yale University
Box 11A Yale Station
New Haven, CT 06520

Dr. Marilyn Hoyson
Western Psychiatric Institute & Clinic
University of Pittsburgh School of Medicine
3811 O'Hara Street
Pittsburgh, PA 15261

Dr. Bonnie Jamieson
Western Psychiatric Institute & Clinic
University of Pittsburgh School of Medicine
3811 O'Hara Street
Pittsburgh, PA 15261

Dr. David Johnson
202 Pattee Hall
University of Minnesota
150 Pillsbury Drive, S.E.
Minneapolis, MN 55455

Dr. Roger Johnson
202 Pattee Hall
University of Minnesota
150 Pillsbury Drive, S.E.
Minneapolis, MN 55455

Dr. Linda Levy
School of Psychology
New York University
New York, NY 10003

Ms. Joan Lieber
Department of Special Education
University of California
Santa Barbara, CA 93106

Dr. C. Julius Meisel
University of Delaware
Department of Educational Studies
Newark, DE 19716

Dr. Susan Munson
University of Georgia
Exceptional Education Division
Aderhold Hall
Athens, GA 30602

Dr. Frank Murray
113 Willard Building
University of Delaware
Newark, DE 19716

Dr. Charles Peck
College of Education
Washington State University
Pullman, WA 91168

Dr. John Salvia
Division of Special Education
Pennsylvania State University
State College, PA 16801

Dr. Melvyn Semmel
Department of Special Education
University of California
Santa Barbara, CA 93106

Dr. Gary Siperstein
Center for Human Services
University of Massachusetts
Boston, MA 02125

Dr. Philip Strain
Western Psychiatric Institute & Clinic
University of Pittsburgh School of Medicine
3811 O'Hara Street
Pittsburgh, PA 15261

Dr. Pamela Winton
2802 Legion Avenue
Durham, NC 27707

Dr. Mark Wolraich
University Hospital School
University of Iowa
Iowa City, IA 52242

Dr. Roland Yoshida
Fordham University
113 W. 60th Street
New York, NY 10023

Professor Edward Zigler
Department of Psychology
Yale University
Box 11A Yale Station
New Haven, CT 06520

Foreword

"Mainstreaming the Handicapped" was the title of the ninth College of Education symposium at the University of Delaware. In previous years participants had taken up such topics as "Theories of Instruction," "The Psychological Prerequisites of Reading," "Desegregation in Delaware," "Evaluation Techniques," "Ethnography," "Infant Communication," "Vouchers and Tax Credit Schemes," and "The Case for Public Education."

It was once said of Rousseau that the only element of consistency in his writings was that he wrote them; and the only common theme in our symposia has been that each topic sufficiently interested our faculty and students to organize an annual symposium on the topic.

The climate at Delaware is hospitable to the concept of mainstreaming, both as a political and as an intellectual ideal. Nearly half a decade ago the university merged its regular and special education teacher education programs into one certification program. This was done on the logic, as Finn and Resnick point out in the April 1984 issue of the *Educational Researcher*, that the features of instruction that improve learning among those children likely to be labled EMR, perhaps even diagnosed that way, are features that can be implemented productively in a variety of educational settings to the benefit of a wide spectrum of other groups of children.

The research of the last decade after the House and Senate overrode, by margins of 404 to 7 and 87 to 7, President Ford's veto of the Education of All Handicapped Children Act (PL 94–142), continues to confirm the underlying logic of mainstreaming as an educational policy. This research is reviewed in this book, which is based on the revised proceedings of a symposium, held at the University of Delaware on April 6–7, 1984.

The symposium, sponsored by the College of Education of the University of Delaware, was funded by the Committee on Interdisciplinary Research in Education, which operates under a grant from the UNIDEL Foundation. Special acknowledgment is given to Dr. Julius Meisel, editor of this volume, for his leadership in organizing and managing the symposium.

Frank B. Murray
Dean and H. Rodney Sharp Professor

Preface

Mainstreaming is now entering its second decade as an officially sanctioned ideal in the American school system. When the idea was first seriously proposed in the late 1960s, it seemed to many to be a contradiction in terms. Segregation had always been a sine qua non of special education. Since it was often assumed that instruction of academically handicapped children required that they be given a specially designed curriculum administered by a specially trained teacher who used esoteric teaching techniques, it followed that such instruction would have to be delivered in a separate classroom. The logic was persuasive, and it sustained a presumption in favor of the value of special classes that lasted for some time without the benefit of clear cut empirical validation.

The presumption may have continued for an even longer time had not special education begun, in the late 1950s, to seek its clientele among the large pool of academic underachievers that existed at the time. This population had always been around; it seems to have been built into the fabric of compulsory education in the United States. By the early 1960s, however, a combination of rising educational standards, widespread use of norm-referenced standardized tests, and escalating school enrollments caused the population of underachievers to swell to the point of attaining national scandal status.

The message of the special educator was simple. Many academic underachievers were in fact suffering from "hidden" handicaps. Though often concealed from the untrained eye of regular educators, such handicaps were easily detected by specially trained diagnosticians using specially designed tests. The secret often lay in an artful reading of the numbers.

The message found a receptive audience among administrators, who were among the first in history to have to face the problems of mass public education on a truly grand scale. By 1970, special education had begun to look like a second education system nearly everywhere in the country. It had its own bureaucracies at the federal, state, and local levels, its own professional organizations and journals, and its own teachers trained in separate university departments of special education. The growing need for separate classroom space was met in many instances by buildings abandoned during the great school building of the 1960s.

Ironically, the hey day of segregated special education occurred just at that point in history when we, as a society, were becoming more sensitive to the social and legal implications of segregation in all its forms. The courts of the day were particularly aggressive in seeking out and condemning bureaucratic practices that abridged individual liberties without sufficient justification. The inability of special education to justify its separatist ways would soon become its Achilles Heel. By 1966, the principle of least restrictive placement had already been formulated in a federal court decision. Although the decision came out of a case involving institutional placement, it was only a matter of time before it became apparent that the principle applied as well to the placement of handicapped children in segregated classes.

There were a few individuals within special education who, even before 1970, spoke out against the practice of labeling and segregating academic underachievers, but they were largely ignored. Eventually, forces within the field began to fuel the change process. The philosophy of normalization, which originated in Europe, gained acceptance among professionals in this country during the early 1970s. In the opening chapter of this volume, Edward Zigler and Nancy Hall discuss in detail the relationship between normalization and the mainstreaming movement. Zigler and Hall critically examine the impact that the normalization ideal and its various practical applications have had on the daily lives of handicapped individuals.

Despite the inevitability of mainstreaming, its implementation has not always been smooth. The Education of All Handicapped Children Act of 1975 stated that, *to the extent possible*, handicapped children should be educated with nonhandicapped peers. The legislators who framed the act wisely left to educators the task of determining the limits of the possible. This, however, has not turned out to be an easy task, and the past 10 years have witnessed both confusion and some painful trial and error learning.

There has been no clear consensus on what the goals of mainstreaming should be. This point is made forcefully by Roland Yoshida in Chapter 2 of this volume. He critically reviews the various goals that have been proposed for mainstreaming programs and suggests some directions for future evaluation research efforts.

The remainder of this volume is devoted to an in depth review of what we have learned about mainstreaming in the past 10 years. Mainstreaming has attracted many researchers from a variety of disciplines and different theoretical points of view, and they have brought to bear on its problems a rich and varied methodology. This is especially apparent in Part II. The chapters in this section report on and discuss research bearing, either directly or indirectly, on the predicted outcomes of mainstreaming.

In Chapter 3, Michael Guralnick sets forth a series of propositions that are derived from general developmental principles and that predict overall positive outcomes for preschool mainstreaming programs. Guralnick supports these propositions with references to a large body of existing research on preschool mainstreaming. In Chapter 4, Frank Murray also draws upon developmental principles to predict positive cognitive outcomes for developmentally delayed children who are mainstreamed. He reviews his own research and that of others. He shows that, under certain conditions, cognitively immature children make predictable gains on tasks that require interaction with children who are performing at expected cognitive levels.

The remaining chapters in Part II report the results of field-based research done with school-age academically handicapped children. In Chapter 5, Gary Siperstein and John Bak review existing and new literature that deals with the reasons why nonhandicapped children tend to have negative attitudes toward their mentally retarded peers. Siperstein and Bak also present an interactive model that will serve not only to help interpret previous research, but also to guide future research. In Chapter 6, Julius Meisel reports in detail on how mainstreaming is likely to affect the social comparison behavior of academically handicapped children. Using methods designed to study social comparison in classroom environments, Meisel has produced evidence suggesting that, when given a choice, handicapped children prefer to compare themselves with classmates who perform at a higher level both socially and academically. In Chapter 7, Jay Gottlieb, Linda Levy, and Barbara Gottlieb report on a study designed to determine whether or not the play behavior of mainstreamed learning disabled (LD) children differs in any important way from that of nonhandicapped children, and whether those differences are related to sociometric status. Gottlieb and colleagues found that, although LD children tend to be nominated as play companions less often than nonhandicapped classmates, direct observation on the playground revealed few quantitative or qualitative differences in the play behavior of the two groups.

Part III deals with mainstreaming's consequences for those persons who perform the adult roles involving education and care of handicapped children. In Chapter 8, John Salvia and Susan Munson argue that the attitudes of regular class teachers toward handicapped children have a great effect on the outcomes of mainstreaming programs. Their work contains a thorough review of the literature that supports this argument, as well as suggestions about what can be done to promote positive attitudes. In Chapter 9, Pamela Winton talks about how mainstreaming may produce stress for families of handicapped preschool children. Winton reviews the results of her own investigations into the causes of this stress, and identifies resources that are both available and needed to help families cope. In Chapter 10, Mark Wolraich discusses the impact that deinstitutionalization and mainstreaming have had on health professionals and their dealings with schools. Wolraich argues that these moments have resulted in changes in existing roles and creation of new roles, both of which have important implications for medical education programs.

The chapters in Part IV exemplify the leading edge of intervention research in mainstreaming, as well as current thinking about the future direction of both mainstreaming programs and mainstreaming research. The section opens with Chapter 11, a broad-based conceptual work by Melvyn Semmel, Joan Lieber, and Charles Peck, who call for a new framework within which to study special education environments and their effects. They argue that the practice of comparing effects across various administrative arrangements has led to over simplistic and often contradictory results, and they propose that we use instead empirically derived systems to classify and compare special education environments. In Chapter 12, Frank Gresham argues convincingly that unless mainstreaming programs include planned strategies to increase the social acceptability of handicapped students and to change negative attitudes toward them, mainstreaming in general is doomed to fail. Gresham cites literature from a variety of disciplines that supports his well articulated position.

In Chapter 13, David and Roger Johnson discuss the application of their cooperative learning model to mainstreaming programs. They review the results of a comprehensive series of studies that document the superiority of cooperative learning arrangements in maximizing several important outcomes among mainstreamed handicapped students. Finally, in Chapter 14, Phillip Strain, Bonnie Jamieson, and Marilyn Hoyson describe a comprehensive program for mainstreaming children with autistic and autistic-like characteristics. Their program incorporates a number of new and innovative ideas to maximize the social integration of children who by definition can be expected to exhibit pronounced deficits in social development.

I ORIGINS AND GOALS OF MAINSTREAMING

1 Mainstreaming and the Philosophy of Normalization

Edward Zigler, Nancy Hall
Yale University

In recent years there has been a major emphasis on the treatment and placement of the mildly retarded. It is this group that workers in the field have been particularly concerned about for the last 10 to 15 years, and about which we have become perhaps too optimistic. The predominant ideology in the United States today regarding this group concerns normalization, the theory being that workers in the field should strive to provide for the mentally retarded an experience that resembles as closely as possible the cultural norm.

Although at first glance this would seem to be an incontrovertible point of view, it has split and polarized the intellectual community concerned with mental retardation. Care must be taken that we do not adopt an all-or-nothing attitude towards normalization. There will always be a need for the institution, and there are a number of eminent workers who have shown us that there can be habitable and humanized institutions. Unfortunately, many of the forces at work, such as that represented by the judicial system, depict the issues surrounding normalization as win–lose, either–or choices, driving out the moderate middle ground position. Those who polarize the situation by promoting either normalization or institutionalization to the complete exclusion of the other do the situation and its complexity a grave injustice.

After more than a decade of promoting normalization it remains a basically ephemeral construct, backed by relatively little sound research. The characterization of normalization as "a banner in search of some data" (Zigler, 1976) is still a fair one. As yet we have no clearly articulated operational definition of normalization, with the result being that we are not able to set down clear guidelines for the formulation and implementation of social policies based on the normalization ideology (Zigler, 1985).

ORIGINS OF THE MAINSTREAMING MOVEMENT

One of the social policy manifestations of normalization that has been widely promulgated in the past decade is mainstreaming. Mainstreaming is usually viewed as an outgrowth of Public Law 94–142, the Education for All Handicapped Children Act of 1975, which provided the legislative leverage for handicapped children and their families to gain access to often-denied educational services. Under the protection of this law, these children have gained an inlet into a network of essential services, and their families have been supported in the desire for a voice in the education of their children.

Even though the term mainstreaming does not actually appear in the wording of the legislation, the administrators of institutions and school systems have typically interpreted the phrase "least restrictive alternative" to mean integrated classes. The authors concur with Gottlieb's charge (1981) that the least restrictive alternative is still unknown. What is the operation by which we define it? All too often, school systems, pressed by this legislation's failure to pay for the services it mandates, have been forced to equate "least restrictive" with least expensive (Zigler & Muenchow, 1979). Caught between a federal mandate and state and local budget cuts, school administrators may have little choice about the placement of handicapped children. In the long run, the law may even result in a failure by school systems to provide sufficient special classes. The use of high quality but expensive private services for handicapped children may also be severely curtailed if school systems cannot pay for them. One of the top priorities, when considering the merits of various settings—home, institution or group home, special class, private school, or regular classroom—must be to respect certain basic principles of development, the most crucial of these being the principle of continuity. We cannot, with impunity, continue to move the retarded about like cattle under the banner of normalization. The positive effects of any setting must be weighed against the possible damaging effects of a move.

Public Law 94–142 may have built-in flaws. Ironically, the very law that was designed to safeguard the options of handicapped children and their parents may, in the end, act to constrict their choices and result in disservice to the very children the legislators sought to help, by forcing schools to place them in programs that are not equipped to meet their needs. The normalization principle and the practice of mainstreaming may have deleterious effects on some children by denying them their right to be different.

The variability that is so essential to our understanding of handicapped individuals is ignored by these trends. Underlying the very idea of normalization is a push toward homogeneity, which is unfair to those children whose special needs may come to be viewed as unacceptable. We must face the fact that normalization can entail nonacceptance of an individual's differences. This attitude could prove to be damaging both to individual children and adults and to the progress of the field as a whole.

It will take more than a rewriting of social policy to bring about the changes in social attitude that are required here. Training is needed for the teachers affected by this mandate. More research is necessary to determine just how PL 94–142 is being implemented across the nation. Specific criteria for determining who should be mainstreamed, and to what extent, are still, after almost 10 years, conspicuous by their absence.

In the face of this relative lack of research and education on the most compassionate and efficacious implementation of mainstreaming, why has it been so widely championed and so heavily promoted? Is this widespread implementation justified? Gottlieb (1981) has reviewed in some detail the reasons behind the push toward the mainstreaming of handicapped children and, in examining the evidence in support of these reasons, has found them to be sorely lacking.

The first argument Gottlieb reviews claims to demonstrate the superiority of regular over special classrooms with regard to pupil achievement. Gottlieb's thorough search fails to uncover much evidence in favor of this argument, and suggests that a truly appropriate course for stimulating higher academic achievement in educable mentally retarded (EMR) children has still not been found. The authors feel it should be noted that, with very few exceptions, the studies that gave rise to the purported superiority of regular classroom placement (Kirk, 1964) were measures of cognitive ability, and excluded social competence indices.

A second concern of investigators in the 1960s and 1970s revolved around the stigma and the social isolation that were thought to be associated with placement in a special classroom. Mainstreaming, it was felt, would increase the level of acceptance of EMR children by their nonhandicapped peers. Gottlieb points to three areas of research that are relevant to this argument. First, he reports that the devaluing of retarded children by their peers is not as global as critics of the segregated classroom seem to feel, and that indeed, many EMR children are as well-accepted as nonretarded children. He then goes on to describe the results of work which shows that the social status of EMR children placed in regular classrooms can be improved. This is an area in which special programs for teachers would be useful. Where social isolation does exist, it is likely to be exacerbated by placement in a regular classroom, in which the handicapped child's behavioral differences take on an increased visibility through comparison with his classmates. In this case, mainstreaming may cause as many problems as it corrects.

A third force in the push towards mainstreaming was a direct outgrowth of the civil rights movement, on whose heels it followed. Many critics noted that classes for the handicapped contained a disproportionate percentage of minority students, so that a side effect of special class placement was often racial segregation. Gottlieb's data on this point indicate that this was indeed the case, but, regardless of the extent of mainstreaming, it continues to be true. Special classes are still racially imbalanced, and moving children to racially segregated regular classrooms does not alleviate the problem.

Finally, proponents of mainstreaming point to the value of individualized curriculum in a regular classroom. Again, the available data do not support this point, but suggest that there are few differences in teaching methods between regular and special classrooms. Gottlieb (1981) sums up this and his other arguments by saying:

> . . . mainstreaming evolved from a disenchantment with self-contained classes. The changes that occurred were entirely administrative. New educational techniques or approaches were not introduced. The main expectation was that EMR children would do no worse in mainstreamed classes than in self-contained classes (Semmel, 1979). The expectation was not that they would do better. To date, the expectation has been confirmed [p.124].

THE EFFECTS OF MAINSTREAMING

In examining some of the effects of mainstreaming that have been documented, the best that can be said about the body of data is that they are inconclusive and often contradictory. In addition to the possibility of increasing or decreasing social stigma, mainstreaming may have an effect on a number of other behavioral variables, such as expectancy of success, responsivity to social reinforcement, outerdirectedness or imitativeness, self-image and wariness of adults. Motivational factors such as these have the potential to impact on such cognitive and achievement measures as IQ score and academic performance, in addition to relating directly to social competence. There is little evidence that mainstreamed retarded children exhibit more socially competent behaviors with regard to these motivational variables than do nonmainstreamed retarded children. The one statement that can be made with certainty is that the effects of mainstreaming on the behavior of mildly retarded children are extremely complex (Caparulo & Zigler, 1983). One must consider the degree and definition of the mainstreaming in question, the social histories of the children, age, and gender, to name but a few of the variables that have been shown to account for variation in behavior. We cannot assume that mainstreaming is a simple variable that has a unidirectional effect on the children involved.

The variation in the effects of mainstreaming points out the fact that we *must* define the "appropriate education" that is guaranteed by the Education for All Handicapped Children Act. It is time to work on defining the criteria for the appropriateness of an educational program, to recognize the need for a differentiated approach to this problem and in doing so attend to the daily experiences of retarded children in a variety of settings.

EVALUATION OF MAINSTREAMING

One of the most important components of any program of services is evaluation, and mainstreaming represents no exception to this rule. Here again, objective and well-defined criteria are essential. The best evaluation of mainstreaming, which is yet to come, would look at adults who experienced a variety of mainstreamed and nonmainstreamed programs during their school years. How does classroom placement effect these individuals later in life? With either adults or children, it is clear that we cannot view cognitive measures, such as IQ, to be the most useful tool for evaluation, but should strive for a more global picture of optimal human development. Social competence must be our ultimate criterion for the evaluation of programs for the handicapped.

Consider the situation of familial retarded individuals in Sweden (Zigler, Balla & Hodapp, 1984). Sweden purports to have no retarded individuals in this category. In reality, the percentage of familial retarded in Sweden is the same as it is in the United States, but there they are not labeled as retarded. These children pass from grade to grade till adulthood. Following their graduation and entry into society, however, these individuals often find that, because they were not labeled as retarded, they were not able to benefit from the excellent special education programs that would have prepared them for competent functioning in an adult world. Many, in fact, return to the school system and ask to be labeled retarded and educated appropriately so that they can find employment. Care must be taken that we do not duplicate this system in the United States. We should be cautious that we do not mainstream handicapped children away from training programs that will enable them to become socially competent and independent adults.

AN ECOLOGICAL APPROACH

We are beyond the point at which we can cling to the simplistic notion of some model retarded individual for whom there is a single undisputable optimal placement. The time has come instead for us to adopt a more complex systems approach in which relevant subsystems are viewed as being in interaction. An ecological model, such as that defined by Bronfenbrenner (1979), would typify such a systems approach. But any global view of the retarded would minimally have to include the retarded individual, the family (regardless of whether the individual resides at home), the workers in any nonfamily residential setting, and teachers and administrative personnel responsible for the care and education of the individual.

Both family and nonfamily residential settings exist as part of a larger community. This system includes, as integral parts, the professionals and paraprofessionals who work on the problems of the mentally retarded in medicine, psychology, and other social services. Within this system there is tremendous complexity associated with the interaction of these different disciplines. There is another relevant plane of interface: The plane between the private or for profit and governmental and nonprofit sectors. The legal system at all levels is also inextricably bound up in how we view and treat the placement of our retarded citizens, and is a strong force behind the move towards an increasing degree of normalization and mainstreaming. Another facet of this system is represented by the media, which is charged with reporting accomplishments as well as failures, and can have an enormous impact on how the field is viewed by the general public.

In addition to attending to the complexity of their world, we must be mindful of the heterogeneity of retarded individuals. There is a wide range of behaviors in those whose IQs range from 0 to 70, and an equally wide variety of factors that impinge on these behaviors. It is essential that we appreciate fully the considerable variability that exists even among the severely and profoundly retarded, and it is because of this complexity that we cannot allow ourselves to be sanguine about simplistic views of the treatment of the retarded. The retarded individual may have exacerbating physical handicaps and medical problems. There may be accompanying emotional or behavioral problems, or a concurrent psychopathology. Even in the absence of relatively major complications such as these, we must take care not to ignore the effects of less controversial variables. The age of the retarded individual, for example, is an important determinant of problems and social reactions. The needs and the adaptation of retarded individuals change as the decades go by. For some time the field has been so child-centered that we have underinvestigated the needs of the retarded adult. The lifespan approach which has had such a positive impact on developmental psychology could be put to good use by workers in the mental retardation field.

Gender is another important variable that should be taken more seriously. Mental retardation and developmental disability do not swamp sex role effects. As we make progress in the field of mental retardation we still have not produced a major study concerning the intersect of mental retardation and gender. Recognizing that such variables affect the retarded with as much force as they affect any of us may require that we humanize both ourselves and our approach to retarded persons.

What seem to be such simple and noncontroversial variables as chronological age (CA) and mental age (MA) must also be investigated thoroughly. Those of us who champion a developmental approach to retardation would argue for comparison of subject groups matched for mental age; other theorists believe that chronological age is the more important matching criterion. Until this issue is settled, researchers must continue to examine the controversy from both sides.

Another characteristic of importance is the individual's level of retardation, which has been shown to affect the way in which others interact with the individual (Zigler, Balla, & Styfco, in press). Level of retardation is largely determined by yet another highly relevant variable, namely etiology. We have long argued that researchers must distinguish between those whose retardation stems from an organic dysfunction and those whose retardation may be defined as cultural–familial. Numerous behavioral differences are associated with this etiological distinction.

The deviance in the life of a mentally retarded individual is not limited to that accounted for by the retardation itself. Leaving aside questions of cause and effect, we must simply note that the retarded are more likely to have experienced a high degree of social deprivation than are those with higher IQs.

In recognizing the variability among retarded individuals and the various factors that impinge on their development and behavior, we must acknowledge the need for an interdisciplinary effort on their behalf. Pediatricians and geneticists, psychologists and psychiatrists, policy makers and educators alike must join forces in a cooperative effort if we are to achieve any real progress toward solving the problems of retardation.

We should be wary of those who tell us that we need not examine all alternatives and to proceed on the basis of common sense. This often turns out to be more common than sensible. It is also important to know and to bear in mind the history of this field if we are to escape Santayana's prophecy that in forgetting our history we would be forced to relive it. Many of our new ideas are actually old ideas. The treatment of the handicapped has progressed in cycles, dominated by trends that seem to have had an average lifespan of about a decade. Think back to Seguin (1866) with his emphasis on moral training, promising that normal development for the retarded would follow as a result of the right treatment. There sprang up at this time a proliferation of state schools, and the prevailing mood was one of boundless optimism. This effort did not, of course, make the retarded normal, and the pendulum swung in the opposite direction, toward a time of unwarranted pessimism. Then it was felt that nothing could be done for the retarded and they were warehoused in large institutions, often sterilized, and frequently, dehumanized. The current era of normalization represents another move toward optimism. Let us hope that our expectations for progress in this direction are tempered with realism and compassion.

THE ROLE OF PROFESSIONALS

The relatively new ideology concerning the education and placement of the handicapped makes new demands on professionals and policy makers in the field. How do we define the changing and often controversial roles of such workers? What are the tasks set before them? It was not so very long ago that professionals who worked with retarded individuals were virtually unanimous in their recommendation of institutionalization. Today the zeitgeist is such that parents who consider institutionalization are made to feel guilty and inadequate by professionals. It is troubling that we as scholars and professionals have become so intrusive in the lives of families of the retarded. Our role is not to tell families what decision to make, but to advise them on how best to make it—to give counsel, information, and support where they are needed. One humane and ethical model for such interaction has been proposed by Duff (1983), who speaks of the "moral community." In this model, the family is counseled best by those who know them and their situation best, i.e., their physician, religious counselor, or own family members. Professionals in a truly enlightened society would provide viable and available alternatives from which parents could choose in the best interest of their child.

In the best of all possible worlds, choices regarding placement and education of a handicapped person would be made according to such a model. Teachers and school administrators would also play a role in such decision making. But before this can become truly feasible we must educate our educators. We must also provide specially trained support personnel for these teachers. And we must recognize that such training, and the effective and human integration of handicapped children into mainstream settings, is going to be expensive.

Public Law 94–142 provides for less than 10% of the money needed to implement the changes it mandates. Compare this to, for example, Head Start, for which federal legislation provides 80% of the program's costs. It is clear that our nations's financial priorities have not kept pace with the needs of our handicapped citizens. It is still true, for instance, that economic incentives are provided to families choosing to institutionalize a severely handicapped child.

OUTLOOK FOR THE FUTURE

What lies in the future for normalization and its two most apparent manifestations, deinstitutionalization and mainstreaming? New directions will be affected by, among other things, the course taken by institutions. We have finally seen that the size of a treatment facility per se does not determine its social–psychological characteristics, and tells little about the daily experiences of its residents. The normalization adherents have not yet appreciated the variability of even large institutions. There is some value left in such places: In a comprehensive system of care for the retarded a large institution could serve as the hub of a network of services. For an example of such a system, examine the model developed at the Ellwyn Conference (Crissey, in press).

The future of the field of mental retardation is also being influenced in a constructive way by a strengthened commitment to interdisciplinary work. Only a cooperative effort involving physicians, psychologists, educators, social workers, sociologists, and public policy makers, to name but a few, can lead to real progress in formulating a comprehensive model to help the retarded. The significant improvements in the treatment of the retarded which we have witnessed over the past two decades have been a result of just such interdisciplinary work.

Further improvements depend on our recognition of the importance of continued sound research, and of ongoing and longitudinal evaluations of treatment programs.

The only safeguards we have against fads in treatment trends lie in the results of our research. Solid scientific underpinnings are essential to the development of policies and treatments that are both effective and humane. Quality programs and comprehensive research studies are often expensive and we must take care to make them as cost-effective as possible, tempering our rhetoric with financial realism. Advocacy for rational and compassionate budgetary priorities is essential, but at the same time we should be willing to listen and to compromise in our interactions with decision-makers. We must, as workers concerned with the retarded, support and guide our advocates and policy-makers by sharing with them our knowledge.

There is a new note of optimism among those concerned with the retarded. The heat of the once virulent debate over normalization has cooled in recent years, and a new sanity and synthesis has emerged. Although the principle of normalization is not without merit, we cannot allow ourselves to lose sight of long-term goals in our anxiousness to produce quick and visible results. The positive effects of normalization and its social policy manifestations will be many if we do not allow these policies to become empty slogans by ignoring sound developmental principles. Responsibility for protecting these principles and safeguarding choices for the treatment of the retarded rests with us all.

REFERENCES

Bronfenbrenner, U. (1979). *The ecology of human development: Experiments by nature and design.* Cambridge, MA: Harvard University Press.

Caparulo, B., & Zigler, E. (1983). The effects of mainstreaming on success expectancy and imitation in mildly retarded children. *Peabody Journal of Education, 60* (3), 85–98.

Crissey, M. A. (in press). *The residential institution: A community resource.* Baltimore: University Park Press.

Duff, R. (1983, February). Decision-making in extreme situations; Infant Doe and related matters. Paper presented at the Bush Luncheon in Child Development and Social Policy, Yale University, New Haven, CT.

Gottlieb, J. (1981). Mainstreaming: Fulfilling the promise? *American Journal of Mental Deficiency, 86*(2), 115–126

Kirk, S. A. (1964). Research in education. In H. A. Stevens & R. Heber (Eds.) *Mental retardation: A review of research.* Chicago: University of Chicago Press.

Public Law 94:142, Education for All Handicapped Children Act, November 29, 1975.

Seguin, E. (1866) Idiocy: And its treatment by the physiological method. New York: Wood.

Zigler, E. (1985). Handicapped children and their families. In E. Schopler & G. B. Mesibov (Eds.), *The effects of autism on the family.* New York: Plenum.

Zigler, E. Testimony presented to the Senate and House Appropriations Committee, March 1976.

Zigler, E., Balla, D., & Hodapp, R. (1984). On the definition and classification of mental retardation. *American Journal of Mental Deficiency, 89,* 215–230.

Zigler, E., Balla, D., & Styfco, S. (in press). New directions for the study of the effects of institutionalization on retarded persons. In *Proceedings of the NICHD Conference on Learning and Cognition in the Mentally Retarded,* Nashville, TN, September 16–18, 1980.
Zigler, E., & Muenchow, S. (1979). Mainstreaming: The proof is in the implementation. *American Psychologist, 34*(10), 993–996.

2 Setting Goals for Mainstream Programs

Roland Yoshida
Fordham University

Several articles have described the late 1960s as the period in which legal and professional pressures coalesced to legitimize the principle of mainstreaming (Gottlieb 1981; Meyers, MacMillan, & Yoshida 1980; Semmel, Gottlieb, & Robinson 1979). The movement toward mainstreaming grew out of research evidence that EMR students who were placed in segregated special classes did not seem to achieve any better than their peers who remained in regular classes (Johnson 1950; 1962; Kirk 1964). Although the popularly termed efficacy studies have been cited for conceptual as well as methodological problems (Guskin & Spicker 1968; MacMillan 1971), they nevertheless gave credibility to the argument that, because student performance in special classes was no better than in regular classes, students should not have the added burdens of stigma and separation from normal peers.

The *Zeitgeist* shifted from supporting special classes to one of the concept of normalization and mainstreaming. This concept presumes that regular class placements provide inherently better environments because the handicapped students are exposed more often to "normal" play and learning experiences, and have opportunities to learn socially appropriate behaviors through modeling or imitation. Thus, the handicapped student would be given a better chance to develop competencies for independent living in a mainstream program.

This exciting period of questioning and change resulted in Public Law 94–142, which legitimized mainstreaming. This concept became an accepted tenet in educational planning, programming, and in evaluation. The prevailing mood was optimism.

However, during this period of time, a closely related event occurred—the explosive debate over the relative contributions of heredity and environment to intelligence (Jensen 1969). While most observers focused on the nature/nuture issues, the context in which Jensen placed his article was forgotten, namely the insignificant results from the compensatory education program. Specifically, Jensen (1969) stated:

> The chief goal of compensatory education—to remedy the educational lag of disadvantaged children and thereby narrow the achievement gap between "minority" and "majority" pupils—has been utterly unrealized in any of the large compensatory educational programs that have been evaluated so far [p. 3].

Perhaps this statement was premature (Head Start programs had been legislated only a few years before) and too strong. However, questioning the efficacy of a policy and program is the primary function of evaluation. Although there are several evaluation models, most require the systematic assessment of instructional programs according to the extent to which they match clearly stated program goals and objectives (Maher & Bennett 1984). In reviewing the impact of Head Start, Zigler and Trickett (1978) concluded that, because the goals and objectives of Head Start were originally presented vaguely and then constantly changed throughout the life the program, it was difficult to perform outcome evaluations or to assess the impact of the program.

It has been 16 years since mainstreaming captured the attention of the profession, advocates, and courts, and 7 years since school systems had to comply with Public Law 94—142 and its provisions. The time is nearing when fundamental questions, such as those asked of Head Start, will be posed for mainstreaming. Are we in the same position as Head Start was when Jensen (1969) wrote? There have already been warning signs in the past few years that we may have a hard time making a positive case for mainstreaming. For example, Semmel, Gottlieb, and Robinson (1979) in their review of the mainstreaming literature concluded that there is little evidence that mainstreaming practices resulted in superior performance among handicapped children. Gottlieb (1981) raised the issue even more strongly when he entitled his article, "Mainstreaming: Fulfilling the Promise?"

How will we respond to this question? I chose to begin answering this question by determining what the literature can tell us about the nature of what Gottlieb terms "the Promise," or in evaluation terms, the goals of mainstreaming. Unless the personnel in each school district define these goals, they cannot determine whether their programs are consistent with these goals, cannot define criteria for determining the success of the program, and more importantly, cannot be held accountable for outcomes about which they are unaware. Other papers have raised this point (Jones, Gottlieb, Guskin, & Yoshida 1978; MacMillan & Semmel 1977); however, the literature is nearly nonexistent on demonstrating the efficacy of the concept or any program being offered in a school district.

Given the state of the literature and the amount of time mainstreaming has been policy, it is time to address what may seem to be an obvious yet incomplete task. In order to do so, I have reviewed three definitions of mainstreaming currently used in the literature and, for each definition, have derived goal statements from it, and presented examples from the literature of instructional programs that could be derived from the goal statements. Before presenting the analysis, I would like to state some caveats to this evaluation problem.

Three conditions must be considered in planning the evaluation of mainstream programs. First, given the methodological problems of the special class versus regular class efficacy studies, it seems futile to use this research/evaluation model in mainstreaming designs. By definition, students selected to return to less restrictive environments differ on the variables of IQ, achievement, and adjustment; just as the large scale study of decertified EMR students who were transitioned to regular classes as a result of the *Larry P.* case found (MacMillan, Meyers, & Yoshida, 1976; Meyers, MacMillan, & Yoshida 1980). Second, although placement in the least restrictive environment and mainstreaming are nationwide policies, their implementation varies considerably on a district, school, and even classroom basis (Semmel, Gottlieb, & Robinson 1979; Weatherly & Lipsky 1977), a legacy of our tradition of local control over education. It is not presently realistic to propose national goals and performance standards for mainstreaming, nor is it necessarily desirable. Finally, mainstreaming currently operates within the regular education setting; special education children are a minority and special education a junior partner (if even perceived as a partner) in the integration of these children. This organizational situation necessarily limits the extent to which a "mainstreaming program" can be institutionalized in the regular program. Attempting to make causal attributions of student performance to such "programs" may be difficult and frustrating. There are just too many alternative hypotheses to contend with. However, as we shall see, one definition (Wang 1981) proposes to place special students on an equal basis with nonhandicapped students in the regular classroom.

DEFINITIONS OF MAINSTREAMING AND DERIVED GOAL STATEMENTS

The Continuum of Service Definition

Responding to the least restrictive alternative provisions of Public Law 94–142, several authors have proposed classifying mainstreaming settings according to the extent to which handicapped students are educated in proximity to nonhandicapped learners (Chiba & Semmel 1977; Deno 1970; Lowenbraun & Affleck 1978). For example, Lowenbraun and Affleck (1978) describe placement and service options ranging from special class placement (where the child is primarily assigned to a self-contained classroom with some contact with nonhandicapped students for academic or non-academic activities during the school day) to services-to-teacher placement (in which the handicapped child is placed full time in the regular classroom and the teacher receives materials, and instructional advice to aid the implementation of an appropriate program).

The continuum of services scale represents not only types of settings, but also has been interpreted to mean that less restrictive placements are more desirable than more restrictive ones. The U.S. Department of Education Annual Reports to Congress (1981, 1982) have reported efforts by state and school districts to increase the movement of the handicapped to less restrictive environments. Thus, the goal of mainstreaming derived from this definition would be the transitioning of students to less restrictive placements and their continued maintenance in those settings.

However, focusing on placements may prove so satisfying to school district personnel that determining goals for the instructional program and the students themselves may become secondary or of no importance. For example, Meyers, MacMillan, and Yoshida (1975) found in their study of decertified EMR students that, although district personnel were most concerned about complying with the *Larry P.* consent decree and orders by the State Department of Education to decertify and transition students to regular class, personnel at neither the district nor building level knew whether the decertified students were achieving or adjusting socially in their new classrooms. Very few were given any transitional help; rarely were any instructional or social goals stated for these students. School district personnel were aware of student status only if the students were referred again for special class. Apparently, district personnel were satisfied that these students were succeeding if they merely remained in regular class.

Although this example may not reflect the exact situation currently confronting providers of service to mainstreamed children, it illustrates many of the conditions that occur when school policy changes and new directions have to be implemented. The policy directs school personnel to focus on placements and not program goals. Also, much of the research and evaluation work on mainstreaming used a two-group design of comparing special education students in special classes versus those who were in mainstreaming environments, such as regular class or resource rooms (for example, Iano, Ayers, Heller, McGettigan, & Walker 1974; Meyers, MacMillan, & Yoshida 1975; Prillaman 1981; Scholom, Schiff, Smerdlik, & Knight 1979; Schumaker, Wildgen, & Sherman 1982; Sheare 1978; Walker 1974). However, as Semmel et al., (1979) stated, "Available evidence suggests that amount of time in the regular classes, without consideration of quality of instruction, has little impact on academic or social outcomes" (p. 268). To help determine the quality of instruction, school personnel must know what goals direct instruction for individual and groups of mainstreamed children as well as the extent to which instruction is actually based on those goals. In short, the goal of merely placing children in less restrictive environments is a legally necessary, but not educationally sufficient, condition for student success.

The Kaufman et al. Definition

The continuum of service definition focuses primarily on the location and time handicapped learners spend in various placements. Moving from a unidimensional perspective on mainstreaming, Kaufman, Gottlieb, Agard and Kukic (1975) proposed the following definition:

> Mainstreaming refers to the temporal, instructional and social integration of eligible exceptional children with normal peers. It is based on an ongoing individually determined educational needs assessment requiring classification of responsibility for coordinated planning and programming by regular and special education administrative, instructional, and support personnel [pp. 40–41].

Although this definition has been cited for the shortcoming that very few, if any, mainstreaming programs can fulfill all of its features (MacMillan & Semmel 1977; Semmel, Gottlieb, & Robinson 1979), it does call attention to other crucial dimensions of a mainstreaming program, namely instructional and social integration of handicapped children with nonhandicapped peers.

Consistent with this definition, there are several studies that have attempted to test various treatments to increase the handicapped student's acceptance in the less restrictive environment (for example, Ballard, Corman, Gottlieb, & Kaufman 1977; Johnson & Johnson 1981; Knowles, Aufderheide, & McKenzie 1982; Madden & Slavin 1983; Vandell, Anderson, Ehrhardt, & Wilson 1982). Although these studies generally lasted less than a year and were experimental, several of them were successful in improving the social status of mainstreamed students or in increasing their interpersonal interactions with nonhandicapped peers (Ballard, et al., 1977; Johnson & Johnson 1981). Some have resulted in improvement in academic achievement as well (Knowles, Aufderheide, & McKenzie 1982; Madden & Slavin 1983). Such results should provide encouragement to school personnel. Programs do exist that, though limited in duration and impact on the total instructional program of mainstreamed children, help teachers begin to define an educational program based on more specific goals for such students.

In short, the goal of transition to a less restrictive environment is only the first step. Traditional program goals, such as achievement and social adjustment, should be stated for mainstreamed students. Contributers to this volume have expressed various goals for mainstreamed children that have been suggested by their own research work. For example, Guralnick stated his goals of the mainstreaming program at the pre-school level in such a way that they addressed the developmental needs of the handicapped student. Gresham's goals were more specific and reflected his concern that students develop social skills to adjust to new environments, such as the less restrictive classroom. Finally, Johnson and Johnson seem concerned that mainstreamed students learn how to cooperate and work well with peers. With literature that ties educational goals to programs becoming more available, school district personnel should gain the confidence to specify desired outcomes for mainstreamed students as well as for mainstreamed programs. We can begin to know what will be expected to be taught to children and what the school district believes it can accomplish with mainstreamed children.

Wang's Full Integration Definition

Wang (1981) presents the most ambitious definition for integrating mainstreamed students into the regular class environment. She states that ". . . the term mainstreaming is used here to mean an integration of regular and exceptional children in a school setting where all children share the same resources and opportunities for learning on a full-time basis" [p.196].

Wang has also reported on the only complete educational program designed to achieve the full integration of handicapped students. The program is entitled the Adaptive Learning Environments (ALEMS) and has five major components as follows: (a) a prescriptive learning curriculum, which is a series of highly structured and hierarchically organized lessons for academic skills development; (b) an exploratory learning component, which provides handicapped and nonhandicapped students with learning options apart from the district-wide prescribed learning curriculum; (c) a clearly stated classroom management system in which students are taught self-management skills so that they behave appropriately in the classroom; (d) a family involvement program; and (e) a team teaching structure. This program has been pilot tested with two teachers and an aide who worked with 45 handicapped and nonhandicapped students between 5 and 8 years. Preliminary results indicate that presenting self-management skills to these students, especially to those who are low-achieving, increases their on-task time and the number of tasks they complete.

Although a final assessment of this project has yet to be reported, it is instructive for our purposes that Wang has stated goals for both handicapped and nonhandicapped students, and has described a program to achieve those goals. Whether those goals are the ones other professionals would choose is another matter. At least, we have had the opportunity to know what accomplishments were attempted, which gives us a basis for making a judgment about the success of the program as well as the progress of mainstreamed students.

CONCLUSION

We are at another crossroad in the development of special education. Similar to Dunn (1968) for special classes and Jensen (1969) for compensatory programs, Gottlieb (1981) has raised the question of efficacy of mainstream programs. The current literature provides little support for the continued implementation of this policy. Although there are many sources of problems that attenuate the efforts to develop a supportive body of information, none seems more potent than our lack of commitment to or perception of the need to state goals and objectives for mainstreaming. Perhaps this is the nature of implementing and evaluating social policy in schools. As Trow (1970) stated:

> Whether advertised or not, it is important that innovation is commonly done for its sake and only secondarily for its outcomes. Because that fact reduces the relevance of systematic evaluation of innovation, it reduces the significance of the manifest functions of evaluation—to tell the innovator what he has achieved and how successfully—as compared with its chief latent function— to legitimize an innovation and contribute to its continuation and extension [pp. 291–292].

Thus, the best we can do is provide the numbers of children who are in particular environments, which tells us even less than the information Dunn (1968) used to question the special class.

I am concerned that under the pressure to implement social policy, we have forgotten the fundamental conditions for educating handicapped children in the mainstream. Every district needs to define a curriculum based on goals. Without goals, the evaluator is at a loss in designing an evaluation plan. More importantly, teachers have little direction about what to do with mainstreamed children except maintain them in whatever way possible in their classrooms. Finally, school personnel are unable to explain whether, in Gottlieb's terms: The promise has been achieved.

REFERENCES

Ballard, M., Corman, L., Gottlieb, J., & Kaufman, M. J. (1977). Improving the social status of mainstreamed retarded children. *Journal of Educational Psychology, 69,* 605–6ll.

Chiba, C., & Semmel, M. (1977). Due process and least restrictive alternative: New emphasis on parental participation. *Viewpoints, 53*, 17–29.

Deno, E. (1970). Special education as developmental capital. *Exceptional Children, 37*, 229–237.

Dunn, L.M. (1968). Special education for the mildly retarded—Is much of it justifiable? *Exceptional Children*, 35, 5–22.

Gottlieb, J. (1981). Mainstreaming: Fulfilling the promise? *American Journal of Mental Deficiency, 86*, 115–126.

Guskin, S., & Spicker, H. (1968). Educational research in mental retardation. In N. R. Ellis (Ed.), *International review of research in mental retardation* (Vol. 3) (pp. 217–278). New York: Academic Press.

Iano, R. P., Ayers, D., Heller, H. B., McGettigan, J. F., & Walker, V. S. (1974). Sociometric status of retarded children in an integrative program. *Exceptional Children, 40*. 267–271.

Jensen, A. R. (1969). How much can we boost IQ and scholastic achievements? *Harvard Educational Review, 39*, 1–123.

Johnson, G. O. (1950). A study of the social position of mentally handicapped children in the regular grades. *American Journal of Mental Deficiency, 55*, 60–89.

Johnson, G. O. (1962). Special education for the mentally handicapped: A paradox. *Exceptional Children, 19*, 62–n69.

Johnson, R. T., & Johnson, D. W. (1981). Building friendships between handicapped and nonhandicapped students: Effects of cooperative and individualistic instructions. *American Educational Research Journal, 18*, 415–423.

Jones, R. L., Gottlieb, J., Guskin, S., & Yoshida, R. K. (1978). Evaluating mainstreaming programs: Models, caveats, considerations, and guidelines. *Exceptional Children, 44*,588–601.

Kaufman, M. J., Gottlieb, J., Agard, J. A., & Kukic, M. (1975). Mainstreaming: Toward an explication of the construct. In E. L. Meyen, G. A., Vergason, & R. J. Whelan (Eds.), *Alternatives for teaching exceptional children* (pp. 35–54).Denver: Love.

Kirk, S. A. (1964). Research in education. In H. A. Stevens & R. Heber (Eds.), *Mental retardation* (pp. 57–99). Chicago: University of Chicago Press.

Knowles, C. J., Aufderheide, S. K., & McKenzie, T. (1982). Relationship of individualized teaching strategies to academic learning time for mainstreamed and nonhandicapped students. *Journal of Special Education, 16*, 449–456.

Lowenbraun, S., & Afflect, J. Q. (1978). *Least restrictive environment*. Seattle: University of Washington.

MacMillan, D. L. (1971). Special education for the mildly retarded: Servant or savant? *Focus on Exceptional Children, 2*, 1–11.

MacMillan, D. L., Meyers, C. E., & Yoshida, R. K. (1976). Regular class teachers' perceptions of transition programs for EMR students and their impact on the students. *Psychology in the Schools, 15*, 99–103.

MacMillan, D. L., & Semmel, M. I. (1977). Evaluation of mainstreaming programs. *Focus on Exceptional Children, 9*, 1–14.

Madden, N. A., & Slavin, R. E. (1983). Effects of cooperative learning on the social acceptance of mainstreamed academically handicapped students. *Journal of Special Education, 17*, 171–182.

Maher, C. A., & Bennett, R. E. (1984). *Planning and evaluating special education services*.Englewood Cliffs, NJ: Prentice-Hall.

Meyers, C. E., MacMillan, D. L., & Yoshida, R. K. (1975). *Correlates of success in transition of MR to regular class*. (Final Report, Grant OEG 0-73-5263) Pomona, CA: The Neuropsychiatric Institute/Pacific State Hospital Research Group.

Meyers, C. E., MacMillan, D. L., & Yoshida, R. K. (1980). Regular class placement of EMR students, from efficacy to mainstreaming: A review of issues and research (pp. 176–206). In J. Gottlieb (Ed.), *Educating mentally retarded persons in the mainstream*. Baltimore, MD: University Park Press.

Prillaman, D. (1981). Acceptance of learning disabled students in the mainstream environment: A failure to replicate. *Journal of Learning Disabilities, 14*, 344–346, 368.

Scholom, A., Schiff, G., Smerdlik, M. E., & Knight, T. (1979). A three year study of learning disabled children in mainstreamed and self-contained classes. *Education, 101*, 231–238.

Schumaker, J. B., Wildgen, J. S., & Sherman, J. A. (1982). *Journal of Learning Disabilities, 15*, 355–358.

Semmel, M. I., Gottlieb, J., & Robinson, N. M. (1979). Mainstreaming: Perspectives on educating handicapped children in the public schools. In D. Berliner (Ed.), *Review of research in education* (Vol. 7) (pp. 223–279). Washington, DC: American Educational Research Association.

Sheare, J. B. (1978). The impact of resource programs upon the self-concept and peer acceptance of learning disabled children. *Psychology in the Schools, 15*, 406–412.

Trow, M. (1970). Methodological problems in the evaluation of innovation. In M. C. Wittrock, & D. E. Wiley (Eds.), *The evaluation of instruction: Issues and problems* (pp. 289–305). New York: Holt.

U. S. Department of Education. (1981). *Third annual report to Congress on the implementation of Public Law 94–142: The Education for All Handicapped Children Act*. Washington, D. C.: U. S. Dept. of Education.

U. S. Department of Education. (1982). *Fourth annual report to Congress on the implementation of Public Law 94–142: The Education for All Handicapped Children Act*. Washington, D.C.: U. S. Dept. of Education.

Vandell, D. L., Anderson, L. D., Ehrhardt, G., & Wilson, K. S. (1982). Integrating hearing and deaf preschoolers: An attempt to enhance hearing children's interactions with deaf peers. *Child Development, 53*, 1354–1363.

Walker, V. S. (1974). The efficacy of the resource room for educating retarded children. *Exceptional Children, 40*, 288–289.

Wang, M. C. (1981). Mainstreaming exceptional children: Some instructional design and implementation considerations. *Elementary School Journal, 81*, 195–221.

Weatherley, R., & Lipsky, M. (1977). Street-level bureaucrats and institutional innovation: Implementing special-education reform. *Harvard Educational Review, 47*, 171–197.

Zigler, E., & Trickett, P. K. (1978). IQ, social competence, and evaluation of early childhood intervention programs. *American Psychologist, 33*, 789–798.

II MAINSTREAMING'S EFFECTS ON HANDICAPPED AND NONHANDICAPPED CHILDREN

3 The Application of Child Development Principles and Research to Preschool Mainstreaming

Michael J. Guralnick
The Ohio State University

The field of child development serves as one of the basic sciences for educational practice and, in the case of early childhood mainstreaming, has often been relied on to provide a developmentally based rationale for encouraging integrated or mainstreamed program models (Guralnick, 1978, 1982). Yet, despite the compelling nature of many developmental principles and corresponding research findings applied to early childhood mainstreaming, these principles and research have not often been examined closely in this context nor been subjected to the level of empirical scrutiny that should accompany important educational innovations.

In this chapter, three topics in the field of child development that are relevant to preschool mainstreaming are considered: (a) the social responsiveness of peers in mainstreamed settings; (b) the extent to which mainstreamed environments are rich, challenging, and stimulating; and (c) the degree to which broad developmental (and educational) principles apply to all children, handicapped or not. In considering these topics, specific expectations are derived from the literature on normal child development as well as corresponding developmental studies focusing on handicapped children. Because the three topics to be discussed tend to constitute the essence of a developmental/educational rationale for mainstreaming, these expectations are phrased as positive statements in order to facilitate discussion. Specifically, each proposition is phrased to suggest that as a result of the operation of certain principles and processes derived from the developmental literature, mainstreamed experiences should prove to be more beneficial to handicapped children than specialized or segregated settings. Each statement is then followed by an analysis of existing research on preschool mainstreaming, designed to evaluate whether or not these positive expectations can in fact be supported on an empirical basis.

RESPONSIVENESS OF PEERS

Responsiveness has been a central construct in developmental psychology over the years. A responsive caretaker (one who responds quickly and appropriately) has been associated with the promotion of social, cognitive, and language development in young children (Wachs & Gruen, 1982). Although the construct itself can take many complex forms and occasionally eludes sound scientific definitions (Cairns, 1979), many prominent theorists have suggested that responsiveness to a child reaching out to the social environment creates a generalized sense of efficacy for social interactions (Lewis & Goldberg, 1969). Moreover, the role and importance of responsiveness can be extended to relationships with one's peers (Guralnick, in press).

Consistent with the principle of stating the proposition in the positive form, it is proposed that *children in mainstreamed settings will be more responsive to the social bids and social interactions of handicapped children than in settings containing only handicapped children*. On the surface, this proposition seems eminently reasonable as the responsiveness of playmates is at a very high level in typical preschools. For example, for social bids relating to offering objects or rough and tumble play, children usually achieve a positive response at least 75% of the time (Tremblay, Strain, Hendrickson, & Shores, 1981). Although the degree of responsiveness will vary with the content and purpose of a social initiation, children attending preschools for normally developing children can certainly be characterized as being highly responsive. Overall, children tend to receive appropriate responses from peers on at least two thirds of the occasions, and interactions with other children eventually dominate most social situations (e.g., Garvey & Hogan, 1973; Holmberg, 1980; Wright, 1980).

In part, the success of child–child social interactions can be attributed to the fact that by the time young children are ready for preschool they have developed an extensive array of social and communicative skills that maximize their chances of achieving an appropriate response (Mueller, Bleir, Krakow, Hegedus, & Cournoyer, 1977; Guralnick, 1981a, in press). In addition, their partners become more adept respondents, as children learn to attend to and interpret social cues more readily and develop a set of shared "meaning factors" that promotes responsiveness (Garvey, 1975).

In contrast, developmental research on the peer relations of young handicapped children in specialized programs reveals that handicapped children often experience extraordinary difficulties in their efforts to establish relationships with their peers. This is especially the case for heterogeneous groups of developmentally delayed children (Crawley & Chan, 1982; Field, 1980; Guralnick &

Weinhouse 1984; Mindes, 1982). A recent study focusing on developmentally delayed children provides specific information with regard to the nature of these difficulties (Guralnick & Groom, in press). In this investigation, a heterogeneous but highly representative sample of 33 moderately and mildly delayed children (mean chronological age = 61.7 months; mean IQ = 59.2) typically found in specialized community early intervention programs were observed in free play situations over a 13-week period during the middle of the school year. Overall, the results revealed that these developmentally delayed children exhibited a much reduced level of social interaction. However, the inability of these children to obtain a satisfactory or appropriate response from peers to their initiations was most noticeable. In particular, the most frequent behavior that was an initiation consisted of efforts to gain the attention of their peers. Unfortunately, these attempts were successful only one-third of the time. Attempts to utilize peers as resources or to direct their activities were successful on slightly over 40% of the occasions. Comparisons with normally developing samples at equivalent developmental levels to the delayed group revealed that the delayed children were much less successful in their bids to obtain a response from peers (Doyle, Connolly, & Rivest, 1980; Wright, 1980).

Observations of other disability groups have yielded similar outcomes. For example, comparisons between sighted and blind preschool children in specialized settings indicated that not only are blind children less socially interactive, but their social bids are responded to in a significantly smaller proportion of instances than sighted children (Markovits & Strayer, 1982). Relatively high levels of ignoring a peer's verbal or physical social bids were noted for the blind group. Similarly, dyads of hearing-impaired children are less successful in achieving an appropriate response to their social bids than are dyads composed only of normally hearing children (Vandell & George, 1981).

Responsiveness in Mainstreamed Settings

The question of interest is, however, whether normally developing children are actually more responsive to the social bids and ongoing social interactions of handicapped children in mainstreamed as contrasted with specialized settings? Perhaps the most persuasive evidence to date that this is the case has been provided by a series of intervention and generalization studies by Strain working with autistic preschool children (1983, 1984a).

In one study (Strain, 1984a), comparisons between two integrated (one integrated setting included normally developing kindergarten children; the other a similar kindergarten group but with instructions to engage the autistic children in play) and two specialized settings (one specialized setting consisted of the children's usual classroom and classmates; the other consisted of new children with similar handicaps) with regard to positive social interactions were carried out. These interactions were comprised of both initiations and responses to those initiations and were obtained for each of six autistic children. Interestingly, even prior to the implementation of peer training procedures, Strain noted that the positive social interactions (including responses) of the autistic children were higher in integrated settings than in specialized settings. In fact, as might be expected, social interactions were virtually nonexistent in the two specialized settings he evaluated. Perhaps most striking, however, was the finding that when the six autistic children were trained through a peer confederate procedure in a separate experimental setting, marked improvements occurred when the children were placed in the two integrated settings compared to very modest increases in positive social interactions in either of the two segregated situations. Clearly, the peer training procedure had an effect, but only when the autistic child was in a more responsive social environment. When the normally developing children in the integrated setting were asked to initiate interactions with the autistic children and to engage them in play, the level of positive social interactions by the autistic children began to approximate those of their normally developing classmates. The quality of these interactions was likely to have differed from those of normally developing children, but the increased initiations and particularly the responses of the normally developing children appeared to have created a major impact on the peer related social behavior of the autistic children. This increased responsiveness, as well as other factors, may well create future opportunities for fostering the development of more sophisticated social skills.

These findings were directly supported in a more recent study by Strain (1984b) who first asked 68 normally developing preschool children enrolled in 10 different mainstreamed classes to identify "friends" through a standard sociometric procedure. The children were considered by the school system to be severely handicapped and primarily included those who were diagnosed as mentally retarded or autistic (IQ range = 25–55). Selecting from this population of handicapped and nonhandicapped children, 30 of the nonhandicapped children identified at least one handicapped child as well as other nonhandicapped children as "friends." Following this, direct observations of the social interactions of the nonhandicapped–handicapped pairs were obtained during various portions of the school day and these data were compared with observations of the same 30 nonhandicapped children as they interacted with one randomly selected nonhandicapped friend identified through the same sociometric procedure.

Although it is interesting to note that the handicapped children who were selected as friends were older and more cognitively advanced than those not selected, the most important finding for this discussion was that related to the responsiveness of the nonhandicapped children to social initiations. For initiations related to showing affection, organizing play, playing in a rough and tumble fashion, and sharing, the average probability of receiving a positive response from a nonhandicapped friend to an initiation of another nonhandicapped friend was .72. Similarly, the probability of receiving a response from the nonhandicapped friend to a social initiation by the handicapped friend was also high, at .69. Accordingly, although the overall frequency of initiations was much lower on the part of the handicapped children, their chances of being responded to positively by nonhandicapped friends were as high as those of other designated nonhandicapped children. It is not known whether handicapped friends of the handicapped children would have been just as responsive, but on the basis of other studies that have established the lower responsiveness of even mildly delayed preschool age children (e.g., Guralnick & Groom, in press), it is very unlikely that such high levels of responsiveness would be obtained. In fact, the handicapped children in the Strain study were far less responsive to the initiations of even nonhandicapped friends than were other nonhandicapped children (.74 vs .37).

A somewhat different picture emerges, however, when evaluations are carried out on handicapped children with different or less severe disabilities. For example, in a study of hearing-impaired children in a mainstreamed program, it was found that hearing-impaired partners were actually slightly more responsive than hearing partners when children were paired in play situations (Vandell & George, 1981).

A recent study of the communicative interactions and effectiveness of mildly delayed children in a mainstreamed setting also has a bearing on the issue of responsiveness (Guralnick & Paul-Brown, in press). Briefly, 32 children, ages 4 to 6 years (12 nonhandicapped, 7 mildly delayed, 5 moderately delayed, and 8 severely delayed children) were observed during free play interactions. In order to allow children to move about freely, yet record all of their social and communicative interactions, target children wore wireless microphones as part of a radiotelemetry system while being videotaped through a one-way mirror in an adjacent room. Their social exchanges were then transcribed and coded in terms of a wide range of communicative characteristics. In addition, the effectiveness of two types of communicative behaviors was analyzed: (a) behavior requests—statements related to obtaining goods or services from a peer, and (b) informational requests—questions relating to any topic. Although the study was much more comprehensive, the responsiveness issue closely corresponds to the general communicative effectiveness of the mildly delayed children in the sample as they interacted with other mildly delayed or nonhandicapped companions; therefore discussion is limited to those outcomes.

Accordingly, a companion's immediate response to either a request or question of the mildly delayed children was coded in terms of: (a) whether the request was in fact recognized as a behavior or informational request as indicated by an acknowledgment or other similar response; however, the request was not immediately complied with or responded to; (b) whether compliance or an appropriate response to the question occurred; and (c) whether the companion ignored the request or indicated that it lacked clarity. Focusing on the mildly delayed children when addressing other mildly delayed companions or normally developing children, responsiveness analyzed in this way did not differ between these two companion groups. Mildly delayed children obtained a clear response to their informational and behavior requests about 50% of the time from both nonhandicapped and mildly delayed companions. About 25% of the time, their companions recognized that a question or request was presented but did not comply or provide the information immediately. Accordingly, in this study, responsiveness by nonhandicapped or mildly delayed children to other mildly delayed children in free play did not seem to differ for these types of requests. It should be noted that the mildly delayed children were about one year older than their nonhandicapped classmates, and were highly similar in terms of developmental level.

From the relatively limited database that exists, it seems fair to state that the contention that children in mainstreamed settings are likely to be more responsive to the social initiations of handicapped children than children in specialized settings must be retained as viable. In particular, research indicates that an unusually low rate of social interactions exists in general on the part of handicapped children in specialized settings. This rate is much lower than what would be expected on the basis of their developmental levels. Research also indicates an equally low probability of success in achieving a response to a social bid. When settings are altered by the inclusion of nonhandicapped children, important and sometimes dramatic changes in responsiveness occur, especially when combined with explicit peer-mediated training activities. However, when the responsiveness of the partner in existing mainstreamed settings is analyzed, more equivocal results have been obtained. Although there is some suggestion that the more severely handicapped children may find nonhandicapped children far more responsive than other handicapped classmates, so many factors must be considered such as the type of handicap, whether training was provided, the chronological ages and developmental levels of the subjects, the nature of the programs they were involved in, and numerous others (Guralnick, 1981b), that it is only possible to speculate about this suggestion until more information is obtained.

A RICHER, CHALLENGING, AND MORE STIMULATING ENVIRONMENT

The second major principle suggests that from the perspective of handicapped children, *mainstreamed environments will be richer, more challenging, and more stimulating than specialized settings*. There is an important corollary proposition to this as well, suggesting that *as a result of these environmental challenges, development will proceed at a faster rate in mainstreamed settings*.

It is important to note that this principle extends beyond interactions with peers (responsiveness focused exclusively on peers in the previous section).[1]

[1]It is somewhat artificial to have separated out the topics of responsiveness and stimulation (initiations) in the natural flow of events. However, these are conceptually useful distinctions and numerous studies have established separate measures for each dimension.

Rather, it includes the overall social and environmental stimulation provided by teachers, explicit and implicit classroom demands, and of course the interactions by peers, primarily in the form of social and communicative initiations, overall activity level, and as potential models for handicapped children in the setting.

Intuitively, it seems reasonable to expect that mainstreamed environments would have more stimulating characteristics and a greater potential for promoting development than specialized settings. After all, classroom structure, the nature of teacher directed activities, and the availability of certain types of toys and materials can all influence the level of social interactions and perhaps even other aspects of development as well (Huston-Stein, Friedrich-Cofer, & Susman, 1977; Miller & Dyer, 1975; Rogers-Warren & Wedel, 1980; Shure, 1963; Vandenberg, 1981). From the perspective of teachers and classroom organization, it is reasonable to anticipate a faster pace, greater overall demands, and an orientation to development pitched at a higher and more intense level in mainstreamed than in specialized classes. Unfortunately, comparisons between specialized and mainstreamed programs along these dimensions have rarely been carried out. With the exception of a recent study by Bailey, Clifford, and Harms (1982), virtually no systematic data are available on this issue. Consequently, the remainder of this section is focused on peer interactions.

When stimulation from peers in mainstreamed settings is considered, a much stronger developmental framework to support expectations regarding the benefits of mainstreamed programs is available. For example, numerous laboratory and naturalistic studies have suggested that a young child's social and communicative interactions adjust to the level of one's companions (Cairns, 1979). Although there are certainly limits to the extent to which interaction patterns can be altered simply by the behavior of one's companions, the more active and interactive levels of social and communicative behavior likely to be exhibited by nonhandicapped children may well have a positive impact on handicapped companions. Moreover, where disparities exist between children's developmental levels, there is some suggestion that these heterogeneous groupings can be beneficial. Goldman (1981) found that children in mixed age classes of 3- and 4-year-olds tended to play in a more mature fashion than children in same age classes. However, results of laboratory type studies have been inconsistent on this issue, suggesting benefits for some and not other children (Lougee, Grueneich, & Hartup, 1977), or even finding a suppressive effect on the younger children (Langlois, Gottfried, Barnes, & Hendricks, 1978).

Extensive evidence is now available that developmentally appropriate adjustments are made by preschool-age children in accordance with the cognitive and linguistic levels of younger companions (e.g., Shatz & Gelman, 1973) with regard to their abilities to adjust their social and communicative interactions to younger companions in the mixed age (and therefore mixed developmental level settings). The nature of these adjustments are such that they appear quite capable of promoting the communicative development of the younger companion (Guralnick, 1981a).

Finally, developmental research has established that more competent children are observed more and imitated more than less competent children (Grusec & Abramovitch, 1982; Peterson, Peterson, & Scriven, 1977; Vaughn & Waters, 1981), suggesting potential benefits through observational learning for handicapped children in mainstreamed settings.

Anyone visiting mainstreamed and specialized classes likely will be struck by the differences in the level of activity, overall conversation among peers, and quality of social play in these two settings. This is distressing from a developmental perspective because the role and importance of peers in promoting child–child social and communicative development is well established (Hartup, 1979; Guralnick, 1981c). Unfortunately, recent developmental research focusing on handicapped children's peer relations has clearly confirmed these observations, at least for children considered developmentally delayed. Specifically, the extent to which delayed children initiate social interactions and the quality of their play with peers occurs at a very low level, even when comparisons are made with normally developing children at equivalent developmental levels (Field, 1980; Guralnick & Weinhouse, 1984). In the study by Guralnick and Groom (in press) noted earlier, it was observed that developmentally delayed preschool children not only engaged in relatively few peer related social interactions but, more importantly perhaps, was the fact that those specific behaviors commonly associated with socially competent functioning, such as leading others, using them as resources, or showing affection, were notably absent. There was also very little conversation and very limited involvement in socially interactive activities with peers in these specialized settings. Similar, though less severe, discrepancies have been reported for children with other disabilities as well (Darbyshire, 1977; Higgenbotham & Baker, 1981; Markovits & Strayer, 1982).

Mainstreamed Programs as Stimulating Environments

With this as background, the research focusing on the challenging nature, richness, and stimulation value of peer interactions in mainstreamed settings is examined. First, the concepts of stimulation and richness require clarification. It is not just overall stimulation or the general level of input that is of developmental significance, but rather the level of input as adjusted or appropriately adapted to the social understanding, linguistic, and cognitive levels of those to whom it is directed. In one series of studies designed to determine if adjustments do occur on the part of nonhandicapped preschool children in mainstreamed settings, the language and communicative interactions of nonhandicapped children were evaluated as they interacted with companions of similar chronological age but different developmental levels, during both laboratory type dyadic interactions and during free play (Guralnick & Paul-Brown, 1977, 1980). These studies were limited to children with developmental delays and the outcomes may not at all be generalizable to children with other types of handicapping conditions.

The findings of these investigations can be summarized as follows. For the most part, the results have been quite clear. Nonhandicapped children, despite contradictions among age, physical size, and developmental level of their companions are nevertheless able to adapt appropriately to the level of their delayed companions. Syntactically, normally developing children reduce their mean length of utterance and the complexity of their speech when they address less developmentally advanced children. Similarly, these nonhandicapped children adjust the semantic diversity of their speech to the level of the listener and introduce proportionately fewer new ideas in conversations with children with less sophisticated skills. To enhance the clarity of their communications to children with more severe delays, normally developing children use physical guidance, repetitions, and demonstrations of what they mean more often to children with significant delays. Moreover, they tend to use requests for action more frequently to the more delayed children, in part as an excellent way of testing the understanding of children with limited verbal skills.

More detailed analyses have also revealed that nonhandicapped children's speech to children at different developmental levels, although adapted to the level of the listener, contains sufficient variability such that a *progressive* linguistic environment is provided; that is, the input to these children has many of the characteristics that we know are compatible with a press for communicative development (Guralnick, 1981a). Certainly, for the moderately and severely delayed children in these samples, the quality of linguistic input from peers in specialized settings would be vastly different.

These findings have been verified and extended in a recent study by Guralnick and Paul-Brown (1984) by tracking sequences of social/communicative exchanges between pairs of children when they are engaged in matters of social importance. Perhaps nothing is more important to children in social play sequences than getting a playmate to do what you want them to do; that is, sequences involving behavior requests. Accordingly, behavior request episodes were identified for nonhandicapped children as they interacted with other nonhandicapped children, or mildly, moderately, or severely delayed companions in a dyadic situation. Those sequences were followed, exchange by exchange, until some resolution to the original behavior request was reached. To ensure a high level of motivation, only those sequences in which the nonhandicapped children persisted with the request at least one more time, were analyzed. The intent in analyzing these sequences was as follows: *first*—to determine how successful normally developing children were in achieving compliance to their requests from children at vastly different developmental levels; *second*—to examine how they went about seeking that compliance and what strategies were employed; and *third*—to evaluate whether creative, flexible strategies were employed and whether the normally developing children were persistent in their efforts.

Carrying out this analysis, it was found that overall success in achieving compliance, often requiring many cycles of interchanges, was similar for the four companion groups. Success rates averaged about 50%, although it was somewhat less (30%) to severely delayed children. On the basis of the results of nonhandicapped child to other nonhandicapped child pairings, as well as data from the general developmental literature (Garvey, 1975; Levin & Rubin, 1983), this is a reasonable rate of success.

This degree of success could be understood readily when the strategies these nonhandicapped children employed to gain compliance were examined. In fact, ten separate specific adaptive strategies were identified; that is, strategies that added to or clarified the nature of the original behavior request. These strategies included motivating or prodding their companion, justifying their request, demonstrating or exemplifying, adding relevant information, simplifying the request, focusing their attention, etc. Many of these strategies, especially the verbal and nonverbal ones, were combined in one communicative act; in fact, 62 different combinations were used. Overall, 80% of the communicative interactions to children in all groups were adaptive.

In addition to overall adjustments, certain special adaptations were made to children who were less developmentally advanced. There was more demonstration and exemplification, but fewer efforts to justify or mitigate requests. More multiple combinations of strategies were used to less advanced children, such as concurrently repeating, using attentionals, and demonstrating; strategies similar to those parents and teachers might use in order to gain compliance from a child with significant developmental delays.

Evidence for flexibility and persistence on the part of the nonhandicapped children was also obtained. Children often extended their efforts to achieve compliance into long cycles of exchanges, with an overall mean of 5.13 exchanges per behavior request episode. During these exchanges, communicative interactions were rarely stereotyped, with different approaches or strategies being tried in adjacent cycles within an episode. These results are consistent with those of McHale (1983) in her work with elementary school children in which she observed how remarkably persistent and creative nonhandicapped children could be in order to engage autistic children in play. The potential for peer initiated activities of nonhandicapped children in mainstreamed settings appears to be substantial.

There are, however, some contradictory findings. For hearing-impaired children, available data suggest that appropriate adjustments do not occur very readily (Arnold & Tremblay, 1979; Vandell & George, 1981). In their analysis of dyadic interactions within the context of a mainstreamed program, Vandell and George commented that " . . . hearing children did not appear systematically to vary their interaction strategies to accommodate the special needs of deaf partners. To the contrary, they simply continued to use simple vocalizations which were effective with hearing but not deaf partners." (p. 624) Proper training and other experiences may be effective in addressing this problem. However, Vandell has indicated (personal communication) that these interaction patterns are very difficult to modify.

The social and communicative environment of a handicapped child, as provided by normally developing children in mainstreamed settings, may be highly stimulating and adapted to the level of one's companions in certain circumstances. However, the content of what is being said and the behavioral context are equally important. Although limited empirical data are available, there is cause for concern with regard to this issue. Children with significant delays, for example, can easily be assigned demeaning roles (Strain, 1984b), and even more mildly handicapped children are likely to be assigned to lower status levels and not receive truly egalitarian treatment by nonhandicapped classmates (Guralnick & Paul-Brown, 1984).

In addition to the richness and potential stimulation value of communicative exchanges directed to handicapped children, existing research suggests that opportunities for observational learning readily occur for handicapped children, especially during parallel play episodes (Guralnick, 1980). Strong but anecdotal evidence indicates that delayed imitation of normally developing children occurs frequently (Devoney, Guralnick, & Rubin, 1974).

Taken together, these process studies focusing on peer interactions do indeed suggest that for children with a wide array of handicapping conditions, mainstreamed programs often provide a rich, adapted, and challenging environment; one that in many ways is not possible to achieve in specialized settings. Whether these process results actually translate into better outcomes for handicapped children, as suggested by the corollary proposition that development will proceed at a faster rate in mainstreamed settings, is a more significant question but one much more difficult to answer.[2]

Comparisons Between Mainstreaming and Specialized Settings

Efficacy questions—in this case, those requiring a determination of whether developmental outcomes for handicapped children are superior in mainstreamed in contrast to specialized settings (Guralnick, 1981d)—have always been extraordinarily difficult to address. How experimental questions might best be phrased and those specific approaches most likely to yield answers to those questions are topics that are well beyond the scope of this chapter and are discussed by others in this volume. Instead, those few efficacy type studies are reviewed.

[2]Although the focus is on the stimulation and challenging aspects of the environment for this proposition, the role of responsiveness as described earlier must be considered as an influential factor as well.

It appears that only three studies have been published that attempted to address the difficult design problems faced by efficacy research in this area. Two of these, one by Field, Roseman, De Stefano, and Koewler (1981) and one by Guralnick (1981e), solved the problems of random assignment of subjects to different programs and finding specialized and mainstreamed programs that were equivalent across critical variables through the use of a within-subjects design. Both studies evaluated the peer related social interaction patterns of both handicapped (a range of developmentally delayed children) and nonhandicapped children when in the presence of heterogeneous groups of children (i.e., mainstreaming) in comparison to their peer interactions when in more homogenous groups (i.e., only with other handicapped children). This design clearly limits the generalizability of findings and the questions that can be asked, but nevertheless can provide some valuable information.

The results of these studies were straightforward—no dramatic changes occurred. Children appeared to play and interact socially at about the same level and rate irrespective of the presence of more advanced playmates. Two positive outcomes were noted. First, the presence of nonhandicapped children was associated with lower levels of inappropriate play on the part of severely delayed children (Guralnick, 1981e). Second, there was a strong tendency for both nonhandicapped and some handicapped children to increase their rate of social interactions when in the mainstreamed groupings (Field et al., 1981). These outcomes, although statistically significant, appeared to be less meaningful from an educational perspective. Other efforts of a more widescale nature, such as the one reported by Cooke, Ruskus, Apolloni, and Peck (1981) in northern California, have also failed to find consistent outcomes suggesting that mainstreaming provides unique benefits in terms of developmental growth. Nevertheless, it is important to note that none of the studies reported any adverse effects for either the handicapped or nonhandicapped children as a consequence of mainstreaming.

Given both the expectations from the developmental literature and the results of process studies of mainstreaming, it is important to consider why placement in mainstreamed settings has produced such limited effects to date. From my perspective, these outcomes should not dissuade others from pursuing mainstreaming, both programmatically or experimentally, as the existing efficacy studies have so many limitations that it appears most reasonable to defer judgment at this time. In view of the more favorable results from the process studies, when some of the experimental design issues can be resolved and quality programs selected for comparative purposes, more optimistic outcomes may emerge. At the same time, the available evidence suggests that a cautious outlook may be warranted. Specifically, there has been a tendency to overstate the expectations for mainstreaming as a strategy, in and of itself, for improving the social and cognitive development of young handicapped children. As we have seen, certain principles and findings suggest the potential for promoting development beyond that of specialized programs, but the expectation of radical change simply as a result of mainstreaming is not, in my opinion, logically or developmentally justifiable.

APPLICATION OF DEVELOPMENTAL PRINCIPLES TO EDUCATIONAL PROGRAMS

The final principle differs from the previous two in that it is much broader in scope and more indirect evidence must be relied on to test its implications. The proposition in relation to mainstreaming states as follows: *Developmental principles apply to all children, handicapped or not, so despite special needs, educational programs can be expected to accommodate handicapped children within their usual programmatic and curricular structure.*

The validity of this principle appears to be less of a concern for children with sensory, motor, health, communicative, or behavioral disabilities; at least in theory. There is no question that structural, architectural, programmatic, and curricular alterations, some major, may be necessary to accommodate children with these disabilities and that additional resources, especially for children with behavioral disorders, may well be required (see Walker & Hallau, 1981). There is likely to be relatively little concern that the early education/intervention program's developmental model would be inappropriate for these children. It is the modifications of teaching procedures, the ability to provide appropriate therapeutic strategies, the form environmental adaptations must take, and the extent to which each child's program can be individualized that are the primary issues.

For children with mild developmental delays, where no organic basis for the delays can be discerned, there is little argument that normal developmental principles and accompanying educational strategies apply. It has now been well established through developmental research that the pattern, organization, and sequence of development for these youngsters parallels that of nondelayed children (see Zigler & Balla, 1982). Although there are other issues, especially instructional ones that must be considered, the principle of continuity of development clearly applies to this subgroup of handicapped children.

For those children with more significant developmental delays and for whom a clear or presumed biological basis for their delays exists, the issue is somewhat different. Whether the organization, sequence, and pattern of development is similar for these children is still a much debated issue. There is evidence, especially for young children with Down syndrome that, when matched in terms of developmental level with normally developing children, many of the major developmental processes of these children are similar to nondelayed peers. For example, cognitive, affective, and affiliative/exploration systems seem to operate in a manner similar to nondelayed children (Cicchetti & Sroufe, 1978; Cicchetti & Pogge-Hesse, 1982). However, despite these similarities, it is clear that children with significant delays, most with an established organic basis for their disabilities, differ in important ways from nondelayed children, even when matched in terms of developmental level. It is not possible to provide details in this chapter, but it should be noted that such differences have been found in terms of quality of spontaneous play with objects (Krakow & Kopp, 1982), their peer relations (Guralnick & Groom, in press), the quality of their pretend play (Hill & McCune-Nicolich, 1981), and their ability to appropriately sustain attention, to organize stimuli to solve problems, and to develop strategies that would enable them to be less impulsive (Kopp, Krakow, & Johnson, 1983; Krakow & Kopp, 1983). Again, these studies matched children on the basis of mental age and, where appropriate to the task, on language variables as well; yet differences were still obtained.

Developmental research has been most instructive in pointing out that the differences that do emerge are those associated with special deficits in processing information, difficulties in attending to salient stimuli, and general problems in discrimination (Kopp, 1983), but are not related to the organizational structure or sequential pattern of development. Unusual problems in social development, especially in establishing peer relations, would be expected from these deficits, as the subtleties and complexities of information that must be processed in a social learning task are substantial. Despite these differences, the evidence suggests the tenability, in general terms, of a developmental approach for the vast majority of handicapped children.

The contention remains then, that accommodations to handicapped children that must be made reside primarily in the areas of assessment and planning, the pacing of the presentation of new concepts, the organization of materials and curricula to ensure proper acquisition of information and skills, the careful application of all the educational procedures at our disposal, ranging from behavioral strategies of prompting, shaping, and reinforcement to the teaching of explicit cognitive strategies, and numerous others. It also resides in environmental adjustments, special efforts to ensure that concepts have indeed generalized, a particular emphasis promoting social relationships, and a need to address potential motivational problems, among others. In essence, there are more quantitative rather than qualitative differences, and so the question remains, "Is it feasible to make these accommodations within the mainstreamed setting?"

Feasibility of Mainstreamed Programs

As I have noted (Guralnick, 1982), in order to answer the question of feasibility, two issues must be considered. First, it is important to determine if the philosophy and developmental/educational model of an early education program remains intact despite the accommodations that must occur to handicapped children. Simply, does the program look and behave the same way on a day-to-day basis? Second, it is essential to evaluate whether the educational and developmental needs of all children, handicapped and nonhandicapped, in the setting are being met. In this case, indices of developmental outcome must be obtained.

In an excellent review article, Peck and Cooke (1983) have summarized a series of demonstration programs which appear to have collected sufficient data to respond to the feasibility question. The label 'demonstration projects' is, I believe, a fair one, reflecting earlier comments that efforts to obtain random samples, to collect data using external evaluators, to deal with questions of statistical regression, or to locate appropriate comparison groups, are extremely difficult if not impossible to achieve when attempting to evaluate the impact of mainstreaming. But these demonstration projects cannot and should not be dismissed simply because of one or another imperfection, as they may be able to contribute important information to our understanding of the feasibility issue. Many projects have added important evaluation components to their work and, in some instances, have developed quite sophisticated data collection techniques and devised creative means for making comparisons to specialized programs. Most often, appeal has been made to normative standards, usually pointing to the rates of development of both the handicapped and nonhandicapped children who participated in the programs.

In my view, the results of a sufficiently large number of demonstration projects are available to suggest that mainstreamed programs in a variety of forms are indeed feasible. For example, in a report by Bricker and her colleagues (Bricker, Bruder, & Bailey, 1982), standardized measures consisting of the Bayley and McCarthy scales in addition to well-tested criterion referenced instruments were administered on a pre- and post-test basis to three different toddler and preschool classes. Each class was composed of a heterogeneous grouping of developmentally delayed, multiply handicapped, orthopedically handicapped, cerebral palsied, or hearing-impaired youngsters. In addition, approximately one-third to one-half of the children were normally developing. The results over a 7-month period using these measures revealed that the normally developing children showed typical developmental changes (gains in developmental age kept pace with the time in the program), and one group even gained significantly in average IQ score. The handicapped children did especially well, with average increases in mental age ranging from 4 to 11 months over the 7-month period, with a significant increase in IQ being found for one of the preschool classes (74 to 81 on the McCarthy). All groups made highly significant progress on the criterion referenced instruments.

Even more positive outcomes associated with participation in mainstreamed programs can be found in a recent report by Strain (in press) for autistic preschoolers. Five carefully diagnosed autistic children with minimal functional speech, scoring within the mild to severe range of retardation, exhibiting stereotypic and self-stimulating behaviors but virtually no positive interaction with peers, and ten normally developing children were drawn randomly from a large sample of early intervention classes in which half the children were normally developing. The Learning Accomplishment Profile (LAP) was used as a measure of developmental achievement. In addition, data based on direct observations of on-task, language frequency, and positive interactions with peers were obtained over a one-year period. With regard to developmental changes, the autistic children were functioning at about 60% of age level for each of the eight domains of the LAP on entry into the program. By the end of the year, and following direct instruction in each of the eight developmental domains, all five autistic children were functioning at about 90% of expected level based on their chronological age. The application of a comprehensive peer-mediated package to improve positive social interactions was also highly successful as the handicapped children's interactions began to approximate those of the normally developing children in the setting. It should be noted that for both the developmental and social interaction outcomes, multiple baseline techniques were used to demonstrate that it was the program itself that was responsible for these changes.

To evaluate whether the program met the needs of the normally developing children, Strain (in press) applied the LAP teaching procedures to those normally developing children who were below age level in any domain. Important gains were made in each of these targeted domains, but not in those that were at age level and for which direct instruction was not attempted. Consequently, the specific effects of instruction within the program were also observed for the normally developing children. In addition, the observational data collected in the classroom for the normally developing children were compared to other nonhandicapped children in ten nursery schools in the local area. Comparison children in the nursery schools were selected as very outstanding by their teachers, thereby providing a conservative comparative test. These comparisons revealed that the mainstreamed and nursery school samples of normally developing children were highly similar.

Earlier reports of demonstration programs had also suggested the feasibility of mainstreaming. Ispa and Matz (1978) found that mildly handicapped and nonhandicapped children in a cognitively oriented mainstreamed program made considerable advances over a one-year period in terms of cognitive development (pre- to post-testing on the McCarthy), averaging about two months of progress for every month enrolled in the program. Similar, though less dramatic outcomes for mildly and moderately handicapped children enrolled in community programs have been reported by Galloway and Chandler (1978).

Not all demonstration type project reports have been as successful as those just presented. A few reports expressing difficulty mainstreaming or integrating disturbed children (Smith & Greenberg, 1981), visually handicapped children (Simon & Gillman, 1979), and hearing-impaired children (Vandell & George, 1981), can be found in the literature. On balance, however, the evidence for the feasibility of mainstreamed programs in terms of appropriate developmental gains is impressive, especially because the positive reports included children with a wide range of handicaps, were carried out in community and university settings, and consisted of different program and integration models.

Few of these demonstration type projects commented on the integrity of their program's model, the second component of feasibility, tending to concentrate on describing developmental outcomes for both the handicapped and nonhandicapped children. However, from discussions in their reports, it is reasonable to surmise that their philosophy and program model were appropriate for all children and that the day-to-day activities were consistent with that model. Some of the most persuasive evidence supporting this second component of feasibility is the array of available anecdotal evidence. Local conference presentations, the numerous models that currently exist, the rapidly accumulating favorable reports by teachers and preschool administrators with regard to how mainstreaming works for them, should not be ignored. For example, many Head Start programs continue to report favorable results as more experience is gained with the process (evaluation of the process of mainstreaming handicapped children in Project Head Start, Phase I, 1978). A Canadian group has developed a very interesting model for rural mainstreaming through the provision of mobile teams to provide support to community programs (Crozier, unpublished). At an even more comprehensive level, Sweden's daycare services have been especially designed to accommodate both handicapped and nonhandicapped children, selecting and arranging materials appropriately and even providing books illustrating handicapped and nonhandicapped children playing together (Bergstrom & Gold, 1974). These perceptions are based less, I suspect, on developmental outcomes than they are on issues of social integration and the ability of their staff to continue to work within their own models of development and education.

CONCLUSION

General developmental principles and research derived from the literature on both normally developing and handicapped children have been examined as they applied to specific issues of mainstreaming at the preschool level. Expectations related to the issues of peer responsiveness, the existence of a richer, more challenging, and more stimulating environment, and the applicability of developmental models to all children, have been explored. The implementation of mainstreamed programs is a complex process and is subject to so many different and sometimes unknown factors and patterns of interaction that numerous and unexpected outcomes are possible. Nevertheless, the available evidence clearly indicates that there is no reason, at this point, to alter the view that preschool mainstreaming is potentially a valuable educational option. In fact, there is reason to suggest that mainstreaming as a concept and as a practice be pursued in a positive and activist manner, while retaining a focus on careful evaluation.

Continuing to explore preschool mainstreaming in an activist fashion is perhaps the most crucial point of this discussion because, in the final analysis, it will be our willingness to test to its fullest this public policy, this social process, this educational innovation, this treatment strategy, this value system, and whatever else we choose to call mainstreaming. Only by pressing to provide adequate resources and well-trained personnel, by continuing to develop innovative models, and by maximizing so-called programmatic factors that are likely to be associated with successful outcomes, will a fair assessment of the potential and effectiveness of mainstreaming become possible. As that process proceeds, the answers to the important questions of who can and should be mainstreamed, under what conditions, and toward what ends, will be well within our reach.

REFERENCES

Arnold, W., & Tremblay, A. (1979). Interaction of deaf and hearing preschool children. *Journal of Communication Disorders, 12*, 245–251.

Bailey, D. B., Jr., Clifford, R. M., & Harms, T. (1982). Comparison of preschool environments for handicapped and nonhandicapped children. *Topics in Early Childhood Special Education, 2*, 9–20.

Bergstrom, J. L., & Gold, J. R. (1974). *Sweden's day nurseries: Focus on programs for infants and toddlers*. Washington, DC: The Day Care and Child Development Council of America.

Bricker, D., Bruder, M.B., & Bailey, E. (1982). Developmental integration of preschool children. *Analysis and Intervention in Developmental Disabilities, 2*, 207–222.

Cairns, R. B. (1979). *Social development: The origins and plasticity of interchanges*. San Francisco: W. H. Freeman.

Cicchetti, D., & Pogge-Hesse, P. (1982). Possible contributions of the study of organically retarded persons to developmental theory. In E. Zigler & D. Balla (Eds.), *Mental retardation: The developmental-difference controversy* (pp. 277–318). Hillsdale, NJ: Lawrence Erlbaum Associates.

Cicchetti, D., & Sroufe, A. (1978). An organizational view of affect: Illustration from the study of Down's syndrome infants. In M. Lewis & L. A. Rosenblum (Eds.), *The development of affect* (pp. 309–350). New York: Plenum.

Cooke, T. P., Ruskus, J. A., Apolloni, T., & Peck, C. A. (1981). Handicapped preschool children in the mainstream: Background, outcomes, and clinical suggestions. *Topics in Early Childhood Special Education, 1*(1), 73–83.

Crawley, S. B., & Chan, K. S. (1982). Developmental changes to the free play behavior of mildly and moderately retarded preschool-aged children. *Education and Training of the Mentally Retarded, 17*, 234–239.

Crozier, S. *The Mobile Team Program*. Unpublished, Alberta Children's Hospital, Canada.

Darbyshire, J. O. (1977). Play patterns in young children with impaired hearing. *The Volta Review, 79*, 19–26.

Devoney, C., Guralnick, M. J., & Rubin, H. (1974). Integrating handicapped and non-handicapped preschool children: Effects of social play. *Childhood Education, 50*, 360–364.

Doyle, A., Connolly, J., & Rivest, L. (1980). The effect of playmate familiarity on the social interactions of young children. *Child Development, 51*, 217–223.

Field, T. M. (1980). Self, teacher, toy, and peer-directed behaviors of handicapped preschool children. In T. M. Field, S. Goldberg, D. Stern, & A. M. Sostek (Eds.), *High-risk infants and children: Adult and peer interactions* (pp. 313–326). New York: Academic.

Field, T., Roseman, S., De Stefano, L., & Koewler, J. H., III. (1981). Play behaviors of handicapped preschool children in the presence and absence of nonhandicapped peers. *Journal of Applied Developmental Psychology, 2*, 49–58.

Galloway, C., & Chandler, P. (1978). The marriage of special and generic early education services. In M. J. Guralnick (Ed.), *Early intervention and the integration of handicapped and nonhandicapped children* (pp. 261–287). Baltimore, MD: University Park Press.

Garvey, C. (1975). Requests and responses in children's speech. *Journal of Child Language, 2*, 41–63.

Garvey, C., & Hogan, R. (1973). Social speech and social interaction: Egocentrism revisited. *Child Development, 44*, 562–568.

Goldman, J. A. (1981). Social participation of preschool children in same- versus mixed-age groups. *Child Development, 52*, 644–650.

Grusec, J. E., & Abramovitch, R. (1982). Imitation of peers and adults in a natural setting: A functional analysis. *Child Development, 53*, 636–642.

Guralnick, M. J. (Ed.). (1978). *Early intervention and the integration of handicapped and nonhandicapped children.* Baltimore: University Park Press.

Guralnick, M. J. (1980). Social interactions among preschool children. *Exceptional Children, 46*, 248–253.

Guralnick, M. J. (1981a). Peer influences on the development of communicative competence. In P. Strain (Ed.), *The utilization of classroom peers as behavior change agents* (pp. 31–68). New York: Plenum.

Guralnick, M. J. (1981b). Programmatic factors affecting child–child social interactions in mainstreamed preschool programs. *Exceptional Education Quarterly, 1*(4), 71–91.

Guralnick, M. J. (1981c). The development and role of child–child social interactions. In N. Anastasiow (Ed.), *New directions for exceptional children: Socioemotional development* (pp. 53–80). San Francisco: Jossey-Bass.

Guralnick, M. J. (1981d). The efficacy of integrating handicapped children in early education settings: Research implications. *Topics in Early Childhood Special Education, 1*(1), 57–71.

Guralnick, M. J. (1981e). The social behavior of preschool children at different developmental levels: Effects of group composition. *Journal of Experimental Child Psychology, 31*, 115–130.

Guralnick, M. J. (1982). Mainstreaming young handicapped children: A public policy and ecological systems analysis. In B. Spodek (Ed.), *Handbook of research on early childhood education* (pp. 456–500). New York: The Free Press/Macmillan.

Guralnick, M. J. (in press). The peer relations of young handicapped and nonhandicapped children. In P. S. Strain, M. J. Guralnick, & H. M. Walker (Eds.), *Children's social behavior: Development, assessment, and modification.* New York: Academic.

Guralnick, M. J., & Groom, J. M. (in press). Correlates of peer related social competence in developmentally delayed preschool children. *American Journal of Mental Deficiency.*

Guralnick, M. J., & Paul-Brown, D. (1977). The nature of verbal interactions among handicapped and nonhandicapped preschool children. *Child Development, 48*, 254–260.

Guralnick, M. J., & Paul-Brown, D. (1980). Functional and discourse analyses of nonhandicapped preschool children's speech to handicapped children. *American Journal of Mental Deficiency, 84*, 444–454.

Guralnick, M. J., & Paul-Brown, D. (1984). Communicative adjustments during behavior-request episodes among children at different developmental levels. *Child Development, 55*, 911–919.

Guralnick, M. J., & Paul-Brown, D. (in press). Communicative interactions of mildly delayed and normally developing preschool children: Effects of listener's developmental level. *Journal of Speech and Hearing Research.*

Guralnick, M. J., & Weinhouse, E. M. (1984). Peer related social interactions of developmentally delayed young children: Development and characteristics. *Developmental Psychology, 20*, 815–827.

Hartup, W. W. (1979). Peer relations and the growth of social competence. In M. W. Kent & J. E. Rolf (Eds.), *Primary prevention of psychopathology*: Vol. 3. Social competence in children (pp. 150–170). Hanover, NH: University Press of New England.

Higgenbotham, J., & Baker, B. M. (1981). Social participation and cognitive play differences in hearing-impaired and normally hearing preschoolers. *The Volta Review, 83*, 135–149.

Hill, P. M., & McCune-Nicolich, L. (1981). Pretend play and patterns of cognition in Down's syndrome children. *Child Development, 52*, 611–617.

Holmberg, M. C. (1980). The development of social interchange patterns from 12 to 42 months. *Child Development, 51*, 448–456.

Huston-Stein, A., Friedrich-Cofer, L., & Susman, E. J. (1977). The relation of classroom structure to social behavior, imaginative play, and self-regulation of economically disadvantaged children. *Child Development, 48*, 908–916.

Ispa, J., & Matz, R. D. (1978). Integrating handicapped preschool children within a cognitively oriented program. In M. J. Guralnick (Ed.), *Early intervention and the integration of handicapped and nonhandicapped children* (pp. 167–190). Baltimore: University Park Press.

Kopp, C. B. (1983). Risk factors in development. In M. M. Haith & J. J. Campos (Eds.), *Handbook of child psychology: Vol. 2. Infancy and developmental psychobiology* (pp. 1081–1188). New York: Wiley.

Kopp, C. B., Krakow, J. B., & Johnson, K. L. (1983). Strategy production by young Down syndrome children. *American Journal of Mental Deficiency, 88*, 164–169.

Krakow, J. B., & Kopp, C. B. (1982). Sustained attention in young Down syndrome children. *Topics in Early Childhood Special Education, 2*(2), 32–42.

Krakow, J. B., & Kopp, C. B. (1983). The effects of developmental delay on sustained attention in young children. *Child Development, 54*, 1143–1155.

Langlois, J. H., Gottfried, N. W., Barnes, B. M., & Hendricks, D. E. (1978). The effect of peer age on the social behavior of preschool children. *The Journal of Genetic Psychology, 132*, 11–19.

Levin, E. A., & Rubin, K. H. (1983). Getting others to do what you want them to do: The development of children's requestive strategies. In K. E. Nelson (Ed.), *Children's language* (Vol. 4, pp. 157–186). Hillsdale, NJ: Lawrence Erlbaum Associates.

Lewis, M., & Goldberg, S. (1969). Perceptual-cognitive development in infancy: A generalized expectancy model as a function of mother–infant interaction. *Merrill-Palmer Quarterly, 15*, 81–100.

Lougee, M. D., Grueneich, R., & Hartup, W. W. (1977). Social interaction in same- and mixed-age dyads of preschool children. *Child Development, 48*, 1353–1361.

Markovits, H., & Strayer, F. F. (1982). Toward an applied social ethology: A case study of social skills among blind children. In K. H. Rubin & H. S. Ross (Eds.), *Peer relationships and social skills in childhood* (pp. 301–322). New York: Springer-Verlag.

McHale, S. M. (1983). Social interactions of autistic and nonhandicapped children during free play. *American Journal of Orthopsychiatry, 53*, 81–91.

Miller, L. B., & Dyer, J. L. (1975). Four preschool programs: Their dimensions and effects. *Monographs of the Society for Research in Child Development, 40* (5,6).

Mindes, G. (1982). Social and cognitive aspects of play in young handicapped children. *Topics in Early Childhood Special Education, 2*(3), 39–52.

Mueller, E., Bleir, M., Krakow, J., Hegedus, K., & Cournoyer, P. (1977). The development of peer verbal interactions among two-year-old boys. *Child Development, 48*, 284–287.

Peck, C. A., & Cooke, T. P. (1983). Benefits of mainstreaming at the early childhood level: How much can we expect? *Analysis and Intervention in Developmental Disabilities, 3*, 1–22.

Peterson, C., Peterson, J., & Scriven, G. (1977). Peer imitation by nonhandicapped and handicapped preschoolers. *Exceptional Children, 43*, 223–224.

Rogers-Warren, A., & Wedel, J. W. (1980). The ecology of preschool classrooms for the handicapped. In J. J. Gallagher (Ed.), *New directions for exceptional children: Ecology of exceptional children* (pp. 1–24). San Francisco: Jossey-Bass.

Shatz, M., & Gelman, R. (1973). The development of communication skills: Modifications in the speech of young children as a function of listener. *Monographs of the Society for Research in Child Development, 38*(5).

Shure, M. B. (1963). Psychological ecology of a nursery school. *Child Development, 34*, 979–992.

Simon, E. P., & Gillman, A. E. (1979). Mainstreaming visually handicapped preschoolers. *Exceptional Children, 45*, 463–464.

Smith, C., & Greenberg, M. (1981). Step by step integration of handicapped preschool children in a day care center for nonhandicapped children. *Journal of the Division for Early Childhood, 2*, 96–101.

Strain, P. S. (1983). Generalization of autistic children's social behavior change: Effects of developmentally integrated and segregated settings. *Analysis and Intervention in Developmental Disabilities, 3*, 23–34.

Strain, P. S. (1984a). Social interactions of handicapped preschoolers in developmentally integrated and segregated settings: A study of generalization effects. In T. Field, J. Roopnarine, & M. Segal (Eds.), *Friendships in normal and handicapped children* (pp. 187–207). Norwood, NJ: Ablex.

Strain, P. S. (1984b). Social behavior patterns of nonhandicapped and nonhandicapped-developmentally disabled friend pairs in mainstream preschools. *Analysis and Intervention in Developmental Disabilities, 4*, 15–28.

Strain, P. S. (in press). Outcomes for normally developing and autistic-like children in an integrated preschool. *Journal of the Division for Early Childhood.*

Tremblay, A., Strain, P. S., Hendrickson, J. M., Shores, R. E. (1981). Social interactions of normally developing preschool children: Using normative data for subject and target behavior selection. *Behavior Modification, 5*, 237–253.

Vandell, D. L., & George, L. B. (1981). Social interaction in hearing and deaf preschoolers: Successes and failures in initiations. *Child Development, 52*, 627–635.

Vandenberg, B. (1981). Environmental and cognitive factors in social play. *Journal of Experimental Child Psychology, 31*, 169–175.

Vaughn, B. E., & Waters, E. (1981). Attention structure, sociometric status, and dominance: Interrelations, behavioral correlates, and relationships to social competence. *Developmental Psychology, 17*, 275–288.

Wachs, T. D., & Gruen, G. E. (1982). *Early experience and human development.* New York: Plenum.

Walker, J. A., & Hallau, M. G. (1981). Why the "H"in ECEH? Considerations in training teachers of young handicapped children. *Journal of the Division for Early Childhood, 2*, 61–66.

Wright, M. J. (1980). Measuring the social competence of preschool children. *Canadian Journal of Behavioral Science, 12*, 17–32.

Zigler, E., & Balla, D. (1982). *Mental retardation: The developmental-difference controversy.* Hillsdale, NJ: Lawrence Erlbaum Associates.

4 Micro-Mainstreaming

Frank B. Murray
University of Delaware

It is regrettable that the language of the mainstreaming legislation (PL 93–380 and PL 94–142) focused so squarely on the setting and environment, the context of instruction, rather than the features of effective instruction. The definition of "the least restrictive environment" was often taken as a physical place rather than as a set of the psychological features or conditions that promote normal social interactions among pupils of widely different ability. It was taken as an arrangement of classroom furniture and seating proximity rather than as a social system that required genuine commerce between pupils, made equitable demands on instructional time, and gave equitable opportunities for achievement and progress.

In the end, the practice of mainstreaming derives from several strong theoretical claims that the major principles of human learning and development hold uniformly across our species. It derives as well from the putative empirical result that the aggregate cognitive benefits are greater—or at least no worse—in mixed groups of pupils than they are in segregated groups (e.g., Goldberg & Passow, 1962; Eyler, Cook, & Ward, 1983). However, both the theoretical and empirical claims that support mainstreaming practices can be contested on several grounds (Rosenbaum, 1980).

There has been a tendency among researchers to view mainstreaming simply in terms of physical integration of pupils rather than as a defining set of psychological features for genuine interaction between pupils. This tendency is apparent not only in the research literature on placement of handicapped pupils, but also in the literature on heterogeneous grouping of pupils in general. As a result, there is no clear or firm conclusion about the cognitive benefits—to either party—that come from instructional settings in which pupils of markedly mixed academic ability are placed. The conventional wisdom that lower ability pupils benefit more than they would in segregated classrooms and that high ability pupils do about as well as they would if they were placed only with peers of comparable academic promise can no longer be put forward with assurance.

Stephens (1967) reviews literature from several sources that indicates mainstreaming, or the creation of groups of mixed ability pupils, would, in itself, have no positive or negative differential effect on pupil achievement because comparable levels of academic achievement can be had in either segregated or integrated groups. However Rosenbaum (1980) also cites evidence from several sources—some of which were comprehensive reviews of the literature—which as a collection, indicate that positive, mixed, and negative effects of mainstreaming on academic achievement can be demonstrated for all ability levels—talented, average, and slow pupils. This confusing outcome could occur in several ways. Ability grouping by itself may be a weak and ineffectual factor whose effects on pupil achievement are swamped by more potent factors, such as the teacher's style, curriculum quality, and so forth. Or it may be that true ability groupings are rarely implemented because it is simply not possible to create convincing and lasting groups of children who differ in their ability consistently over a wide range of educational tasks (Balow, 1963). Grouping admittedly may reduce the variation in one or two pupil characteristics in a classroom, but obviously it never completely eliminates differences in those characteristics and it may have no effect on other important characteristics that are uncorrelated with the characteristics that formed the basis of the original classification. Or it may be that teachers group children into subgroups in either case so that no meaningful contrast between segregated and integrated ability organizations can be had (Schofield & Sagar, 1983).

Thus, it may very well be that the confusion that remains after 50 years of research on ability grouping stems from the fact that few researchers have been able to guarantee that the groups under investigation were critically different from one another and that the pupils were treated differently by their teachers or classmates. One exception in the research literature, an exception that is often unrecognized by educational researchers (e.g., Walker, 1984), is a body of work in developmental psychology that deals with the effects on cognitive development of social interaction and social conflict between cognitively advanced and cognitively immature children. The outcomes of this research are instructive for the issue of mainstreaming because the critical conditions for mainstreaming are met, namely pupils who differ qualitatively in their intellectual competence are placed in a situation that requires social interaction of some sort. Most important of all, the research clearly shows that the cognitively immature children make substantial gains in cognitive growth at no cost to the cognitive status of the cognitively advanced children (Murray, 1982).

AN EXAMINATION OF SOCIAL INTERACTION TECHNIQUES

Since the middle of the 1970s, there has not been any legitimate doubt that conflict and interaction among peers in small classroomlike settings are effective ways to promote cognitive development and the acquisition of some conceptual information in the curriculum. Murray (1972) and Silverman and Stone (1972) reported success with training procedures based on the rather simple micro-mainstreaming experimental manipulation of having immature pupils argue with their advanced peers until they all came to an agreement or stalemate about the solutions to various problems. When tested alone after the interaction, 80% to 94% of the lower level pupils made significant gains in performance compared to very much lower rates of success reported in studies of more traditional training attempts (Beilin, 1977; Murray, 1978). These gains fulfilled several demanding criteria for genuine accomplishment. Not only do most immature children make significant gains as a result of social interactions with advanced children, but the gains are of substantial magnitude. For example, in Murray (1972) 8 out of 15 children who scored 0 out of 12 on the pretest had scores of 11 or 12 out of 12 on the various posttest. What has not been clear in this research is what in the social interaction experience produced these gains. A number of factors come to mind, and research since 1973 has treated many of them.

The social interaction effect can be had in different size interaction groups of one on one (Silverman & Geiringer 1973; Silverman & Stone, 1972), two on one (Murray, 1972), and three on two (Botvin & Murray; 1975) in kindergarten, first, second, third, and fifth grades with normal and learning disabled, although not with those disabled with communication disorders, (Knight-Arest & Reid, 1978); with blacks and whites; and with middle and low socioeconomic status (SES) groups. Borys and Spitz (1979), however, did not find social interaction to be especially effective with mentally retarded institutionalized adolescents (IQ = 66, mental age (MA) = 10 years, chronological age (CA) = 20 years), but these persons are not likely to be a part of the typical mainstreaming manipulation.

No unusual information or instruction is presented in the interaction; that is, no researcher has reported children saying anything or manipulating the stimuli in any way that has not been said or demonstrated in the less effective "nonsocial" training procedures, namely, cognitive conflict, cue reduction, phenomenal-real discrimination, verbal rule instruction, reversibility, and the various learning paradigm procedures (Murray, 1978).

Analyses of the course of the interaction yield no surprises either, except perhaps that agreement is often reached quickly. Miller and Brownell (1975) found that nearly half the agreements were reached in less than 50 seconds and rarely took longer than 4 or 5 minutes. It is also surprising that the advanced children do not prevail because of any greater social influence or higher IQ or because they are particularly better arguers. In arguments about best TV shows and so forth, the advanced children won only 41 of 90 arguments, lost 38, and stalemated 11, which leads Miller and Brownell (1975) to conclude that relative social influence was not a factor in their findings.

Growth occurs only for the children who yield, which they do 60–80% of the time (Silverman & Geiringer, 1973). The advanced children seem to initiate discussion slightly more often, state their answer slightly more often, give good reasons, counter the others slightly more often, move stimuli more often, and appear slightly more flexible in their arguments than the immature children who repetitiously focus on their original opinion and its justifications (Miller & Brownell, 1975; Silverman & Stone, 1972). No differences between the pupils are found in their modes of communication, considered apart from their content, nor between yielders and nonyielders in this regard (Silverman & Geiringer, 1973); thus, the clues to the success of the procedure are not apparent in the analysis of the form or content of interactions between the children.

Despite the magnitude of the success of the social interaction procedures, the authenticity of the children's newly acquired solutions may still be questioned even though, taking the studies as a whole, the principal criteria for genuine solutions are met. It may have been possible for the immature children in these studies to have merely parroted or imitated the correct response because a thoughtless repetition of the right answer could have inflated the posttest performance. Although some researchers controlled for such a response set with inclusion of items for which the "right answer" would be inappropriate, a most demanding test of whether the children did more than imitate their tutors would be the degree to which they explained their new judgments by justifications that differ from those given by the advanced pupils during the social interaction sessions. Silverman and Stone (1972) report only one instance out of 14 in which a newly trained child gave an explanation not originally offered by his partner in the interaction. However, Botvin and Murray (1975) report significant differences in the types of reasons given by advanced children during the interaction and by the immature ones on the posttest. Forty-nine percent of the original advanced children gave one kind of reason for their answers during the interaction, and 61% of the immature children tended to give another kind of reason when they solved the problems correctly on the posttest. Similarly, Perret-Clermont (reported in Doise, Mugny, & Perret-Clermont, 1975) found that over half the children she studied introduced one or more arguments or explanations that had not occurred during the social interaction session. There is evidence that the newly acquired solution has a different basis of justification than what is used by the advanced children (Gelman, 1978; Murray, 1981). Although these latter studies bolster considerably the contention that the immature were not merely imitating the others, they do not indicate whether the training procedures merely addressed or activated a pre-existing competence.

The group of social interaction training procedures, incidentally, does address the directionality of development issue. From a social learning theory perspective, particularly in the dyad interactions, there is no a priori reason to think that the advanced children should not be as affected as the immature ones are by the interaction, especially when the social influence of one is no less than the other (Miller & Brownell, 1975; Silverman & Geiringer, 1973). Yet, shifts from correct to incorrect solutions simply are not reported in any significant degree in the literature. Why should the correct solution be a more firmly held position than an incorrect one from a social learning perspective is not clear because environmental and linguistic support for errors is very great (Murray, 1981). For example, because there are so many more large–heavy and small–light objects in the world than large–light and small–heavy, it is not unreasonable to expect errors in children's concepts of weight to result, as it commonly does, from transformations of the size and shape of objects. In fact, it is a puzzle in social learning theory why the errors eventually break down because they seem to serve the child so well who for so long thinks that heavy objects are larger than lighter objects.

Silverman and Geiringer (1973) found five cases (of 23) and Miller and Brownell (1975) found one eight instances (of 69) where the advanced yielded his or her position during the social interaction session, but in virtually no case did even these correct children regress to an incorrect answer on the posttests. Thus, the directionality requirement of development is sustained in these studies, although it remains to be seen whether more direct or systematic attempts to shift children from the correct to the incorrect answer would succeed. Still, a heavy burden is placed on social learning theory to explain the single direction of the behavioral change that results from the social interaction procedures.

The Genevan account for the efficacy of the social interaction treatments in facilitating development, centers on the claim that logic has its origins in children's need to prove their point of view to others, coupled with the shock of their thought coming up against that of others. Logic and necessity, the critical ingredients in persuasive argument, have their origins in the breakdown of the equilibrium of egocentrism as a result of the child's cooperation with others. The efficacy of the social interaction studies makes sense from the Genevan perspective, although the changes occur over intervals that are too short to be consistent with the general Genevan position that development is a slow process. The question of how much time it takes to advance to a higher, more advanced level on the other hand, is somewhat meaningless because it involves the quantification of a quality. The Genevan explanation, however, lacks parsimony, and it should come as no surprise that it might be possible to explain the workings of social interaction procedures with more parsimonious mechanisms, such as imitation or modeling.

MODELING AND IMITATION

Several researchers (Charbonneau & Robert, 1977; Charbonneau, Robert, Bourassa, & Gladu-Bisonnette, 1976; Rosenthal & Zimmerman, 1972; Sullivan, 1969; Waghorn & Sullivan, 1970; Zimmerman & Lanaro, 1974) have demonstrated that children who were incorrect can acquire the correct answer merely by observing adults model or perform the tasks correctly, and other researchers (Botvin & Murray, 1975; Cook & Murray, 1973; J. Murray, 1974) have confirmed the result with child models, often showing greater gains here than with adult models.

In a direct comparison of the power of modeling and social interaction procedures, Botvin and Murray (1975) showed they yield equivalent success. In both cases, the gains met the traditional justification, transfer, and durability criteria. As Murray (1972) in his study of social interaction and Rosenthal and Zimmerman (1972) in their study of modeling both used the Goldschmid and Bentler (1968) Concept Assessment Kit, Forms A and B, as the dependent measure, another comparison of the two procedures is possible, at least indirectly. Both studies yielded equivalent posttest scores (Forms A and B) with children of the same age and background. The posttest scores for children who could solve no problems correctly on the pretests were essentially the same in the two studies and met all the major criteria for being correct. There is some evidence (Charbonneau & Robert, 1977; Charbonneau et al., 1976) that some children exposed to a modeling experience fail in the end to meet the full range of the criteria for genuine achievement (viz., duration and generalization). Also it appears that the cognitive growth that results from modeling is constrained by the intellectual and cognitive level of the observer (Murray, 1974) to a greater degree than it appears to be for children in the social interaction experience. It appears that some children rotely memorize the model's response algorithms, but this fact itself does not rule out the possibility that in other circumstances they would respond at a more advanced level. Highly competent persons may still use rotely memorized algorithms as a problem-solving approach in a situation for which they perceive them to be an appropriate, or at least an economical, strategy.

The modeling effects, like the interaction ones, have been shown to hold across various age groups (4 to 8 years), SES levels, language and ethnic groups, and IQ levels. Moreover, they cannot be explained away as merely the assimilation of the information presented by the model because often the information presented outside a modeling condition fails to produce stable conservation gains (Rosenthal & Zimmerman, 1972) and because the gains are sometimes based on reasons different from those given by the model (Botvin & Murray, 1975; Murray, 1974). Rules and explanations given by the model often, but not always, enhanced the gain, to be sure (Rosenthal & Zimmerman, 1972; Sullivan, 1969; Waghorn & Sullivan, 1970), but the effect cannot be attributed solely to their presence. Something more is contributed by the modeling aspect of the information transmission. The social attribute of the message appears to be critical for cognitive growth.

Unlike the children in the social interaction condition who may yield temporarily to the wrong approach but still give the correct response on the pottests, some researchers (Rosenthal & Zimmerman, 1972) report that advanced children who observe children making errors regress and imitate the model somewhat. These reports of regression require close examination because potentially they are a serious threat to the strong directionality claims of developmental theories. Moreover, they pose practical and ethical constraints on mainstreaming as a useful educational practice.

A closer look at Rosenthal and Zimmerman's (1972) 17 children whose mean scores significantly declined after exposure to an adult model who made errors, reveals that the children had a mean score of only 8.59 out of 12 on the Goldschmidt-Bentler (1968) assessment kit and could, on that basis alone, be thought to be not that advanced in the first place. Cook and Murray (1973), on the other hand, had 12 children with perfect scores on the Goldschmid-Bentler kit observe a child model with a score of 0 and found no regression. The observers maintained perfect scores on the modeled tasks and on the transfer tasks. Murray (1974) also found no evidence of regression after his subjects observed a child model make errors.

These regression effects are not found when children serve as the model. Robert and Charbonneau (1977, 1978) argue convincingly that regression reports in modeling procedures are artifactual and a function of social control and submissiveness to social influence features of the procedure. They found that extinction or regression occurred only in the presence of adults, and even then it appeared that the children only temporarily adopted the errors simply to conform to perceived social demands (Robert & Charbonneau, 1978). Kuhn (1972) found little evidence of regression in the modeling of classification in a study that provided a fine-grained portrayal of regression and progression in terms of the Piagetian substages. The directionality assumption of the developmental model is not seriously threatened by the results of modeling and imitation attempts to extinguish the correct response in either "natural" or newly trained children. Still, the potential for regression in some circumstances is a nagging problem for unqualified mainstreaming implementation.

Although it is plausible that the social interaction effects are explainable as essentially modeling effects, competing explanations are equally plausible. For example, it is possible that given the very short durations of the interactions, the immature children merely acquiesced to terminate the argument and simply pretended to be advanced. Their pretense would not fully explain all the results of the interaction studies. It might be expected that the dissonance between their pretense and true belief, discounting the likelihood of the sufficient justification of the experimental procedure, could motivate cognitive change, as it typically does, in the direction of the subject's public position (viz., the correct response). In this account, the immature would come to believe their public position and genuinely be correct.

Murray, Ames, and Botvin (1977) investigated the dissonance or role-playing hypothesis in two experiments that dramatically confirmed it. Children with initial scores of 0 scored 14.5 out of 16 in one experiment and 6 out of 8 in the other experiment after they pretended to believe the correct answer publicly. All demanding criteria, including resistance to extinction, were met. In the extinction condition, the newly trained children pretended to be wrong publicly with no ensuing evidence of regression. Thus, they gave all the signs of genuine understanding of the solution—justification, transfer, durability, and countersuggestion resistance. Those who were initially correct and who pretended to be wrong also gave no signs of regression, even after a second dissonance manipulation. They maintained nearly perfect scores on the pretest and throughout the posttests. However, there were signs of regression among those whose understanding was incomplete where their pretenses conflicted with their original judgments. An interesting case was that of those children with a shaky grasp of a problem who pretended to give the right answer. On problems where their pretense conflicted with their initial position, they made the maximum gain, but on problems where there was no conflict (i.e., where there was originally a correct judgment without a correct reason), they made only half the gains that could have been made, despite the fact that all the information needed to solve the problem was presented in the pretense.

The picture that is emerging from these "social" training procedures supports a unidirectional and nonreversible change in children's performance on some tasks, which is supported by something more than the presentation of additional useful information. There is support in these studies for the *development* construct and perhaps for the Genevan *equilibration* construct. There is no support for social learning theories because these are unable to explain the general failure of experimenters to undo correct performance through social interaction, conflict, modeling, or dissonance. In social learning theory, it should be as easy to shift children from correct to incorrect responses as it is to shift them from incorrect to correct answers. Change should be symmetrical, but the evidence points more certainly to an asymmetrical change.

If the effects of social conflict, interaction, modeling, and dissonance are greater or more potent than the effects from the presentation of the same informational content in nonsocial formats, the question of the 'contentfree' motivational aspects of these procedures naturally arises. Unique effects of these procedures are confounded with the information contained in them. It may be possible to unconfound these and generate the unique motivational feature of each by confronting immature children with modeled, dissonant, etc. information that conflicts with their incorrect judgment but is still equally incorrect. Thus, any gain could not be attributed to the presentation of the correct answer. For example, a child who thought that a glass of water poured into a taller, narrower glass held more liquid than when it was poured into a shorter, wider glass could be confronted by a peer who argues it contains less, by a model who states it contains less, or by his or her own public pretense that it contains less.

Both Murray (1974) and Cook and Murray (1973) found that children who were wrong and who observed other children who were wrong made slight but significant gains. Doise, Mugny, and Perret-Clermont (1976) found that when children were told by an adult that a displaced stick, which the child thought was longer, was shorter when viewed from its other end, a significant number of them (9/20) came to understand that the length of the stick was constant. Even though they were presented with erroneous information, apparently the fact that it conflicted with their initial position promoted some cognitive growth, although not as much growth as when they received correct information. In that case, nearly all the children were correct on the posttests.

Ames and Murray (1982) also subjected children to conflicting judgments in social interaction dyads, in a model, in a pretense, and in a "nonsocial" information presentation. All social procedures—social interaction, dissonance, modeling—had significant effects on the immature children. Virtually all the children changed their responses to at least one of nine tasks presented, but just a few children (12%) changed only to the correct answer. Most (57%) changed to another incorrect judgment (i.e., the conflicting version), and about 31% changed to the correct answer on some tasks and to another error on some others. The changes to the correct answer on the posttests were virtually all from children in the social interaction group. Significant differences in correct performance were found between the social interaction and all other groups in mean posttest scores. Insignificant differences were found among all the other groups and the retesting control. Still, the gains were modest, with final mean posttest scores slightly better than 4(sd = 5) out of 18. These modest gains nevertheless did fulfill the justification, transfer and durability criteria. Three children with scores of 0 scored 16–18 out of 18, and eleven scored between 5 and 15.

This approach provides some support for cognitive motivation, but little support for a unique equilibration function in any procedure but the social interaction condition. Here it is shown that conflict qua conflict is not only cognitively motivating but that the resolution of the conflict is likely to be in the progressive directions described by the equilibration model. In this limited way, two wrongs come to make a right. Lower change rates from these social procedures occur when incorrect information content is presented than when correct information content is presented. This indicates that correct and incorrect information are not equivalent. The child more easily changes from incorrect to correct than the other way around.

FINAL CAUTIONS

The cognitive tasks used to demonstrate the effects that have been cited previously are developmental tasks. They are tasks, like those on IQ tests, that have strong relationships with the age, particularly the mental age, of the child who attempts to solve them. These tasks, while measures of important intellectual accomplishments, are only measures of a small portion of the school curriculum (Murray, 1979). They are about the child's mastery of the notion of necessity, about information that must be true, that could not be otherwise. The child's grasp of information that is merely true, and does not have to be true, may be altered in several other ways in the kinds of social interaction situations described earlier. The Miller & Brownell study (1975), for example, shows that the outcome of social conflict procedures could go either way when children argue about some topics (e.g., favorite television shows). There is certainly the potential for conceptual regression and the acquisition of errors in the social interaction circumstance, particularly when the subject of the conflict is merely a matter of information, when the information is simply wrong. Thus, the expectation that the result of micro-mainstreaming, or the social interaction that occurs between at least two children of qualitatively different intellectual levels, will be positive, or in the direction of more sophisticated levels of thinking, is only warranted at this time for the kinds of tasks that already have a significant developmental component. Nevertheless, the research indicates that when mainstreaming—or micro-mainstreaming—is truly implemented, the effects on cognitive growth are likely to be positive for all members of the group. When pupils tutor each other on ordinary topics in the curriculum, for example, cognitive benefits invariably accrue to the tutor as well as the tutee (Hufnagel, 1984).

It must be recognized that the implementation of mainstreaming, even the circumscribed micro-mainstreaming procedures that have been reviewed here, have consequences that extend beyond the pupil's mastery of the set curriculum. The examination of these social consequences, as Rosenbaum notes (1980), needs to be undertaken on their own merit as well as how they help explain the 50 years of confusion that exists on the question of whether it is wiser to segregate pupils of different levels of ability or to integrate them.

REFERENCES

Ames, G., & Murray, F. (1982). When two wrongs make a right: Promoting cognitive change by social conflict. *Developmental Psychology*, *18*, 892–895.

Balow, I. H. (1963). Does homogeneous grouping give homogeneous groups? *Elementary School Journal*, *63*, 28–32.

Beilin, H. (1972). Inducing conservation through training. In G. Steiner (Ed.), *Psychology of the 20th century, Piaget and beyond* (Vol. 7). Zurich: Kindler.

Borys, S., & Spitz, H. (1979). Effect of peer interaction on the problem-solving behavior of mentally retarded youths. *American Journal of Mental Deficiency*, *84*, 273–279.
Botvin, G., & Murray, F. (1975). The efficacy of peer modeling and social conflict in the acquisition of conservation. *Child Development*, *46*, 796–799.
Charbonneau, C., & Robert, M. (1977). Observational learning of quantity conservation in relation to the degree of cognitive and conflict. *Psychological Reports*, *44*, 975–986.
Charbonneau, C., Robert, M., Bourassa, G., & Gladu-Bissonnette, S. (1976). Observational learning of quantity conservation and Piagetian generalization tasks. *Developmental Psychology*, *12*, 211–217.
Cook, H., & Murray, F. (1973). Acquisition of conservative through the observation of conserving models. Paper presented at the meetings of the American Educational Research Association, New Orleans, March.
Doise, W., Mugny, G., & Perret-Clermont, A-N. (1975). Social interaction and the development of cognitive operations. *European Journal of Social Psychology*, *5*, 367–383.
Doise, W., Mugny, G., & Perret-Clermont, A-N. (1976). Social interaction and cognitive development: Further evidence. *European Journal of Social Psychology*, *6*, 245–247.
Eyler, J., Cook, V., & Ward, L. (1983). Resegregation: Segregation within desegregated schools. In C. Rossell & W. Hawley (Eds.), *The consequences of school desegregation*. (pp. 126–162). Philadelphia: Temple University.
Gelman, R. (1978). Cognition development. *Annual Review of Psychology*, *29*, 297–332.
Goldberg, M. L., & Passow, A. H. (1962). The effects of ability grouping. *Education*, *82*, 482–487.
Goldschmid, M., & Bentler, P. (1968). *Concept assessment kit-conservation manual*. San Diego, CA.: Education and Industrial Testing Service.
Hufnagel, P. (1984). Effects of tutoring on tutors. Unpublished doctoral dissertation, University of Delaware.
Knight-Arest, I., & Reid, D. (1978). Peer interaction as a catalyst for conservation acquisition in normal and learning disabled children. Paper presented at the eighth annual symposium of The Jean Piaget Society, Philadelphia, May.
Kuhn, D. (1972). Mechanisms of change in the development of cognitive structures. *Child Development*, *43*, 833–844.
Miller, S., & Brownell, C. (1975). Peers, persuasion, and Piaget: Dyadic interaction between conservers and nonconservers. *Child Development*, *46*, 992–997.
Murray, F. (1972). The acquisition of conservation through social interaction. *Developmental Psychology*, *6*, 1–6.
Murray, F. (1978). Teaching strategies and conservation training. In A. M. Lesgold, J. W. Pellegrino, S. Fokkema, & R. Glaser (Eds.), *Cognitive psychology and instruction* (pp. 419–428). New York: Plenum.
Murray, F. (1979). The generation of educational practice from developmental theory. *Educational Psychologist*, *14*, 30–43.
Murray, F. (1981). The conservation paradigm: Conservation of conservation research. In D. Brodzinsky, I. Sigel, & R. Golinkoff (Eds.), *New directions in Piagetian theory and research* (pp. 143–175). Hillsdale, NJ. Lawrence Erlbaum Associates.
Murray, F. (1982). Teaching through social conflict. *Contemporary Educational Psychology*, *7*, 257–271.
Murray, F., Ames, G., & Botvin, G. (1977). The acquisition of conservation through cognitive dissonance. *Journal of Educational Psychology*, *69*, 519–527.
Murray, J. (1974). Social learning and cognitive development: Modeling effects on children's understanding of conservation. *British Journal of Psychology*, *65*, 151–160.
Robert, M., & Charbonneau, C. (1977). Extinction of liquid conservation by observation: Effects of model's age and presence. *Child Development*, *48*, 648–652.

Robert, M., & Charbonneau, C. (1978). Extinction of liquid conservation by modeling: Three indicators of its artificiality. *Child Development*, *49*, 194–200.

Rosenbaum, J. (1980). Social implications of educational grouping. In D. Berliner (Ed.), *Review of research in education, Vol. 8, American Educational Research Association*, 361–401.

Rosenthal, T., & Zimmerman, B. (1972). Modeling by exemplification and instruction in training conservation. *Developmental Psychology*, *6*, 392–401.

Schofield, J., & Sagar, H. (1983). Desegregation, school practices, and student race relations. In C. Rossell, & W. Hawley (Eds.), *The consequences of school desegregation*, Philadelphia: Temple University.

Silverman, I., & Geiringer, E. (1973). Dyadic interaction and conservation induction: A test of Piaget's equilibration model. *Child Development*, *44*, 815–820.

Silverman, I., & Stone, J. (1972). Modifying cognitive functioning through participation in a problem-solving group. *Journal of Educational Psychology*, *63*, 603–608.

Stephens, J. M., (1967). *The process of schooling*. New York: Holt, Rinehart, & Winston.

Sullivan, E. (1969). Trasnsition problems in conservation research. *Journal of Genetic Psychology*, *115*, 41–45.

Waghorn, L., & Sullivan, E. (1970). The exploration of transition rules in conservation of quantity (substance) using film mediated modeling. *Acta Psychologica*, *32*, 65–80.

Walker, S. (1984). Issues and trends in the education of the severely handicapped. In E. Gordon (Ed.), *Review of research in education, Vol. 11*, (pp. 93–124). American Educational Research Association, Washington, D.C.

Zimmerman, B., & Lanaro, P. (1974). Acquiring and retaining conservation of length through modeling and reversibility cues. *Merrill-Palmer Quarterly of Behavior and Development*, *20*, 145–161.

5 Understanding Factors That Affect Children's Attitudes Toward Mentally Retarded Peers

Gary N. Siperstein
John J. Bak
University of Massachusetts/Boston

As a result of legislative mandate and court action, almost every classroom in our elementary public schools contains a child who has been formally identified and diagnosed as having a specific disability. It is more the rule than the exception that the child is at risk for experiencing social problems. Children with disabilities experience rejection or isolation when they are with nondisabled peers. This is particularly true for children with mental disabilities—the children who make up the largest portion of the disabled population and who are the subject of this chapter.

In this chapter, we document how children's attitudes toward mentally retarded peers are the result of a complex interaction between their own personal characteristics, those of their mentally retarded peers, and the environment in which they interact. The purpose of this chapter is not only to document the negative attitudes that exist toward mentally retarded children, but also to identify reasons for that negativity. We introduce an attitude model to help explain the interaction between the different factors that affect children's attitudes, discuss our own research in light of this model, and conclude with implications and suggestions for future research.

INTERPRETING RESEARCH CONCERNING CHILDREN'S ATTITUDES TOWARD MENTALLY RETARDED PEERS

Definition of Attitudes

To understand the negative reactions children have toward their mentally retarded peers, we must first address the concept of attitudes. The definition of attitude has created heated debate since Thurstone's article "Attitudes can be measured" appeared in 1928. Only a rough consensus has emerged from this debate. Most investigators today embrace a definition of attitudes that encompasses one or more of the following components: cognition, affect, and behavioral intentions. Some investigators view attitudes as only cognitions and affect, treating behavioral intentions and subsequent behavior as a separate factor, possibly determined by cognition and affect. Others view attitude as a purely emotional response, and define cognition as a form of belief.

In this chapter, we do not seek to test different attitude theories. Our concern for defining attitudes arises from a need to develop an understanding of how attitudes can help us explain the interaction between mentally retarded and nonretarded children, and not from a concern for any particular attitudinal theory. It is for this reason that we ask the reader to accept our broader definition of attitudes, best summarized by Campbell (1950): "Social attitude is (or is evidenced by) consistency in response to social objects (p. 31)." We expand this definition here to include three different types of responses: cognitive (beliefs and attributive responses), affective (feelings and judgments), and behavioral (intentions and overt behaviors).

A Model for the Study of Attitudes and Attitude Change

To help the reader visualize the three components of an attitude and the important factors that affect these components, we have provided a schematic model (Fig. 5.1). This model, reflecting a basic theory of social perception, was adapted from Triandis's (1970) model of how persons from different cultures interact. The system of relationships shown in Fig. 5.1 provides us with a framework with which we can explore the effects of certain input variables. These include (a) the characteristics of the perceiver (needs, values, personality traits, etc.), (b) the characteristics of the target (physical characteristics, behavioral characteristics, etc.), (c) background variables that affect the perceiver (previous experience with similar targets, judgements made about the target by others, etc.) and (d) the social context in which the perceiver processes the stimulus information about the target (the influence of significant others in the social situation, the norms and roles governing the perceiver's behavior in the social situation, etc.). These input variables influence the output variables of cognition, affect, and behavioral intentions, which ultimately determine the perceiver's overt behaviors toward the target.

There are specific aspects of this model that warrant elaboration. Of central importance is that it allows us to focus on how children perceive their peers (particularly their mentally retarded peers) and how children process information transmitted by the characteristics of mentally retarded peers. Using the model, we can examine those characteristics children perceive, those that provide them

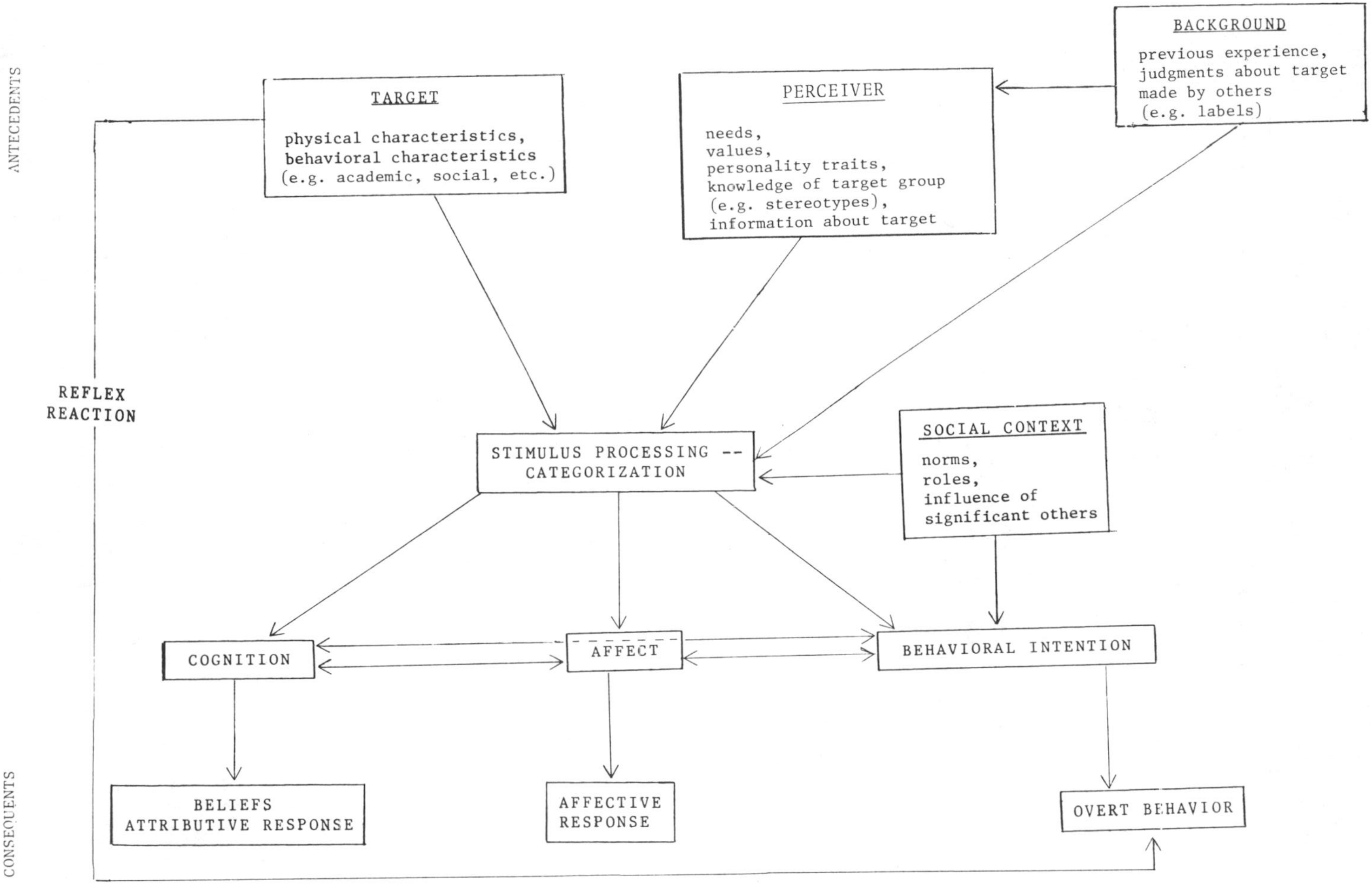

Fig. 5.1 Interactive model of children's attitudes toward their peers

with information about the target, and finally, those that allow children to categorize and thus place the mentally retarded child into a particular group. The group into which the mentally retarded child is placed may be one toward which children respond either positively or negatively.

By focusing on the stimulus processing aspect of children's interactions with their disabled peers, we are better able to identify how children form a first impression by selecting information from the complex array of characteristics exhibited by another peer. Only through understanding this process will we then be able to approach the task of changing not just the perceiver who is doing the observing, but also the targets and their characteristics. This latter approach (altering the characteristics of mentally retarded children) seldom has been taken by researchers reporting in the attitude change literature. However, the idea of change in mentally retarded children is central to the principle of normalization.

Most person-perception research, including the earliest work by Asch (1952); Bruner, Shapiro, and Taguiri (1958), and others, has not taken into account either information that a person has stored in memory or available situational information. Person-perception research has only focused on the characteristics, or cues, (i.e., the present information) that a target emits and a perceiver processes. A strength of our model is that it takes into account not only the characteristics of the target that act as cues to the perceiver, but also the perceiver's information about mentally retarded people as a group, as well as the information supplied by the situational context in which the perceiver interacts with the target.

Although not articulated in our model, our notion of characteristics that act as cues is somewhat more inclusive than past definitions of cues. Secord (1958) defined a cue (in our model, a characteristic) as an aspect of the larger perceptual field which may be differentiated with varying degrees of clarity. He held that a cue is not necessarily a single stimulus element, that it may be a configuration of elements, as in a patterned facial expression. For our purposes, characteristics may include such things as group membership in a race, minority or ethnic group, the wearing of glasses, or other types of category groupings both highly diffuse and highly specific.

The contention that children, acting as perceivers, respond to mentally retarded children as targets through the process of categorization, is in part supported by Campbell and Yarrow's (1961) person-perception research with children. They found that not only do children categorize others into broad groupings based on physical appearance, social interaction, etc., but also that children's categorization process was consistent to each perceiver across time and target persons. This finding is important because it demonstrates that we are not dealing with an idiosyncratic process by which children categorize others based on characteristics that act as cues A, B, and C at one time, but as cues D, E, and F at another time. The stability of this process is fundamental to our model and our underlying contention that target characteristics provide the cues that form the basis for perceivers' positive and negative, cognitive and affective responses, and behavioral intentions.

Past Research on Children's Attitudes Toward Mentally Retarded Peers

The mentally retarded, as a subgroup of children with disabilities, have the highest prevalence rate in our public schools within segregated and integrated settings. They also have been the most examined subgroup in attitudinal research. Gottlieb (1975) has shown in a survey of the literature that the attitudes of children and adults toward the retarded tend to be negative, especially after extended contact. Among children, there is little doubt that the retarded are perceived more negatively than their normal peers.

As early as 1950, Johnson found that mentally retarded children in public schools were not as accepted as their more normal peers. This finding has held up consistently, whether or not mentally retarded children have been integrated into regular classrooms. Attitudes toward both partially segregated educable mentally retarded and integrated children have been shown to be more negative than attitudes toward normal children (Baldwin, 1962; Dentler & Mackler, 1961; Goodman, Gottlieb, & Harrison, 1972; Lapp, 1957; Rucker, Howe, & Snyder, 1969). Only Renz and Simenson (1969) have found no differences in the social acceptance of normal and mentally retarded children.

Several efforts to engender children with more positive attitudes toward the mentally retarded have not met with much success. Although studies have shown some short-term positive changes (children participating expressed more positive attitudes immediately after the treatment period ended), these changes did not persist after a short period of time (Chennault, 1967; Lilly, 1971; McDaniel, 1969; Rucker & Vincenzo, 1970).

The social problems of the mentally retarded child have been aggravated by the fact that physical integration in public schools has not promoted social integration of the mentally retarded with their nonretarded peers. In fact, there is evidence of the reverse. The more contact that the nonretarded have had with their mentally retarded peers, the more negative their attitudes have become (e.g., Goodman, Gottlieb & Harrison, 1972). Because of these social problems, our research over the past 10 years has attempted to address both the factors that stigmatize a mentally retarded child in the eyes of his nonretarded peers, and those variables that mediate the stigmatization process.

By using the interactive model presented in Fig. 5.1 as a guideline, we have systematically studied (a) the characteristics of the mentally retarded child (target) that may or may not stigmatize the child in the eyes of the perceiver, (b) the characteristics of the nonretarded child (perceiver) that may affect how the mentally retarded child's behavioral and physical characteristics are processed and categorized, (c) the background variables, such as people's judgements made about the mentally retarded (labels), and the contact the nonretarded child has had with other mentally retarded children, and (d) the social context in which the nonretarded and mentally retarded child interact, which may include the influence of significant others and group pressure from nonretarded peers. In the following sections, we review our past research and show how our programmatic approach has led us to postulate certain basic tenets concerning nonretarded children's attitudinal responses to their mentally retarded peers.

CHILDREN'S ATTITUDES TOWARD MENTALLY RETARDED PEERS: RESULTS OF A PROGRAMMATIC RESEARCH EFFORT

Survey of Children's Knowledge about Mental Retardation

The first step toward understanding the attitudes of nonretarded to mentally retarded peers was to determine how nonretarded children perceived and characterized (as a function of their own age—a perceiver characteristic) their mentally retarded peers. Over 1000 students in grades 4 through 12 answered four critical questions:

1. What does it mean if a boy or a girl is mentally retarded?
2. What do you think are the common causes of mental retardation?
3. Do mentally retarded boys and girls look different from other boys and girls?
4. How do you think mentally retarded boys and girls feel?

The results showed that many children confused mental retardation with other sensory handicaps such as blindness and deafness (Siperstein & Bak, 1980). They also tended to view the mentally retarded child as being severely handicapped; they frequently described a Down's syndrome child's appearance. Lastly, most of the students in low grades described mentally retarded people as having negative feelings in either being aware that they are different or unaware of their condition.

Overall, the major conclusion drawn from our survey was that most children, like adults (Gottlieb & Siperstein, 1976) have an image of the mentally retarded child as one who has physical stigmata and is severely impaired. This is in contrast to actual prevalence figures, which show that severely mentally retarded with organic causes make up the smallest percentage of the mentally retarded population. This led us to examine more closely the nature of children's stereotypes of mentally retarded peers.

Assessment of Children's Stereotypes of Mentally Retarded Peers

The Role of Stereotypes. Stereotypes are included in our attitude model as perceiver characteristics. Past research on stereotypes shows that cues (or in our terms, characteristics) are selectively processed so that perceivers see consistency in the attributes of others; perceivers then categorize people based on their preconceived notions of the relationship between these characteristics and specific groups of people. The literature indicates that people tend to evaluate others in terms of their membership in certain categorical groups.

This stereotyping is fundamental to the way children process information regarding their mentally retarded peers. Children's stereotypes are beliefs about the characteristics of groups of targets, such as the mentally retarded. Although these stereotypes often may include a kernel of truth, there is usually much misinformation in them. Stereotypes obstruct the judgemental process that a child engages in because the stereotype provides a sense of absolutism. Within a stereotype there is a tendency to overstress the similarity among the members of the group—in this case, the mentally retarded.

What are the stereotypes that children hold toward the mentally retarded that affect their response toward a particular mentally retarded child? Not since an early study by Willey and McCandless (1973) had there been a large-scale assessment of children's social stereotypes of their handicapped peers. Given the importance of stereotypes and the negative way children responded to their mentally retarded peers, we undertook a series of studies to assess children's stereotypes.

The first need was to develop an attitude instrument that would be meaningful to children, thus helping to ensure valid responses. We developed an attitude instrument that would measure children's judgemental responses and reflect their stereotypes by first attempting to see the social world of children through their own eyes. To do this we designed an instrument in cooperation with children, using their own terminology, specifically, their own lexicon for depicting peers.

The Development of an Adjective Checklist to Measure Children's Attitudes. The instrument decided on to measure children's social stereotypes was an adjective checklist. This idea was borrowed from early personality studies that dealt with self-characterization (Barron, 1953; Gough, 1952). We believed that an open-ended checklist format would give an accurate picture of children's judgements about their peers. Past researchers have usually relied on a forced choice format in assessing children's beliefs, for example, the semantic differential. However, children in classroom situations are not forced to make judgements about others. In developing first impressions, some children are more apt to generalize beyond observed characteristics, whereas others are more apt to infer hidden traits regardless of a child's characteristics. Furthermore, some children employ more elaborate vocabulary in communicating their judgements.

Thus the open-ended format of an adjective checklist from which children can choose as many or as few trait descriptors as they please, does not restrict children's stereotypic response.

To develop the adjective checklist, over 300 children in grades 1 through 8 were asked to list all the words they would use to describe someone they liked and someone they didn't like. We then selected the 100 adjectives most frequently chosen and administered that list to over 200 children. They were asked to rate each word as to its positive or negative value. From this list, 34 adjectives were selected that children nearly unanimously agreed were either positive or negative. The adjectives depicted affective feelings, physical appearance, and academic and social behavior. Within each of these four categories, there was an equal number of positive and negative trait descriptors. (See Siperstein, 1980, for a complete description of the adjective checklist and other measures of children's attitudes.)

To assess the factor structure underlying the adjective checklist, the scale was administered to over 2,000 children in grades 2 through 8. Each child was asked to use the checklist four times to describe four target children: a peer who was the child's friend, and three peers who were mentally retarded, emotionally disturbed, and crippled. This data was summarized by tabulating the frequency of times children used each of the adjectives in their judgement of the four target children.

A three-factor structure in children's judgements of the target appeared. The first factor depicted a bright, socially able classmate (smart, friendly, nice). The second factor depicted a dull, socially inept classmate (dumb, careless, greedy), while the third reflected a negative empathetic response by the perceiver toward the target (lonely, unhappy, ashamed). These three factors appeared to describe, respectively, a popular child, a rejected child, and a withdrawn child.

This factor structure was then used to analyze children's stereotypic responses as a function of the target condition and the children's age. It was found that more than half of the children in grades 4 through 8 characterized the mentally retarded child using mainly the negative empathetic factor and using only slightly the negative factor (which reflected academic/social incompetence). The mentally retarded were perceived as slow, weak, lonely, and sad, but also as friendly. Another finding was that children's stereotypes of the three different disability groups became more differentiated with increasing age. All the children were able to differentiate the emotionally disturbed child from the mentally retarded in their stereotypic responses. Further, children in the upper grades were more apt to include in their stereotypes of the disability groups trait descriptors that reflected negative affect. This was especially true for the mentally retarded and emotionally disturbed target children. The results that grew out of the development of the adjective checklist prepared us to compare more directly the stereotypes of mentally retarded children with those of children in other disability groups.

Children's Judgements of Mentally Retarded and Other Disabled Children: A Comparison of Stereotypes. Our initial research concerning children's stereotypes of the mentally retarded and their comparison to stereotypes of other disability groups clearly indicated that children perceived mentally retarded children as being the most severely disabled. Children had a more positive stereotype of physically disabled children. To understand better children's differential stereotypes, we decided to build upon research conducted by Richardson, Hastorf, Goodman, and Dornbusch (1961), who had attempted to identify in adults a social preference hierarchy among the disability groups. The goal was to assess elementary school children's preferences for peers who had different disabilities (mental retardation, visual impairment, hearing impairment, physical impairment). We sought to compare groups along several dimensions that have been shown to underlie social acceptance in the classroom: academic behavior, social behavior, and physical appearance (see Siperstein, 1980).

A set of photographs depicting children in wheelchairs, wearing hearing aids, wearing dark glasses and using canes, and having Down's syndrome was shown to over 50 fourth- through sixth-grade students. Using paired comparisons and ranking procedures, children were asked to judge each of the target children along the previous three dimensions. Similar to findings of Richardson et al., we found a definite hierarchy in children's judgements of the different disability groups. Overall, children judged the mentally retarded lowest on all four dimensions. They were most consistent in their judgements of the disability groups on the academic dimension, and were much less consistent on the social and appearance dimensions. It is possible that the children had an easier time judging the disability groups when their estimates were based on how well a child with a given disability would perform in a classroom.

In addition to judging the disability groups along the dimensions of academic behavior, social behavior, and physical appearance, children also indicated which target they would most like to have as a member of their classroom. This question represented a measure of social distance. We found that fourth-grade children did not differentiate the different disability groups in terms of who should join their classrooms. In contrast, sixth-graders least preferred a mentally retarded child as a new member of their class.

Combining these results with our previous findings from children's responses on the adjective checklist, we see that as children get older they have a more negative stereotype of mentally retarded children. Perhaps more importantly, it appears that the physical characteristics of a target with a disability, especially one with Down's syndrome, can evoke consistent judgements about both overt attributes and, more particularly, covert attributes. Furthermore, children's judgements about both the covert and overt characteristics of a mentally retarded peer are associated with their judgements concerning the social distance between them and the peer.

The Effects of Target Characteristics on Children's Attitudes

The Effects of Academic Behavior and Physical Appearance. Utilizing our understanding of children's stereotypes of the mentally retarded, we designed a study that addressed children's attitudinal responses toward their mentally retarded peers (Siperstein & Gottlieb, 1977). This study took into account the mentally retarded child's behavior and appearance—specifically, those behavioral and appearance characteristics that children most associated with the mentally retarded. Thus, we studied the effects of academically incompetent behavior and the physical stigmata associated with mental retardation—Down's syndrome. These two factors, academic incompetence and Down's syndrome appearance, were the most mentioned attributes of a mentally retarded child's behavior and physical appearance.

Our study employed a procedure and design in which over 100 fourth through sixth-grade children were presented with audio tapes and photographs of mentally retarded target children whose behavior and appearance characteristics varied. The results showed conclusively that children's attitudes are most negative toward a peer who exhibits incompetent academic behavior. Furthermore, when target children were generally competent, if they appeared mentally retarded as a result of Down's syndrome, children were not as positive toward them as they were to other children who appeared normal. Thus we found not only that children were affected by their peers' academic behavior, but also that physical stigmata were salient in children's perceptions of others—children did not easily dismiss physical appearance when they evaluated others. Physical appearance, which connotes mental retardation, showed itself potent enough to diminish the favorable judgements children usually make of competent peers.

Children evaluated targets using the adjective checklist. Similar to our previous findings, we found that children's descriptions of targets on this measure generalized beyond the specific attributes of the target (academic behavior and physical appearance) depicted on our stimulus materials. For example, children described the academically incompetent child as socially incompetent and unhappy. Thus, the children's final judgements about the target child contained more than the actual descriptors presented. Not only was there evidence that children differentially judged their peers as a result of academic behavior and physical appearance, but it was found that children were less inclined to engage in activities with the academically incompetent or physically stigmatized target child. These activities represented things children do both in and out of the classroom (e.g., working on a class project, talking on the telephone, watching TV together, and riding bicycles). Thus, we saw that children's cognitive judgements had an impact on their behavioral intentions.

The Effect of Social Behavior on Children's Attitudes. This study examined the effects of the target characteristic of social competence on children's attitudes

(Siperstein & Bak, in press). We chose to study this characteristic because recent studies have shown that isolation and rejection among nonretarded children can be attributed to the absence of prosocial behavior and the presence of antisocial behavior (Asher & Gottman, 1981; Dodge, 1983). Children who exhibit withdrawn or aggressive behavior are most often, respectively, isolated or rejected within the social hierarchy of a classroom. We wished to determine if such social behaviors would further stigmatize a mentally retarded child who experiences academic problems, and to see if prosocial behaviors would keep children from responding negatively toward mentally retarded peers.

Using a design similar to that described in the previous study, we presented over 100 fourth through sixth-grade children with mentally retarded target children who exhibited mild or moderate retardation in both academic behavior and physical appearance. The mildly and moderately retarded children were depicted as exhibiting either the prosocial, withdrawn, or aggressive behavior associated with popularity, isolation, and rejection among nonretarded children.

The results indicated that children judged withdrawn and aggressive targets negatively and were less inclined to interact with them. This finding was expected. More importantly, children responded favorably toward the mentally retarded targets who exhibited prosocial behavior. Thus, the target characteristic of prosocial behavior appeared strong enough to ameliorate the negative attitudes often caused by poor academic performance and abnormal physical appearance.

An unexpected finding occurred among children who viewed the withdrawn and aggressive targets. Although these children were extremely negative in their judgements and behavioral intentions toward nonretarded targets who exhibited withdrawn or aggressive behavior, they were not as negative toward the targets when they were mildly retarded (poor academic behavior), or moderately retarded (poor academic behavior, poor speech, Down's syndrome appearance). The targets' personal characteristics (particularly the Down's syndrome appearance) seemed to act as de facto labels. Because children perceived the targets as mentally retarded, they seemed to employ a different and less harsh (although in this case, still negative) standard. This protective effect is examined more closely in our investigation of labels.

The Effect of Labels (Background Variables) on Children's Attitudes

The Effect of the Label "Mentally Retarded." In addition to studying children's reactions to a mentally retarded target child as a function of the target's physical and behavioral characteristics, we also examined background factors that affect the perceiver's response to the target. The factor we studied most closely concerned the judgements about the target made by others which are then reflected in a label. Throughout the literature, labeling has been considered deleterious to the person labeled. Legislative action banning the use of labels has resulted from research that has documented some of labeling's harmful effects. Dexter (1964), for example, has suggested that most of a labeled person's behavior is the result of significant others' (teachers', parents', and peers') expectations of him as a result of the label. Mercer (1973) takes the labeling issue one step further by theorizing that handicapping conditions, such as mental retardation, are not an intrinsic characteristic of the person labeled, but rather a role learned through the personal interactions between the labeled and the labelers.

Evidence demonstrating the adverse effects that a label has on the way people treat the mentally retarded is neither complete nor conclusive (MacMillan, Jones, & Aloia, 1974). There are those who have pointed out the potential benefits of labeling children. Guskin (1962) believes that a label assists adults in understanding the child's behavior, and allows them to be less critical. MacMillan, Jones and Aloia (1974) discuss how a label such as "mentally retarded" tends to reduce cognitive dissonance in the individuals observing the behavior of an unlabeled mentally retarded person. It provides people with the framework to understand certain behaviors.

We believe that the type of child to whom a label is applied determines, to a great extent, what the effect of the label will be. Children have positive and negative personal characteristics. Past researchers confounded labels with negative characteristics, and then blamed the label for resulting poor attitudes. In our research, we have attempted to find the conditions under which a label, such as mentally retarded, can have either a positive or negative effect. Our objective has been to learn how to eliminate or reduce the stigmatizing potential of labels.

The question addressed in our research was whether labels have more or less of a negative impact on children's attitudes than the negative behavior or appearance characteristics of a mentally retarded child. We also wished to determine the effects on the perceiver when the target child exhibits negative behavioral and physical characteristics in the presence of a label (Budoff & Siperstein, 1978). Employing procedures similar to those described in the previous study, we presented over 100 sixth-graders with audiotapes and photographs of target children who either were or were not labeled mentally retarded.

Our findings indicated that children have more favorable attitudes toward labeled than toward unlabeled targets when a target exhibits academically incompetent behavior or is physically stigmatized. This indicates that the mentally retarded label serves a protective function. It may cause children to apply a different set of standards when judging the labeled mentally retarded child than when judging a nonretarded child. The label helped override the stigmatizing aspects of negative behavioral and physical characteristics.

The Effects of the Idiomatic Label, "Retard." In a follow-up study, we varied two different labels while taking into account the academic incompetent behavior and physical appearance of the mentally retarded child (Siperstein, Budoff, & Bak, 1980). The specific question asked was whether or not idiomatic labels, such as "retard," which are part of children's lexicon of insults, have more of an effect on mentally retarded peers' social acceptability than the clinical label "mentally retarded." It was possible that the clinical label had not stigmatized the target child in the previous studies because either the label had been denied, or the clinical label may have protected the target child who exhibited incompetent behavior. To compare the effects of the two labels on children's attitudes toward their mentally retarded peers without confounding the effects of a target child's academic behavior and physical appearance, the target's behavior and appearance were varied, as well as the labels.

More than 100 fifth and sixth-grade children saw a target child whose academic behavior, physical appearance, and label was systematically varied. The results of the study indicated that the idiomatic label "retard" had a greater power to stigmatize the mentally retarded child than the clinical label "mentally retarded." Children expressed extremely negative judgements and behavioral intentions toward the target child who was labeled "retard" and who was academically incompetent. In contrast, children were generally neutral or slightly positive in their response to the academically incompetent child when he was labeled "mentally retarded." These findings suggest that the clinical label provides a way for children to understand the mentally retarded child's poor performance.

In the absence of a label in the preceding study, children were overly critical of a child possessing characteristics such as academic incompetence. Since children may not have been able to attribute the aberrant behavior or appearance to a disability, as they could when the target was labeled "mentally retarded," they may have been more likely to apply the standards they used to judge their more normal peers. To children, a "retard" may not really be a mentally retarded person. He therefore does not receive special dispensation because children see him as responsible for his actions.

The results of this study and previous ones have important implications for people who support the movement to abandon the use of labels. The findings question the validity of the movement's central thesis (here oversimplified) that a label is bad and the absence of a label is good. In the aforementioned studies, we have emphasized the effects of target children's negative behavior and physical characteristics, both alone and in combination with a label, on nonretarded children's attitudinal responses. In our next study, we examine another set of variables—perceived similarities between perceiver and target—to see if they also can act to ameliorate the negative attitudinal responses brought on by mentally retarded children's behavior and appearance.

The Effect of Perceived Similarity on Children's Attitudes

The Effect of Directly Matching Similar Target and Perceiver Characteristics. Our next objective was to study what target and perceiver characteristics would mediate children's negative responses to a mentally retarded peer. To identify these factors, we searched the literature in social cognition and found that "perceived similarity" by a perceiver toward a target person has been well documented as a major factor underlying interpersonal relationships and the development of friendship between able-bodied children. Two studies were designed that examined the ability of perceived similarity (between nonretarded and mentally retarded children) to reduce the stigmatizing potential of a mentally retarded child's negative characteristics.

Much research has shown that similarities in attitude, sex, socioeconomic status, and race are predictive of interpersonal attraction. Some researchers have suggested that, no matter what the dimensions of comparison, similarity is preferred to dissimilarity (Byrne, 1969). Similarity theory, initially postulated by Festinger (1954), holds that one's identity varies as a function of his standing relative to other people, and the clearest and most satisfying sense of self comes from associating with similar others. Whether similarity is a powerful agent for interpersonal attraction because of one's need to evaluate oneself (Festinger's theory of social comparison processes, 1954), or because it acts as a reinforcer by legitimizing one's conduct and abilities (Morse & Gergen, 1970), one thing is certain: Knowing how two children are similar helps in forecasting the type of interpersonal interaction that will take place. This research has been limited to examining relationships between normal persons.

The negative attitudes nonretarded children hold toward any mentally retarded child may be due to the fact that the mentally retarded child's negative physical characteristics or inappropriate behaviors may blind children to existing similarities. To test this assumption, a study was conducted to determine the power of perceived similarity to mediate children's attitudinal responses to a mentally retarded child who exhibited negative physical and behavioral characteristics (Siperstein & Chatillon, 1982). The design we used was similar to that used in the earlier studies previously mentioned; we presented over 100 fifth and sixth-grade children with a target child who was academically incompetent and who had Down's syndrome. In addition, we manipulated the factor of perceived similarity by presenting the mentally retarded target as either similar or not similar to the perceiver. This was done by matching the items we depicted the target as liking with the items the perceivers had already told us they liked (e.g., specific foods and after school activities).

The results conclusively showed that elementary school children would respond positively in both their judgements and behavioral intentions toward a mentally retarded peer who exhibited negative behavioral and physical characteristics when that peer was perceived as similar to themselves. Unexpectedly, we found that a background variable—previous experience with the mentally retarded—interacted with the effects of perceived similarity. Children who were familiar with mentally retarded children from the segregated classes in their schools, did not respond as positively to the mentally retarded child as did children who were unfamiliar with mentally retarded peers and did not have them in their schools. We concluded that it was more difficult for children who saw mentally retarded peers in segregated classes to perceive similarities than it was for children who have had no previous school experience with the mentally retarded. Thus, the positive effects of perceived similarity must be viewed within the context of the past experiences of the nonretarded child.

The results of this study provide insight into why past attempts to change children's attitudes toward the mentally retarded have not met with much success. For example, when Chennault (1967) and Lilly (1971) paired unpopular mentally retarded children with the most popular normal children, their underlying hypothesis was that children look to the popular child for direction in developing friendships with new peers. They found that the social positions of the mentally retarded were raised, but only temporarily. It is probable that children look to the popular child for guidance in initially interacting with a new peer, particularly one who might be visibly handicapped. However, lasting friendships are governed more by the similarity between the child and the new peer.

The Effect of Naturally Occurring Similarities. In the natural social context of the classroom, children's personality characteristics are seldom matched exactly to those of another peer, as they were in the previous study. Children must find out about a peer and then make their own judgements about similarities and the likelihood of friendship. In this study, we sought to determine if children would become more favorably inclined toward mentally retarded target peers after they had a chance to learn about the targets' personal preferences and to see that these target children were similar, at least in general, to their own classmates if not to their individual selves.

The design and procedures employed were similar to those used in previous studies. Nearly 100 fourth through sixth-grade children first viewed videotapes of either a nonretarded, mildly, or moderately retarded target reading material that reflected his or her ability level. They then viewed another videotape showing a teacher interviewing the same target about personal likes, dislikes, and favorite activities in and out of school. We believe that the interview format provided information about the mentally retarded child's social behavior in a way that would elicit perceptions of similarity from the nonretarded subjects.

The results indicated that the positive effects of similarity were still evident in this more naturalistic context. Children, after first observing a mildly or moderately retarded child reading, were negative or neutral in their judgements and negative in their behavioral intentions. After children were given the opportunity to observe the mildly or moderately retarded target being interviewed, they saw themselves as more similar to the targets and they changed their judgements in a positive direction as a result. The mentally retarded target children, after being seen in the interview as liking the same things and engaging in the same activities as nonretarded children, were judged as more friendly and happy. However, children did not significantly change their behavioral intentions toward the mentally retarded peer.

It was apparent from this study that children were more willing to change their judgements and beliefs about a specific mentally retarded child than they were willing to change their behavioral intentions. This demonstrates how attitudinal change can occur in one aspect of a person's attitude but not another. This differentiation within the concept of attitude becomes more important as we begin to work with children in actual classroom situations. The following study examines more closely the processes that affect children's perceptions of new peers in the social context of the classroom.

Effects of Peer Group Discussion (Social Context) on Children's Attitudes

In this study, we sought to examine children's attitudes toward their mentally retarded peers in a social context that allowed children to recreate the patterns of their daily interpersonal interactions (Siperstein, Bak, & Gottlieb, 1977). This approach was taken because past research on adult attitudes had indicated that group discussion among adults made their individual attitudes more extreme in the direction toward which they were tending before group discussion. There was reason to believe that some of the negative attitudes expressed by children individually were not as extreme as some of the behaviors of social rejection we had observed or heard about in classrooms. One of the possible reasons for the discrepancy was that children alone might have been less inclined to be negative than when they were among their peers. Thus it was necessary to recreate a realistic social context where children would be more inclined to express attitudes as a function of more naturally occurring processes.

To do this, we employed a design in which we presented a target child to approximately 100 fifth and sixth-grade children who viewed the target in small groups. The target child exhibited negative behavioral characteristics and physical characteristics (Down's syndrome). The difference between this study and previous ones was that the children were permitted to discuss among themselves how they felt about the target after they had responded to the target on their own. The children were also instructed to reach a consensus about their attitude toward the target child.

The initial results were as expected—children responded negatively toward the mentally retarded target who exhibited academic problems and who had a Down's syndrome appearance. The children became more negative toward the incompetent physically stigmatized target child after group discussion, but they did not become more positive toward a competent, normal-appearing child. By analyzing the specific individual judgements of each group, we were able to find that children who were extremely negative toward the mentally retarded target, made other members of the group who were neutral or slightly negative become more extreme in their feelings and behavioral intentions.

We hypothesized that children who changed toward the extreme negative pole were initially inhibited by what they thought was a limit of acceptability for certain attitudes. However, as a result of group discussion these children saw others as being closer to the imagined limit than they had realized. Thus it made it easier for them to change toward the position that was more closely aligned to their own natural feelings. The individuals in the group who were responsible for the negative change were probably masking their initial negative feelings toward the mentally retarded child. It is also possible that children who shifted were bowing to group pressure to conform and were more negative after group discussion than they were on their own.

From these results, it is apparent that we cannot adequately assess children's attitudinal responses toward their mentally retarded peers without taking into account peer group pressures that are part of children's social context. Future research directed toward changing children's attitudes needs to consider not only the individual child, but the child within the context of his or her peer group. More successful change strategies may be those that are directed at the group rather than the individual child.

FUTURE DIRECTIONS IN RESEARCH CONCERNING CHILDREN'S ATTITUDES TOWARD MENTALLY RETARDED PEERS

Establishing Ecological Validity

For research to have maximum practical and theoretical impact, it must faithfully relate to and represent what occurs in real-life settings. A small but growing number of researchers have already made clear the challenge of establishing ecological validity in future investigations (e.g., Berkson & Romer, 1980; Bronfenbrenner, 1976). In our own line of research, this challenge raises several questions. Are there are situations in the classroom where labels take on a protective function and others where they serve to stigmatize? What is the value of perceived similarity in initial interactions between nonretarded and mentally retarded peers?

To begin answering such questions, we are currently expanding our research in two new directions. One is an investigation of the relationship between laboratory findings and children's reactions to real mentally retarded peers in their classrooms. The other takes an observational approach to studying the factors associated with the acceptance and rejection of mentally retarded children.

Assessing the Relationship Between Laboratory and Field Research Findings. In this study, we compare children's attitudinal responses to mentally retarded targets presented within a laboratory situation via videotapes, to their responses to mentally retarded peers integrated into their classrooms. It is hypothesized that children who respond favorably to integrated peers will be more inclined to respond in a positive way toward mentally retarded targets in the videotapes. The results will help us understand the generalizability of children's attitudinal responses toward specific mentally retarded peers. A study by Miller and Gibbs (1984) provides some evidence of such a relationship. Using our measures to assess children's judgements and behavioral intentions of their peers, the study found a relationship between adolescents' responses to the learning handicapped in general, and their behaviors as tutors to specific learning handicapped children.

Employing an Observational Approach. In this study, we attempt to determine whether mentally retarded children's academic and social characteristics remain consistent across different learning environments. The personal characteristics of mentally retarded children can either stigmatize the mentally retarded or act as de facto labels to protect them from the otherwise negative reactions of their nonretarded peers. If these characteristics change in different settings (regular vs. special education classrooms, for example), it can be expected that mentally retarded children's acceptance may show a concommitant change. They may be accepted in one setting but not in another. We hypothesize that mentally retarded children's behavioral characteristics are not set, but are variable according to background factors similar to those we have begun to identify among nonretarded children. By understanding the exact role that different educational settings have on mentally retarded children's specific behaviors, we will help improve the ecological validity of our attitude model.

Using an Inclusive Definition of Attitudes

Future research would benefit from using an inclusive definition of attitudes. In our work, it has been found that children's attitudinal responses are not singular. Different aspects of one response toward the same mentally retarded peer may be simultaneously positive and negative. This strongly suggests that there is a need to continue to take a more broadly analytical approach to assessing children's attitudes. We must continue to examine the components of children's attitudes—beliefs, feelings, behavioral intentions—and how they relate to children's actual behaviors. By taking this approach, we will be better prepared to study children not only in controlled laboratory situations, but also in real-life situations where nonretarded children are in contact with mentally retarded children.

Summary and Conclusion: The Importance of Using a Model

The studies reported here document that children's attitudes toward their mentally retarded peers are a complex phenomenon. Children's attitudes are not simply negative; they are a blend of positive and negative, changing across time, place and setting, and dependent on specific perceiver, target, and background variables. We have proposed a model both to help describe this dynamic process and to synthesize different areas of relevant research. Before making final comment on this model, we use it to summarize our major findings.

The work we have done has shown the importance of investigating the effects of perceiver and target characteristics and background variables on children's attitudes. We have attempted to show how such characteristics and variables act alone and in combination to affect children's attitudes. In our initial investigation of children's stereotypes of mentally retarded peers (part of the perceiver's background), it was learned that children do not define the mentally retarded uniformly. Most had a stereotypic notion of the mentally retarded that aligned closely with a severely retarded child. It is important to keep this finding in mind, for it helps explain how children process information about mentally retarded peers.

In examining the influence of the mentally retarded target's characteristics on children's attitudes, evidence was found that children could be affected either positively or negatively by such characteristics. Poor academic behavior, abnormal physical appearance, and social incompetence were all characteristics that contributed to negative attitudes. However, labels (a background variable) could mediate the negative effects and make children respond in a more protective way toward the mentally retarded targets. Also, when similarities between target and perceiver characteristics (common likes and dislikes in food, entertainment, and play activities) were made salient to children, they (the perceivers) responded quite favorably to the targets. When exploring the role of the social context in affecting children's attitudes, it was found that children who have negative leanings toward the mentally retarded could become more negative as a result of group discussion.

The attitude model used has provided us with a broader view of how nonretarded children respond to their mentally retarded peers. It has given us a way to organize, investigate, and interpret the interactive effects of many pieces in the attitude puzzle: target characteristics, perceiver characteristics, the social context of the interaction, and background variables such as labels. Perhaps more importantly, it has prepared us to take a more ecological approach in current and future research. Relating our findings to what actually occurs in classrooms is of critical importance. It is our hope that this and other such models will help to spur new investigations that will advance the understanding of relationships between mentally retarded and nonretarded peers and help further improve the process of social integration.

ACKNOWLEDGMENT

The work reported in this paper was made possible in part by funding from the National Institute for Child Health and Human Development Grant Number HD14772-01.

REFERENCES

Asch, S. E. (1952). *Social psychology*. Englewood Cliffs, NJ: Prentice-Hall.

Asher, S. R., & Gottman, J. M. (Eds.) (1981). *The Development of Children's Friendships: Description and Intervention*. New York: Cambridge University Press.

Baldwin, W. D. (1962). The social position of the educable mentally retarded in the regular grades in the public schools. *Exceptional Children, 29*, 106–112.

Barron, F. (1953). An ego-strength scale which predicts response to psychotherapy. *Journal of Consulting Psychology, 17*, 327–333.

Berkson, G., & Romer, D. (1980). Social ecology of supervised communal facilities. Communal facilities for mentally retarded adults, I: Introduction. *American Journal of Mental Deficiency, 85*, 219–228.

Bronfenbrenner, U. (1976). The experimental ecology of education. *Educational Researcher, 5*, 5–15.

Bruner, J. S., Shapiro, D., & Taguiri, R. (1958). The meaning of traits in isolation and in combination. In R. Taguiri and L. Petrullo (Eds.), *Person perception and interpersonal behavior* (pp. 277–288). Stanford: Stanford University Press.

Budoff, M., & Siperstein, G. N. (1978). Low income children's attitudes toward the mentally retarded: Effects of labeling and academic behavior. *American Journal of Mental Deficiency, 82*, 474–478.

Byrne, D. (1969). Attitudes and attraction. In L. Berkowitz (Ed.), *Advances in experimental social psychology*, (Vol. 4) (pp. 35–89). New York: Academic Press.

Campbell, D. T. (1950). The indirect assessment of social attitudes. *Psychological Bulletin, 47*, 15–38.

Campbell, J. D., & Yarrow, M. R. (1961). Perceptual and behavioral correlates of social effectiveness. *Sociometry, 24*, 1–20.

Chennault, M. (1967). Improving the social acceptance of unpopular educable mentally retarded pupils in special classes. *American Journal of Mental Deficiency, 72*, 455–458.

Dentler, R. A., and Mackler, B. (1961). Mental ability and sociometric status among retarded children. *Psychological Bulletin, 59*, 273–283.

Dexter, L. A. (1964). *The tyranny of schooling: An inquiry into the problem of "stupidity"*. New York: Basic Books.

Dodge, K. A. (1983). Behavioral antecedents of peer social status. *Child Development, 54*, 1386–1399.

Festinger, L. (1954). A theory of social comparison processes. *Human Relations, 7*, 117–140.

Goodman, H., Gottlieb, J., & Harrison, R. H. (1972). Social acceptance of EMR's integrated into a nongraded elementary school. *American Journal of Mental Deficiency, 76*, 412–417.

Gottlieb, J. (1975). Attitudes toward retarded children: Effects of labeling and academic performance. *American Journal of Mental Deficiency*, 1975, *79*, 268–273.

Gottlieb, J. & Siperstein, G. N. (1976). Attitudes toward mentally retarded persons: Effects of attitude referent specificity. *American Journal of Mental Deficiency, 80*, 376–381.

Gough, H. G. (1965). *The Adjective Checklist Manual*. Palo Alto, California: Consulting Psychologist Press.

Guskin, S. L. (1962). The influence of labeling upon the perception of subnormality in mentally defective children. *American Journal of Mental Deficiency, 67*, 402–406.

Johnson, G. O. (1950). A study of the social position of mentally handicapped children in the regular grades. *American Journal of Mental Deficiency, 55*, 60–88.

Lapp, E. R. (1951). A study of the social adjustment of slow-learning children who were assigned part-time to regular classes. *American Journal of Mental Deficiency, 62*, 254–262.

Lilly, M. S. (1971). Improving social acceptance of low socioeconomic status, low achieving students. *Exceptional Children, 37*, 441–447.

MacMillan, D. L., Jones, R. L., & Aloia, G. F. (1974). The mentally retarded label: A theoretical analysis and review of research. *American Journal of Mental Deficiency, 79*, 241–261.

McDaniel, J. W. (1969). *Physical disability and human behavior*. New York: Pergamon.

Mercer, J. R. (1973). *Labeling the mentally retarded*. Berkeley: University of California Press.

Miller, C. T., & Gibbs, E. D. (1984). High school students' attitudes and actions toward "slow learners." *American Journal of Mental Deficiency, 89*, 156–166.

Morse, S., & Gergen, K. J. (1970). Social comparison, self-consistency and the concept of self. *Journal of Personality and Social Psychology, 16*, 148–156.

Renz, P., & Simenson, R. J. (1969). The social perception of normals towards their EMR grade-mates. *American Journal of Mental Deficiency, 74*, 405–408.

Richardson, S. A., Hastorf, A. H., Goodman, H., & Dornbusch, S. M. (1961). Cultural uniformity in reaction to physical disabilities. *American Sociological Review, 26*, 241–247.

Rucker, C. N., Howe, C. E., & Snyder, B. (1969). The participation of retarded children in junior high academic and nonacademic regular classes. *Exceptional Children, 35*, 617–623.

Rucker, C. N., & Vincenzo, F. M. (1970). Maintaining social acceptance gains made by mentally retarded children. *Exceptional Children, 36*, 679–680.

Secord, P. F. (1958). Facial features and inference processes in interpersonal perception. In R. Taguiri & L. Petrullo (Eds.), *Person perception and interpersonal behavior* (pp. 300–315). Stanford: Stanford University Press.

Siperstein, G. N. (1980). *Instruments for measuring children's attitudes toward the handicapped*. Unpublished manuscript, University of Massachusetts, Boston.

Siperstein, G. N., & Bak, J. J. (1980). Students' and teachers' perceptions of the mentally retarded child. In J. Gottlieb (Ed.), *Educating mentally retarded persons*, (pp. 207–230). Baltimore: University Park Press.

Siperstein, G. N., & Bak, J. J. (in press). Social behavior: How it affects children's attitudes toward mildly and moderately mentally retarded peers. *American Journal of Mental Deficiency*.

Siperstein, G. N., Bak, J. J., & Gottlieb, J. (1977). Effects of group discussion on children's attitudes toward handicapped peers. *Journal of Educational Research, 70*, 131–134.

Siperstein, G. N., Budoff, M., & Bak, J. J. (1980). Effects of the labels "mentally retarded" and "retard" on the social acceptability of mentally retarded children. *American Journal of Mental Deficiency, 84*, 596–601.

Siperstein, G. N., & Chatillon, A. C. (1982). Importance of perceived similarity in improving children's attitudes toward mentally retarded peers. *American Journal of Mental Deficiency, 86*, 453–458.

Siperstein, G. N., & Gottlieb, J. (1977). Physical stigma and academic performance as factors affecting children's first impressions of handicapped peers. *American Journal of Mental Deficiency, 81*, 455–462.

Thurstone, L. L. (1928). Attitudes can be measured. *American Journal of Sociology, 33*, 529–554.

Triandis, H. C. (1970). *Person perception: A review of the literature and implications* (Tech. Rep. 3). Chicago: Illinois Studies of the Culturally Disadvantaged.

Willey, N. R. & McCandless, B. R. (1973). Social stereotypes for normal, educable mentally retarded, and orthopedically handicapped children. *Journal of Special Education, 1*, 283–288.

6 The Social Comparison Behavior of Academically Handicapped Students in Mainstream Classes

C. Julius Meisel
University of Delaware

This chapter reviews what is known and what has long been assumed about the social comparison behavior of school-age handicapped children. The chapter is divided into two parts. The first part reviews the major issues and includes a critical examination of the assumptions that are often made about the social comparison behavior of children, its likely consequences for low-performing children, and the implications of these assumptions for school placement of academically handicapped children. The second part reviews my work on the social comparison behavior of mainstreamed academically handicapped children.

THE ISSUES

Social comparison is the process whereby people evaluate their own abilities or opinions by comparing them with the abilities or opinions of others (Festinger, 1954). In the past several decades, social psychologists have studied this process extensively to determine when and how it takes place and what its social and psychological consequences are. Suls and Miller (1977) have offered the most extensive review to date. Although most of these studies were done with adult subjects, there is evidence that social comparison is used for self-evaluation by children as young as 7 or 8 years old (Ruble, Feldman, & Boggiano, 1976; Ruble, Boggiano, Feldman, & Loebl, 1980). Whether or not the behavior develops as a result of the school experience, is not known. What is known is that the school environment stimulates a great deal of social comparison among students (Pepitone, 1972; Suls & Sanders, 1979; Veroff, 1969). Despite this, there has been relatively little study of the social comparison behavior of school and many questions about how it develops and what its consequences are remain to be answered (Levine, 1983).

Presumed Effects of Social Comparison on Self Esteem

It is interesting that arguments both for segregated placement of handicapped children as well as for mainstreaming of those same children have been based on assumptions about their social comparison behavior and its likely consequences. A major argument in favor of segregated placement, for example, has been that handicapped students are likely to feel better about themselves (i.e. have greater self esteem or more positive self evaluations) when placed with other handicapped students than they would if they remained in regular classes. The presumption underlying this argument is that in regular classes, handicapped students tend to have only higher performing peers as standards of comparison and the results of such comparisons are likely to have negative effects on self-esteem.

One of the principal arguments for mainstreaming, on the other hand, has been that integration provides the handicapped child an opportunity to model nonhandicapped peers (e.g. Altman & Talkington, 1977; Dunn, 1968). Implied in this argument is a suggestion that mainstreamed students will find their own behavioral repertoires deficient in comparison to those of higher performing peers, and will, as a result, be motivated to imitate the behavior of those peers. Presumably, the imitation would be stimulated by a desire to reduce a comparative discrepancy in some area of social or academic performance.

By the late 1960s, the argument that segregated classes are likely to be beneficial for the self-esteem of handicapped students had begun to wane. This was due in part to the results of studies showing that educable mentally retarded (EMR) students were more likely to make self-derogatory statements *after* placement in special classes than before (Meyerowitz, 1965), and that EMR students in special classes were more likely to make self-derogatory statements than counterparts who remained in regular classes (Carroll, 1967). Recently, however, there has been some shift back to a position favoring segregated placement for mildly handicapped students. This shift has been stimulated by the work of investigators who have used direct measures of self-esteem to study the issue. Their results seem to support the presumed benefits of special class placement for the self-esteem of handicapped students (Battle, 1979; Battle & Blowers, 1982; Coleman, 1983; Strang, Smith, & Rogers, 1978).

Battle (1979) and Battle and Blowers (1982) reported results of research among elementary children in a Canadian school district who were placed for the first time in special classes. Using a measure developed by Battle, they showed that scores obtained from children following special placement were significantly higher on the average than baseline scores obtained prior to placement. Coleman (1983) reported results of a large study done in a Texas school district. He found that children placed in special education resource room programs (partially mainstreamed) had higher average scores on the Piers-Harris Self Concept Scale (Piers, 1969) than children at the same grade level who remained entirely in regular classes, but who were described by their teachers as having "sufficient academic difficulty to warrant special education placement" (p. 40).

The Contribution of Social Comparison Theory

Battle and Blowers (1982) and Coleman (1983) both drew on elements of social comparison theory to explain their results. A major component of that theory is the so-called similarity hypothesis. Proposed initially by Festinger (1954), this hypothesis holds that humans have a tendency to choose for social comparison purposes others who are similar to themselves on the dimension being compared. Although qualified extensively, the hypothesis remains a viable one, particularly regarding the social comparison choices of adults. (See Gruder, 1977, or Singer, 1981 for discussions of the relevant issues and summaries of available evidence.) Battle and Blowers (1982), Coleman (1983), as well as others, have pointed out that special classes make available to handicapped students a large block of similar performing peers who they can utilize for social comparison. This, they argue, is likely to have a positive effect on self-esteem rather than the negative effect that has been claimed by some proponents of mainstreaming. Coleman (1983), put it this way:

> These data lend substantial support to the value of social-comparison theory in understanding the influence of special education placement on children's self concepts. . . To varying degrees, special education removes children from regular-classroom environments where their abilities likely appear inadequate in comparison to the immediate reference groups (particularly on academic dimensions). The special education classroom creates a social comparison group far more homogeneous with regard to ability . . . Rather than lowering self perceptions of ability we might expect such transitions to bolster children's images of themselves (p. 42).

Inherent in Coleman's argument is a rather sobering prediction regarding the likely effects of mainstreaming on self-esteem. Because the mainstreamed student is likely to have mostly superior others available for comparison, the presumption is that this will tend to have a depressing effect on self-esteem. Some support for this line of reasoning can be found in the second part of the study by Strang et al. (1978) cited earlier. These authors did an experiment in which they attempted to simulate social comparison effects on self-esteem. Twenty academically handicapped elementary school children, all mainstreamed for part of their academic day, were administered the Piers-Harris Self Concept Scale (Piers, 1969) on a pretest–posttest basis. For the second administration (6 months after mainstreaming began), students were divided into experimental and comparison groups. Experimental children were tested while in regular class and were given instructions to think of regular class peers when responding. Comparison children were tested in segregated classes and were given no special instructions. Significant differences were found between the groups on change scores. The self-concept scores of the experimental children declined on the average, whereas those of comparison children tended to increase. Strang et al. (1978) suggested that the decline of self-concept among the experimental children was due to their having been restricted by the procedures to comparing themselves with an academically superior group:

> When similar others are available, children use those who are similar and disregard those who are not similar, thus protecting their self concepts from possible diminution. On the other hand, when similar others are removed as a source of comparison, self concept declines if those remaining are superior on the relevant ability dimension. (p. 496)

Although the manipulation employed by Strang et al. (1978) produced a plausible simulation, it is a simulation nonetheless and requires the assumption that the observed effects closely approximate those that would be obtained under more natural conditions. More importantly, the arguments of all the aforementioned investigators (Battle & Blowers 1982; Coleman, 1983, Strang et al., 1978) are based on assumptions regarding social comparison behavior among children which, although reasonable, have yet to be supported by any direct evidence.

Social comparison theory has been fashioned almost entirely with data gathered from studies of adult social comparison behavior, and most of these studies have been done in laboratories or under other strictly controlled conditions. It is not known to what extent their results apply to the social comparison behavior of children under naturally occurring conditions. Suls and Mullen (1982), in their review of the available literature relevant to social comparison among children, suggested that the social comparison behavior of young children may differ markedly not only from that of adults but from that of older children as well.

Even the assumption, long held by many, that comparison with brighter students is likely to have adverse consequences for lower achieving students, has never been critically examined. Levine (1983), in a critical review of the literature relating to social comparison among children in schools, suggests that potential benefits of such comparisons for lower achieving students are often overlooked. Even among adults, who demonstrate a preference for comparing with similar others, there is evidence of a strong interest in superior others (Wheeler, Shaver, Jones, Goethals, Cooper, Robinson, Gruder, & Butzine,

1969). Thornton and Arrowood (1966) have speculated that comparison with superior others on positively valued measures serves a self-enhancement purpose. Some investigators have even speculated that among school children comparison with high-performing classmates has the effect of increasing achievement motivation (Masters, 1971; Schunk, 1983).

It seems clear that much more evidence concerning the development and consequences of children's social comparison behavior will be needed before social comparison factors can be considered in making placement decisions for handicapped children. Especially needed are naturalistic studies that can help determine to what extent the results of studies done under controlled conditions apply to social comparison in the classroom.

STUDIES OF THE SOCIAL COMPARISON BEHAVIOR OF HANDICAPPED STUDENTS

In 1981, I began the first in a series of three investigations aimed primarily at developing a methodology for studying the social comparison behavior of academically handicapped students who were integrated full time into regular classrooms. Two of these studies (Meisel, 1983; Meisel & Sheaffer, in press) are reviewed here. Despite the methodological focus and small scale of these studies, they have produced some interesting findings. At the very least, the data generated offer some insight into the complex nature of children's social comparison behavior.

Two major criteria were used in the selection of classroom sites for these studies. First, it was necessary that students in the classrooms selected be at least 7 years old. Previous research has suggested that this is the age at which children begin using social comparison for self-evaluation purposes (Ruble, Feldman, & Boggiano, 1976; Ruble et al., 1980) Second, classrooms were sought that contained a relatively large proportion of mainstreamed handicapped children. In these classrooms the handicapped students have two potential reference groups available to them, one composed of other handicapped students and the other composed of nonhandicapped students. This allows a clear-cut choice and makes it possible for the observer to document preferences.

Methodologically, all three studies used an auditing method to elicit overt social comparison behavior. In an auditing procedure members of a group (in this case, members of classrooms) are given access to scores of all other members of the group on some measure that they share in common. The common measure is typically referred to as the *comparison measure*. In the variation of the procedure used in these studies, the students were first required to audit their own scores on the comparison measure, and then were permitted to audit the scores of whomever else in the class they wished. The major assumption of this procedure is that classmate-audits made subsequent to self-audits are acts of social comparison.

The major substantive questions asked in all of these investigations were: (1) whether handicapped students would tend to audit classmates less frequently than their nonhandicapped peers, and (2) whether handicapped students prefer to audit classmates who are similar to themselves. Both questions have been suggested by existing social comparison theory.

Regarding the first question, Festinger (1954) hypothesized that when individuals are in a group of dissimilar others they will tend to cease comparing themselves with those others. It is at least conceivable that many handicapped students have found social comparisons in general to be punishing and have learned, therefore, to avoid them. To the extent that this is true, one might expect handicapped children to audit less often, on the average, than their nonhandicapped peers.

The second question arose out of interest in determining whether or not Festinger's similarity hypothesis (Festinger, 1954) is applicable to the comparison choices of mainstreamed handicapped children. The prior expectation was that the handicapped students would tend to audit similar others. Similar for purposes of these studies was operationally defined in two ways: (1) as other students with handicapped labels, and (2) as others who perform similarly regardless of whether or not they are labeled.

STUDY ONE

Subjects

The first study (Meisel, 1983) was done in a fifth-grade class with 8 academically handicapped and 22 nonhandicapped students enrolled. The students ranged in age from 9 years, 8 months to 11 years, 6 months (mean = 10 years, 7 months). Of the 8 academically handicapped students, 5 were classified learning disabled and three socially/emotionally maladjusted. The proportion of females among handicapped students (.25) was smaller than the proportion in the class as a whole (.53). The proportion of black students in the handicapped group (.38) was slightly greater than the proportion in the class (.33).

Procedures

The comparison measure in this first study was the number of daily points accumulated by each student in a point distribution system that was operating in the classroom prior to the study. In this class, students could earn up to 10 points each day based on such things as attention and participation during class activities, assignment completion, and general conduct during class. Points were accumulated for a 5-day period after which those who attained a minimum of 40 points received an activity reward.

The auditing method used in this study differed somewhat from the one used in Study Two, which will be discussed later. Prior to the onset of the study, students were typically told by the teacher how many points they received each day. When the study began, students were able to learn of their cumulative point totals only by asking the investigator or an assistant who was present in the classroom each day. After receiving their own totals, students were then free to ask for the totals of as many classmates as they wished. This continued for 6 weeks, with each student's self- and classmate-audits being carefully recorded.

Results

At the end of the 6 weeks, each student's auditing record was examined to determine the extent and nature of his or her auditing. Table 6.1 summarizes the auditing records for the eight handicapped students. In column one, these students are listed according to their rankings on the comparison measure (number of points earned). The second column lists the total number of classmate audits that each made. The mean number for all handicapped was 7.4 audits. This was compared with the mean for the nonhandicapped students (16.4). A Mann-Whitney U Test indicated that these means were significantly different ($U = 5.95$, $p < .01$). The suggestion in these results is that handicapped students were less likely to use social comparison than their nonhandicapped peers.

The third column of Table 6.1 lists the number of different classmates audited by each handicapped student. In parentheses next to each entry is the number of other handicapped students audited. When looked at in this way, it seems safe to conclude that not handicapped student showed any clear preference for auditing other handicapped students. However, the totals in column three do not take into account the number of times each classmate was audited. It was thought to be at least possible that, although handicapped students audited proportionately

Table 6.1
Summary of Auditing Records of Handicapped Students in Study One

Students	*Total Number of Audits*	*Number of Classmates Audited (Number Handicapped)*	*Number of Regularly Audited Classmates*	$\overline{RPA}$
14	4	4 (1)	–	7.00
16	4	3 (1)	–	10.00
17	17	4 (0)	1	5.29
20	10	3 (0)	1	10.90
23	3	3 (1)	–	13.00
26	13	2 (0)	1	13.30
27	5	1 (0)	1	26.00
28	6	4 (2)	–	11.67

fewer handicapped classmates, they might have been auditing those classmates more frequently than they audited nonhandicapped classmates.

Indeed, close inspection of each student's auditing record revealed that most students audited several classmates on an occasional basis, but tended to audit only one or two on a regular basis. It seemed reasonable to assume that the performance of the classmates audited on a regular basis was more likely to be of comparative interest to students than the performance of those audited only occasionally. Despite the reasonableness of this assumption, however, it turned out to be difficult to decide where to draw the line between regularly and occasionally audited classmates. It was decided, therefore, to impose an arbitrary but conservative criterion, defining "regularly" audited classmates as those whose scores students audited following at least 75% of the times that they audited their own scores. The last column in Table 6.1 lists the numbers of classmates meeting the 75% criterion for each handicapped student. Four of the students audited no one with sufficient regularity to meet the criterion. The remaining four each audited one classmate at the 75% level. In all cases, those meeting the criterion were nonhandicapped classmates. The apparent conclusion to be drawn from these data is that, when given a choice, the majority of mainstreamed handicapped students in this study preferred comparison with nonhandicapped classmates.

The next question asked was whether or not the classmates that the handicapped students audited were ones who were similar to them in performance. To answer this question students were ranked on average daily point acquisition for the 6 weeks of the study. Each student's own rank was then compared to the rank(s) of the classmate(s) he or she regularly audited.

Fig.6.1 graphically represents these data for the students, both handicapped and nonhandicapped, who audited at least one classmate at the 75% level. As can be seen, most students regularly audited classmates who were quite discrepant in rank (either above or below). Particularly surprising was the tendency for low-ranked students to regularly audit classmates ranked in the upper third of the class on the comparison measure.

The above analysis appears to offer convincing evidence that few students preferred comparison with classmates similar to themselves in rank on the comparison measure. The analysis suffers, however, from the fact that it is confined to the discrepancy between handicapped students and regularly audited classmates. Because of this, it was decided that a measure was needed that would numerically capture what appeared obvious visually, but would, at the same time, include information about all of the auditing choices each student made. With the help of colleagues,[1] a measure called *mean rank per audit* ($\overline{\text{RPA}}$), was

---

[1]The author would like to acknowledge the assistance of Joel R. Levin and Carol Joyce Blumberg, who provided critical insight and suggestions for the development of the mean rank per audit statistic.

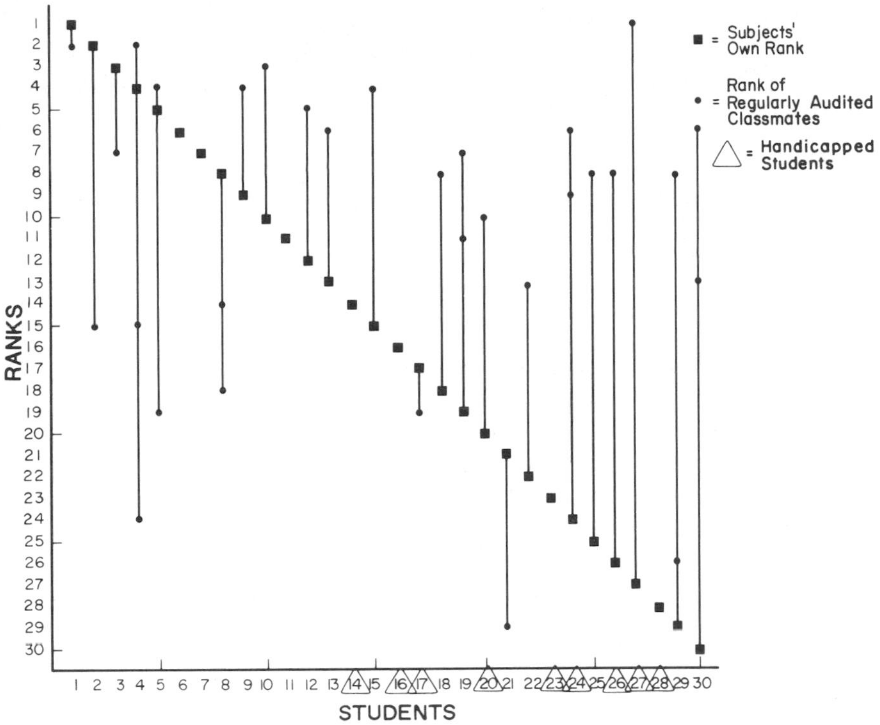

Fig. 6.1

formulated. It is an expression of the average distance above or below their own rank that students covered each time they audited a classmate. The $\overline{\text{RPA}}$ for an individual student is obtained using the following equation:

$$\overline{\text{RPA}}_i = \frac{\Sigma\, W_{ik} \bullet \mid \text{difference in rank} \mid}{N_i} \qquad (1)$$

The numerator of Equation (1) is obtained by summing for each student the weighted difference between his or her own rank and the rank(s) of every classmate audited (absolute rank difference). The weighting factor, W_{ik}, is simply the number of times that, student, i, audited each of the classmates, k, included on his or her auditing record. This allows differences with frequently audited classmates to contribute more heavily to the magnitude of $\overline{\text{RPA}}$ than those with less frequently audited classmates. The denominator (Ni) is the total number of classmate-audits made the student.

The last column of Table 6.1 gives the $\overline{\text{RPA}}$ for each of the handicapped students. These ranged from 5.29 to 26 ranks per audit. For example, in the case of student 14, each time he audited a classmate he was, on the average, auditing someone who was 7 ranks from him. In every instance these were classmates ranked above him. In fact, close inspection of the data revealed that seven of the eight handicapped students audited only classmates ranked above them. Only student 7 audited a lower ranked classmate. The mean for all handicapped students was 12.16 ranks per audit. The mean for nonhandicapped students was 10.76. These data suggest that few students, handicapped or nonhandicapped, were auditing classmates similar to themselves in performance.

Discussion

The data from this first study produced what appeared to be somewhat inconsistent results. The apparent tendency of handicapped students to audit classmates significantly fewer times than their nonhandicapped peers did is consistent with a view that academically handicapped children are likely to avoid social comparisons because frequently they find that the results of such comparisons are aversive. Such a view, however, is not consistent with the fact that, given the opportunity to audit anyone in their class, handicapped students, even those performing low on the comparison measure and those with low auditing rates, chose to audit classmates performing much higher than themselves.

A possible explanation for the apparent inconsistency is that all eight handicapped students began the study auditing higher performing classmates and some, having found this aversive, reacted by ceasing auditing altogether rather than by turning to auditing lower performing classmates. These auditing "dropouts" may have had the effect of reducing the average auditing rate for all handicapped students. The fact that several of the handicapped students had auditing rates that were close to the average for nonhandicapped students seems to support this explanation.

Another possible explanation for the relatively low auditing rates among several of the handicapped students is that the depressed rates were an artifact of the auditing procedure itself. Because students had to request classmate scores from an adult, the possibility existed that some handicapped students may have been more reticent than other students about making such requests. It was this possibility that called for the development of a less obtrusive auditing method.

The tendency for handicapped students in this study to prefer comparison with higher performing peers remained a surprising result. Especially surprising was the finding that several handicapped students persisted in auditing higher performing peers despite their own continued low performance. One of several questions this raises is whether or not this would have been the case had the comparison measure been an academic one rather than a measure of compliance with classroom rules. It may be argued that, in general, a deficiency in points awarded for conduct is less likely to have aversive consequences for a student than a deficiency on some more strictly academic measure.

STUDY TWO

Subjects

Subjects in the second study were members of a fourth-grade class who ranged in age from 9 years 4 months to 11 years 9 months. All members of the class for whom parental permission was obtained participated. This included 11 academically handicapped and 18 nonhandicapped students. One handicapped student was classified socially/emotionally maladjusted, the remaining 10 were classified learning disabled. Ten of the 11 had been in special classes previously, for periods ranging from 1 to 3 years. Seven of these had spent at least 1 year in a totally segregated class.

Five of the 11 handicapped students were female and 5 were black. The proportions of males and females among the handicapped students were nearly equal to what they were in the class as a whole. However, the proportion of black students among the handicapped (.45) was greater than in the class as a whole (.28).

Procedures

The procedures used in this study were different from those in the first study in two important ways. First, the comparison measure was an academic rather than a social measure. As had been the case in the previous study, the comparison measure was the number of points students received each day in a point distribution system. In this class, however, points were awarded for completion and correctness of arithmetic homework and seatwork rather than for appropriate conduct. The average number of daily points earned by each student over the 6 weeks of the study was later found to correlate highly with students' arithmetic achievement scores ($r = .71$).

The second important difference was the use of a less obtrusive auditing method. As was the case in the first study, teachers discontinued telling students how many points they earned at the onset of the study. Instead, they entered each student's daily point total into a time-sharing mainframe computer, using a terminal and telephone connection provided by the investigator. For 2 days prior to the study, the students were trained to use the terminal to access information about their own and classmates' performance. To obtain visual display of their own cumulative point total on a given day in any 5-day accumulation period, students entered their own single- or double-digit code number. After seeing their own total, students were permitted to see the point total(s) for as many classmates as they wished by entering the code(s) for those desired. A wall chart posted near the terminal listed the codes for all class members. Time for auditing was allotted at the beginning and end of each day. The computer kept a running record of each student's auditing choices. The record included the name(s) of classmates whose scores each student asked for (if any), as well as the order in which they were requested each time.

Results

To answer the question of whether or not the handicapped students audited classmates as frequently as their nonhandicapped peers, the total number of classmate audits made by each student during the 6 weeks of the study was counted and compared for each group. The total number of audits for handicapped students ranged from 26 to 142 (mean = 81.364) and for the nonhandicapped the range was 30 to 126 (mean = 65.889). Although it appeared that handicapped students were auditing at a higher rate than nonhandicapped students, a Mann-Whitney U Test comparing the two means of the two groups indicated that they were not significantly different ($U = 199$, $p < .1321$). Clearly, handicapped students in this classroom did not exhibit the significantly lower auditing rate apparent among handicapped students in the previous study.

Determing whether or not handicapped students audited similar others began with close examination of each one's auditing record. Table 6.2 contains summaries of those records. In column one, handicapped students are listed according to rank on the comparison measure. The figures in column two make it readily apparent that handicapped students did not prefer to audit handicapped classmates. In fact, nearly every student audited every classmate at least once during the 6 weeks of the study. Of more interest may be the figures in column three, which contains the numbers of classmates audited on a regular basis by each handicapped student. In parenthesis after each entry is the number of other handicapped students contained in the overall figure. The proportions of the total

Table 6.2
Summary of Auditing Records of Handicapped Students in Study Two

Students	*Total Number of Audits*	*Number of Different Classmates Audited*	*Number of Classmates Meeting 75% Criterion (Number of Handicapped)*	$\overline{RPA}$
4	142	28	9 (4)	11.79
8	139	27	5 (4)	9.86
9	71	22	5 (2)	8.46
16	26	18	1 (0)	7.93
21	88	27	2 (1)	9.82
23	63	26	5 (2)	11.13
24	58	25	5 (1)	11.42
26	88	27	3 (1)	13.48
27	92	28	2 (0)	12.83
28	64	23	0 –	12.88
29	64	25	0 –	13.88

that these subsets represent ranged from .00 to .80. However, in only one case was the proportion greater than .50, and the mean proportion (.34) was only slightly below the proportion of handicapped children in the class as a whole (.38). In summary, only one of nine handicapped students who audited classmates on a regular basis appeared to prefer comparison with handicapped peers.

To determine whether or not handicapped students were auditing classmates similar in performance, each one's rank on the comparison measured was compared to the rank(s) of regularly audited classmates. Fig. 6.2 displays the results of this analysis. As was the case with students in the previous study, those who regularly audited classmates made choices across a fairly wide range of ranks. Again, there was a tendency for low ranked students to audit higher ranked students and vice versa. Seven of the 11 handicapped students were ranked in the lowest third of the distribution. Five of these had auditing choices that met the 75% criterion. All five regularly audited someone in the *highest* third of the distribution. The two lowest of these five did not audit anyone on a regular basis who was in the bottom third of the distribution.

Finally, Equation (1) was again used to determine the $\overline{\text{RPA}}$ for each student. The last column of Table 6.2 contains the results for all handicapped students. They ranged from 7.93 to 13.88 ranks per audit. The grand mean (11.23) was

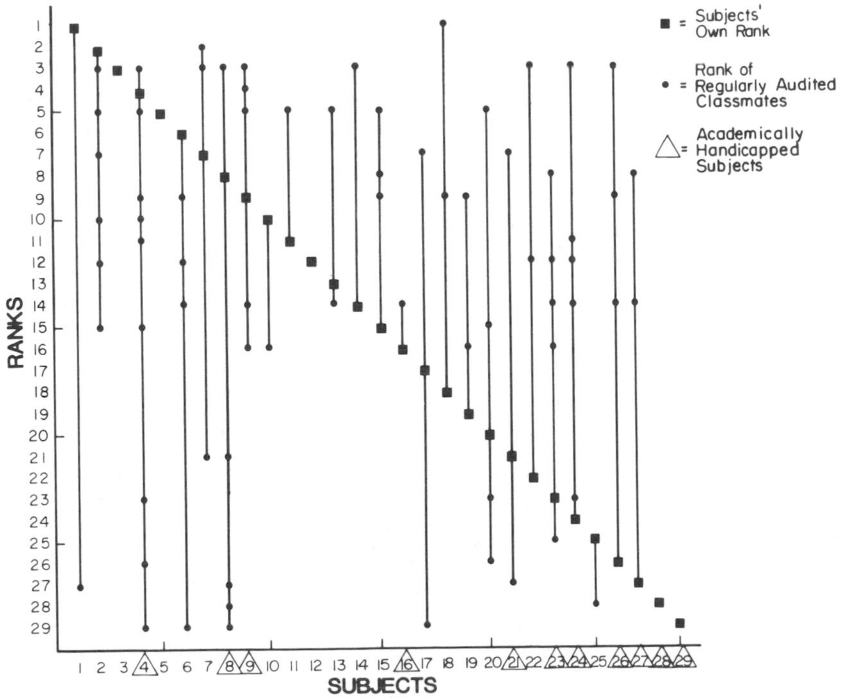

Fig 6.2

somewhat higher than the grand mean for nonhandicapped students (8.82) but slightly lower than the grand mean for the handicapped students in the first study (12.16). However, it may be interesting to note here that, despite the differences in comparison measures and auditing methods used, the overall means for the two classes studied, 11.46 and 9.81 respectively, were remarkably similar. They suggest that children in the age range 9 to 11 years generally do not prefer comparison with others who perform similarly to themselves.

Discussion

The fact that handicapped students in this second study did not exhibit a significantly lower auditing rate like their fifth-grade counterparts in the previous study leaves open the question of whether or not mainstreamed children are likely to use social comparison as often as nonhandicapped age peers. Because the auditing method used in the second study is more likely to have elicited the kind of free operant responding usually desired in a naturalistic study, the no difference in rate hypothesis suggested by the results of this study is probably the most tenable.

On the question of whether handicapped students prefer comparison with similar others, the results were quite consistent with what had been found previously. Whether similarity was defined in terms of others similarly labeled or others performing similarly, the results of this study suggest that most mainstreamed students, like most of their age peers, do not prefer comparison with similar others. Especially surprising was the tendency for those ranked low on the comparison measure to prefer comparison with those ranked well above them. This has been a consistent finding in two classrooms studied so far. It is particularly noteworthy because students in those classes were at different grade levels and because both the auditing method and comparison measures used were different in each case. It is difficult to reconcile this finding with the notion that mainstreamed students are likely to avoid comparison with higher functioning classmates in order to protect their self-esteem. Although such an assumption may still be valid in many instances, there are at least some cases in which it is not.

The above finding may be good news for those who predict that mainstreamed students will benefit from the higher standard of performance that is likely to prevail in regular classes. This prediction assumes, first of all, that the higher standards will actually be used by mainstreamed students to measure their own performance. Although not conclusively proving the validity of this assumption, the data from the two studies reviewed certainly add to its credibility.

The "benefit prediction" further assumes that in instances where the handicapped students find their own performance deficient relative to that of comparison others, they will be motivated to improve that performance to the point where it matches or surpasses the comparative standard. It is assumed that having superior others to compare with will have a positive effect on the mainstreamed students' achievement motivation. This assumption has never been tested directly, although there is some evidence from studies with adults that make it at least a tenable hypothesis. For example, Seta (1982) found that college students improved their performance on a laboratory task that they had previously worked on alone after being paired with a superior performing co-actor. No such improvement was found when students were paired with co-actors performing at or below their own level.

Whether or not continued comparison with higher performing classmates has a positive effect on a student's performance is no doubt dependent on a number of intervening variables. One factor that is important is the extent to which the student perceives matching or surpassing the comparative standard to be a real possibility. Richer (1976) speculated that the perceived possibility of upward mobility is an important determiner of whether low-ability students profit or become discouraged when placed in heterogeneous ability groups.

Close inspection of each student's daily performance in Study Two revealed that most of those in the lowest third of the rankings had occasions on which they obtained as many, or in some cases more, points than the higher ranked classmates they regularly audited. For some of them this may have been a powerful reinforcer, and receiving that reinforcer on a rather thin schedule was more likely to have aided rather than hindered maintenance of auditing by low-ranked students. In some cases this same reinforcer operated to help maintain achievement motivation.

The analyses and discussion to this point have assumed that the students in these studies audited classmates primarily for purposes of self-evaluation. The tendency to use the terms auditing and social comparison as if they were synonymous rests on this assumption. It is recognized that this is an unproven assumption. In fact, it is likely that some auditing done by students in both studies was not motivated by a desire to make performance comparisons with the specific classmates audited. It was due in part to recognition of this possibility that some of the analyses related to the question of similarity included only data on regularly audited classmates. This decision was based on the assumption that classmates audited on a regular basis were more likely to have been serving as comparison standards than those audited only occasionally. Put in terms used in reference group theory, the assumption is that regularly audited classmates are more likely to be members of the student's *comparative reference group* (Kelley, 1952). Although this seems to be a reasonable assumption, it is an assumption nevertheless, and remains to be empirically validated.

There is one possible noncomparative use of auditing that deserves mention, because it applies primarily to the choices of the lower ranked students focused on in this review. It is possible that in some instances these students audited higher performing peers because they obtained vicarious satisfaction from the success of the latter. This is analogous to the behavior of a sports fan who checks the newspaper or tunes in to a media commentator to learn the standings of favorite teams. Auditing of this kind is likely to increase in frequency and regularity when those teams are doing well.

SUMMARY AND CONCLUSIONS

Whether the placement of academically handicapped children into classes with higher performing age peers is likely to have a positive or negative effect on self-esteem and, at least implicitly, on achievement motivation, has been an issue debated for some time in special education. Similar debates surface from time to time in general education revolving about the issue of homogeneous versus heterogeneous ability groups (See Richer, 1976). Until recently, positions on these issues have relied entirely on speculation or speculative interpretation of indirect evidence. Only in the past several years have there been efforts to gather direct evidence concerning the factors that influence how children evaluate themselves. Already, it is clear that these influences are many, that they interact in complex ways, and that they change as children progress through school. It is likely to be some time before a full picture emerges, and before this information can be used in any meaningful way for making placement decisions.

The two studies reviewed in this chapter have produced evidence suggesting that fourth- and fifth-grade children generally do not prefer comparison with similarly performing classmates, and that, in this aspect at least, the social comparison behavior of mainstreamed students is not likely to differ from that of their age peers. Because most academically handicapped children are likely to be ranked low on many school measures, this finding means in practical terms that they are likely to prefer comparison with higher performing classmates. What long term implications this might have for self-esteem or achievement motivation is not yet known. The finding that low-performing students in the two studies reviewed here continued to regularly audit higher performing classmates over a 6-week period suggests, however, that the results of such comparisons were not overwhelmingly aversive. Other indirect evidence also suggests that comparison with higher performing peers can have a positive effect on achievement motivation. More research is needed to determine for whom and under what conditions this is likely to be the case.

REFERENCES

Altman, R., & Talkington, L. W. (1977). Modeling: An alternate behavior modification approach for retardates. *Mental Retardation, 9,* 20–23.

Battle, J. (1979). Self-esteem of students in regular and special education classes. *Psychological Reports, 44,* 212–214.

Battle, J., & Blowers T. (1982). Self-esteem of students in regular and special education classes. *Journal of Learning Disabilities, 15,* 100–102.

Carroll, A. W. (1967). The effects of segregated and partially integrated school programs on self-concept and academic achievement of educable mental retardates. *Exceptional Children, 34,* 93–99.

Coleman, M.J. (1983). Self-concept and the mildly handicapped: The role of social comparisons. *Journal of Special Education, 17,* 37–45.

Dunn, L. M. (1968). Special education for the mildly retarded—Is much of it justifiable? *Exceptional Children, 35,* 5–22.

Festinger, L. (1954). A theory of social comparison processes. *Human Relations, 7,* 117–140.

Gruder, C. L. (1977). Choice of comparison persons in evaluating oneself. In J. M. Suls & R. L. Miller, (Eds.). *Social comparison processes.* (pp. 21–41). New York: John Wiley.

Kelley, H. H. (1952). The two functions of reference groups. In G. E. Swanson, T. M. Newcomb, & E. L. Hartley (Eds.), *Readings in social psychology* (2nd ed.) (pp.410–414). New York: Holt.

Levine, J. M. (1983). Social comparison and education. In J. M. Levine & M. C. Wang, (Eds.), *Teacher and student perceptions: Implications for Learning.* Hillsdale, NJ: Lawrence Erlbaum Associates.

Masters, J. C. (1971). Social comparison by young children. *Young Children, 27,* 37–60.

Meisel, C. J. (1983, April). *Some influences on the social comparison choices of mainstreamed handicapped children.* Paper presented at the meeting of the Council for Exceptional Children, Detroit.

Meisel, C. J., & Sheaffer, B. (in press). Social comparison choices of mainstreamed academically handicapped children. *The Journal of Special Education.*

Meyerowitz, J. H. (1965). Self-derogations in young retardates and special class placement. *Child Development, 33,* 443–451.

Pepitone, E. A. (1972). Comparison behavior in elementary school children. *American Educational Research Journal, 9,* 45–63.

Piers, E. V. (1969). *The manual for the Piers-Harris self-concept scale.* Nashville: Counselor Recordings and Tapes.

Richer, S. (1976). Reference-group theory and ability grouping: A convergence of sociological theory and educational research. *Sociology of Education, 49,* 65–71.

Ruble, D. N., Boggiano, A. K., Feldman, N. S. & Loebl, J. H., (1980). Developmental analysis of the role of social comparison is self-evaluation. *Developmental Psychology, 16,* 105–115.

Ruble, D. N., Feldman, N. S., & Boggiano, A. K. (1976). Social comparison between young children in achievement situations. *Developmental Psychology, 12,* 192–197.

Schunk, D.H. (1983). Developing children's self-efficacy and skills: The roles of social comparative information and goal setting. *Contemporary Educational Psychology, 8,* 76–86.

Seta, J. J. (1982). The impact of comparison processes on coactors' task performance. *Journal of Personality and Social Psychology, 42,* 281–291.

Singer, E. (1981). Reference groups and social evaluations. In M. Rosenberg & R. H. Turner, (Eds.), *Social Psychology: Sociological perspectives* (pp. 66–93). New York: Basic Books.

Strang, L., Smith, M. D. & Rogers, C. M. (1978). Social comparison multiple reference groups, and the self-concepts of academically handicapped. *Journal of Educational Psychology, 70,* 487–497.

Suls, J. M., & Miller, R. L. (Eds.). (1977). Social comparison processes: Theoretical and empirical perspectives. Washington, D.C.: Hemisphere.

Suls, J. M. & Mullen, B. (1982). From the cradle to the grave: Comparison of self-evaluation across the life span. In J. M. Suls (Eds.), *Psychological perspectives on the self* (pp. 97–125). Hillsdale, NJ: Lawrence Erlbaum Associates.

Suls, J. M. & Sanders, G. S., (1979). Social comparison process in the young child. *Journal of Research and Development in Education, 13,* 79–89.

Thornton, D. A., & Arrowood, A. J. (1966). Self-evaluation, self-enhancement, and the locus of social comparison. *Journal of Experimental Social Psychology, Suppl. 1,* 40–48.

Veroff, J. (1969). Social comparison and the development of achievement motivation. In C. P. Smith (Ed.), *Achievement-related motives in children* (pp. 46–101). New York: Sage.

Wheeler, L., Shaver, K. G., Jones, R. A., Goethals, G. R., Cooper, J., Robinson, J. E., Gruder, C. L., & Butzine, K. W. (1969). Factors determining choice of a comparison other. *Journal of Experimental Social Psychology, 5,* 219–232.

7 The Play Behavior of Mainstreamed Learning Disabled Children

Jay Gottlieb
Linda Levy
New York University

Barbara W. Gottlieb
Herbert H. Lehman College
City University of New York

It is well-established that the quality of children's social relationships during childhood has an enormous influence on adjustment during adulthood (e.g., Cowen, Pederson, Babigan, Izzo, & Trost, 1973). The overriding importance of social relationships for all children and their eventual effects during later years are ample testament to their importance for handicapped children, whose handicaps are often caused by or associated with poor social relationships, as is the case with children classified as emotionally disturbed or mentally retarded. Historically, a considerable proportion of research in the fields of emotional disturbance and mental retardation has been devoted to elucidating the social dimensions of these particular handicapping conditions. Far fewer studies have been directed to the social dimensions of learning disabled children, the third of the so-called high-incidence handicapping conditions. As recently as 1980, Torgesen and Dice estimated that only 9% of the research in the field of learning disabilities was devoted to social issues. Of the research that has been devoted to social issues of learning disabilities, few if any, of the studies have been conducted in naturalistic environments outside of the classroom context.

This chapter reviews some of the research devoted to the social aspects of learning disabilities and presents some recent data on that topic. Our primary intent is to expand the range of research interest beyond the classroom and into other environments that affect children's social development. We begin our treatment of the topic with a brief review of the role of play in child development.

THE DEVELOPMENT OF PLAY BEHAVIOR

Play behavior, its origins and significance, has been a topic of longstanding interest. Herbert Spencer, expanding the ideas of Friedrich von Schiller, developed what is known as the Schiller-Spencer Hypothesis, that play resulted from surplus neural energy. Stanley Hall believed that it represented a recapitulation of the stages of man's development and Karl Groos felt that it served the purpose of practicing and completing hereditary skills (Millar, 1968).

Most current theorists emphasize the function of play in facilitating and enhancing intellectual and social development (Piaget, 1962; Singer, 1973). Play follows and reflects stages of general intellectual development outlined by Piaget in his equilibration theory of the development of thought. According to Piaget, the child expands his world of knowledge when his existing frame of reference is in conflict with a new experience. This disequilibration causes him to construct new logical schemes. Two complementary processes are used to resolve conflicts and contradictions; assimilation and accommodation. Assimilation refers to the accumulation of experiences that fit in with already existing schemes—ideas or concepts— and accommodation refers to changes in one's existing schemas as a result of reality-based adjustments. For example, assimilation is seen in the child repeatedly using a newly learned word or gesture. He is assimilating it into his repertoire. Accommodation is seen when a child, having only experienced soft toys that respond to being pushed and gently fondled, is given his first hard toy. He may learn hammering, banging, etc. These represent accommodations to gain satisfaction from his play.

Early play experiences are regarded by Piaget as pure assimilation activity wherein the very young child enjoys the pleasure of exploration of newly discovered actions and objects. These activities depend largely on the child's sensory-perceptual development and motor apparatus and their proper functioning. At around the age of 18 months, the repertoire expands and symbolic play appears. The child now uses substitute objects as ludic (playful) symbols of absent and remembered things. This symbolic representation serves as an intermediate stage in the development of the child's linguistic communication system by enabling him to re-experience objects in their absence. Ludic representations are ultimately replaced by words. Symbolic play, therefore, is based first in the earlier sensory motor period and relies on proper functioning of the sensory motor system, and is also important in laying the foundation for language development. In the last stage of play, games with rules, the cognitive function of play shifts to serve accomodation of the individual to social group norms.

Although each successive stage appears at a later chronological age, earlier forms of play continue in the later periods (Piaget, 1962). Children with educationally handicapping conditions have been found to exhibit delays in the appearance of symbolic play in early childhood (Higgenbotham & Baker, 1981; Lovell, Hoyle, & Siddall, 1968). Because development is sequential, this finding suggests that the appearance of the later stage, games with rules, might also be delayed.

PLAY BEHAVIOR OF PRESCHOOL AND ELEMENTARY SCHOOL AGE CHILDREN

For a considerable period of time, the sequential nature of play among preschoolers in terms of both cognitive aspects (Smilansky, 1968) and social stages (Parten, 1932) has been documented. Scales developed in these studies have been used to assess the play of nonhandicapped children (Vandenberg, 1981), handicapped children (Darbyshire, 1977), and socioeconomically deprived children (Smilansky, 1968). Parten's scale of social interactions traces development of extent of involvement with another child, that is, onlooking, parallel play, associative play, and finally, cooperative play.

Among nonhandicapped children, there is empirical documentation of the relationship between cognitive and social maturity, and both activity choice and social interactive behavior (Vandenberg, 1981). Singer (1977) has studied symbolic play and found that engaging in symbolic play is related to "more positive affective states, greater self-restraint and less aggressive and disruptive behavior, more social cooperation, and generally what looks like a better preparation for the necessary constraints of the classroom" (p. 136).

Preschool children with educationally handicapping conditions, in general, have been shown to engage in less mature patterns of social interaction and cognitive play than nonhandicapped children (Higgenbotham & Baker, 1981; Thompson, 1980). They also show delays in shifting to symbolic play (Eifermann, 1971; Lovell, et al., 1968) or an absence of symbolic play (Smilansky, 1968). There is a relationship between the extent of the handicapping condition and the degree of the child's play difficulty (Guralnick, 1981). Although these findings have, as yet, not been explored for elementary school aged children, it could be expected that educationally handicapped children's play, in general, will continue to show similar patterns of delay and difficulty in middle childhood. This is, in part, to be expected because as children become older the nature of their play becomes increasingly more sophisticated.

Playing games with rules is the expected form of play during the elementary school years, although earlier forms of play also persist. The play behaviors of earlier stages do not entirely disappear at the next stage, but rather become subsumed by more complex behavior. Millar (1968) noted that: "Play which consists of movements in space, handling objects, and the perceptual control this involves, is characteristic of the first eighteen months of life when it first develops, it is not confined to this period. Play with more complex skills embodying simpler ones is quite as frequent in childhood and later although differences between individuals increase" (p. 136).

In order to categorize playground activities, three criteria exist for distinguishing games with rules from earlier games. First, is the nature of the relationship between the playmates. In the earlier stages, children may play in parallel or association with each other (Parten, 1933), but in games with rules, attainment of a mutual level of relating must exist. According to Anna Freud (1965), at the minimum the child must relate to other children "as helpmates in carrying out a desired task such as playing, destroying, causing mischief of some kind, etc. the duration of the partnership being determined by the task, and secondary to it (p. 257)."

Piaget (1962) provides the second and third criteria of rule-governed games. He explains that rules imply the relationship between at least two people or, in the case of the solitary player, there is the generalization from such a relationship. Implicit in the rules are the ideas of *regularity* and *obligation,* both of which presuppose two individuals.

Summarizing the above, on the playground one would expect to see sensory motor games, symbolic games, and games with rules. Sensory motor games would involve motor or kinesthetic activities, which seem to be their purpose; symbolic games, which entail some imagination or representation of one object by another; and games that are governed by rules. Three criteria distinguishing the earlier games from the games with rules are: (a) mutuality in social relationships; (b) a sense of regularity in the activity; and (c) a sense of obligation among the players.

Partial confirmation that nonhandicapped children show a steady increase in playing games with rules as they age was provided by Eifermann (1971), who found this form of game to increase in frequency through sixth grade, but thereafter found it to reach a plateau. One study addressed this form of play with educationally handicapped children. Darbyshire (1977), studying 3 to 8-year-old hearing-impaired children, concluded that games with rules were the form of play that was most disturbed. Because learning disabled children often have difficulties following directions, maintaining attention, tolerating frustration, and dealing with a variety of verbal and spatial concepts, it is expected that they may not be able to engage in this type of play as well as their nonlearning disabled peers. In fact, if Darbyshire's findings generalize to learning disabled elementary school children, greater difficulties may be observed than those found among preschool children.

But, in what ways and in which situations could we anticipate that learning disabled have more severe problems at play than nonlearning disabled children? Unfortunately, the literature on this point is scant, although we will review some data on this topic later in the chapter. At this time, we offer our considerations for areas in need of a sound data base in order to broaden our understanding of the social difficulties experienced by all children, including those who are classified by schools as learning disabled (LD).

ECOLOGICAL FACTORS IN PLAY: GROUP COMPOSITION AND GROUP SIZE

Group involvement is an important aspect of the elementary school child's social life. Playgroup size has been shown to follow a developmental pattern among preschoolers: There is increasing ability to play in larger groups as the child gets older (Parten, 1933). Normative information on group size involvements is not available for elementary school children, to our knowledge. However, in the two studies of elementary school children that investigated the effect of group size on social interactions, a relationship was found (Hare, 1952; Hutt & Vaizey, 1966). Hare found greater cohesiveness in discussion groups composed of 5 members than those comprised of 12 members. Hutt and Vaizey found an increase in aggressiveness in larger playgroups of both nonhandicapped and brain-injured children. The brain-injured children, however, reacted with greater aggressiveness to smaller increments in group size. A difference in total amount of social interaction was also demonstrated: The increase in group size was related to diminished interaction among nonhandicapped children and increased interaction among the brain-injured children.

Smaller group size has also been found to be a positive factor affecting preschoolers' play. Loo (1978) found that 5-year olds showed less aggressiveness and more positive social interactions in groups of 4 rather than 8 children. Also, McGrew (1970), studying the effects of group size on social behavior among preschoolers, found a tendency toward more integrated social organization in the maintenance of closer peer proximity in groups of 8 to 10 compared to groups twice as large. In the higher density groups, children avoided each other more and engaged in more solitary activity. More recently, Thompson (1980), studied the effect of group size (2, 3 or 4 children) on cognitive play and social behavior in delayed and nondelayed toddlers. It was expected that small group size would be most conducive to higher levels of cognitive play and positive social interactions and that delayed children would show more extreme behaviors in the larger groups. Thompson found that groups of 3 children, whether delayed or nondelayed, resulted in the most prosocial behavior and the highest levels of cognitive play. In the larger group size, the delayed children showed earlier cognitive play behaviors and more immature and negative social behaviors than they exhibited in smaller groups. Finally, Peterson and Haralick (1977) found that an interaction of group size and the ratio of handicapped to nonhandicapped children was critical to the social acceptance of preschool handicapped children.

The fact that playgroup size appears to affect quality of play and is related to development in children should be an indication that it offers possibilities for studying the social life of learning disabled children. Theory and research into social aspects of learning disabled children should focus on a variety of environments, not only play groups, however. Three primary environments where research attention is needed are the classroom, the home, and the playground and other unstructured free-play situations. Unquestionably, the bulk of research to date has focused on classroom environments, the site where children are most accessible and where they become classified as handicapped. The pivotal role of parents in the development of their learning disabled children's functioning is also well acknowledged (Lerner, 1985), although there is far less active research with parents of learning disabled children than with parents of mentally retarded children, for example. Finally, play situations, although important for development, have received scant attention, probably because both professionals and parents believe that this environment is less pivotal than the classroom. In the following pages, we comment on the importance of research on play with learning disabled populations, and present the results of one research program that studied LD children during unsupervised play situations.

LEARNING DISABLED CHILDREN AT PLAY

Barker's studies in ecological psychology have indicated convincingly that environments influence and at times dictate behavior (Barker, 1965). This is an important consideration for the study of learning disabled children because in the overwhelming majority of situations the diagnosis of learning disabilities is influenced by adverse performance in a single environment, the academic classroom. Yet, there is a growing, although still very small, body of literature that attempts to depict social problems of learning disabled children as manifest beyond the classroom. By studying the social aspects of learning disabilities, the intent is to demonstrate that academic difficulty creates problems for the child, not only in the classroom but outside the classroom as well.

As with all children, there is little doubt that the environment influences their behavior. Indeed, the susceptibility of learning disabled children's behavior to environmental factors is amply attested to by their improved behavior in small, structured classes. Because learning disabled children are viewed as often being especially sensitive to their environments, de Hirsh (1973) described some LD children as *plastic*. Quite possibly, the behavior of learning disabled children may be not so much deviant as exaggerated, that is, a more severe reaction to the environment than appears in non LD children. Learning disabled children may react either with greater degrees of aggressiveness or greater degrees of inhibition than other children. A general hypothesis that could be offered is that learning disabled children would show more extreme forms of behavior, either aggressiveness or withdrawl, when confronted with stressful situations. Because playgroup size has been shown to be a cause of stress (McGrew, 1970), it could be anticipated that learning disabled children would tend to spend more time alone or at least in smaller groups than non LD peers. This hypothesis suggests that the predicted solitary play of learning disabled children is volitional, an assertion that may be only partially correct.

The availability of ample data that LD children tend to be socially rejected more than non LD children suggests (e.g., Siperstein, Bopp, & Bak, 1978) that if, in fact, LD children are found to play alone more frequently than non LD peers, this condition may also be the result of peers' play preferences rather than the volition of the learning disabled youngster. Regardless of the theoretical underpinning for the hypothesis that LD children play alone more often than non LD peers, data are required to test the generalizeability of social deficits that learning disabled children are said to possess. Recognize, of course, that in our example of playgroup size we are implicitly assuming that solitary play has negative consequences for children. To our knowledge, there are no data to support this assumption, consequently the assumption itself requires empirical confirmation.

Another area of importance with respect to the play of learning disabled children is a description of the children with whom they play. It is not sufficient to know simply the number of children with whom learning disabled children typically play. It is equally, if not more important, to develop an understanding of the characteristics of children with whom they play. Do LD children consistently play with children younger than themselves because their agemates find them immature? Does their peer group include an overrepresentation of low-ability children like themselves who may form the socially isolated or rejected clique in the peer group? Are they part of the group of children whom teachers might refer to as "troublemakers"? At the present time, there is very little research addressing these issues. To the extent that the field of learning disabilities views social aspects of this handicapping condition as being of importance, these issues must begin to be addressed. The general absence of concern in the field is exemplified by a recent paper describing techniques for assessing the ecology of learning disabled children (Heron & Heward, 1982). Although these authors stressed the classroom and included the home as an important environment, the playground or other play environments were absent from their discussion.

The general omission of play from discussions of social concerns of learning disabled youngsters is especially surprising in view of the fact that a fair number of studies have examined the sociometric status of learning disabled children. Although an underlying asumption of sociometric measurement is that it reflects actual behavioral choice should the opportunity arise, few studies have made this connection and none to our knowledge with learning disabled youngsters. In fact, it is probably accurate to state that the major avenue of inquiry with respect to social aspects of learning disabilities has been with identifying their sociometric status (Bruininks, 1978; Bryan, 1974; 1976; 1978; Garrett & Crump, 1980; Pullis & Smith, 1981; Scranton & Rykman, 1979; Siperstein, Bopp, & Bak, 1978). A second line of research has been devoted to seeking a variety of correlates of learning disabled children's low popularity (Bachara, 1976; Bruck

& Hebert, 1982; Bryan, 1974; 1976; Dickstein & Warren, 1980; Greiger & Richards, 1976; Horowitz, 1981; Keogh, Tchir, & Windeguth-Behn, 1974; Pearl & Cosden, 1982; Wong & Wong, 1980). No line of research has focused on stability of sociometric status across different environments. If learning disabled children's primary area of deficit is in academics, then it is both logical and expected that their sociometric status should suffer when measured in an academic environment. This does not automatically lead to the assumption, however, that LD children should also suffer sociometrically in environments where they may not have obvious and pronounced difficulties, such as in free-play situations.

At this point, we present the findings from a research program that we conducted designed to study the free play of learning disabled children and their nonhandicapped age-mates. Our purpose in this investigation was to determine the extent to which learning disabled children were adversely affected in their play when the situation was not under adult supervision. We were interested in studying, not only quantitative differences between learning disabled and nonhandicapped elementary school children, but also qualitative differences that might exist between the two groups.

LEARNING DISABLED CHILDREN AND THEIR NONHANDICAPPED CLASSMATES AT PLAY

During the spring semester of the 1982 academic year, observations were conducted on 37 learning disabled children from grades three, four, and five, and their classmates. Observations were conducted at four elementary schools located in two relatively affluent suburban communities. All observations were conducted during the lunch break when the children's play activities were not structured either by the teachers or the playground aides.

The learning disabled children were designated as such by their child study team, and, for the most part, attended resource room programs for about one hour daily, with the remainder of the school day being spent in regular classrooms. Children not classified as learning disabled were selected on the basis of their being classmates of the learning disabled children. Each was matched for age and gender with a learning disabled child. Children who were believed by teachers to have major emotional problems were excluded from the sample.

Observational Instrument

An observational instrument was developed that combined 10-second momentary time-sampling of behavioral categories with ethnographic techniques suggested by Spradley (1980). The instrument allowed us to observe major categories of behavior: play activities, nonplay activities, prosocial behaviors, neutral behaviors, aggressive behaviors, and another category of interest, group size. Each of these categories was subdivided into more refined categories.

Play Activities Play activities represented a generic class and the social interactions that emerged during these activites. The play activities were classified as one of three types: sensory-motor play, symbolic play, and games with rules, with the three types of play implying a hierarchy in terms of their complexity and the cognitive demands they required. Sensory-motor play involved physical, kinesthetic and /or perceptual activity that was purposeful, rather than appearing to be random physical movement. Symbolic play had dramatic or make believe elements. Games with rules involved mutuality of social relationships and a sense of obligation among the players who abided by the rules of the game.

In addition to the categories of play behavior that were coded, a number of other categories were also coded. These included *nonplay activity,* which was defined as the absence of play, and included circumstances when the child was *isolated* and not talking to or playing with anyone else but did appear to be self-absorbed in an activity.

Another category, *prosocial behavior* represented positive involvement with other children. Among the categories of prosocial behavior that were noted were *approach, active, passive,* and *playfight.* Approach behavior was observed when a child made an attempt to join an activity. Active behavior was noted when the child was fully participating in as active a way as the particular activity permitted. This was distinguished from passive behavior in which the child was only semi-involved in an ongoing activity with peers. Playfight connoted aggressive behavior that was appropriate for the activity, such as when children were wrestling or playing karate.

The next major category of behavior that was recorded involved *neutral behavior,* and included the subcategories of no interaction, onlooks, and non-assertive. No interaction was recorded when the child was not interacting with anyone else and did not appear to be involved in a solitary activity. It was the latter qualifier that distinguished no interaction from isolated play. Onlooks was used when the child was observed looking at other children playing. Nonassertive was coded when one of two events occurred: the child was aggressed against by another, or he yielded to a request by another.

The final major behavioral category that was coded was *aggressive behavior,* and was comprised of two subcategories: aggress and disrupt. The former subcategory was used when the child was in physical contact with another that was intended to harm the other child. Disrupt was used when the behavior stopped short of physical violence but was intended to interfere with the ongoing activity of other children.

Training Observers and Collecting the Data

A total of 12 observers collected the observational data. Observers were either graduate students in psychology or education, or had a keen interest in the behavior of learning disabled children. Training was conducted in phases, beginning with group discussion and written material to provide observers with some of the theoretical background of the topic, and ending with several weeks of direct practice on the playground. An observer was said to be trained when his or her reliability, indicated an agreement of at least 75% to 80% with the primary investigator.

Once an observer achieved the necessary level of reliability, he or she was assigned at random to one of the four schools. Each observation session on a child lasted for 10 minutes, divided into 60 10-second intervals, with an equal number for observing and recoding of behavior. Each child was observed for nine intervals of 10 minutes each, a total of 90 minutes.

Sociometric Data Collection

In addition to direct observations of children on the playground, sociometric data were also collected. A roster-and-rating sociometric questionnaire developed by Singleton and Asher (1977) was used. In this instrument each child rates every other child in the class on a 1–5 continuum. The roster-and-rating sociometric method is especially preferred for learning disabled children because it avoids reliance on the children's memory of their classmates and on their ability to spell the names of their classmates, a skill that is necessary in traditional sociometric assessment. In the research being reported here, two sociometric questionnaires were used, one for work and the other for play. Administration of the questionnaires was conducted during the last 3 weeks of observations, toward the end of the school year, either immediately before or immediately after the children's lunch period.

Data Transformation and Analysis

Both the observational data and the sociometric data were tallied and transformed prior to the actual statistical analyses. Frequencies of the observational data were transformed using the formula log + .5 as recommended by Bock (1975). This transformation normalizes the frequency distribution that often is highly skewed in the case of observational categories. The sociometric data were also transformed within each classroom, using a z-transformation for both same-sex and opposite-sex ratings. Analysis of the observational data was conducted using one-way multivariate analyses of variance for each major category of behavior. Sociometric data analyses consisted of one-way or two-way univariate analyses of variance, depending upon the specific questions being addressed.

Results

The first set of questions with which we were concerned were with comparisons of the natural play patterns of learning disabled and nonlearning disabled children. To what extent are learning disabled children's play patterns either qualitatively or quantitatively different from their nonhandicapped peers?

Our first analysis was to determine whether learning disabled children were observed playing less often than their nonhandicapped peers and whether there were any differences among children in the third, fourth, and fifth grades. A two-way analysis of variance on frequency of observed play was conducted and none of the resulting F values were statistically significant. This indicated that there were no quantitative differences in the frequency of play that was observed for learning disabled and nonlearning disabled children across the three grade levels.

Our second general question was whether learning disabled children would play more sensory-motor games and fewer games with rules than nonlearning disabled children. Our general hypothesis was that if learning disabled children operate on a lower cognitive level than their nonhandicapped classmates, this difference might also be manifest in the level of their play. As part of this question, we were also interested in whether there would be differences in type of play for children in grades three, four, and five. This question was addressed statistically by a two-way multivariate analysis of variance with LD/non LD and grade level as the independent variables and the three types of play (sensory-motor, symbolic, and games with rules) as the dependent measures. Again, no significant differences emerged for either independent variable. Thus, there were no overall differences in the developmental quality of play between learning disabled and nondisabled youngsters as we observed it.

Our third general question concerned the number of children with whom learning disabled and nonlearning disabled children played. Specifically, we studied whether learning disabled children played with fewer children in smaller size playgroups. This question was tested in a one-way multivariate analysis of variance with LD/non LD as the independent variable and the frequency of play in the five different playgroup sizes as the dependent measure. Results indicated a significant multivariate effect, with lambda $= .83$, and Rao's approximation $(5,62) = 2.46$. ($p < .04$). In order to determine the specific playgroup size that differentiated LD from non LD children, tests of simple effects were computed, with each of the playgroup sizes analyzed separately. Only the group size 1 condition significantly differentiated the LD and non LD children. LD children were observed playing alone significantly more often than non LD were observed playing alone ($F = 10.16$, $df = 1, 66$, $p = .002$). No other significant differences between LD and non LD children were found for the four other group size conditions. In other words, no trend was evident indicating a corresponding decrease in the percentage of time that LD children spent playing in groups of increasingly larger size.

We next analyzed the data for neutral and aggressive behaviors. Here we were specifically interested in whether LD children played more aggressively than their non LD classmates, and whether they exhibited more neutral behavior, especially in the no interaction subcategory. Results of this analysis revealed no significant multivariate effect. That is, LD children did not differ from their non LD peers in frequency of neutral and/or aggressive behavior. When the no interaction subcategory was analyzed by itself, rather than being part of the multivariate neutral category, the results indicated that LD children did not interact significantly more often than non LD children ($F = 6.76$, $df = 1{,}66$, $p < .01$). This finding differs from the previous finding that LD children played alone more often than non LD children in that the present finding indicated that the behavior of LD children was neither activity nor socially oriented.

The next analyses concerned the sociometric data. We had several interests with these data. First, we wished to determine whether our data replicated prior studies and indicated that learning disabled children occupied an inferior sociometric status than nonlearning disabled youngsters. Second, we wished to determine whether the inferior ratings, if they occurred, resulted primarily from ratings of members of the same sex, or were the result of ratings by members of the opposite sex. Finally, we wished to determine whether sociometric status correlated with observed behavior in natural settings. We were especially interested in being able to relate low sociometric status to increased frequency of solitary play.

In order to determine whether the LD children occupied a lower sociometric status than their nonhandicapped classmates, sociometric scores for the play ratings were converted to z scores and subjected to a t test. The resulting value of 2.37 was significant at the .02 level and revealed that the LD children received lower ratings as play companions than non LD children. These data therefore compare favorably with prior data on this topic.

When the sociometric data were analyzed for gender differences, several significant findings emerged. First, the significant differences in sociometric status between LD and non LD children was attributable primarily to same-sex ratings. Female LD children were rated most negatively by other girls; male LD children were also rated negatively by other boys, but much less so than girls ratings discussed above. No significant differences were found among any of the opposite-sex ratings. Overall, the low sociometric status of LD children in this sample was the result of LD girls being rated very negatively by other girls.

A final analysis for purposes of this report was the correlation between same-sex sociometric ratings and frequency of isolate play. The resulting correlation coefficient of $-.46$ indicated that the lower children were rated sociometrically by same-sex peers the more they tended to play in an isolate fashion.

Additional post hoc analyses of the sociometric and play data suggested that the significant correlation between same-sex sociometric ratings and isolate play was accounted for by a subset of approximately one-third of the LD children. That is, these one-third of the children had low sociometric ratings and played alone. The remaining two-thirds had average sociometric ratings and played with others to the same extent as their nonhandicapped peers. At this time, we do not know the additional characteristics of these LD children that differentiate them from higher sociometric status LD children, but this subset of one-third was responsible for all statistically significant differences that emerged in this investigation.

The overall set of data that emerged from the research reviewed is that there are no differences either in the quality or the quantity of play exhibited by LD children when compared to non LD classmates who are matched for age and gender. Differences that resulted were in the number of children with whom LD children played. The major difference was that they tended to play alone somewhat more frequently than non LD children. However, when they did play with other children, they played in the same size groups as their handicapped peers. As a final qualification, only a minority of LD children did play alone more often.

These data call into question a general tendency in the literature to attribute qualitative differences to the social aspects of learning disabilities. Although there may indeed be differences in the social experiences of LD and non LD children, these differences may lie primarily in academic settings and much less so in nonacademic settings, which constitute the bulk of the children's waking hours. Furthermore, it appears that even in academic settings, rather than generalize about perceived differences between LD and non LD children, the major emphasis should be on similarities between them and to identify the subsample of LD children who might, in fact, contribute to the overall group differences that are reported in the literature. It is most important to recognize that, at least in the present research, the majority of LD children did not differ from their non LD peers.

CONCLUSIONS

One of the glaring weaknesses in our understanding of handicapped children is with their life experiences outside the classroom. By far, the bulk of research data to date has focused on academic experiences in a classroom situation despite the fact that children spend no more than 4 to 5 hours daily in academic activities. Our research, conducted with mildly learning disabled youngsters of elementary school age, suggests that for the majority of such children, there are not many differences in play behavior, at least the way that we observed it. We have no information on the play of more severely learning disabled children or of LD children of different chronological ages. Also, our entire sample of children was from middle- and upper-middle class backgrounds, and no generalizations can be made beyond this socioeconomic grouping. Furthermore, we did not attempt to assess the relationship to self-esteem of variations of play as we observed it.

It appears to us that perhaps as much research effort should be directed toward identifying the strengths of handicapped children as is devoted to their weaknesses. We have spent too much time searching for the differences between handicapped and nonhandicapped children and too little time looking for similarities. Certainly, the first course of action must be to obtain adequate descriptors of learning disabled children, a fact that has so far proven elusive. Casual perusal of the children in our sample suggested differences among them. Other than in their level of acceptance by peers, we have no concrete social data on the extent of these differences. We do know, however, that peer sociometric status relates fairly powerfully to children's unsupervised play. Perhaps other social factors are equally or more important.

REFERENCES

Bachara, G. (1976). Empathy in learning disabled children. *Perceptual and Motor skills, 43*, 541–542.

Barker, R. (1965). Explorations in ecological psychology. *American Psychologist*, 1965, *20*, 1–4.

Bock, D. (1975). *Multivariate statistical methods in behavioral research.* New York: McGraw-Hill.

Bruck, M., & Hebart, M. (1982). Correlates of learning disabled students' peer-interaction patterns. *Learning Disability Quarterly, 5*, 353–362.

Bruininks, V. (1978). Actual and perceived peer status of learning-disabled students in mainstream programs. *The Journal of Special Education, 12*, 51–58.

Bryan, T. (1974). An observational analysis of classroom behaviors of children with learning disabilities. *Journal of Learning Disabilities, 7*, 34–43.

Bryan, T. (1976). Peer popularity of learning disabled children: A replication. *Journal of Learning Disabilities, 9*, 49–53.

Bryan, T. (1978). Social relationships and verbal interactions of learning disabled children. *Journal of Learning Disabilities, 11*, 107–115.

Cowen, E., Pederson, A., Babigan, H., Izzo, L., & Trost, M. (1973). Long term follow-up of early detected vulnerable children. *Journal of Consulting and Clinical Psychology, 41*, 438–446.

Darbyshire, J. (1977). Play patterns in young children with impaired hearing. *The Volta Review, 79*, 19–26.

Dickstein, E., & Warren, D. (1980). Role taking deficits in learning disabled children. *Journal of Learning Disabilities, 13*, 378–382.

Eifermann, R. (1971). Social play in childhood. In R. Herron & B. Sutton-Smith (Eds.), *Child's Play*. New York: Wiley.

Freud, A. (1963). The concept of developmental lines. *Psychoanalytic Study of the Child, 18*, 245–265.

Garrett, M., & Crump, W. (1980). Peer acceptance, teacher preferences, and self-appraisal of social status among learning disabled students. *Learning Disability Quarterly, 3*, 42–48.

Greiger, R., & Richards, H. (1976). Prevalence and structure of behavior symptoms among children in special education and regular classroom settings. *Journal of School Psychology, 14*, 27–38.

Guralnick, M. (1981). The social behavior of preschool children at different developmental levels: Effects of group composition. *Journal of Experimental Child Psychology, 31*, 115–130.

Hare, A. (1952). A study of interaction and consensus in different sized groups. *American Sociological Review, 17*, 261–267.

Heron, T. E., & Heward, W. L. (1982). Ecological assessment: Implications for teachers of learning disabled students. *Learning Disability Quarterly, 5*, 117–125.

Higginbotham, D., & Baker, B. (1981). Social participation and cognitive play differences in hearing-impaired and normally hearing preschoolers. *The Volta Review, 83*, 135–149.

de Hirsch, K. (1973). The concept of plasticity and language disabilities. In S. Sapir, & A. Nitzburg (Eds.), *Children with learning problems* (pp. 477–516). New York: Brunner/Mazel.

Horowitz, E. (1981). Popularity, decentering ability, and role-taking skills in learning disabled and normal children. *Learning Disability Quarterly, 4*, 23–38.

Hutt, C., & Vaizey, M. (1966). Differential effects of group density on social behavior. *Nature, 209*, 1371–1372.

Koegh, B., Tchir, C., & Windeguth-Behn, A. (1974). Teachers' perceptions of educationally high risk children. *Journal of Learning Disabilities, 7*, 367–374.

Lerner, J. W. (1985). *Learning disabilities: Theories, diagnosis, and teaching strategies* (4th ed.). Boston, MA: Houghton Mifflin.

Lerner, J. W., Egan, R. W., & James, K. W. (1981). *Learning Disabilities: Theories, Diagnosis, and Teaching Strategies*. Boston: Houghton-Mifflin.

Loo, C. (1978). Density, crowding, and preschool children. In A. Baum, & Y. Epstein (Eds.). *Human responses to crowding*. (pp. 371–388). Hillsdale, NJ: Lawrence Erlbaum Associates.

Lovell, K., Hoyle, H., & Siddall, M. (1968). A study of some aspects of the play and language of young children with delayed speech. *Journal of Child Psychology and Psychiatry, 9*, 51–59.

McGrew, P. (1970). Social and spatial density effects on spacing behavior in preschool children. *Journal of Child Psychology and Psychiatry, 11*, 197–205.

Millar, S. (1968). *The psychology of play*. London: Penguin.

Parten, M. (1932). Social participation among preschool children. *Journal of Abnormal and Social Psychology, 27*, 243–269.

Parten, M. (1933). Social play among preschool children. *Journal of Abnormal and Social Psychology, 28* 136–147.

Pearl, R., & Cosden, M. (1982). Sizing up a situation; LD children's understanding of social interactions. *Learning Disability Quarterly, 5*, 344–352.

Peterson, N., & Haralick, J. (1977). Integration of handicapped and nonhandicapped preschoolers: An analysis of play behavior and social interaction. *Education and Training of the Mentally Retarded, 12*, 235–245.

Piaget, J. (1962). *Play, dreams, and imitation in childhood*. New York: W. W. Norton, 1962. London: Routledge and Kegan Paul.

Pullis, M., & Smith, D. (1981). Social-cognitive development of learning disabled children. *Topics in Learning and Learning Disabilities, 1*, 43–55.

Scranton, T., & Ryckman, D. (1979). Sociometric status of learning disabled children in an integrative program. *Journal of Learning Disabilities, 12*, 49–54.

Singer, J. (1973). *The child's world of make believe*. New York: Academic Press, 1973.

Singer, J. (1977). Imagination and make-believe play in early childhood: Some educational implications. *Journal of Mental Imagery, 1*, 127–144.

Singleton, L., & Asher, S. (1977). Peer preferences and social interaction among third-grade children in an integrated school district. *Journal of Educational Psychology, 69*, 330–336.

Siperstein, G., Bopp, M., & Bak, J. (1978). Social status of learning disabled children. *Journal of Learning Disabilities, 11*, 98–102.

Smilansky, S. (1968). *The effects of sociodramatic play on disadvantaged children*. New York: Wiley.

Spradley, J. (1980). *Participant observation*. New York: Holt, Rinehart and Winston.

Thompson, L. (1980). *Effects of group size on social and representational behaviors of delayed and nondelayed preschool children*. Unpublished doctoral dissertation, George Peabody College for Teachers of Vanderbilt University.

Torgesen, J., & Dice, C. (1980). Characteristics of research on learning disabilities. *Journal of Learning Disabilities, 13*, 531–535.

Vandenberg, B. (1981). Environmental and cognitive factors in social play. *Journal of Experimental Child Psychology, 31*, 169–175.

Wong, B., & Wong, R. (1980). Role-taking in normal achieving and learning disabled children. *Learning Disability Quarterly, 3*, 11–18.

III THE IMPACT OF MAINSTREAMING ON TEACHERS, PARENTS, AND HEALTH PROFESSIONALS

8 Attitudes of Regular Education Teachers Toward Mainstreaming Mildly Handicapped Students

John Salvia
Susan Munson
The Pennsylvania State University

Early efforts in special education were directed toward the most severely handicapped. The treatment goals for these individuals were quite different from the educational goals for children who attended school. When special education was incorporated into the public schools, it was viewed as a place of refuge for students who could not complete the prescribed educational curriculum when implemented by the traditional educational methods. Even the mildly handicapped individuals who attended public schools [educable mentally retarded (EMR), emotionally disturbed (ED), and learning disabled (LD) students] were believed to be so different from normal students that they could not meet the goals established. This general feeling was expressed by S. A. Kirk and G. O. Johnson 30 years ago when they defined a mentally retarded student as "one who is unable to profit sufficiently from the curriculum of the public schools, but who can be educated to become socially adequate and occupationally competent, provided special educational facilities are furnished" (1951, p. 13). Today, handicapped students are still those who cannot attain the goals established for the lowest track for normal students. For these students, the rules are changed—they do not have to achieve the same goals as the students in regular classes.

Although special education grew and prospered as more and more students were enrolled, four things happened in the late 60s and early 70s to halt and reverse the growth of special education. First, the results of a series of methodologically flawed efficacy studies altered the views of special educators (e.g., Lilly, 1971). These studies often showed no advantage in academics for handicapped students in special classes over handicapped students in regular classes (cf Kirk, 1964; Guskin & Spicker, 1968; Hirshoren, Schultz, Manton, & Henderson, 1970). Second, special educators came to believe that the labels they were using with handicapped students were stigmatizing and that they produced harmful effects independently of other factors, such as the children's performances (e.g., Dunn, 1968). Third, the diagnostic procedures used to place students in special education came to be looked on as racially and ethnically biased (e.g., Mercer, 1970). Fourth, special educators began to believe that educational segregation, by itself, was evil and should be avoided unless absolutely necessary (Burgdorf & Bersoff, 1980).

These four trends affected parents and professionals, who in turn brought lawsuits and lobbied legislators. The eventual result was a social policy that mandated education for handicapped pupils in the least restrictive environment (LRE). This requirement is represented in Public Law 93–380, section 504 of the Rehabilitation Act of 1973, and Public Law 94–142. The latter represents the judicial, legislative, and societal preference for the integration of handicapped students to the maximum extent appropriate (Turnbull & Turnbull, 1978). According to the law, a handicapped pupil should be removed from the regular class setting only when the severity of the handicap is such that achievement is unsatisfactory despite the provision of supplemental aids and services.

The responsibility for implementing the principle of least restrictive environment now falls to both regular and special educators. Successful mainstreaming is especially dependent on positive attitudes by regular classroom teachers (RCTs). These attitudes are influenced, in part, by the official attitudes of significant regular educators and in part by the individual RCTs' attitudes and expectations for handicapped students.

INFLUENCES ON REGULAR CLASS TEACHERS' ATTITUDES

Official Attitudes

Concern with the impact of LRE and mainstreaming for RCTs has been evident in publications of the National Education Association (NEA). The Teachers' Rights Committee of NEA identified concerns and problems of regular teachers in complying with Public Law 94–142 during the first year of implementation. The committee found that there was general support of the rights of handicapped children, but it also identified the LRE provision as the most controversial. Problems cited most often included: (1) lack of preparation to teach handicapped pupils; (2) overcrowded classrooms; and (3) inflexible and inadequate time and teaching schedules (Massie, 1978). Subsequently, the NEA passed a resolution based on the needs and concerns of the teacher membership. The 1983 NEA Representative Assembly reiterated the original resolution and incorporated additional items to be considered in LRE programs. The resolution included the following items regarding LRE:

1. Shared planning by all professionals to create on-going communication and a favorable experience for all children.
2. Adequate preparation of staff and students.
3. Modification of class size, scheduling (with released time), and curriculum.
4. Appropriate methods, materials, and support services with systematic evaluation.
5. The rights of teachers to dissent and not to be evaluated on the basis of the IEP.
6. Changes in funding of special education services and provision of incentives for participation in activities mandated by law.
7. Involvement of teachers and the organization in advisory panels and United States Office of Education on-site monitoring activities.

Similar concerns were expressed by the American Federation of Teachers (AFT) over the LRE provisions of the law. Zettel (1982) reported comments made by AFT President, Albert Shanker. Shanker urged that the following circumstances be documented by regular classroom teachers: (1) the wholesale return of handicapped students; (2) decrease in special education personnel; (3) lack of in-service training; and (4) large class sizes that diminish the quality of education for all (Zettel, 1982, p. 33).

The Official Stereotypes

Some of what RCTs know about handicapped pupils can be inferred from descriptions of handicapped students offered in introductory special-education texts. A recent survey indicated that 15 states had a requirement that preservice RCTs complete coursework related to exceptional children (Smith & Schindler, 1980). This coursework usually involved one introductory-level special-education course. The content focus was general information and the characteristics of exceptional individuals. If this is "the" special-education course provided to RCTs, a cursory review of the contents of several popular introductory textbooks should provide a general idea of the information that RCTs have about handicapped students. Despite cautions that handicapped groups are variable and that the use of disability categories are not particularly useful for educators, these texts reflect an adherence to categorically ascribed characteristics.

The presentation of characteristics specific to categories of exceptional persons may promote stereotypic expectations in RCTs for specific types of handicapped students. Table 8.1 contains selected descriptions of exceptional students that were taken from five popular texts introducing special education. The texts portray EMR, ED, and LD students more negatively than they portray physically, sensorily, and communication handicapped pupils. EMR, ED, and LD students are described in terms of limited intellectual abilities, low achievement, and disruptive behavior patterns. The reported learning problems would require that

Table 8.1
The Official Stereotypes

Handicapping Condition	*Dimensions*	*Characteristics*
Mental Retardation	Cognitive	• Exhibit an overall decrease in the ability to learn (1, 2). • Difficulties in rate of learning, level of learning in academic areas, memory, transfer of training, abstract learning (1, 5). • Difficulties in selective attention (2, 3).
	Physical	• Domain in which the least differences are observed in comparison to normal children except for severe levels of retardation (1, 2).
	Behavior-Social	• Display a range of emotional and social behaviors which are similar to nonretarded children (1). • May exhibit dependency, poor self-concept, expectancy for failure and experience limited peer acceptance (3).
Learning Disabled	Cognitive	• Difficulty in major academic areas such as reading, math, language (1,2,3,4,5). • Achievement level is often 18 months to two years behind grade level (5). • Academic difficulties are not due to low intelligence (1). • Exhibit difficulties in attention and memory skills (2,3).
	Physical	• Hyperactive (1,2,3,4,5). • Restless and fidgety (4). • Exhibit fine or gross motor incoordination (1,3).
	Behavior-Social	• Exhibit poor social perception skills (1). • Exhibit any one or a combination of the following behaviors: disruptive, inconsistent, irritable, withdrawn, dependent. (1,2,5).
Emotional Disturbance	Cognitive	• Intelligence level may be in the dull normal range (2). • Exhibit lowered achievement levels and learning problems (1,3,4).
	Physical	• May exhibit hyperactive behaviors, such as high activity level (5).
	Behavior-Social	• Inappropriate classroom behaviors include aggressive behavior such as fighting, disrespect, and disobeying the teacher (3). • Described on the basis of deviant syndromes such as underachieving, irrepressible, or incorrigible (1).
Physically Handicapped	Cognitive	• The severity of physical involvement is not predictive of the level of intellectual functioning (1). • May exhibit learning problems, but these problems may be resolved (3). • Are able to make "healthy adjustments" (2).

Table 8.1 (*continued*)
The Official Stereotypes

Handicapping Condition	*Dimensions*	*Characteristics*
	Physical	• Described as exhibiting specific physical or organic dysfunctions (1,2,3,4,5).
	Behavior-Social	• Exhibit the same range of emotions as other age-mates (1). • No specific characteristics related to personality type (2).
Speech and Language	Cognitive	• Exhibit wide variability in levels of cognitive functioning (1,2).
	Communication	• Exhibit difficulties in articulation, language, voice or fluency (1,5).
	Behavioral-Social	• No generalizable personality types (2). • May experience feelings of frustration or anxiety (1).
Hearing Impaired	Cognitive	• Normal distribution of intelligence levels (1,2,3). • Evaluation instruments and procedures used to determine intelligence are not appropriate for this group (1). • Deaf may function at a retarded level (1). • May have an impact on achievement levels (2,5). • May exhibit behaviors characteristic of LD, EMR, and ED children (2).
	Behavior-Social	• May exhibit a lack of responsibility or independence (3).
Visually Impaired	Cognitive	• Achievement may not be affected (2). • Cognitive abilities are usually within a normal range (5). • Potential to be an "effective learner" (3). • Normal curriculum may be used with adaptations in materials (5).
	Physical	• Exhibit delayed motor development (1,3).
	Behavior-Social	• Low peer acceptance may occur (2). • Self-regard depends on other people's attitudes and reactions toward them (1,3).

REFERENCE LIST FOR OFFICIAL STEREOTYPE, TABLE 1

Cartwright, G. P., Cartwright, C. A., Ward, M. E. (1981). *Educating special learners*. Belmont, CA.: Wadsworth.

Hallahan, D. P., & Kauffman, J. P. (1982). *Exceptional children. Introduction to special education*. Englewood Cliffs, NJ: Prentice-Hall.

Haring, N. G. (1982). *Exceptional children and youth*. Columbus, OH: Charles E. Merrill.

Schulz, J. B., & Turnbull, A. P. (1984). *Mainstreaming handicapped students. A guide for classroom teachers*. Boston: Allyn and Bacon.

Smith, R. M., Neisworth, J. T., Hunt, F. M. (1983). *The exceptional child*. New York: McGraw-Hill.

RCTs adjust the educational programs for these students; the reported disruptive behaviors would pose a threat to the maintenance of discipline and control in the classroom.

For physically, sensorily, and speech impaired students, no specific set of characteristics (intellectual, behavioral, achievement, or personality) was typically offered. Less emphasis was placed on the diminished ability of the pupil to learn or to behave appropriately. The texts suggest that adaptations in the physical environment, materials, and prosthetic and communication devices facilitated normal functioning. The reader is told that a wide range of ability levels and personality characteristics may be found in individuals so labelled. Finally, the role of others in the social adjustment of these handicapped students was often emphasized. Because the attitudes and behavior of others can significantly affect the self-esteem and adjustment of these children, more responsibility was placed on the normal individual to act in positive and appropriate ways.

Regular Class Teachers' Expectations for Handicapped Students

RCTs are led to believe by the texts that some handicapped students will be difficult to teach because of learning and behavior problems. These lowered expectations have been directly verified in a number of two-phase experiments. The first phases of these experiments directly assessed expectations by having subjects (Ss) complete a checklist of hypothetical students. In one study of this kind, Reschly and Lamprecht (1979) found that 36 experienced teachers who were enrolled in graduate school held different expectations for educable mentally retarded (EMR) students than they did for nonhandicapped students. Foster and Keech (1978) asked highly experienced RCTs (mean experience = 10.8 years) to complete two dependent measures: a 35-item checklist based on the California Test of Personality and a 23-item checklist assessing potential problems in language, perception, attention, and personality on a 5-point scale. They found that the RCTs had lower expectations for EMRs than they had for normals. Other studies by Foster and several colleagues used the same dependent measures. Ysseldyke and Foster (1978) investigated the expectations of 75 elementary RCTs who were randomly assigned to one of three groups (normal, LD, ED). Each group was asked to complete the form for a fourth-grade boy. Hypothetical normal children were rated higher than LD and ED pupils; LD and ED students were rated equally negatively. Foster, Algozzine, and Ysseldyke (1980) found that 36 certified, elementary RCTs and 36 graduate students in special education held lower expectations for ED than for normal students.

Students aspiring to be RCTs have also served as subjects in a number of very similar investigations. Salvia, Clark, and Ysseldyke (1973) assessed the expectations of 117 special and 48 regular educators-in-training for the performance of retarded individuals in several areas. They found that, when compared to normal children, expectations for retarded students were lower on the five characteristics investigated (attitudes and reactions toward adults, attitudes toward tasks, attitudes toward own performance, motor reactions, and verbalizations). Foster, Ysseldyke, and Reese (1975) assessed the expectations of 38 special-education majors for labels of ED and normal. They found that the teachers-in-training held more negative expectations on the measures.

The second phase of these experiments followed a different tack. All subjects watched the same videotape(s); however, depending on the experimental condition, Ss were told that the child depicted in the videotape was normal or handicapped. Ss rated the student, and differences in ratings were attributed to different expectations held for the types of handicaps. In the second phase of their study, Reschly and Lamprecht (1979) found that their 36 teachers initially held different expectations for EMR and normal students, but these expectations were reduced and eliminated by longer exposure to videotapes.

Salvia, Clark, and Ysseldyke (1973) found that expectations interacted with children and were modified for individual pupils. However, when expectations did operate, they operated as would be predicted: Ss held lower expectations for retarded students than for normal students. The next series of studies not only used the checklist developed by Foster Ysseldyke, & Reese (1975), they used the same 12-minute videotape of a fourth-grade boy completing four tasks (the reading recognition subtest of the Wide Range Achievement Test, the general information subtest of the Peabody Individual Achievement Test, several perceptual-motor tasks, and free play). Foster and Keech (1977) showed that 50 RCTs held different expectations for EMRs and normals for personality traits, academic performance, and behavior problems. Ysseldyke and Foster (1978) found the expectations for LD and ED were unaffected when 75 RCTs viewed a real child: ED and LD children were still viewed more negatively than normal students; there were no differences in the ratings of LD and ED students. Foster, Algozzine, & Ysseldyke (1980) found that RCTs and graduate students in special education held lower expectations for ED students than they held for normal students. Foster, Ysseldyke, and Reese (1975) found that teachers-in-training rated the fourth grader lower when he was labeled ED.

Other studies did not use the two-phase approach: Ss simply evaluated the videotaped performance of a labeled student. Taylor, Smiley, and Ziegler (1983) studied the effect of the MR label on the perceptions of teachers and teachers-to-be. They found "a label of mentally retarded resulted in significantly lower ratings on teacher acceptance (although this was involved in a significant interaction with the attribute condition), prediction of reading, prediction of spelling, and prediction of arithmetic" (p. 47). Minner (1982) studied the expectations of 66 regular, experienced, vocational teachers who watched a videotape and read a vignette of students described positively or negatively and labeled (LD or

EMR) or unlabeled. "The presence of the labels. . . lowered the initial academic and social expectations of the teachers in the sample" (p. 452). Three other studies used Foster's videotape. Foster, Schmidt, and Sabatino (1976) examined the expectations of 44 elementary RCTs and found that they held lower academic expectations and greater expectations for behavior problems when the boy was labeled LD. Foster and Salvia (1977) found that the label of LD produced negative expectations for 88 certified elementary RCTs even when the teachers were cautioned to be objective. Simpson (1981) studied the expectations of 34 RCTs using Foster's videotape and found that the ED label produced greater perceptions of emotional disturbance and decreased predictions of successful learning in a regular elementary class.

Other studies using different methodology have reached similar results. Gillung and Rucker (1977) used a modified version of the Rucker-Gable Educational Programming Scale to assess the effects of labels and behavioral descriptions on the attitudes of 176 RCTs and 82 SCTs. They concluded, in part, that "regular teachers have lower expectations for children who are labeled than children with identical behaviors who are not labeled" (p. 465). Using the Leary Interpersonal Checklist, Moore and Fine (1978) compared the perceptions of LD, EMR, and normal students held by teachers of EMRs, LDs, or regular-class students. They found that the three types of teachers generally viewed handicapped students in similar ways: the EMR "child was seen as a borderline cooperative-over-conventional, docile-dependent subject; the LD child was viewed as skeptical-distrustful; and the normal 10-year-old was seen as competitive-exploitative" (p. 256).

Siperstein and Bak (1980) report three investigations they conducted. In the first they asked 30 RCTs "who had very little or no contact with mentally retarded children" to describe a mentally retarded child (p. 221). Three out of four teachers responded with general statements about nondisruptive behavioral differences. Several teachers reported such pupils "cannot function in a classroom situation" and "cannot be expected to learn to cope with any kind of teaching or instruction" (p. 222). In the second study, they asked RCTs about the actions, looks, and feelings of a mentally retarded person. About 80% offered negative characterizations of how he or she might act (e.g., disoriented); about 40% indicated a mentally retarded pupil feels "rejected and isolated." In the third study, prospective teachers were asked about the actions, looks, and feelings of a mentally retarded person. Generally, teachers-to-be used negative traits to depict either a very active or a very withdrawn child (p. 224).

As can be anticipated, not every study produced label effects. We found studies that produced mixed effects e.g., Fogel & Nelson, 1983] or no effect (e.g., Yoshida & Meyers, 1975). Nonetheless, it seems very clear that RCTs anticipate lower performances from EMR, ED, LD youngsters than they expect from nonhandiapped students.

RCT'S PERCEPTIONS OF MAINSTREAMING

A belief in the general philosophy of mainstreaming handicapped children is a significant factor underlying RCTs' attitudes and willingness to accept these children in their classrooms (Larrivee & Cook, 1979; Ringlaben & Price, 1981). The bases for these beliefs reside in the value of handicapped children as useful members of society and the responsibility of the public schools to educate these children (Stephens & Braun, 1980). The degree to which RCTs believe in the philosophy of mainstreaming has been inferred from their willingness to accept handicapped children in their classrooms.

Levels of acceptance of handicapped children by RCTs have been somewhat discouraging. A survey of 200 teachers of mainstreamed EMR children revealed that only 38% of the teachers supported the concept of mainstreaming. Of that same sample, only 40.5% were willing to accept an EMR student in their classroom (Childs, 1979). In a similar study, 50% of 139 RCTs disagreed with the efficacy of regular classroom instruction for the handicapped, but 65% of the same group of teachers expressed little understanding of the legislation mandating mainstreaming (Horne, 1983).

RCTs' willingness to mainstream handicapped children has been shown to be differentially affected by several variables. These variables have been grouped into three clusters for discussion purposes: (1) child-related variables; (2) teacher-related variables; and (3) variables related to the educational environment in which mainstreaming is to occur.

Child-related Variables

Labels. Assessment of teacher attitudes toward children with various deviance labels has generated consistent evidence of the existence of a heirarchy of acceptance for various handicapping conditons. The perceptions of disabilities held by RCTs [as well as those held by SCTs and nonteachers] can be differentiated on the basis of several dimensions, including: (1) physical; (2) cognitive; and (3) behavioral–emotional (Schmelkin, 1982).

Physically handicapped students (PHs) are usually identified as the most acceptable handicapped students for placement in the regular classroom (Parish & Copeland, 1978; Parish, Dyck, & Kappes, 1979). Williams (1977) obtained similar findings when RCTs were asked which of four types of handicapped children would be acceptable for mainstreaming. Physically handicapped children were consistently rated as most acceptable. However, Panda and Bartel (1972) found that crippled children were included in a subgroup with the mentally and retarded speech impaired and were ranked after blind and deaf. A similar ranking of various disability groups was reported for teachers in a rural setting. Again, crippled children were ranked after blind and deaf (Leyser & Abrams, 1982).

Children with cognitive disabilities tend to be rated consistently lower than normal children or children with physical problems. Shotel, Iano, and McGettigan (1972) assessed teacher attitudes toward ED, LD, and EMR children in schools with and without special-education resource-room programs. Teachers rated MR children more negatively than they rated ED and LD children in terms of acceptability for integration into regular classrooms. EMR children were also rated as having less potential for social and academic adjustment in the regular class. A follow-up interview with the respondents revealed that the EMR students continued to be identified as low achievers in the regular classroom. Similarly, Hirshoren, and Burton (1979) found that the MR students were the least preferred of the five types of handicapped students investigated. Moore and Fine (1978) found that teachers were more willing to accept LD than EMR students in their classrooms, with or without assistance, for part of the day. Moreover, 50% of the same sample disapproved of the placement of EMR students in the regular class for any part of the day. Williams (1977) investigated the acceptance of EMR, LD, ED, and PH students for mainstreaming by RCTs and found that EMR and ED students were rated equally as the least acceptable group for placement in their classes. The situation is less positive for more severely retarded students (Harth, 1981). For disabilties other than mental retardation, RCTs are also less willing to educate pupils with moderate and severe levels of disability.

Students with behavioral or emotional handicaps are also rated as less preferred group with which to interact (Jones, 1974). These pupils quite often share the position with the EMR as the most negatively evaluated for acceptance in mainstreamed settings. Harasymiw and Horne (1976) investigated RCTs' attitudes toward ED, EMR, and PH children on a measure of social distance. No significant differences were identified between teachers in an experimental integration program and a control group of RCTs on their rankings of labeled hypothetical children. The ED were rated more negatively than the EMR or PH. Similar ratings were reported as to the unacceptability of ED children for mainstreaming on measures of social distance (Horne, 1983; Parish & Copeland, 1978; Parish, Dyck, & Kappes, 1979).

Pupil Behavior Investigations have focused on pupil behaviors commonly associated with the behavioral-emotional dimension to determine the reasons for the negative reactions of teachers toward children exhibiting such behaviors or toward the labels themselves (Harasymiw & Horne, 1976; Horne, 1983; Parish & Copeland, 1978; Parish, Dyck, & Kappes, 1979; Williams, 1977). Algozzine (1976) compared the ratings of RCTs, SCTs, and special-education students who had completed student teaching, on the disturbingness of four areas of child behavior (social facility, social defiance, physical symptoms, and socialized delinquency). Significant differences were identified between SCTs and special-education student teachers and the RCTs. RCTs rated the behaviors as more disturbing than either of the special-education respondent groups, and the socially defiant behaviors were significantly more disturbing than the three other dimensions of pupil behavior. The pupil's sex was also a critical factor for teachers' willingness to tolerate disturbing behaviors. Behaviors exhibited more often by boys were significantly more disturbing to RCTs than those behaviors prevalent among girls (Schlosser & Algozzine, 1979). Unacceptable boy behavior included acting out, aggressiveness, and immaturity; more acceptable girl behavior was characterized as withdrawn and neurotic.

Coleman & Gilliam (1983) investigated the extent to which behaviors exhibited by ED students differentially affected the attitudes of elementary, mostly female, RCTs. Behavioral vignettes describing a white, middle-class boy, with average intelligence but below-grade achievement were used. Each vignette included one of seven clusters of behaviors to determine the differential disturbingness of each. Results indicated that two behavioral clusters significantly affected teacher ratings: The most favorable ratings were directed toward students who avoided peer interactions; the least favorable attitudes were directed toward students who exhibited aggressive interactions with peers and teachers.

Teacher-related Variables

Four categories of variables affect RCTs attitudes toward mainstreaming: general demographics, educational background, teaching experience, and perceived competence to teach the handicapped.

General Demographics. Teachers' race as a mediating variable in attitudes toward MR students was investigated by Kennon and Sandoval (1978). Comparisons were made between black and white teachers of EMRs and black and white RCTs attitudes toward MRs. No significant differences were reported between EMR teachers and RCTs' attitudes toward the MR as well as no differences between EMR majority and minority groups. The impact of age, sex, and marital status have received limited attention. Ringlaben and Price (1981) found no significant relationship between sex of the respondents and perceptions of mainstreaming effects. Stephens and Braun (1980) found that sex, age, and marital status were not significant predictors of teachers' willingness to integrate handicapped students.

Educational Background. Knowledge about handicapped children gained through formal study seems to be a factor in the development of positive attitudes. In several studies, RCTs' willingness to accept handicapped children in their classes has been significantly related to the number of special-education credits accrued (Mandell & Strain, 1978; Ringlaben & Price, 1981; Stephens & Braun, 1980). Knowledge gained in special-education coursework also interacts with the presence of special-education programs in the school and the teachers' prior experience with handicapped children to positively affect RCTs' willingness to mainstream (Williams, 1977). In spite of the supposed importance of special-education coursework, Ringlaben and Price (1981) reported that 86% of the respondents in their study had none.

The specific content of the courses taken is important. Courses and workshops that focus on diagnosis and learning problems of handicapped children are significantly related to positive attitudes. Courses in behavior management, special materials, and alternative teaching strategies do not appear to be related (Mandell & Strain, 1978).

Advanced degrees also seem important as a factor in willingness to teach handicapped children (Hudson, Graham, & Warner, 1979). Teachers with Master's degrees are more positive about adapting and locating materials even though the majority of the respondents felt that adequate materials were not available. These teachers were also more positive about their skills in teaching handicapped students.

Attitudes of RCTs differ as a function of the level at which teaching occurs; they become less positive as grade level increases from elementay to secondary (Larrivee & Cook, 1979). A similar decrease was reported when the sample of teachers ranged from kindergarten through eighth grade; teachers at the seventh and eighth grades were less willing to mainstream (Stephens & Braun, 1980). One study that sampled teachers from kindergarten through twelfth grade did not identify a grade-level effect (Ringlaben & Price, 1981). Grade level did not have a significant impact on the positiveness of RCTs' attitudes in studies only focusing on elementary teachers (Hudson, Graham, & Warner 1979; Mandel & Strain, 1978). Thus, the major impact of grade level appears after the intermediate grades. This decrease in willingness to mainstream has been attributed to the increased concern with subject matter and the decreased concern with individual student differences (Stephens & Braun, 1980).

Teaching Experience. A positive relationship between teaching experience in regular classes and positive attitudes toward both handicapped pupils and mainstreaming has not been documented (Jordan & Proctor, 1969; Stephens & Braun, 1980). In fact, an inverse relationship was found to exist between years of teaching experience and positiveness of teacher attitudes (Mandell & Strain, 1978). Teachers with more than 7 years of experience had lower expectations for handicapped students than those teaching for less than 7 years (Gilling & Rucker, 1977).

Conflicting results have been reported for the importance of prior teaching experience in special education. Some have reported a relationship between experience teaching handicapped students and willingness to integrate handicapped children (Mandell & Strain, 1978; Williams, 1977). Others have not (Shotel, Iano, & McGettigan, 1972; Jordan & Proctor, 1969).

Perceived Competence. RCTs' perceptions of their ability to meet the academic and social needs of handicapped pupils in their classes are a predictor of favorable attitudes toward mainstreaming (Larrivee & Cook, 1979; Stephens & Braun, 1980). RCTs may indeed be willing to mainstream but at the same time perceive themselves as incompetent to do so (Keogh & Levitt, 1976). Lack of skill was one of the reasons most often reported by RCTs for their unwillingness to participate in mainstreaming programs (Williams, 1977).

To provide a meaningful educational program for mildly handicapped children, RCTs need to develop additional skills. In developing in-service training programs, RCTs have been questioned to ascertain the specific skills they believe they need to acquire. RCTs have indicated needs in instructional methods, materials, and behavior management in order to teach handicapped students (Hudson, Graham, Warner, 1979; Shotel, Iano, & McGettigan, 1972). RCTs self-reported training needs by category of handicapped condition are listed in Table 8.2 The lack of requests for consulting teachers and school psychologists was noteworthy. It may be that the services are unavailable or that they are of little value to the RCT.

When teachers are provided with appropriate in-service training, there appears to be a significant positive impact on attitudes toward mainstreaming (Mandell & Strain, 1978). Larrivee (1981) investigated the effects of two in-service programs on the attitudes of RCTs toward mainstreaming. Short-term in-service programs (6 weeks) were not as effective as long-term programs providing in-class demonstrations and follow-up visits. Specific skill training had differential effects on teachers' attitudes toward managing certain types of handicapped children. An experimental training program for RCTs improved attitudes toward

Table 8.2
Differential Training Needs of Regular Class Teachers
(Williams, 1977)

	Handicapping Condition			
Expressed Needs	*LD*	*SED*	*PH*	*EMR*
Inservice training in the psychology of the handicapped	X			
Inservice training in instructional methodology	X	X	X	X
A visiting teacher				
Regular visits from a school psychologist				
Specialized curricular materials	X		X	X
Regular visits from someone who worked successfully with a handicapped student	X	X	X	

managing EMR, LD, TMR, deaf and multiply handicapped students, but not ED and blind students (Harasymiw & Horne, 1976).

Variables Related to the Educational Environment

Variables in the classroom and school setting have been investigated to ascertain their impact on RCTs' attitudes toward teaching handicapped students in those environments. Time, class size, and the availability of support services have been investigated.

Time. Constraints placed on the time available to the teacher to individualize instruction and to manage the educational program for handicapped children was identified as a significant deterrent to positive attitudes (Williams, 1977). In a survey of 1512 RCTs, 83% of 151 respondents felt that inadequate time was available to plan for and to teach exceptional pupils (Hudson, Graham, & Warner, 1979). NEA also advocated the need for released time for RCTs accepting handicapped students into their classes.

Class Size. Class size is closely related to the time constraints placed on RCTs. Mandell and Strain (1978) suggested a class size of 25–28 as optimal for placement of a handicapped child. Larrivee and Cook (1979) reported conflicting results in that no relationship was identified between class size and positive attitudes toward mainstreaming. Reduction of class size was recommended by both the National Education Association and the American Federation of Teachers. These organizations have proposed polices for reducing class size by three to four students for every handicapped child place in a regular class.

Availability of Support Services. Teachers and teacher organizations have cited the need for support services as a condition for effective mainstreaming. Fifty-eight percent of the 151 respondents sampled from two states felt that support services were not available to them (Hudson, Graham, & Warner, 1979).

It does not appear that the mere availability of services that someone names "support" services has an impact. In some research, the availability of support services for the RCT has had a significant impact on their willingness to integrate handicapped students (Larrivee & Cook, 1979); Moore & Fine, 1978). In other research, it has not (Shotel, Iano, & McGettigan, 1972). However, the type of support services provided must be considered. For example, opportunities for team teaching in conjunction with support services predict favorable teacher attitudes toward mainstreaming; the presence of teacher aides do not (Mandell & Strain, 1978). The mere presence of special-education classes receives mixed support. Williams (1977) reported that the presence of a special-education program in the school was one of three critical variables correlated with positive attitudes toward mainstreaming. The attitudes of the resource teachers are important because RCTs may model them (Guerin & Szatlocky, 1974). Shotel, Iano, McGettigan, (1972) reported that the presence of special education in the building was not adequate support for the RCT.

The attitudes of school administrators may be critical to the success of mainstreaming programs (Guerin & Szatlocky, 1974). Adminstrative support as perceived by the RCTs has been identified as a significant factor in positive teacher attitudes toward mainstreaming in some studies (Larrivee & Cook, 1979), but not in all (Mandell & Strain, 1978).

CONCLUSIONS AND IMPLICATIONS

Both professional education organizations and RCTs hold lower expectations for handicapped students. The lowest of these expectations are reserved for those students with cognitive and behavioral disabilities, as well as those with more severe handicaps. Morever, professional education organizations and RCTs generally seem unwilling to accept the integration of handicapped students into regular classrooms.

The expectations and attitudes of RCTs are certainly understandable given the relationship of special and regular education over the last 50 years. RCTs have been able to transfer students who were unable to meet the goals and objectives of the regular curriculum to SCTs who readily accepted responsibility for these students. SCTs, state education codes, and parent advocacy groups have all told RCTs that cognitively and behaviorally handicapped students have trouble meeting or cannot meet the goals of regular education. RCTs can observe that teachers trained to work with handicapped students receive different training and different certification. RCTs can observe that SETs have substantially smaller classes. RCTs can observe that SETs have different materials and different back-up services. Finally, RCTs can observe that handicapped students meet different educational goals than the students in regular classes.

RCTs seem willing to accommodate handicapped students, at least in part, as a function of their perceived competence to do so. Integration of students with communication disorders, visual impairments, hearing impairments, and sometimes mild learning disabilities, is usually viewed more positively than the integration of students with other handicaps (cf Antonak, 1980). These students are often in "pull-out" programs for remediation; instruction of these special students in the regular classroom does not typically require that the RCT make instructional modifications. Specialists provide direct instruction in areas where instructional modifications are necessary, and the handicapped students are left to master the remainder of the curriculum taught by the usual methods. What modifications a RCT must make are environmental: altered lighting, acetate covers for written materials, preferential seating, written directions, facing the class when speaking, oral tests, etc. In sharp contrast, RCTs are reluctant to mainstream students for whom they must alter basic instruction. Mentally retarded, emotionally disturbed, severely handicapped, and sometimes learning-disabled students *do* require modifications in the goals that RCTs hold for their students and in the methods by which they are taught. For teaching handicapped students, RCTs lack educational background (Ringlaben & Price, 1981) and teaching competencies (Keogh & Levitt, 1976). To accommodate handicapped students in classes, RCTs want additional training, released time (presumably to plan the special modifications, consult with parents and resource people, etc.), and smaller class sizes—adjustments that SCTs have had for years.

Knowing what RCTs expect and believe they need to teach handicapped students is only a small consideration in mainstreaming. Other important considerations include increasing instructional competencies of RCTs (as opposed to providing so many hours of in-service training), altering the preservice training of RCTs to reflect the need to develop teaching competencies (as opposed to imparting only factual information about characteristics and causes), and, most importantly, altering the goals of regular education to allow incompetent students who are not handicapped to complete compulsory schooling.

REFERENCES

Algozzine, R. (1976). The disturbing child: What you see is what you get? *Alberta Journal of Educational Research, 22*, 330–333.

Antonak, R. F. (1980). A hierarchy of attitudes toward exceptionality. *Journal of Special Education, 14*, 231–241.

Burgdorf, R. L. & Bersoff, D. N. (1980). Equal educational opportunity. In R. L. Burgdorf (Ed.), *The legal rights of handicapped persons: Cases, materials and text*. Baltimore: Paul H. Brookes.

Childs, R. E. (1979). Perceptions of mainstreaming by regular classroom teachers who teach mainstreamed educable mentally retarded students in the public schools. *Education and Training of The Mentally Retarded, 14*, 225–227.

Coleman, M. C. & Gilliam, J. E. (1983). Disturbing behaviors in the classroom: A survey of teacher attitudes. *Journal of Special Education, 17*, 121–129.

Dunn, L. (1968). Special education for the mildly handicapped—is much of it justifiable? *Exceptional Children*, 35, 5–22.

Fogel, L. & Nelson, R. O. (1983). The effects of special education labels on teachers' behavioral observations, checklist scores, and grading of academic work. *Journal of School Psychology, 21*, 241–251.

Foster, G., Algozzine, B., & Ysseldyke J. (1980). Classroom teacher and teacher-in-training susceptibility to stereotypical bias. *Personnel and Guidance Journal, 59*, 27–30.

Foster, G. & Keech, V. (1977). Teacher reactions to the label of educable mentally retarded. *Education and Training of The Mentally Retarded, 12*, 307–311.

Foster, G. & Salvia, J. (1977). Teacher response to label of learning disabled as a function of demand characteristics. *Exceptional Children, 43*, 533–534.

Foster, G., Schmidt, C. & Sabatino, D. (1976). Teacher expectancies and the label "learning disabilities." *Journal of Learning Disabilities, 9*, 58–61.

Foster, G., Ysseldyke, J., & Reese, J. (1975). I wouldn't have seen it if I hadn't believed it. *Exceptional Children, 41*, 469–473.

Gillung, T. & Rucker, C. (1977). Labels and teacher expectations. *Exceptional Children, 44*, 464–465.

Guerin, G. R. & Szatlocky, K. (1974). Integration programs for the mildly handicapped. *Exceptional Children, 41*, 173–179.

Guskin, S. & Spicker, H. (1968). Educational research in mental retardation. In N. Ellis (Ed.), *International review of research in mental retardation: Vol. 3*. New York: Academic Press.

Harasymiw, S. & Horne, M. (1976). Teacher attitudes toward handicapped children and regular class integration. *Journal of Special Education, 10*, 393–400.

Harth, R. (1981). Personality relevant and personality irrelevant attitude differences toward educable and trainable retarded children. *Education and Training of The Mentally Retarded, 16*, 213–216.

Hirshoren, A. & Burton, T. (1979). Willingness of regular teachers to participate in mainstreaming handicapped children. *Journal of Research and Development in Education, 12*, 93–100.

Hirshoren, A., Schultz, E., Manton, A., & Henderson, R. (1970). *A survey of public school special education programs for emotionally disturbed children*. (ERIC document reproduction service No. EDO050540).

Horne, M. (1983). Attitudes of elementary classroom teachers toward mainstreaming. *Exceptional Child, 30*, 93–98.

Hudson, F., Graham, S. & Warner, M. (1979). Mainstreaming: An examination of the attitudes and needs of regular classroom teachers. *Learning Disabilities Quarterly, 2*, 58–62.

Jones, R. (1974). The hierarchical structures of attitudes toward the exceptional. *Exceptional Children, 40*, 430–435.

Jordan, J. & Proctor, D. (1969). Relationships between knowledge of exceptional children, kind and amount of experience with them and teacher attitudes toward their classroom integration. *Journal of Special Education*, 3, 433–439.

Kennon, A. & Sandoval, J. (1978). Teacher attitudes toward the educable mentally retarded. *Education and Training of the Mentally Retarded, 13*, 139–145.

Keogh, B. & Levitt, M. (1976). Special education in the mainstream: A confrontation of limitations. *Focus on Exceptional Children*, 8, 1–11.

Kirk, S. (1964). Research in education. In H. Stevens & R. Heber (Eds.), *Mental retardation, a review of research*. Chicago: University of Chicago Press.

Kirk, S. & Johnson, G. (1951). Educating the retarded child. Boston: Houghton Mifflin.

Larrivee, B. (1981). Effect of inservice training intensity on teachers' attitudes toward mainstreaming. *Exceptional Children, 48*, 34–39.

Larrivee, B. & Cook, L. (1979). Mainstreaming: A study of the variables affecting teacher attitude. *Journal of Special Education, 13*, 315–324.

Leyser, Y. & Abrams, P. (1982). Teacher attitudes toward normal and exceptional groups. *Journal of Psychology, 110*, 227–238.

Lilly, S. (1971). Special education: A teapot in a tempest. *Exceptional children, 37*, 43–49.

Mandell, C. & Strain, P. (1978). An analysis of factors related to the attitudes of regular classroom teachers toward mainstreaming mildly handicapped children. *Contemporary Educational Psychology, 3*, 154–162.

Massie, D. (1978). Update on education of the handicapped. *Today's Education, 676*, 60–73.

Mercer, J. (1970). *Sociological perspectives on mild mental retardation*. In H. C. Haywood (Ed.), Socio-cultural aspects of mental retardation. New York: Appleton-Century-Crofts.

Minner, S. (1982). Expectations of vocational teachers for handicapped students. *Exceptional Children, 48*, 451–453.

Moore, J. & Fine, M. (1978). Regular and special class teachers' peceptions of normal and exceptional children and their attitudes toward mainstreaming. *Psychology in The Schools, 15*, 253–259.

Panda, K. & Bartel, N. (1972). *Teacher perception of exceptional children. Journal of Special Education, 6*, 261–266.

Parish, T. & Copeland, T. (1978). Teachers' and students' attitudes in mainstreamed classrooms. *Psychological Reports, 43*, 54.

Parish, T., Dyck, N., & Kappes, B. (1979). Stereotypes concerning normal and handicapped children. *Journal of Psychology, 102*, 63–70.

Reschley, D. & Lamprecht, M. (1979). Expectancy effects of labels: Fact or artifact? *Exceptional Children, 46*, 55–58.

Ringlaben, R. & Price, J. (1981). Regular classroom teachers' perceptions of mainstreaming effects. *Exceptional Children, 47*, 302–304.

Salvia, J., Clar, G., & Ysseldyke, J. (1973). Teacher retention of stereotypes of exceptionality. *Exceptional Children, 39*, 651–652.

Schlosser, L. & Algozzine, B. (1979). The disturbing child: He or she? *Alberta Journal of Educational Research, 25*, 30–36.

Schmelkin, L. (1982). Perceptions of disabilities: A multidimensional scaling approach. *Journal of Special Education, 16*, 161–177.

Shotel, J., Iano, R., & McGettigan, J. (1972). Teacher attitudes associated with the integration of handicapped children. *Exceptional Children, 38*, 677–683.

Simpson, R. (1981). Further investigation and interpretation of the expectancy effect generated by disability labels. *Diagnostique, 7*, 101–108.

Siperstein, G., & Bak, J. (1980). Students' and teachers' perceptions of the mentally retarded child. In J. Gottleib (Ed.), *Educating mentally retarded persons in the mainstream.* Baltimore: University Park Press.

Smith, J. & Schindler, W. (1980). Certification requirements of general educators concerning exceptional pupils. *Exceptional Children, 46*, 394–396.

Stephens, T. & Braun, B. (1980). Measures of regular classroom teachers' attitudes toward handicapped children. *Exceptional children, 46*, 292–294.

Taylor, R., Smiley, L. & Ziegler, E. (1983). The effects of labels and assigned attributes on teacher perceptions of academic and social behaviors. *Education and training of the mentally retarded, 18*, 45–51.

Turnball, H. & Turnball, A. (1978). *Free appropriate public education, law and implementations.* Denver: Love.

Williams, R. (1977). An investigation of regular class teachers' attitudes toward the mainstreaming of four categories of mildly handicapped students. *Dissertation Abstracts International, 38*, 2708A.

Yoshida, R. & Meyers, C. (1975). Effects of labeling as EMR on teachers' expectancies for change in a student's performance. *Journal of Educational Psychology, 67*, 521–527.

Ysseldyke, J. & Foster, G. (1978). Bias in teachers' observations of emotionally disturbed and learning disabled children. *Exceptional Children, 45*, 613–615.

Zettel, J. (1982). Implementing thc right to a free appropriate public education. In J. Ballard, B. Ramirez, & F. Weintraub (Eds.), *Special education in America: Its legal and governmental foundations.* Reston, Va.: Council for Exceptional Children.

9 The Consequences of Mainstreaming for Families of Young Handicapped Children

Pamela J. Winton
University of North Carolina

All parents face the questions of how much to protect their children and when to allow or encourage independence. Salvador Minuchin, the well-known family therapist and theorist, has stated that the major task for today's American family is to provide an emotionally supportive environment for their children while at the same time encouraging the development of independence and autonomy (Minuchin, 1974).

For parents of young handicapped children, these issues are of even greater concern. Handicapped children are at risk along many dimensions. Yet at the same time, their parents read and hear about concepts such as normalization, which emphasize the importance of allowing handicapped children to take risks in order to grow and develop to their maximum potential. The father of a sensory-impaired child expressed the dilemma faced by many parents with this comment:

> I believe that parents should love their handicapped children as they are and work with everything they've got to help them reach their highest potential. But there is a fine line involved in doing this, almost a paradox. To love them as they are might tempt parents not to encourage them to achieve their highest potential, but rather to be content. On the other hand, placing emphasis on the child's reaching his or her highest potential could lead parents to dwell on what the child can't do. The result could be that it is harder to love them as they are (Winton, Turnbull, & Blacher, 1984, p. 55).

The first time many parents face this issue directly is when their handicapped child reaches preschool age. Because existing research on the consequences of mainstreaming for families of young handicapped children is scarce, it is necessary, when addressing the issue, to draw from research indirectly related to the question and to utilize models and theories of family functioning developed by other disciplines.

The first part of this paper examines the ecological context within which preschool mainstreaming occurs. Taking a broad look at mainstreaming as it exists as part of the deinstitutionalization movement provides an understanding of how it affects all families of handicapped children, regardless of their child's current placement.

The second part of the paper focuses on a series of research studies (Blacher & Turnbull, 1983; Turnbull & Winton, 1983; Turnbull, Winton, Blacher & Salkind, 1983; Winton & Turnbull, 1981; Winton, Turnbull & Blacher, in press) that suggest specific ways in which considering and experiencing preschool mainstreaming affects families. The research is presented within the framework of a sociological model (Hill, 1958) that makes it possible to consider variables, such as family resources and family's perceptions of stressful events, which may affect each family's unique reaction to mainstreaming. Included in this part of the paper are research findings that suggest ways additional variables, such as race and socioeconomic status, may interact to mediate impact. The final part of the paper addresses implications for practice and further research.

ECOLOGICAL CONTEXT WITHIN WHICH PRESCHOOL MAINSTREAMING OCCURS

The ecological context within which preschool mainstreaming occurs can be described by using a family-systems approach. From a family-systems perspective, three of the different types of change that families characteristically experience during the course of the life cycle include: (1) sociohistorical change, (2) functional change, and (3) developmental stages and transitions (Benson & Turnbull, in press). Preschool mainstreaming is discussed within the context of each of these three types of change.

Mainstreaming Within the Context of Sociohistorical Change

Mainstreaming, as part of the normalization movement, is a sociohistorical phenomenon in that in the not-so-distant past many parents of handicapped children did not have the opportunity to participate in their child's growth and development. From the 1900s to the 1950s a common form of treatment was to place handicapped children in residential institutions. Parents were generally not held responsible for their institutionalized child. In fact, frequently they were told to forget they had ever had the child. The prevalent thinking during this period is reflected in the following statement made by a physician:

> Very frequently it will be the duty of the physician to convince the parents that the child would be better off in the state school than at home and to help with the procedures necessary to have the child admitted to the public institution. Even though the building may be old and crowded and the food scorned by Duncan Hines, the child will be among equals and will be able to compete with them, whereas in the home community the child will always be either overprotected or cruelly rejected by social contacts (Reed, 1963).

The changes since that time in terms of expectations for families have been tremendous. Parents are expected to function in a decision-making role in conjunction with educational institutions, to function in a socialization role in regard to integrating their child into the community, and to carry out the functions and tasks necessary to care for the handicapped child within the family setting. In addition, with the responsibilities of care being placed on the family as opposed to institutions supported by society, parents have had to become more politically aware and involved, because allocations of money and resources to assist families are very much dependent on the political tides. The sociohistorical change just described has culminated in legislation that has increased the rights and responsibilities of parents of handicapped children, based on the assumption that this will further the best interests of the handicapped child (Benson & Turnbull, in press). From a family systems theory perspective, one of the by-products of the increase in parents rights and responsibilities is that families must undergo functional change in order to accommodate their new roles. This change has left many parents feeling as if they should be constantly involved with their handicapped child. One mother stated:

> I think you always are going to feel more pressure if your little one is handicapped, there's no way around it. When you get a little one that doesn't do anything until you're the catalyst . . . it almost becomes an obsession . . . because you feel like he'll be sitting there, and you know that you're either going to sew or you could get him to learn his 'k' sound (Winton & Turnbull, 1981, p. 15).

Mainstreaming Within the Context of Functional Change

One way of conceptualizing the family is to do so as a social system with a set of roles that allow various tasks to be performed effectively (Goldenberg & Goldenberg, 1980; Rollins & Galligan, 1978). These tasks, which the family performs as a system, can be referred to as the functions of the family system. Nine basic family functions, serving both individual and family needs, have been identified in the literature (Turnbull, Summers, & Brotherson, 1983). They are: economic, physical, rest and recuperation, socialization, self-definitional, affectional, guidance, educational, and vocational. When additional demands are placed on a family, as is the case when there is a young handicapped child in the home, it undergoes a renegotiation of roles in order to accommodate the additional demands. The father of a 5-year-old multiply handicapped child describes the additional demands placed on caretaking functions alone, as follows:

> Our household routine is like a three-ring circus in the mornings. Nancy and I both have to be at work at 8:00. Because Megan is totally dependent on us, often we feel like we've put in a full day of effort before we even arrive at our jobs. I wake Megan and put her on the potty and then I get dressed. Nancy bathes Megan and dresses her while I prepare breakfast. Then I feed Megan and brush her teeth while Nancy dresses. We are all under stress, because Megan has never slept through the night. It is hard to keep up such a busy routine when we desperately need sleep (Winton, Turnbull, & Blacher, 1984, p. 4).

Professionals working with handicapped children tend to emphasize the educational functions of parents, overlooking the fact that education is only one of nine family functions. In addition, the most typical form of parent involvement offered by intervention programs focuses on the mother and the handicapped child, with the mother's energies being disproportionately invested in the handicapped child. Such an approach may erode the family support system and be more negative than positive. How often do professionals consider the total impact on a family of asking parents to implement a home intervention program? This quote (Winton, Turnball, & Blacher, 1984) illustrates the affect on one family:

> We are working on a feeding program with Rod at breakfast and dinner. His teacher and occupational therapist set up the program and they use it at lunch. His progress is slow, but in the long run I am committed to helping him do as much as he possibly can for himself. The major problem for me right now is that it takes Rod almost one hour to eat each meal. This creates a real dilemma, because it cuts into my time for my three other children. We also try to set aside about 20 minutes each evening, and more on weekends, to help him learn to use his walker [p. 6].

In their theory of family functioning, Rollins and Galligan (1978) have described how shifts in roles operate in a tandem manner, affecting each member of a family system. Included in their model is recognition that factors such as family size, social status, and personal resources, affect a family's ability to make functional shifts. For example, a large family with older siblings or extended family members living in the home would probably have an easier time implementing a home intervention program than would a single parent or dual-career family with limited time and fewer adult members. Unfortunately, those making policy and those designing intervention programs have not for the most part operated with an understanding of such models and therefore have not taken into account the individual needs and capabilities of families to handle the increased responsibilities as set forth by law.

Mainstreaming Within the Context of Developmental Stages or Transitions

A third type of change that families undergo is developmental stages or transitions, such as the birth of a baby or child entering school. Just as individuals go through stages, so do families. These developmental stages and transitions have been documented as times of stress for individuals and for the family systems in which these individuals reside (Minuchin, 1974). Research indicates that the early stages of parenting (in particular the preschool years) are the most intense, with children presenting more joys and more frustrations to parents (Hoffman & Manis, 1978). Rollins and Galligan (1978) concluded from their review of the literature that it is the caregiving, housekeeping, and financial demands associated with having dependent children in the home that makes this time so intense. When one considers that parenting a handicapped child may mean an increase in the already stressful levels of caretaking and financial demands, then it becomes clear that families of preschool-aged handicapped children are under considerable strain.

An additional source of stress for the families of young children is the child's preschool entry. This transition signals a change in the child's existing relationships with the family as well as the formation of new home-school-peer relationships. For parents of handicapped children, the potential stress is even greater because they are faced with issues such as mainstreaming and questions about what are the child's most pressing needs. A mother of a young handicapped child made this statement (Harrison, 1983) about her need for information as she searched for appropriate services:

> When we first consulted developmental specialists, we hoped for answers about Edward's condition and suggestions for helping him. What we got instead was confusion. Yes, Edward was ready for toilet training. No, he wasn't. Yes, heel cord surgery would help him walk better. No, that was the worst thing we could do. We soon learned that there was no right answer to any question about Edward's care and upbringing [p. 221].

It is no wonder that one parent lamented, "Why can't time stand still? Just when things are really going well in my son's infant program, it is time to make a switch. I wish I could just have one year of relaxation when I wasn't having to worry about what was coming next." (Winton, 1981, p. 81).

In summary, using family-systems theories as a framework, mainstreaming can be viewed as a sociohistorical phenomenon that has caused functional changes in the family systems of handicapped children. Mainstreaming at the preschool level has the potential for causing additional stress for families because it represents a transition at a point in time when families are already stressed by the demands of their young, dependent children.

RESEARCH ON THE CONSEQUENCES OF MAINSTREAMING FOR FAMILIES PRESENTED WITHIN THE FRAMEWORK OF A FAMILY CRISIS MODEL

ABCX Family Crisis Model (Hill, 1958)

The general picture painted thus far is one that portrays mainstreaming as a potential source of stress for all families of young handicapped children. Although the potential is there, no two families react in the same way to stressful events. The Chinese symbol for crisis is two characters, one representing danger and one representing opportunity. In the same way, families have the capacity for both responses. Some families welcome change as a chance to grow, whereas other families are strained to the breaking point by the same event. Family system theorists and sociologists have devised a number of models (Hill, 1958; McCubbin & Patterson, 1983; Rollins & Galligan, 1978) that attempt to describe why families have different reactions to a stressful event. For the sake of simplicity, one of the more parsimonious models, Hill's ABCX Crisis Model, has been chosen as a framework for discussing a series of research studies on the question of the impact of mainstreaming on parents of young handicapped children. The first was a descriptive study involving 30 mothers of preschool-aged handicapped children (Turnbull & Winton, 1983; Winton & Turnbull, 1981). A standardized questionnaire developed as part of that study was used to collect survey data from 100 parents of kindergarten-age handicapped and nonhandicapped mainstreamed children in the second study (Turnbull, Winton, Blacher, & Salkind, 1983; Winton, Turnbull & Blacher, in press). The third study involved collecting sociometric data on parent–parent interaction in a mainstreamed preschool (Blacher & Turnbull, 1983). A thorough description of the studies and the methodology used is available in the journal articles referenced above.

By using Hill's model (1958), it is possible to examine differences in the ways that families react and cope with the particular events and issues surrounding mainstreaming. In this model A (the stressor event)— interacting with B (the family's crisis meeting resources)—interacting with C (the definition the family makes of the event)—produce X (the crisis) . . . (Hill, 1958).

Our research with parents indicated that there are certain issues associated with considering or experiencing preschool mainstreaming that could be called stressor events (A). In the next section, four stressor events identified by parents will be described. Each stressor event is then discussed in terms of family resources (B) and family's perceptions of these events (C).

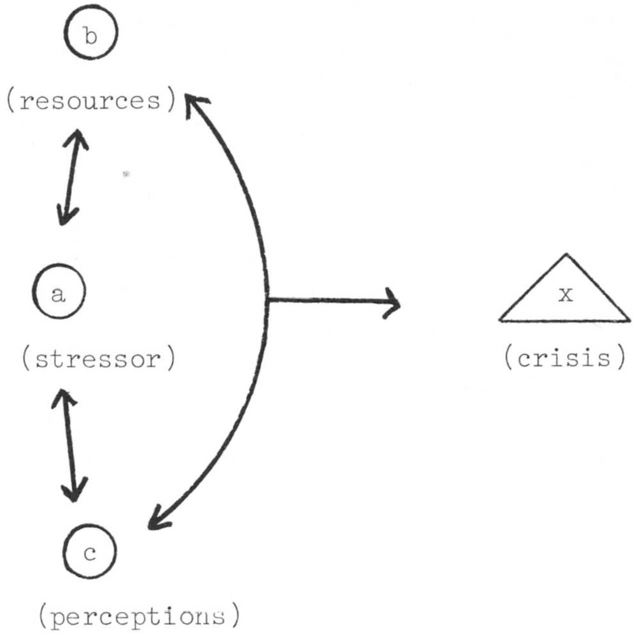

Fig. 9.1 Hills ABCX Crises Model

Note. From Generic features of families under stress by R. Hill, 1958, *Social Casework 49*.

Decision-making Process

The first point at which many parents confront the issue of mainstreaming is when they start to consider the kind of preschool that their handicapped child will attend. Our research indicated that parents who feel a mainstreaming program would be appropriate often have a hard time finding a nonspecialized preschool willing to accept their handicapped child. With the exception of Head Start, publicly supported mainstream preschools are limited. In most communities, there is no one person or place where parents can go to learn about private preschools receptive to handicapped children. One mother commented:

> I am aware of the tremendous struggles that families in this sophisticated and liberal community have in finding help for their impaired children. Often excellent programs exist, but parents and professionals are unaware of them. To a great extent this is because there is a lack of coordinated services, a lack of publicity about services that exist, and uncertain funding—a program may be here today and gone tomorrow. I am appalled by the lack of knowledge about programs that I see among professionals who counsel parents. To take our own example, even though our

> child was diagnosed soon after birth as (1) cerebral palsied; (2) retarded; (3) functionally blind; and (4) hydrocephalic, we were never directed by the followup clinic staff, the pediatrician, numerous psychologists, our opthalmologist, or the neurosurgeon to any program that could help our son.
>
> Every school and preschool our son has attended has been through a chance discovery on our part. He currently attends a wonderful school in San Francisco that I found through a woman I met in a cooking class. Our experiences are not unique. During a meeting at my son's preschool attended by close to 50 parents, almost every set of parents expressed anger that they had found out about the school through word of mouth, not from a professional (Winton, Turnbull & Blacher, 1984, p. xiii).

A research study by Becker, Bender, & Kawabe (1980) validated this mother's perceptions. Their data indicated that the problem may not be that services are not available but that there is not an adequate communication system between service delivery agencies and parents. Our research suggested that professionals may be particularly unaware of mainstreamed preschools. Parents who chose a mainstreamed preschool were more likely to have made the decision without professional help than were parents who had selected a specialized preschool (Winton, 1981). Survey research with parents of young children by Sparling and Lowman (1983) and by Powell (1980) indicated that friends and family are the most frequent first choice sources of information on management of the child's environment (Sparling & Lowman, 1983) and on finding child care (Powell, 1980). However, these traditional sources of information may not be familiar with services for handicapped.

The result is that parents often engage in the painful and lonely process of looking for preschools by themselves. One mother described her search with this comment:

> I won't ever forget when the infant program Christy had been in suggested that I find a regular preschool for her, and I started calling around. I called one preschool that was near us at the Methodist Church. The director was wonderful. She said that they wanted to see Christy and that she would talk to the teacher of the four-year-olds about taking Christy. And then she called me back up and said that the teacher refused to see Christy and that she couldn't have a child with Down's syndrome. She was labeling Christy. And I sat down and I just cried and thought, "She won't even give my child a chance." It wouldn't hurt if she had seen Christy and said, "I don't think it's going to work out;" because I wasn't sure it was going to work out. It was a test situation. I didn't know if Christy could cope with it. But they could have given her a chance to try (Winton, Turnbull, & Blacher, 1984, p. 79).

Another aspect of the stress associated with decision making is the ambiguity surrounding the concept of mainstreaming. Our research indicated that there is a wide variation in parent's knowledge of mainstreaming (Winton, 1981). Most parents have heard of the concepts of normalization and mainstreaming, but some know only enough to be totally confused. One parent's comment that "either they're shoving them into this crazy system or saying, 'keep all handicapped kids together' " (Winton, 1981, p. 117) reflects what she and other parents in our research study described as the battle within the community between those who support mainstreaming and those who oppose it.

A survey we conducted with 50 parents of kindergarten-age mainstreamed handicapped children indicated that a majority of parents (90%) wanted more information about mainstreaming (Turnbull, et al., 1983). Even with an understanding of the term, many parents want to know more. They have questions, such as, what are implications, both long- and short-term, for selecting a mainstreamed preschool?

These questions are difficult to answer. Data from a longitudinal study conducted at UCLA indicated that parents and professionals may hold divergent views of the child at the point of transition to preschool (Bernheimer, Young & Winton, 1983). For instance, the parent may see the greatest need for the child to be the development of social competence, whereas the professional may feel the child needs a program that emphasizes pre-academic skills. This conflict may emerge despite a close relationship when the child was in the infant program.

The possible sources of ambiguity and the general absence of a knowledge base on mainstreaming to which parents can turn, in addition to the absence in most communities of a local clearinghouse for information on available preschool options, suggests that most parents are operating within a number of constraints, rather than with the help of many resources as they enter into the decision-making process.

Family's Crisis Meeting Resources

A family resource that might mediate the stress of such a search is the family's willingness to seek and accept outside help. A source of support during crises identified by family theorists are other individuals who have been through similar experiences (McCubbin & Figley, 1983). Other parents of handicapped children who have been through the decision-making process have been described as being very helpful by some parents. Some families are able to find a helper, an ally who can provide the family with emotional and network support. A factor that affects a family's ability to do this is a phenomenon described by Minuchin (1974) as "rigidity of boundaries." This describes the way families differ in their abilities to allow individuals outside the family to help in times of crisis.

Family's Perceptions of Event

Our research has provided some information on parents' perceptions of the decision-making process (Winton, 1981). These perceptions mediate the stress experienced by families. Parents' perceptions of other mainstreaming opportunities outside the preschool setting influence the decision-making process. If parents perceive that their child has opportunities for normalizing experiences in the neighborhood, at church, and with siblings' activities, then parents may not perceive mainstreaming in the preschool setting as being a pressing need for the child.

Parents' perceptions of their own ability to benefit from mainstreaming also influence the preschool decision. This would include issues such as observing their child among a group of nonhandicapped children. Our research indicated that parents differed in their reactions to these observations. One parent described (Turnbull & Winton, 1983) how hurt she would feel to see her child teased or rejected by nonhandicapped children, even if her child did not notice:

> I really did not want him to go to a private kindergarten. The children there would be capable of doing things that he wouldn't do . . . he would feel left out. I don't guess that he would know the difference but I guess I think it's more for myself . . . I think to myself I wish he could do like the other kids . . . and that sort of makes me feel sad. [p. 60].

A parent's reaction to mainstreaming along this dimension must be considered within the context of a parent's perceptions of the meaning of specialized placement. For instance, the mother of a visually impaired preschooler described her reaction to visiting a specialized preschool when trying to decide on a preschool: "When I saw the kids over there, how badly handicapped they were, I said 'my child doesn't belong here'. There were some severely mentally retarded children there, and I could not help but wonder, 'is this the place for my child?' " (Winton, Turnbull, & Blacher, 1984, p. 80).

On the other hand, the mother of a physically handicapped child described having a completely different reaction to her visit to a specialized preschool. She stated, "Seeing the other kids' conditions . . . more severe than his . . . helped me adjust. I was not aware of so many children being handicapped before then. I realized that we were not the only ones with a handicapped child" (Winton, 1981, p. 114).

These quotes make it clear that the same situation or stressor event is subject to a variety of interpretations, which in turn influence a family's behavioral response to the event.

Another way the family's perceptions interact with the decision-making process is through the parents' perception of their role in decision making. Our research suggests that there is wide variability in parents' perceptions of their role in decision making. Some parents relied totally on the opinions of professionals who worked with their child in early childhood programs, to the point that they did not even visit the preschool selected by these professionals. Other parents conducted extensive searches themselves. One parent visited 15 local preschools.

Factors that might affect involvement are ethnicity, socioeconomic status, and time available. Stack (1975) found that lower income black families were suspicious of service systems, meaning that they might be reluctant to seek professional guidance when deciding on a preschool. Skinner (1983) found time to be a limited resource in dual-career families.

It is important to keep in perspective the information presented previously on the numerous demands on families of preschool-aged handicapped children. For some families the complications of considering mainstreaming might be so great that automatic enrollment in a specialized preschool might be the best option at that time. It is also important to keep in mind that it is the interaction of variables, such as family resources and family's perceptions, that mediate the amount of stress a potential stressor event will create.

Adjustment to Preschool

The next potential stressor event occurs at the point when the child begins preschool and the family forms relationships with the staff of the mainstreamed preschool and adjusts to the services available.

Our research indicated that parents perceive the training and qualifications of teachers in maintreamed preschools to be the greatest drawback to mainstreaming (Turnbull & Winton, 1983). According to Winton, Turnbull, and Blacher (1984), one mother of a blind child commented:

> At first I was very enthusiastic about mainstreaming. I very much wanted my child to attend our church-sponsored preschool. Unfortunately, it just didn't work out for Sandra. The teacher was very uptight about having Sandra in class. Because she didn't want to do the wrong thing, she essentially ended up ignoring Sandra. As long as Sandra would occupy herself listening to records or playing with clay or just fiddling for a long period of time, the teacher would devote herself to the other children. I talked with the teacher about my concerns, and she admitted to me that she would rather not have Sandra. The whole situation was disappointing. It was clear that Sandra's special needs were not being met. [p. 77].

Some parents feel that they have to conduct "inservice" for their child's teachers each year. Other parents feel increased pressure to work with their child at home to help them keep up with the pace of their nonhandicapped classmates. One father describes this situation:

> I am beginning to question whether we made the right decision when we pushed to have Michael placed in a regular kindergarten. His developmental delays have resulted in his not being able to keep up with the progress of the other kids. Every night we work with him on writing his name, counting, and letters. It gets to be a real drag. My wife and I have dropped out of all civic activities. We miss those experiences. It's ironic that Michael's placement in the least restrictive environment of the regular class in many ways requires us to live in a highly restrictive environment. (Winton, Turnbull, & Blacher, 1984, p. 65).

In addition, parents whose children are mainstreamed may have to coordinate special services themselves because these services are less likely to be available in mainstreamed preschools. One mother made this comment: "After driving Ed 10 miles each way to the preschool where he was being mainstreamed, we still had to take him to three additional therapists several times each week. He was spending so much time in the car that we were unable to work with him on his toilet training." (Winton, Turnbull, & Blacher, 1984, p. 79).

The need to provide inservice for teachers, the need to monitor the child's progress and to provide special help at home, and the need to coordinate other special services adds up to an increase in family functions and roles. An increase in the demands on an individual family member will affect the entire family. Even in the case in which most of the additional demands associated with parenting fall on the mother, every family member will be affected. It should also be kept in mind that families of young handicapped children are already experiencing many demands on their time and energy.

Family's Crisis Meeting Resources

McCubbin and Figley (1983) stated that previous experience with stressful events is a factor that may reduce the amount of stress experienced in a stressful situation. Certainly, a family's skills and past experiences in dealing with teachers, monitoring the child's progress, and advocating for changes in classrooms when these seem necessary for their child's success are factors that would seem to facilitate the adjustment to a mainstreamed preschool. One could speculate, however, that performing these tasks time and time again at each new mainstreamed setting might lead to "burnout." Additional variables that might mediate stress are the financial resources to pay for services not provided by the school and to pay for help in carrying out the additional demands placed on family members and extended family and support networks to help with additional demands. Stack (1975) and McAdoo (1983) stated that an extended kin network, characterized by frequent trades in services, is a coping strategy available for lower income black families. For some families, the absence of financial resources may be partially balanced out by this type of informal support system.

Family's Perceptions of Event

For some families, the perceived benefits of mainstreaming outweigh the drawbacks just described. One must consider the willingness of family members to carry out additional functions. One mother made this comment about her experiences in a mainstreamed preschool:

> A lot of times I get tired of having a role. God, I don't want to solve that . . . I'm paying you to take him for 3 hours and, Lady, make it work! Maybe that's a nasty attitude toward teachers, but I kind of feel that way sometimes. It's not worth it to me if I have to figure it out . . . I might as well have him with me at those times. (Winton & Turnbull, 1981, p. 15)

Our research indicated that for many parents an important factor in their selection of a preschool is for them to be able to relax from the responsibility of teaching their child (Winton & Turnbull, 1981). Parents want to know that competent professionals are dealing with their child. One mother, a nurse by training who had a son with spina bifida, expressed her feelings this way (Winton, Turnbull, & Blacher, 1984):

> You've got to have a staff that is smarter than you when it comes to your child's handicap. I'm not a genius; I mean, my background is giving enemas. But you've got to know that the people that are teaching your child know their stuff. Now I drop off Sam in the morning and I feel like, whew, people more competent than I am are taking care of him, and that's a great feeling. [p. 29]

Adjustment to Parent Peer Group

A third stressor event relates to the family's getting used to the parent-peer group at the mainstreamed preschool. Our research indicated that many parents of handicapped children experience a feeling of discomfort and strain when their child first begins a mainstreamed preschool. One parent stated: "When I first started taking Stephanie to Cloverleaf Preschool, it was a little unusual because I felt like most of the parents did not speak to me. It was like they were afraid to get involved in a conversation with me, or they really didn't know how to deal with the situation" (Winton, Turnbull, & Blacher, 1984, p. 82).

Research by Blacher and Turnbull (1983) on parent-to-parent interaction in mainstreamed preschools indicated that families of handicapped children may be isolated. The research suggested that parents are likely to develop closer relationships with the parents that their children make friends with and with parents who live nearby. For handicapped children, making friends may be more problematic. Factors other than proximity of the preschool to home may influence the decision-making process, meaning that the handicapped child is less likely to attend a neighborhood preschool.

Related to the adjustment to a peer group of parents whose children are nonhandicapped is the loss of a support group of parents whose children are handicapped. McCubbin and Figley (1983) described the "comfort in sharing experiences" as being an important way that families can help ease stressful experiences. Parent support groups have been specifically described as being helpful to families of young handicapped children (Klaus & Kennell, 1976).

Family's Crisis Meeting Resources

Past experience in dealing with questions and concerns of parents of nonhandicapped children is a family resource helpful in this situation. Another mediating factor is the parent's personality and ability to use personal resources, such as humor. One mother described how a lively sense of humor helped put the parents of nonhandicapped children at ease at her son's preschool. She said:

"What is really comical is when you meet in the observation room, and they say, 'Mine is the little girl with the blue ribbon, which one is yours?' Then I say, 'Well, mine is the one with the skull cap on and the two braces . . . how can you miss him?' " (Winton, Turnbull, & Blacher, 1984, p. 82).

The availability of a parent support group elsewhere, such as through membership in a parents' advocacy group, is another factor that may mediate the stress associated with the parent peer group in a mainstreamed preschool. One mother whose daughter was mainstreamed offered her views (Winton, Turnbull & Blacher, 1984) on why such contacts are helpful: "If I dealt only with parents of normal children, I would be a crazy person. I need a support group of people who really understand what it is to have a handicapped child, who wonder not only how to handle the child at age 3 or 4, but also think ahead and wonder and worry about what to do when the child becomes adult at ages 20 and 35" [p. 35].

Family's Perceptions of the Event

Family perceptions that may affect the impact of the parent peer group include the perceived needs of parents for the support from families of handicapped children. Our research indicated that families vary tremendously in this respect. Quotes from two highly educated, middle-class mothers, both moving from the same infant program with a support group to programs that did not offer this service illustrate the differences. One mother's response to the switch was this: "I cried for 2 months last spring. I know what was going to happen. I didn't know it would be as drastic. I was hoping that there would be some type of parental support but it just didn't happen" (Winton & Turnbull, 1981, p. 17).

The other mother made this comment about the absence of a mother's support group: "It is definitely refreshing. You really feel bad for the professionals that want to help you but don't know how. You know, the psychologists and the social workers have this concept that every parent with a handicapped child wants to talk about it all the time . . . that's garbage" (Winton & Turnbull, 1981, p. 17).

Our research also suggested that time is a factor. The same mother might have different perceptions at different points in time. For instance, one mother expressed her changing sentiments toward mother groups with this statement: "It was good at that time, and I think I'll always have a feeling for those mothers because we got so close, but I don't miss it now. I don't feel the need for it. I may when he gets older and there are more problems" (Winton & Turnbull, 1981, p. 17).

A mother, who had been heavily involved in advocacy work and had participated in a mother's group in the past, described the change in her attitude with this comment: "When our son was first born we really got involved, and it was tremendously beneficial. But now I just want to draw back and make sure that this little guy gets it at home. When you're putting in so much time that your family is no longer benefiting, then it's time to quit and let somebody else do it. That's where we got" (Winton & Turnbull, 1981, p. 17).

Adjustment to Child's Peer Group

A fourth stressor event is the family's adjustment to their handicapped child's nonhandicapped peer group at school. The nonhandicapped peer group impacts the family in two ways: (1) It provides parents with an opportunity for observing their child among a group of normally developing peers; and (2) it may mean that parents undergo the painful experience of seeing their child rejected or teased by peers. Our research indicated that acceptance of handicapped children by nonhandicapped peers does not occur automatically and that teasing and rejection do sometimes occur (Turnbull & Winton, 1983).

Family's Crisis Meeting Resources

Family resources that may mediate the impact of the adjustment to the child's peer group include the following:

1. Child and family's past experiences in interacting with nonhandicapped children and in dealing with questions and concerns that nonhandicapped adults and children have about handicapped conditions.
2. Opportunities in the past for family members to see their handicapped child among a group of normally developing peers.
3. Family's ability to enhance the child's relationships with nonhandicapped peers by working with the teacher on classroom strategies or planning and implementing out-of-school activities that might accomplish this.
4. Family resources, such as neighborhood, church, extended family, and siblings' activities, like Cub Scouts and soccer, where a handicapped child might have opportunities for "real world exposure" and normalizing experiences.

One mother made this comment about the need to balance her son's specialized preschool experience. She said: "I'm a great believer in the idea that a special setting is great at school, but I also feel that Sam cannot be around handicapped kids all of the time. So, when he comes home, it's just total normalcy. All of his little buddies walk and run and do everything else" (Winton, Turnbull, & Blacher, 1984, p. 70).

Family's Perceptions of Event

Parent's perceptions of their child's need for a specialized environment versus their perceptions of their child's need for real world exposure are likely to mediate the impact of the stress associated with the child's peer group. Our research indicated that parents of young handicapped children view exposure to the real world as being the greatest benefit to preschool mainstreaming (Turnbull & Winton, 1983). A mother whose daughter with cerebral palsy was enrolled in a mainstreamed preschool stated:

> You need to learn to deal with this world the way it's designed to run right now, which is toward the nonhandicapped. You cannot live in a sheltered environment,

> whether it be in your own home or in a private school for the handicapped, and then all of a sudden come of age and be thrown out into that world and never learn to deal with it. She has got to learn to deal with some of the cruelties the other children are going to come up with when they are with her. She's going to have to learn to take care of herself in situations where there is not someone there to protect her (Winton, Turnbull, & Blacher, 1984, p. 68).

Our research suggests that teasing and rejection from peers resolves itself and that it is, in fact, defined by many parents as a useful experience in helping prepare a child for the real world. Related to this issue is a family's willingness to try to provide normalization experiences for their child in the neighborhood and community if these experiences are not available at preschool.

Another perceptual variable is the parents' reaction to seeing their handicapped child among nonhandicapped peers. For some, it heightens anxiety. One mother stated:

> When I pick up Sue, the children are always out on the playground. Sometimes, Sue and some other kids will be playing in the sandbox, and then suddenly the action will move to another part of the playground, and Sue will be left in the sandbox all alone. When I come up she doesn't seem unhappy to be alone . . . sometimes I don't think she even notices. But I just want to grab her up and be her legs and run with her after the other children. I don't know if I'll ever get over that feeling (Winton, Turnbull, & Blacher, 1984, p. 81).

Davis (1963), in his study of families of polio victims, described denial of the extent of a child's problem as sometimes serving a useful function by allowing parents to slowly get used to the idea without being overwhelmed by grief and sorrow at the implications. The same could be said for families of young handicapped children. One parent commented: "Though I've known Ann was handicapped since birth, as long as she was in a program with other handicapped children, I never really had to face it. Seeing her with normal children hit me very hard. I really saw how far she was from the rest of the children" (Cansler & Winton, 1983, p. 71).

Science News reported a study of women with serious breast cancer in which it was found that most managed the stress of their condition by comparing themselves to another woman—real or imagined—who was even worse off. Everyone is better off than someone, the researcher noted (Taylor, cited in Herbert, 1983) as long as they make the right comparison. In some cases, illusions may be more important to mental health than being in touch with reality. Each family's needs for a touch of illusion and a dose of reality differ and evolve over time at an individual pace. Time is clearly a factor. Even though the mother who described the sandbox incident wondered if she would ever get used to seeing her daughter left behind by other children, our research indicated that parents did adjust to these mainstreaming issues over time. A mother whose

Down's syndrome daughter attended a mainstreamed preschool felt that her own sadness over seeing her daughter in the midst of normally developing children had gradually disappeared. She reported that her husband, on the other hand, still had pangs of grief when he saw their daughter on the playground with the other children on the occasional days that he picked her up from school. She felt that she had gotten over her sadness through daily exposure to the situation, whereas the husband had not had enough exposure to adjust to the discrepancies between their handicapped daughter and her nonhandicapped peers (Winton, 1981).

SUMMARY

In summary, our research indicated four potential family stressor events associated with preschool mainstreaming. Using the Family Crisis Model (Hill, 1958) as a framework for presentation of the data helped illustrate how families differ in their definition and response to the identified stressors. However, one thing is clear: All of the stressor events, the decision-making process, the adjustments to teachers, programs, and peer groups, are likely to result in an increase in the demands on families and an accompanying shift in family roles. For professionals working with families, it is important to keep in mind the context within which families are considering and experiencing preschool mainstreaming and the already existing demands on a family's time and energies. One must consider that, in general, transitions are hard for families because they involve a disruption of routines, a shift in roles, and a change in patterns. Things get out of balance. A goal for families during transitions is to make the necessary changes and adjustments in order to return to a state of equilibrium. The choice of mainstreaming certainly makes this more of a challenge. The choice means more uncertainty, more demands, and a great potential for failure.

Why do parents choose mainstreaming? For the most part, parents who choose mainsteaming at the preschool level do it for their child's sake. They perceive it as providing the child with a challenge that will ultimately help them deal with "the real world." At this point, there is no clear research evidence showing this to be a correct assumption. The theme of many of the reports on adolescent handicapped individuals is that they are not prepared for adulthood (Howard, 1978), and presumably this is due to their lack of experience with the challenges of the real world. Research by Dorner (1976) with adolescents with spina bifida indicated that social isolation was much more likely outside of the school setting if the child had attended or now attended a special school, irrespective of the degree of mobility impairment. However, this research does not make it clear that it is the mainstreaming school experience per se that mitigates social isolation. It may be that whatever determines the child's attending a mainstreamed school in the first place, be it personal or family characteristics, is what enhances the his or her social adjustment. Until information is available that can help answer questions about the long-range impact of mainstreaming on children and their families, those families who are choosing mainstreaming for its future value, and perhaps sacrificing some of their present needs as a result, may be operating under false assumptions about the benefits.

RESEARCH DIRECTIONS

Our research has brought to light specific events associated with preschool mainstreaming that are stressful for some families and has provided some preliminary information on variables, such as family resources and family perceptions, that mediate stress. These studies represent a first step. Further research should be done utilizing family systems theory and family crisis models as theoretical frameworks. Such models take into account the interrelatedness of child, family, and community variables and how they interact over time. Strategies for conducting research of this type include the use of methodologies developed by other disciplines, such as naturalistic data collection techniques, and the use of multiple measures. The difficulties in conducting this kind of research are numerous and include operationalizing the critical variables and deciding on outcome measures. For instance, some studies of mainstreaming have used future placement in a mainstreamed setting as a positive outcome measure (Carden-Smith & Fowler, 1983). This approach is based on the assumption that returning to a specialized placement is a failure on the part of the child, family or system. In reality, the return may be a realistic adjustment on the part of the entire system to the changing needs of the child and family.

Specific questions which could be addressed using a model, such as Hill's ABCX Family Crisis Model, include:

1. What specific family resources interacting with which family perceptions lead to lower stress levels associated with stressor events?
2. What family resources interacting with what family perceptions are associated with families who are highly satisfied with preschool mainstreaming experiences?
3. What existing family resources and perceptions interacting with stressor events lead to the creation of new resources and changed perceptions? For instance, some of the families in our research studies were able to create, through their own ingenuity, a mainstreamed preschool situation that worked for their child and for their family. Does this experience make the next transition for this family easier, or do they eventually "burn out" from the ongoing need to create acceptable, least restrictive environments for their handicapped child?
4. Do handicapped children who experience a difficult adjustment to a mainstreamed preschool develop coping skills with later mainstreamed situations?

5. Do training programs developed to help families and handicapped children with transitions from one early childhood program to another make the adjustment to mainstreaming easier?

A final point about future research directions is the importance of providing families with research information on mainstreaming issues. For parents to be able to assess the potential benefits and drawbacks that mainstreaming may offer their family, to be able to investigate the mainstreaming options in their community, and to prepare themselves and their child for transitions into mainstreamed settings, they need current information on these topics. Whenever possible, researchers should make efforts to ensure that their research is translated into products that parents can utilize.

REFERENCES

Becker, L. D., Bender, N. N., & Kawabe, K. K. (1980). Exceptional parents: A survey of programs, services, and needs. *Academic Therapy, 15*, 523–538.

Benson, H. & Turnbull, A. (in press). Approaching families from an individualized perspective. In R. H. Horner, L. M. Voieltz, & H. D. B. Fredericks (Eds.), *Education of learners with severe handicaps: Exemplary service strategies*. Baltimore: Paul H. Brookes.

Bernheimer, L., Young, M. & Winton, P. (1983). Stress over time: Parents with young handicapped children. *Journal of Developmental and Behavioral Pediatrics*, 4, 177–181.

Blacher, J. & Turnbull, A. (1983). Are parents mainstreamed? A survey of parent interactions in the mainstreamed preschool. *Education and Training of the Mentally Retarded, 18*, 10–16.

Cansler, D. & Winton, P. (1983). Parents and preschool mainstreaming. In J. Anderson & T. Black (Eds.), *Mainstreaming in early education* (pp. 67–83) Chapel Hill, NC: Technical Assistance Development System.

Carden-Smith, L. & Fowler, S. (1983). An assessment of student and teacher behavior in treatment and mainstreamed classes for preschool and kindergarten. *Analysis and Intervention in Developmental Disabilities, 3*, 35–37.

Davis, F. (1963). *Passage through crisis: Polio victims and their families*. Indianapolis: Bobbs-Merrill.

Dorner, S. (1976). Adolescents with spina bifida. *Archives of Disease in Childhood, 51*, 439–444.

Goldenberg, I. & Goldenberg, H. (1980). *Family therapy: An overview*. Monterey, CA: Brooks/Cole.

Harrison, H.(1983). *The premature babybook: A parents' guide to coping and caring in the first years*. New York: St. Martin's Press.

Herbert, W. (1983). Copying with illusions. *Science News, 124*, 393.

Hill, R. (1958). Generic features of families under stress. *Social Casework,* 1958, *49*, 139–150.

Hoffman, L. & Manis, J. D. (1978). Influences of children on marital interaction and parental satisfactions and dissatisfactions. In R. M. Lerner & G. B. Spanier (Eds.), *Child influences on marital and family interaction: A life-span perspective* (pp. 165–212). New York: Academic Press.

Howard, J. (1978). The influence of children's developmental dysfunctions on marital quality and family interaction. In R. M. Lerner & G. B. Spanier (Eds.), *Child influences on marital and family interaction: A life-span perspective* (pp. 275–295). New York: Academic Press.

Klaus, M. & Kennell, J. (1976). *Maternal-infant bonding*. St. Louis: C. V. Mosby.

McAdoo, C.(1983). Societal stress: The Black family. In H. McCubbin & C. Figley (Eds.), *Stress and the family: Vol. 1. Coping with normative transitions* (pp. 178–187). New York: Bruner/Mazel.

McCubbin, H. & Figley, C. (1983). Bridging normative and catastrophic family stress. In H. McCubbin & C. Figley (Eds.), *Stress and the family: Vol. 1. Coping with normative transitions* (pp. 218–228). New York: Bruner/Mazel.

McCubbin, H. & Patterson, J. (1983). Family Transitions: Adaptation to stress. In H. McCubbin & C. Figley (Eds.), *Stress and the family: Vol. 1. Coping with normative transitions* (pp. 5–25). New York: Bruner/Mazel.

Minuchin, S. (1974). *Families and family therapy.* Cambridge, MA: Harvard University.

Powell, D. (1980). *Finding child care: A study of parents' search processes.* Detroit: The Merrill-Palmer Institute.

Reed, S. (1963). *Counseling in Medical Genetics, 2nd Ed.* Philadelphia: W. B. Saunders.

Rollins, B. & Galligan, R. (1978). The developing child and marital satisfaction of parents. In R. Lerner & G. B. Spanier (Eds.), *Child influence on marital and family interaction: A life-span perspective* (pp. 71–102). New York: Academic Press.

Skinner, D. (1983). Dual-career families: Strains of sharing. In H. McCubbin & C. Figley (Eds.), *Stress and the family: Vol. 1. Coping with normative transitions* (pp. 26–39). New York: Bruner/Mazel.

Sparling, J. & Lowman, B. (1983). Parent information needs as revealed through interests, problems, attitudes and preferences. In R. Haskins (Ed.), *Parent education and public policy* (pp. 304–323). Norwood, NJ: Ablex.

Stack, C. (1975). *All our kin.* New York: Harper.

Turnbull, A., Summers, J. & Brotherson, M. (1983). The impact of young handicapped children on families: Future research directions. Paper presented at the NIHR State-of-the-Art Conference on Parent's Roles in the Rehabilitation of their Handicapped Children Up to Five Years of Age, Washington, DC.

Turnbull, A. & Winton, P. (1983). A comparison of specialized and mainstreamed preschools from the perspectives of parents of handicapped children. *Journal of Pediatric Psychology, 8*, 57–71.

Turnbull, A., Winton, P., Blacher, J. & Salkind, N. (1983). Mainstreaming in the kindergarten classroom: Perspectives of parents of handicapped and nonhandicapped children. *Journal of the Division for Early Childhood Education, 6,* 14–20.

Winton, P. (1981). Descriptive study of parents' perspectives on preschool services: Mainstreamed and specialized (Doctoral dissertation, University of North Carolina, Chapel Hill, 1981). *Dissertation Abstracts International, 42,* 3562A. (University Microfilms No. 42–08)

Winton, P. & Turnbull, A. (1981). Parent involvement as viewed by parents of handicapped children. *Topics in Early Childhood Special Education, 1*, 11–20.

Winton, P., Turnbull, A. & Blacher, J. (1984). *Selecting A Preschool: A guide for parents of handicapped children.* Baltimore: University Park Press.

Winton, P., Turnbull, A. & Blacher, J. (in press). Expectations of and satisfaction with public school kindergarten. Perspectives of parents of handicapped and nonhandicapped children. *Journal of the Division for Early Childhood Education.*

10 The Consequences for Health Professionals in Mainstreaming Handicapped Children

Mark L. Wolraich
University of Iowa

Health professionals traditionally have played a role in the educational setting through the delivery of health and educationally related services. The initial involvement occurred in the late 1800s in an attempt to prevent and control communicable diseases among the school population. However, physicians rapidly discovered that assessments for communicable diseases frequently identified other health and school related problems. Better continuity and follow-through were attained when the position of the school nurse was introduced into the educational setting. School nurses provided not only direct health care services for illnesses, but also health surveillance (e.g., immunization status or visual screening), health education, health advocacy, and health consultations (such as on health issues relating to sports activities). Traditionally, physicians have also been involved with schools by providing yearly physicals to students who do not have their own physicians.

With the advent of mainstreaming in public schools, the role of physicians and nurses in the educational setting has changed dramatically. Mainstreaming has created new medical issues to be addressed by the educational system. These issues have required a variety of additional types of contributions from health professionals. And further, new types of health professionals not previously involved in public education have been employed to meet the new demands of the educational system. Occupational and physical therapists, in particular, have become part of the educational support team.

A major change in the educational setting has occurred now that schools must provide an education to all children, including children with serious medical and handicapping conditions. Medical collaboration is essential to the school system in order to develop appropriate programs for these children. The law also mandates the provision of multiple assessments and the development of an individualized education plan for these children. This reorganization of the educational structure requires interdisciplinary interactions with medical services, which come under the heading of ancillary services. Thus, the educational system must identify health problems that may affect a child's educational program, and it must provide appropriate medical services. To provide these services, schools have had to develop more intimate relations with the health community. Similarly, health professionals also have to deal more intimately with the educational setting, which has its own goals and terminology and with children they may not have served previously. Many of the more seriously handicapped children were previously managed in institutional settings. Few community physicians have had the opportunity or experience to provide care to that population.

To complicate matters, knowledge in some areas has changed very rapidly in the past several years. One example is the changes that have come about in what used to be called minimal brain dysfunction (now called attention deficit disorder with hyperactivity). The change in name alone reflects some of the change in thinking about the etiology of such terms. Habilitation services, such as bracings for orthopedically impaired children or intermittent catheterizations for urologically impaired children, are also examples of recent progress in available services.

To function appropriately in educational settings, health professionals must be educated in how schools operate in the care of children with disabilities, and in the recent advances in knowledge and technology. Clearly, mainstreaming has had a significant impact on the health profession. This chapter defines that impact and clarifies some of the outstanding issues.

Definitions of Categories to Determine Children's Needs

The impact of mainstreaming on health professionals is most easily described by first defining the two categories of children's needs to be met by the educational and health-care systems. The first category includes children who have high-incidence, low-severity disabilities and the second includes children who have low-incidence, high-severity disabilities. The degree of severity must be taken into account in the provision of services, because the severity of the child's handicapping condition determines to a great extent the impact on his/her life. For example, conditions such as learning disabilities can have a very major impact on a child's life, but such conditions are of a very different nature than profound mental retardation, and as such, will have a different impact requiring a different level of services. The children who fit into the high-incidence, low-severity category generally have conditions falling into the developmental-educational area of service needs. This category would include children with learning disabilities, mild mental retardation, communication disorders, and the less severe behavioral disorders—such as attention deficit disorders (with or without hyperactivity), and conduct disorders. The children who fit into the low-incidence, high-severity category are generally those diagnosed with moderate to profound mental retardation; physical or orthopedic handicapping conditions, such as cerebral palsy and meningomyelocele; severe psychiatric conditions, such as pervasive developmental disorder (autism); and multiple handicapping conditions. These children are less frequent in number and thus of low incidence, but the severity of their disorders is much greater, thus increasing the need for medically oriented services.

CHILDREN WITH HIGH-INCIDENCE, LOW-SEVERITY DISABILITIES

Despite disagreement in both the medical and educational fields, the evaluation and management of learning disabled children rests primarily with the educational system. Health professionals are felt to have little to offer either diagnostically or therapeutically in this area. Some medical contributions have been suggested (Levine, Meltzer, Busch, Palfrey & Sullivan, 1983), and other health professionals also have felt they have a great deal to offer (Ayers, 1972), but these claims have yet to be substantiated.

The Physician's Role As a Third-Party Consultant

Two changes have significantly influenced the physician's role as a consultant in the educational setting. For one, a huge growth has ocurred in the services available to learning disabled children, the most prominent being the program that provides resource rooms for learning. Because of the difficulties in defining learning disabilities, drawing the line as to who is eligible and who is not has been fraught with controversy. The problem has been further exacerbated by the economic recession, which has resulted in reduced allocations for programs. The second change has been the due process system mandated by The Education for All Handicapped Childrens Act of 1975 (PL 94–142). This mandate has provided parents with a method for protesting adverse changes in their child's educational program. The process includes and tends to encourage parents to consult with third parties and to obtain second opinions. Frequently, the parents will seek the advice of their child's physician to help them during those difficult times, particularly if the parents perceive the problem to be neurological in nature.

The physician may often be called on to give advice about the patient's school placement. Since the Task Force on Pediatric Education (1978) determined that pediatric training in this area is inadequate, the fact that most pediatricians feel inadequate in this role is not surprising. For physicians to be of help, they need to be familiar with the benefits and limitations of the educational system. Furthermore, they need to know what the due-process procedures in PL 94–142 entail.

An added problem facing physicians is determining the nature of their patients' school-related problems. Because most of the problems are educational, physicians must depend on school evaluations to determine their nature and extent, or they need to identify their own referral source for obtaining a second opinion. The physicians can do little themselves to accurately determine issues, such as intellectual status or reading level. Often, physicians' frequent decisions concern whether the school is wrong in its assessment or program recommendations; in this case, the physicians need to inform parents of their rights and to advocate for the patient's right to appropriate assessment and programming.

The gap in educationally related training services has left many physicians inadequate in handling such situations. The lack of training referred to earlier was further demonstrated in a study by Dworkin, Shorkoff, Leviton, and Levine (1979), in which 79% of the pediatricians surveyed described their training as inadequate, and in a study by Wolraich (1980), in which pediatric practitioners' mean scores on a multiple-choice exam about developmental disabilities were found to be similar to pediatric residents' mean scores before the residents had any training on the subject. Most physicians are not likely to have had significant professional contact with the school system other than as students or as parents.

With the advent of mainstreaming, physicians need to improve their knowledge about how schools function and their knowledge of educational issues, such as learning disabilities. They need to develop a common terminology with educators to develop adequate communication and to make the necessary contacts in order to insure adequate communication. A good example of an area in which this has been a problem in the past has been in the area of stimulant medication management for children with attention deficit disorders. Despite the fact that stimulant medication has been objectively demonstrated to have positive short-term effects on children's attention behaviors, it has received a bad name because of misuse. In light of what has been discussed, this is not surprising. Physicians have been asked to prescribe an agent that will alter their patient's behavior in the classroom. But if physicians are unfamiliar with what that particular child's behavior entails, and if their communication lines with the teachers are inadequate, they may have to determine the drug's effects on the child's behavior by indirect, and frequently inadequate, means (Sindelar & Meisel, 1982). It would be the same as if they tried to control a patient's diabetes without being able to measure the patient's blood and urine sugar levels.

Two programs have tried to improve training of pediatric residents on a national level. A Task Force on Developmental Pediatrics funded by a grant from the Bureau of Education for the Handicapped is one such program. The Task Force assembled a faculty, prominent in the area of developmental disabilities, to formulate a curriculum, which was then field tested at five sites. The results showed significant improvement in the residents' knowledge. The curriculum has subsequently been implemented at 12 additional sites (Bennett, 1983). The second program was funded through the W.T. Grant Foundation. Under this program, 11 pediatric residency programs were funded to develop their own curriculum in behavioral pediatrics based on their local resources. Based on a report by Friedman, Phillips, and Parrish (1983), five of the residencies were able to establish mandatory rotations and success was dependent on faculty support.

Two important elements of training are instruction in the provisions of PL 94–142, so that physicians can provide appropriate advice to families, as well as instruction in the primary functions of the public school system. This training needs to include issues directly related to the function of teachers and the classroom as well as the financial constraints existing in their community. One invaluable experience is for residents to sit in on a class and visit with the school personnel. This experience is more meaningful to the resident if done within the context of evaluating one of his or her patients. The mainstreaming of children into the public health care and education systems requires enhanced communication between medical and educational personnel if costly due-process hearings are to be minimized.

Screenings to Identify Special Problems

The Education for All Handicapped Children Act also has required the educational system to identify children in need of services so that those who have been overlooked can begin receiving services. It also has suggested the importance of identifying children's problems as early as possible in the hopes that early intervention will minimize the handicap and maximize the child's full potential. This emphasis has led to the concept of screening the children at a preschool age to identify some of the more subtle problems characteristic of the low-severity disabilities. This concept also has created interest in the health community, which historically has been involved in screening children for diseases such as phenylketonuria, hypothyroidism, and tuberculosis. Although a screening program to identify learning and behavioral problems has been developed for physicians (Levine, Oberklaid, Ferb, Hanson, Palfrey & Aufseeser, 1980), the benefits of such a program, particularly in light of its cost, have yet to be proven. Some pediatricians have also adopted pre-kindergarten readiness procedures to use for assessment purposes. These procedures, however, have not been generally employed because of the lengthy time required for such evaluation. Nor is it likely that such assessments will become cost effective compared to what the educational system can provide at no direct cost to the family.

The role of the physician is more likely to be important in identifying underlying etiologies, such as a medical condition that might account for a child's mental retardation, or a hearing loss as a contributing factor to a child's language delay. The physicians' medical approach to a child's problem adds an important dimension to the teacher's educational approach. Determining a specific medical diagnosis may provide some curative or palliative measure, such as treating chronic middle-ear disease to correct the most common cause of childhood hearing loss. Even in cases where remediation is not possible, a diagnosis may provide important prognostic or genetic counseling information, such as in the case of fragile X syndrome. This information often times is useful to the educational system in helping teachers to develop appropriate educational plans.

Medical Therapies in the Educational Setting

Some health-related therapies have been applied to the needs of high-incidence, low-severity students in the school setting. The oldest and most well known of these has been the use of stimulant medication for children with attention deficit disorders, which was mentioned earlier. Stimulant medication has been one of the most extensively studied drug treatments available. Several studies have defined both its benefits and limitations. These medications have been shown to improve children's ability to attend to a task and not be distracted. But they do not necessarily improve school performance and the proven benefits have been limited to short-term effects. However, drug therapy can play a significant role in keeping a child's behavior disorder from disrupting a classroom, if used properly. Teacher input is essential to the physician in determining the effect of the medication. This information is best obtained through direct contact and through teacher-behavior-rating scales. Used appropriately, stimulant medications can be useful adjunctive treatments to school programs in order to help students with attention deficit disorders in regular class placements.

A second therapy related to education, but in the health care domain, is the use of sensory integration therapy to improve learning ability, which has been recommended by occupational therapy. Ayers (1972) has suggested that appropriate exercising to stimulate the vestibular system may help some children with learning disabilities to better integrate sensory stimuli and thereby improve the child's ability to learn. However, the validity of this claim has drawn some disagreement among health scientists. The criticisms waged against the use of sensory integration therapy have suggested that the present research has not been rigorous or extensive enough to warrant its use in the school setting. Another concern is that this therapy recommends spending time on activities not directly related to learning, a practice which needs to be demonstrated to have a definite causal relationship. A review of the literature on this subject has recently been written (Ottenbacher & Short, in press).

CHILDREN WITH LOW-INCIDENCE, HIGH-SEVERITY DISABILITIES

One of the major purposes of the Education for All Handicapped Children Act was to insure that every handicapped child would receive educational services, regardless of the severity of his/her disability. Many children with severe and multiple disabilities were previously excluded from public schools, and for many parents, the only recourse for their child was institutionalization. Now, these children are able to be educated within the public school system and parents are able to keep their child at home. In cases where parents are incapable of caring for the child at home, small group-home programs are available, which make use of community services, thereby avoiding large, isolated, and expensive institutionalized care. This change has presented the educational and health service systems with the new challenge of providing appropriate care for children who have very special needs. The challenge to meet these children's needs has had a very significant impact on both systems.

Attitudes of Health and Educational Personnel

A significant part of the difficulties that have hindered individuals with disabilities in the past and which continue to be a problem has been the attitudes of professionals toward persons with disabilities. For physicians, this has been demonstrated in numerous studies. The most frequently surveyed type of patients are those with Down's syndrome. In one survey (Todres, Krane, Howell, & Shannon, 1977), 51% of the pediatricians felt newborn infants with Down's syndrome should not receive high-risk surgery. In a national survey (Shaw, Randolph, & Mannard,1977), 66% of the pediatric surgeons and over 33% of the pediatricians would not have their own child receive surgery for a life-threatening condition. Furthermore, 43% of the pediatric surgeons and almost 16% of the pediatricians disagreed with the statement "Many children with Down's syndrome are capable of being useful and of bringing love and happiness into the home." However, a more recent survey (Wolraich, 1980) found that slightly less than 6% of the pediatricians felt that high-risk surgery, in the case of Down's syndrome, should *not* be performed, and 68% would have encouraged parents to give consent for surgery. Despite this improvement in medical attitudes, comments such as "The Down's syndrome child . . . can be trained to the point of being a happy family pet" occur in recent medical commentaries (Ravitch, 1983).

Physicians also tend to be more pessimistic about mentally retarded individuals' capabilities than educational personnel. One survey (Wolraich & Siperstein, 1983) found that pediatricians were significantly more pessimistic than special educators or psychologists. A more recent survey (Wolraich & Siperstein, in progress) found that even among professionals interested in providing services to mentally retarded individuals, physicians' attitudes differed from educators' attitudes. Physicians' attitudes continued to be more pessimistic, with the significant difference occurring with regard to moderately mentally retarded individuals. Physicians were also more likely to recommend more restricted living placements. These results are even more significant when one realizes that these were probably the most optimistic physicians because of their interest and experience with mentally retarded patients. Physicians not having a special interest in mental retardation are probably even more pessimistic as was suggested by Wolraich and Siperstein, 1983.

Part of the difficulty has to do with training and with the attitudes physicians bring to training based on their upbringing. Most physicians grew up in a time when mental retardation had severe negative connotations. Also, as was described earlier, physician training in developmental disabilities has been inadequate. Even in existing training programs (Wolraich, 1979; Bennett, 1980; Bennett, 1983; & Friedman, Phillips, & Parrish, 1983), direct experience with persons with developmental disabilities has been provided for only a one-month or, at most, a three-month duration. This type of exposure is not likely to have any impact on the residents' attitudes, as illustrated in a study of those programs attempting to measure attitudes (Wolraich, 1979; & Friedman, Phillips, & Parrish, 1983). Where institutional settings have been used, such as in some psychiatry training programs (Philips, 1960; Cytryn & Milowe, 1966; Raskin, 1972), the experience actually may have a negative impact on the residents' attitudes. However, two studies of nurse training programs did demonstrate a significant positive impact on nursing students' attitudes when training included longitudinal experiences with families that contained a mentally retarded family member (Gibson & Reed, 1974; Haynes, 1975). Most likely, a significant impact on physicians' attitudes will only be made when attitudinal changes occur in society at large. As society becomes more positive about mentally retarded individuals, so will health professionals. Training programs for health professionals should try to incorporate longitudinal experiences with mentally retarded individuals and their families. This training can be provided in the context of continuity clinics, which have already been established in most residency training programs, and by insuring that mentally disabled patients are included in each resident's clinic. House staff should also be presented good role models during their training.

The pessimistic attitudes of physicians have affected the care provided to patients with severe and multiple disabilities. Such attitudes also may inhibit these physicians' future initiative to learn the medical information and to make the recommendations needed to provide appropriate care. Such physicians may perceive the impact of health care on these patients as ultimately inconsequential to bringing about a profound change in their condition. They also may be resistant to supporting the purchase of expensive, but needed, equipment if they feel the patients' ultimate benefit will not be significant. One example of such resistance may be displayed in the management of a severely mentally retarded patient with an intractable seizure disorder. Such physicians may feel that their time could be better spent than on regulating medications to reach a balance between how frequent the patient's seizures occur versus how sedated the patient is from the anticonvulsive medication. However, the degree of this patient's alertness will directly influence the child's school program and only by repeated contacts between the teacher and physician can an optimal balance be attained.

The degree to which the attitude of the professionals can affect their relationship to children with high-severity disabilities, their families, and the school program, cannot be too strongly emphasized. Those health professionals who have an interest in providing needed services must be identified and encouraged to perform those services. Unfortunately, physicians are not presently compensated for the time spent providing these services compared to comparable time spent in other medical areas. Also, attempts should be made to better inform health professionals in the area of developmental disabilities, with more emphasis placed early on in-training programs and postgraduate training on the management of children with multiple and severe disabilities.

What Are Medical Versus Educational Services?

The attempt to place high-severity disabled children in the least restrictive environment sometimes results in difficulties in distinguishing between what are medical and what are educational services that should be provided to meet the children's needs. Is the development of an appropriate wheelchair, which will prevent contractures and skeletal deformities but which also enables a child to interact more effectively with his or her environment, a medical or an educational need? Educational programs have been particularly concerned, because the cost of what has been considered traditional medical equipment and therapies can become a large financial burden. Wheelchairs, bracings, and other adaptive equipment exemplify equipment that may be required to optimize a child's educational program. But educational programs have been reluctant to make that commitment, although many educational agencies are currently providing occupational and physical therapy services.

The educational system's provision of physical and occupational therapy services requires changes to be made in the current service delivery system. Traditionally, physical therapy has been considered a medical therapy, requiring a physician's prescription before treatments can be given. Many states still have this qualification as part of their regulations. In addition, most insurance companies will not pay for such services without a physician's prescription. In many states, the school therapists must first obtain the prescription from a physician before they can institute a program. This is done by sending requests to the student's local physician, referring the student to a specialty center for developmentally disabled children, or contracting with a specific physician. In the latter two cases, the school is required to pay for those evaluations. At times, therapists have had difficulties getting the needed cooperation from local physicians because of the physician's lack of knowledge and/or his/her pessimistic attitude toward more severely involved children. Some states have been reviewing their regulations with the idea of possibly changing the requirements for prescribing therapy.

Another difficulty is that most of this medical equipment, in addition to being expensive, is also individualized to a particular child. Traditionally, most educational equipment, such as books, has remained in the possession of the school and was reused until the equipment wore out. Because much of this expensive medical equipment is tailored to an individual child, it usually is not reuseable. Thus, a number of questions have been raised that need to be addressed. Should the educational system pay for this equipment, and if it does, does this equipment belong to them or does it become the property of the child? How does one weigh the use of therapy or therapeutic equipment as being more important to the child's educational or medical functions and where does one draw the boundary line in determining what the educational system is responsible for?

Another important issue along the same lines involves determining what structural adaptations the school should provide in order for a physically disabled child to be integrated into the public school system. Inaccessible buildings need to be adapted, many times at great expense. Another issue arises regarding new treatments that may be required. The most well-known example of this is the issue of whether teachers should perform clean intermittent catheterization for children whose bladders are unable to function on their own. These children have to be catheterized four to six times a day. They are not able to go to school unless the procedure is done during the school hours. Traditionally, the procedure required the expertise of a nurse because it had to be done under sterile conditions. The present procedure does not require sterile conditions, and parents, as well as the children themselves, are capable of being trained with little difficulty in how to perform the procedure. For those children who are not capable of learning how to perform the procedure, nonmedical personnel in the school can be trained. Whether the school is mandated to perform this procedure in providing the least restrictive environment for children is presently being debated. Whether the person performing the procedure should be a nurse or whether an aide or teacher should be taught to provide the service is also under debate. Attempting to define limits between medical and educational parameters will be a difficult and ongoing task that requires extensive collaboration between educational and health planners.

Changing Health Professional Roles

Many health professionals have assumed new roles in the provision of health and educationally related services, as children with disabilities increasingly are being placed in least restrictive environments. Health and educational systems have made changes in their organizations and in how they deal with children and their problems. Therefore, health professionals, who now work with the educational system because of mainstreaming, have had to adjust to a much different system. Professionals from each discipline have had to acquire special expertise in dealing with developmental and educational aspects of their discipline.

Many educational programs now have physical and occupational therapists on their staff. These therapists have had to learn about how schools function, in order to integrate their therapies appropriately into the students' programs. They also have had to learn to function in an interdisciplinary setting, particularly in staffing conferences mandated by PL 94–142. Many times these professionals are in more independent and decision-making roles than has been the case in traditional rehabilitation settings. Their relationship to the students' physicians still has to be better defined, and the issues of supervision and physician monitoring need to be reviewed. This issue becomes more complicated when equipment, such as bracing, is brought into the picture. This again has traditionally been prescribed by physicians, yet bracing is intimately related to the children's therapy program. This is another example of where the school therapists need to have good communication with the physicians caring for particular children.

Audiologists also can bridge the gap between the health and educational systems. They have historically been involved in the educational system, but with the emphasis on mainstreaming, their role has increased. Now, children with hearing impairments are included in the regular public school system. The audiologists must coordinate their evaluations and therapies with the students' pediatricians and otolaryngologists. Treatment for these students can include surgery, medication, and amplification. The effects of therapy have a direct impact on the students' educational program, in determining what is taught and how it is taught.

Another health professional within the educational system whose role has changed greatly is the school nurse. School nurses traditionally dealt with acute illness in the school, provided health surveillance, and contributed to the health education programs in school. With the addition of more significantly impaired children to the public school setting, the responsibility of school nurses has increased. The school nurse is the only employee of the school system who has been trained within the context of the health system, and as such, serves an essential role as the liaison between the health and educational system. With the increase in the number of high-severity disabled children now within the school system, this role has become very important. Frequently, medical reports provided to the schools may be difficult to interpret because of the medical terminology employed. Having a person available on the educational staff to help interpret the reports and recommendations to educators is an important function that will enhance communication between the two systems. It is extremely helpful for physicians who are not well versed in the functioning of the educational system, to have someone from within the system who also has a medical orientation and can provide the physician with useful information about their patients' school programs.

The school nurse also has become an important community resource to help supervise important health management programs. The school nurse also can play an essential role in insuring the appropriate implementation of a clean intermittent catheterization program. Because children are required to attend school daily, the school nurse is in an excellent position to monitor problems such as skin care, weight management, and bladder or bowel programs. These issues are all frequently important to the wellbeing of children who are severely disabled. Because of time and distance constraints, physicians who do evaluate children for educationally related health issues, rarely attend the child's staffing conference. It is again helpful to have a school nurse present at that conference to help interpret the report and see that the appropriate recommendations are incorporated into the educational plan for that child.

It is ironic that with the increasing need for school nurses because of mainstreaming, there has actually been a decrease in the number of school nurses. With the budgetary problems facing many school systems, the school nurse program has been cut back. The role of school nurse existed before the increased emphasis on mainstreaming, so most of the positions have been funded by community school districts rather than by the support services agencies developed to help the implementation of the mandate. Because these positions already existed, support service agencies didn't need to provide that type of care, so a greater focus was placed on services such as physical and occupational therapy. However, with the growing need for school nurses, these agencies are now finding it necessary to provide more of the nursing services. It is doubtful that these agencies will be able to replace those services to the same extent.

Traditional training has not prepared school nurses for their new role. However, in the past, children with high-severity disabilities were not a major part of the school program. The nurse training programs require the same changes as were discussed for medical training programs in order to better prepare school nurses for their roles within the school setting. As stated earlier, two studies (Gibson & Reed, 1974; Haynes, 1975) have demonstrated that nurse training can have a positive impact on nurses' attitudes about children with disabilities.

Specific Medical Issues Related to High Severity Disabled Children

In the process of developing educational programs for high-severity disabled children some specific medical issues have been identified. A few examples will be discussed to illustrate the problems. Because children with high-severity disabilities occur with low frequency and may require highly specialized programs, school systems try to centralize those programs. In some of the more rural states, this may entail a substantial amount of busing. School districts also try to minimize their expenses by making only some of their older school buildings accessible for physically impaired students, because the cost of making all buildings accessible can be very substantial. This policy also may result in the necessity for a substantial amount of busing. Physicians are sometimes consulted on such issues to determine if the bus rides will be detrimental to a child's health or if any potential hazard might exist as a result of busing (such as the chance for a seizure to occur on the bus trip) and what precautions need to be taken to plan for that possibility. Weighing the benefits of a center-based program against the detriments of excessively lengthy bus trips is a difficult process requiring good communication between school personnel and physicians. Another issue that has been raised concerns children with congenital infections. Children with congenital infections, such as rubella or cytomegalic viruses, can sometimes remain contagious for years. This is primarily a concern for pregnant women. Sometimes school personnel become overly concerned because the potential risks have not been clearly explained. The medical community can be helpful in these circumstances in clarifying the issues for the educational community. While educational programs provide services for children with high-severity disabilities, medically related issues are likely to arise.

Medical Issues Concerning Mainstreaming of High-Severity Disabled Children

The concept of integrating children with high-severity disabilities into the public educational system is also an important concept to apply to the health system. Many of these children were previously institutionalized. Their care was mostly provided by the physicians serving the institution, with occasional consultations provided at tertiary care centers. Most physicians have not had experience working with these children. Also, many often feel uneasy working with these children due to inadequate training and underlying negative attitudes towards them. Thus, parents often are unable to find a primary care physician who they can take their child to and feel comfortable about the care provided. A study by Kanthor, Pless, Satterwhite, & Myers (1974) noted that only 62% of the children received acute care from primary care physicians, and most mothers felt that no one physician could provide overall direction to their children's care. (Primary care refers to short-term acute care and health maintenance care, which is usually provided by a patient's personal physician, such as a pediatrician or a family practitioner; tertiary care refers to sophisticated and highly specialized care frequently provided at centralized medical centers). If high-severity disabled children are to be mainstreamed into the health care community as well as the educational community, primary care physicians will need to be better educated, as was discussed earlier. In addition, health professionals from tertiary care centers need to encourage patients' personal physicians to maintain an active role in the patients' overall management and also to provide continuing medical education about new advances in medical care.

The Impact of Increasing Medical Technology

Advances in medical technology will continue to create new challenges in the public educational systems as long as these systems are required to provide educational services to all children, regardless of the severity of the disability. These new technological advances have increased the physician's ability to sustain life, but sometimes only with the use of sophisticated equipment. For example, many children who would have died of respiratory failure as recently as a few years ago, are now surviving through the use of artificial respirators. Providing them with a meaningful life, including education, will require creativity, significant medical input, and strong financial support from both the health and educational systems. Also, in the future it may be possible to save an even greater number of children who are now beyond the benefits of medical care, which will require greater degrees of sophisticated treatment and ongoing medical management. This possibility even further emphasizes the importance of communication between the health and educational communities.

CONCLUSION

Mainstreaming has not only affected developmentally disabled children and the school program, but also has affected health and educational professionals who provide services to these children. All of the issues that have been discussed in this chapter fall under the broad category of mainstreaming's effect on attitudes, organization, information, and relationships. The impact on professional attitudes, particularly in regard to what up to now has been a group highly discriminated against, has been substantial but still needs to be significantly improved. Changes in health professionals' attitudes may be lagging behind those of educators', but as these professionals have more contact with children with developmental disabilities and their families and as training for health professionals regarding care of developmentally disabled children improves, it is hoped their attitudes will also improve.

The different demands placed on health professionals because of mainstreaming has caused the health community to review how services are delivered to developmentally disabled children. Current practices in supervision, consultation, and financing for services have had to be reviewed and are likely to change with time. Defining the boundaries of educational and health services will be an ongoing process that will change with advances in both medical and educational technology. Changes in the roles of specific health professionals—such as nurses, physical therapists, and occupational therapists—are also taking place. These changes affect not only these professionals' relationship to the educational community but also to other health professionals.

Mainstreaming has brought children into the community who were not only excluded from the public educational system, but who were also excluded from the general health service community. This has resulted in the need for services from professionals who, as of yet, do not have the knowledge to appropriately manage these children's special problems. Many health professionals have become aware of the need for further training in order to cope with this situation. In addition, many training program personnel have become aware of the need to revise their curricula to include the management of developmentally disabled children.

The greatest effect by far is the increased demand for a closer relationship between the educational and health communities. Changes in one clearly affect the other. Enhancing communication between these two communities is therefore essential both for the management of individual cases and for the development of programs and policies.

The overall effects of mainstreaming on health professionals have been beneficial. It has caused physicians to review their attitudes and relationships toward both their patients and toward other professionals. This service-need process is ongoing and is only in its infancy for health and education professionals challenged to provide increasingly specialized, integrated services for disabled children. No doubt, new and difficult problems will arise and need to dealt with in the future as new technologies are developed. But the ultimate effect will be better services provided to developmentally disabled children.

REFERENCES

Ayers, A. J. (1972). *Sensory integration and learning disorders.* Los Angeles: Western Psychological Services.

Bennett F. C. (1980). A three-month residency curriculum in child development and handicapped children. In M. J. Guralnick & H. B. Richardson (Eds.) *Pediatric education and the needs of exceptional children.* Baltimore: University Park Press.

Bennett, F. C., Guralnick, M. J., Richardson, H. B., & Heiser, K. E. (In press). Teaching developmental pediatrics to pediatric residents: The effectiveness of a structured curriculum. *Pediatrics.*

Cytryn, L., & Milowe, I. D. (1966). Development of a training program in mental retardation for psychiatric and pediatric residents. *Mental Retardation, 8,* 68–83.

Dworkin, R. H., Shorkoff, J. P., Leviton, A., & Levine, M. D. (1979). Training in developmental pediatrics. *American Journal of Diseases of Children, 133,* 709–712.

Friedman, S. B., Phillips, S., & Parrish, J. M. (1983). Current status of behavioral pediatric training for general pediatric residents: A study of 11 funded programs. *Pediatrics, 71,* 904–908.

Gibson, B. S., & Reed, J. C. (1974). Training nurses in mental retardation. *Mental Retardation, 12,* 19–22.

Haynes, M. (1975). Teaching mental retardation nursing. *American Journal of Nursing, 75,* 626–628.

Kanthor, H., Pless, B., Satterwhite, B., & Myers, G. (1974). Areas of responsibility in the health care of multiply handicapped children. *Pediatrics, 54,* 779–785.

Levine, M. D., Oberklaid, F., Ferb, T. E., Hanson, M. A., Palfrey, J. S., & Aufseeser, C. L. (1980). The pediatric examination of educational readiness: Validation of an extended observation procedure. *Pediatrics, 66,* 341–349.

Levine, M. D., Meltzer, L. J., Busch, B., Palfrey, J., & Sullivan, M. (1983). The pediatric early elementary examination for 7- to 9-year-old children. *Pediatrics, 71,* 894–903.

Ottenbacher, K., & Short, M. A. (In press). Sensory integrative dysfunction in children: A view of theory and treatment. *Advances in Behavioral and Developmental Pediatrics.*

Philips, I. (1960). Problems of training the professional in the field of mental retardation: A review of a training program. *Journal of American Academy of Child Psychiatry, 5,* 693–705.

Raskin, D. E. (1972). Training psychiatrists in mental retardation. *American Journal of Psychiatry, 128,* 127–129.

Ravitch, M. M. (1983). Big brother comes to the nursery. *Surgical Rounds, 6,* 10–12.

Shaw, A., Randolph, J. G., & Manard, B. (1977). Ethical issues in pediatric surgery: A national survey of pediatricians and pediatric surgeons. *Pediatrics, 60,* 588–599.

Sindelar, P. A., & Meisel, C. J. (1982). Teacher-physician interaction in the treatment of children with behavioral disorders. *International Journal of Partial Hospitalization, 1,* 271–277.

Todres, I. D., Krane, D., Howell, M. C., & Shannon, D. C. (1977). Pediatricians' attitudes affecting decision making in defective newborns. *Pediatrics, 60,* 197–201.

Wolraich, M. L. (1979). Pediatric training in developmental disabilities. *Mental Retardation, 17,* 133–136.

Wolraich, J. L. (1980). Pediatric practitioners' knowledge of developmental disabilities. *Journal of Developmental and Behavioral Pediatrics, 1,* 147–151.

Wolraich, M. L., & Siperstein, G. N. (1983). Assessing professionals' prognostic impressions of mental retardation. *Mental Retardation, 21,* 8–12.

The Task Force on Pediatric Education. (1980). The future of pediatric education. Evanston, IL: American Academy of Pediatrics.

IV NEW DIRECTIONS IN RESEARCH AND INTERVENTION

11 Effects of Special Education Environments: Beyond Mainstreaming

Melvyn I. Semmel
Joan Lieber
University of California, Santa Barbara

Charles A. Peck
Washington State University

A central and enduring concern of empirical researchers in the social–behavioral sciences has involved the parsing of effects due to organismic and environmental variables in explaining human development and achievement (Brody & Brody, 1976; Hunt, 1961; Jensen, 1969). In the applied fields of education, rehabilitation, and clinical psychology, emphasis has often been focused on the differential effects of varying therapeutic environmental arrangements on attainment of desired changes in human behavior (Bandura, 1977; Bloom, 1964; Skeels & Dye, 1939). The purpose of this chapter is to review the current status of theoretical and empirical knowledge relative to similar efforts in the field of special education, with specific reference to outcomes for handicapped children in integrated or mainstream settings.

This area of inquiry has particular importance in the field of special education because of policy mandates placing children with handicaps in the least restrictive environment (LRE). Implementation of this policy is presently proceeding on the basis of its philosophical and ethical justification, but in the absence of an empirical research base (Peck & Cooke, 1983). Our central argument is that policy issues related to mainstreaming, LRE, and other notions emphasizing assumptions about environmental effects on child performance, will not be resolved without a thorough revision of the current concepts of "environment", which dominate policy decision-making. It is equally clear that a revised concept of environment will demand methods of measuring differences among special education alternatives that differ from those characterized in most extant special education research.

We begin with a review of traditional approaches to identifying environmental variables associated with different outcomes for learners with handicaps as well as their contributions and their limitations with respect to current policy issues in special education. Secondly, we review empirical research that suggests some specific instructional variables likely to differentiate educational environments in terms of child outcomes. Finally, we present a revised approach to analysis of special education environments based on recent work from the fields of personality and social psychology. A program of research is outlined showing how this approach to analyzing special education environments may lead to better understanding of environmental contributions to child performance and achievement.

Concepts of "Environment" in Special Education Research

The primary use of the concept of environment in special education research has been with reference to variations in administrative arrangements for the provision of services to learners with handicaps (Semmel, Gottlieb & Robinson, 1979). Environmental categories defined with this approach consist of regular classrooms, resource rooms, self-contained classrooms, segregated schools, and residential institutions (Deno, 1970). The primacy of administrative criteria in distinguishing among special education environments is reflected in the voluminous research literature devoted to comparisons of learning outcomes in regular versus special class settings: the special education "efficacy" research (Guskin & Spicker, 1968; Kirk, 1964; Semmel, Gottlieb, & Robinson, 1979; Strain & Kerr, 1981). The assumption underlying this approach to differentiating special education environments is that specific administrative arrangements are composite proxies for pedagogically meaningful variables affecting child performance and achievement. The extent to which the empirical evidence supports this assumption is evaluated in a subsequent section of the present chapter.

While comparisons of special versus regular class settings have clearly dominated special education research, other conceptualizations of environment have been implicit in investigations of more specific instructional design variables affecting child outcomes. *Instructional design* refers here to consistencies in methods of task presentation, extent of learner participation, and specific reinforcement and feedback strategies employed across instructional tasks and curriculum domains (Bloom, 1976). Two examples of models of instructional design that appear to have substantial effects on child outcomes in special education are the direct instruction model (Becker & Engelmann, 1976) and the cooperative learning model (Johnson & Johnson, 1975; Slavin, 1980). Illustrative empirical reports of effects associated with each of these are reviewed later in the chapter.

A third use of the concept of environment, which has guided a large body of research in special education, has focused on the relationships between antecedent stimuli, specific learner responses, and consequent events. Research focusing on these characteristics of educational environments (typically involving procedural techniques related to instruction) has been most often associated with the concepts and methods of applied behavior analysis (Baer, Wolf & Risley, 1968; Sulzer-Azaroff & Mayer, 1977; Tawney & Gast, 1984). Although the empirical data generated from this research paradigm probably represent the most pragmatic scientific accomplishment of special education researchers (MacMillan & Morrison, 1980; Tawney & Gast, 1984), the particularistic nature of this knowledge-base does not lend itself easily to addressing broader policy issues without substantial leaps of inference. Because of the considerable breadth of the research literature on procedural techniques in regular and special education, and the existence of comprehensive reviews elsewhere (e.g., Lovitt, 1984; Snell, 1983; Sulzer-Azaroff & Mayer, 1977; Tawney & Gast, 1984), this chapter focuses on more macro-level environmental variables assumed to affect child performance: special versus mainstream settings, instructional designs and classroom climate. The following discussion summarizes the most commonly researched of these variables: outcomes of special versus regular class (i.e., mainstream) placement for students with handicaps.

SPECIAL EDUCATION EFFICACY RESEARCH: A REVIEW OF REVIEWS

Administrative concepts of special education environments have been reflected in a long history of efficacy studies dating back to the work of Bennett (1932). The empirical goals of this line of research have remained relatively constant, that is, the comparison of effects of regular versus special class placement for children with handicaps. However, it is important to recognize that the "burden of proof" for specific program arrangements has shifted concomitantly with trends in social and political philosophy (Dunn, 1968; Wolfensberger, 1972). Thus, the earlier efficacy studies (i.e., 1932–1970) reflect emphasis on the potential benefits of special class arrangements, while more recent investigations have sought an empirical justification for the policy of mainstreaming (Meyers, MacMillan & Yoshida, 1980; Strain & Kerr, 1981).

The present evaluation of the efficacy research does not replicate earlier efforts to exhaustively review individual studies. Rather, we have conducted a review of seven major research integration papers (Carlberg & Kavale, 1980; Guskin & Spicker, 1968; Kirk, 1964; Leinhardt & Pallay, 1982; Meyers, MacMillan, & Yoshida, 1980; Semmel, Gottlieb, & Robinson, 1979; Strain & Kerr, 1981). This was done with the goal of clarifying the contribution of these syntheses toward attaining a reliable knowledge-base regarding the effects of administratively categorized special education environments on child outcomes. The reviews of Kirk (1964) and Guskin and Spicker (1968) deal primarily with the early efficacy studies and represent the period when special class placement was preferred for handicapped children. The later reviews include post 1970 studies and reflect the political climate that emerged after the passage of PL 94–142.

Results of Early Efficacy Research

Academic Achievement. There is general agreement across the reviews of the early efficacy studies that academic outcomes were superior in regular class settings. There were, however, exceptions to this consensus (Carlberg & Kavale, 1980; Kirk, 1964; Semmel, Gottlieb, & Robinson, 1979). For example, Semmel, Gottlieb, and Robinson (1979) found no differences due to particular administrative arrangements related to academic achievement. They did conclude, however, that academic behavior (which they distinguish from achievement) was facilitated in resource rooms for EMR, learning disabled, and emotionally disturbed children. Carlberg and Kavale (1980) concluded that *special* class placement was more effective for learning disabled and emotionally disturbed learners, even though they concurred with the general finding that regular class placement contributed to superior academic achievement for EMR children.

Other reviewers found academic outcomes to be differentially related to the functioning level of students. For example, Kirk summarized results differently for children at the lower end of the EMR range, indicating that they had superior achievement in special class settings. A similar distinction was made by Leinhardt and Pally (1982), who cited the Goldstein, Moss, and Jordan (1965) results, which demonstrated different outcomes with high IQ and low IQ students.

Social Adjustment. The most consistent finding from the early efficacy research regarding social adjustment was that EMR children were not well accepted by their nonhandicapped classmates. However, both the Semmel, Gottlieb and Robinson (1979) and Guskin and Spicker (1968) reviews suggested that there is contradictory evidence relative to specific social outcome measures. Although their reviews showed that the social acceptance of EMR children was not facilitated by mainstreaming, they indicated that evidence from self-concept measures was inconclusive. Additionally, Semmel, Gottlieb, and Robinson noted that the actual social behavior of EMR children in regular class settings was indistinguishable from that of their nonhandicapped peers.

As with the academic measures, the conclusions of Carlberg and Kavale were significantly divergent from general opinion. They stated that social outcomes for EMR learners were facilitated in regular class settings. This finding may be partially explained by the specific studies reviewed, because they examined several studies related to social adjustment that were not analyzed by other reviewers. Additionally, their conclusions may have differed because they did not divide studies based on the year in which they were done: More than half of the studies that showed superior social outcomes in regular class settings were post 1970. Several reviews included studies from this era, but considered results separately from earlier efficacy research.

Results of Post 1970 Efficacy Studies

Academic Achievement. Three review papers recognized a fundamental shift in the focus of the post 1970 efficacy studies (Leinhardt & Pallay, 1982; Meyers, MacMillan, & Yoshida, 1980; Strain & Kerr, 1981). Both Meyers, MacMillan, and Yoshida, and Strain and Kerr concluded that EMR children progress at least as well within the regular class setting as they did in self-contained classes. Leinhardt and Pallay concurred with this finding for high-IQ EMR children and for matched populations of EMR students in regular and special classes. However, they concluded that for low-IQ students and for studies that used random assignment, academic achievement was facilitated in self-contained settings. However, these authors suggested that it was not the setting per se that accounted for these results, but rather that innovative and effective experimental programming was instituted within these settings in the post 1970 era.

Social Adjustment. In the area of social outcomes for post 1970 studies, the three reviews reflect conflicting conclusions. While both Meyers, MacMillan and Yoshida (1980) and Strain and Kerr (1981) reported many contradictions in the literature, they concluded that self-concept measures for EMR children were superior in integrated settings. Leinhardt and Pallay (1982) also noted the conflicts in the data but drew a different conclusion: "the consistent finding seems to be that EMR students have better attitudes toward themselves in more isolated settings" (p. 26). Although all authors discussed inconsistencies in the literature, their conflicting conclusions may have resulted from differences in the studies they reviewed.

A general agreement was that handicapped children were not well-accepted within the mainstream (Meyers, MacMillan & Yoshida, 1980; Leinhardt & Pallay, 1982). However, Strain and Kerr (1981) concluded that "all studies reported from the 1970s found that integrated EMR children were viewed more favorably than their special class counterparts" (p. 22). The literature reviewed by Strain and Kerr was limited to teacher reports and measures of peer attitudes, while studies reviewed by Meyers, MacMillan, and Yoshida, and Leinhardt and Pallay included sociometric measures as well.

Methodological and Conceptual Issues in the Efficacy Research

There clearly is little agreement among the seven major reviews relative to the influence of administratively defined environments on academic and social outcomes in special education. The authors are unanimous, however, in concluding that persistent methodological problems present an outgoing hindrance to interpreting results of efficacy research. A number of specific difficulties have been repeatedly cited: (a) nonequivalence of experimental groups; (b) use of dependent measures with unknown reliability and validity for handicapped populations; (c) changes in the nature of the populations defined as "handicapped" (MacMillan, Meyers, & Morrison, 1980); and (d) lack of specification of the treatment variables under study (MacMillan & Semmel, 1977). The specific threats to the validity of research results obtained under these design conditions has been thoroughly explicated elsewhere (Campbell & Stanley, 1963; Cook & Campbell, 1979; Kirk, 1968), and will not be repeated here. However, because of the central conceptual issues implicit in the last problem (d) noted above, some elaboration on problems related to defining mainstreaming as a treatment variable is merited.

The basic strategy employed in efficacy research involved use of between-group designs to compare the effects of special class versus regular class placement on academic and social outcomes (MacMillan & Semmel, 1977). An assumption of these designs is that sufficient homogeneity in the treatment variable exists within each experimental group to allow reasonable prediction of some consistent effects (Kaufman, Gottlieb, Agard, & Kukic, 1975; MacMillan & Semmel, 1977).

Unfortunately, reviewers have noted that this is not typically the case with the efficacy studies in special education. Several differences are evident in the characteristics of classroom settings typically grouped under the same administrative category in special education efficacy research. These include: teacher qualifications (Kirk, 1964); curriculum differences (Semmel, Gottlieb & Robinson, 1979); pupil–teacher ratio, teacher competency (Strain & Kerr, 1981); and variations in classroom climate (MacMillan & Semmel, 1977).

The critical point is that the differences between regular and self-contained classroom environments are not typically as large as differences within each type itself. *This raises the possibility that administrative typologies of special education service settings may be pedagogically unimportant.* We do not infer that service setting characteristics may be irrelevant, but that we have not typically designed research to focus on the most salient characteristics that distinguish various educational environments. Several lines of educational research suggest that variables which are associated with substantive effects on child outcomes may be defined. These are reviewed in the following section as a means of illustrating how pedagogically meaningful distinctions among special education environments might be identified.

INSTRUCTIONAL DESIGN VARIABLES

The predominance of research attention devoted to instructional design variables has focused on factors related to academic achievement. Selected models of instruction and related empirical studies are outlined here.

Instruction Design and Academic Achievement

Following Rosenshine (1979), research on the relationship between instructional design and gains in academic achievement may be considered in three identifiable cycles. During the initial phase, researchers explored the influence of teacher characteristics on student learning. Typical investigations focused on variables related to personality, attitudes, and teacher experience. Unfortunately, findings from this research were inconclusive: Few reliable associations were found between teacher attributes and student achievement.

This led to a second cycle of research directed toward variables more proximal to child outcomes, including a more specific focus on teacher behavior and student–teacher interactions. In a review paper covering this second cycle of research, Rosenshine and Furst (1973) identified several variables that were strongly associated with student achievement: (a) clarity of presentation, (b) teacher enthusiasm, (c) variations in activities during a lesson, (d) content covered, and (e) task-oriented behavior. Subsequent studies indicated that two of these variables (which overlap) remain good predictors of achievement across studies of elementary-aged students: *content covered* and *task-oriented behavior* (Rosenshine, 1979). The first variable, *content covered*, simply refers to the amount of curriculum material presented to students. The second, *task-oriented behavior*, refers to the extent to which the teacher and students maintain a direct focus on academic behavior rather than social or affectively-oriented activities. Data from studies of student–teacher interaction, together with the work of Carroll (1963), Bloom (1976) and others, led to the expansion of academic outcomes research to a third area, emphasizing more direct measures of student instructional participation.

Models of research during the third cycle have typically included three factors (Doyle, 1977): (a) the teacher's arrangement of the learning environment leading to (b) the student's engagement in effective academic learning behavior leading to (c) improved academic achievement. Although third cycle researchers acknowledge the influence of both teacher behavior and student behavior on outcomes, they often focus on either the teacher's role or the student's role in the process. Example of how these roles have been investigated during the third cycle of instructional outcome research are reviewed here.

Models Using Time-on-Task. A critical conceptual shift in thinking about instructional outcome research was articulated in an important paper by Carroll (1963). In this model, amount of learning was predicted by the function: time actually spent divided by the time needed to learn. While some variables in the model consisted of individual characteristics (aptitude, ability, and perseverance) there were others that were environmental in focus (opportunity to learn and quality of instruction). Anderson (1981) describes five major models that have been influenced by Carroll's emphasis on instructional time as a central variable explaining academic outcomes. Three of these approaches, which have been of particular interest for researchers in special education, follow.

Kounin (1970) proposed that managerial success in the classroom exists when there is a high rate of student work involvement and a low rate of student deviancy. He used observations made both during recitation and seatwork activities to identify those teacher behaviors that would lead to greater student time-on-task. The following behaviors were identified as effective: (1) "with-it-ness"—communicating to children that the teacher knows what's going on; (2) "overlapping"—the ability of the teacher to manage two events simultaneously; (3) "smoothness" of pacing in lessons and transitions—preparing materials ahead of time, maintaining a brisk pace of instruction; (4) "group alerting"—the degree to which teachers provide attentional prompts and organizers; and (5) "accountability"—the degree to which teachers demand active participation from students. Although Kounin found significant relationships existed between these teacher behaviors and student outcomes during both recitation and seatwork activities, they were most effective during recitation.

Two later approaches substantially expanded the concepts of time and direct instruction as variables related to academic outcomes. In the Beginning Teacher Evaluation Study (BTES) (Fisher, Berliner, Filby, Marliave, Cahen & Dishaw, 1980), instructional time was conceptualized as consisting of three types: (1) *Allocated time* was defined as the amount of time set aside for learning in a particular content area; (2) *engaged time* was defined as the amount of time that a student attentively spent on task; and (3) *academic learning time* (ALT) was defined as time spent on tasks in which students experience a high success rate. Results of the BTES indicated that there were identifiable classroom situations and accompanying teacher behaviors related to high ALT for students. These included: academically-focused, teacher-directed tasks; teaching activites with clear goals; allocating sufficient time; extensive coverage of content; monitoring of student performance; questioning at a low cognitive level; immediate, academically oriented feedback; teacher control of instructional goals; and teacher selection of material appropriate to the ability level of the students. Results of BTES provided further support for the notion that task-oriented behavior of the teacher and extensive coverage of content are powerfully related to student outcomes.

A second set of important findings regarding the role of time in explaining instructional outcomes came from Stallings and her colleagues (1975). The Follow Through Evaluation Study (Stallings, 1975) examined the relationships between seven different educational models and academic outcomes in reading and math. The model associated most consistently with superior academic outcomes was the "Direct Instruction" model developed by Becker and Engelmann (1976). The Direct Instruction model incorporates many of the variables identified in the other approaches emphasizing instructional time. These include: continuous instruction, clearly specified goals, closely monitored student performance, immediate and academically-oriented feedback, carefully sequenced materials and tasks, direct reinforcement, material that is appropriate to the level of the students, and sufficient time allocated to instruction. Taken with the results of

BTES and Kounin, the Stallings research provided compelling evidence in support of the instructional designs featuring the high rates of task-oriented behavior and maximization of academic content covered.

Studies in Special Education. Several studies related to the instructional models reviewed previously have been carried out with mildly handicapped learners. In an extensive descriptive study, Chow (1981) compared academic learning time for nonhandicapped and learning disabled learners. Repeated observations were made of fifth-and sixth-grade mathematics classes over a two-year period. During year one, Chow found significant differences between learning disabled and nonhandicapped students on allocated and engaged time. Learning disabled students had significantly more time at low and medium success rate, while nonhandicapped students had more time at high success rates. During year two, Chow found that nonhandicapped children demonstrated significantly more engaged time with high success rate than did learning disabled students. In contrast, learning disabled students showed significantly more engaged time with a low success rate. Moreover, Chow indicated that no significant correlations were found between ALT variables and achievement for learning disabled students. These results suggest that learning disabled students were not exposed to appropriately designed learning tasks. This implies that teachers may not sufficiently modify large group instruction when the ability level of the learners is highly discrepant, as in mainstream settings.

In a related study, Leinhardt, Zigmond, and Cooley (1981) investigated the relationship between specific instructional practices and reading outcomes in special day classes for learning disabled children. They found that teachers could structure the learning environment to influence how students spent their time, and that there was a relationship between how students spent instructional time and their reading achievement. The variable most strongly associated with reading achievement was amount of time spent directly on silent reading. Leinhardt, Zigmond, and Cooley suggested that decreases in transition times, management activities, and activities indirectly related to reading (e.g., talking about the story, relating of personal experiences) were associated with increases in reading proficiency.

In another descriptive study, Englert and Thomas (1982) tested the extent to which Kounin's criteria for effective teachers applied in special education environments. Supporting Kounin's original findings, they identified effective teachers as those demonstrating group management strategies that led to a high level of student involvement. These strategies included: occupation of a central position in the classroom from which to monitor student task involvement, active surveillance through visual scanning, and circulation among the students during seatwork tasks.

The results of Chow (1981), Leinhardt, Zigmond, and Cooley (1981), and Englert and Thomas (1982) all indicate that the variables identified repeatedly in regular education outcome research also appear important in effecting instructional gains for students with handicaps. Specifically, the degree of student engagement in instructional activities, as well as the amount of content to which students are exposed, appear to offer a parsimonious characterization of effective special educational environments in terms of academic achievement.

Further support for this proposition comes from a number of experimental investigations that have assessed the effects of more discretely analyzed procedural variables on academic outcomes for learners with handicaps. For example, Pany, Jenkins, and Schreck (1982) used a direct instructional model to teach vocabulary to both learning disabled and nonhandicapped students. They designed several levels of intensity in instruction ranging from requiring the students to use contextual information to define a word, to having the student a) read the word, b) listen to the experimenter define the word, and c) practice the modeled definition. While learning disabled students showed significant gains only with the most intensive instructional procedures, nonhandicapped students learned with the less intensive instruction. This finding supports the notion that the amount of direct instruction required for handicapped children will likely be greater than that required for nonhandicapped students. Simply integrating handicapped children within the mainstream without altering the instructional design may not lead to effective outcomes.

In another study, Maier (1980) explored two aspects of direct instruction: the use of small step increments and the administration of explicit instructions. Learning disabled students, who were randomly assigned to experimental and control groups, heard a story about which they were later questioned. While a control group just had the story read to them, the experimental group had the story divided into three segments and were told to focus on a specific question for each segment. Results indicated that experimental group children had more correct responses to questions which reflected higher mental processes. Again, more direct and intensive instruction appeared to lead to superior outcomes.

Summary: Effects of Instructional Design on Academic Outcomes.

The foregoing review of instructional time as a design variable suggests that the following programmatic characteristics may typify effective special education environments:

1. High student instructional engagement.
2. Rigorous teacher monitoring of student activity.
3. Regular teacher feedback to students.
4. Well-sequenced learning tasks that are appropriate to the learner's achievement level, and broken into incremental steps.
5. Clearly specified performance requirements.

6. Minimization of transition time, management time, and activities indirectly related to academic performance.

Clearly, these characteristics of instruction constitute important variables to be included in any pedagogically meaningful analysis of special education environments. It appears likely, however, that at least some of these characteristics may be difficult to implement in mainstream settings where there is high variance in student cognitive and affective behavior. For example, the large group classroom management strategies identified as effective (Englert & Thomas, 1982; Fisher et al., 1980) may be more difficult to implement when students work at very different levels to maintain a high success rate (See Gerber & Semmel, in press).

Instructional Design and Social Outcomes

Although the direct instructional models previously described here are clearly useful for promoting academic outcomes, they place little emphasis on social development, and likely do not represent optimal approaches to this aspect of classroom programming. Other instructional paradigms, however, have been developed with specific attention to providing conditions likely to facilitate positive child–child social interactions and opportunities for social learning (Johnson & Johnson, 1975; Slavin, 1980; Strain, 1981).

The importance of peer relationships to normal child development has received increased recognition since Hartup's (1970) influential paper. A number of specific instructional models have been developed that utilize cooperatively-oriented small group activities as a method of facilitating development of both positive peer relationships and academic competencies. Each of these models is based on the assumption that students feel positively toward peers who are perceived as contributing to the attainment of their personal goals.

For example, Johnson and Johnson (1975) describe a learning environment that can be structured by the teacher that produces positive goal interdependence among learners. In *cooperative goal structure* students can achieve their learning goal if, and only if, all the other members of the group attain their goal. This structure is contrasted with a *competitive goal structure*, in which attainment of one child's goal is negatively correlated with those of the other children, and an *individualistic goal structure*, in which goals are attained independently. Johnson and Johnson suggest that there are positive feelings generated with cooperative goal structuring because the positive value associated with the efforts of a person who helps to achieve a goal become generalized to the person him/herself.

Models of Cooperative Learning. There are three major models of cooperative learning. In the *Jigsaw* variation (Aronson, Bridgeman, & Geffner, 1978) each member of the group has access to part of the information, which they teach to the other members. Participants in the group are highly interdependent because no individual has access to all information. Rewards, however, are given individually and are based on individual performance. We were unable to uncover empirical evaluation studies focused on the application of this model with handicapped children. Aronson, however, suggests that the model can include "poor readers" who benefit from the modeling presented by the more competent group members. If this instructional design were used with handicapped children, their portion of the lesson would need to be structured carefully so that they would be seen as contributing equally to the effort of the group.

The *Teams-Games-Tournaments* model (Student-Teams-Achievement Division) is a cooperative learning strategy developed by Slavin (1978) and his colleagues. The cooperative aspect of this model lies in its teamwork component. Children of differing ability levels work and train together to prepare for the tournaments (TGT) or quizzes (STAD) that they take. Although children compete during quizzes, the competition occurs between children at the same ability level. Both TGT and STAD were developed for drill and practice on basic skills in reading, mathematics, and language arts.

A third method is the *Small Group Teaching Model* developed by Johnson and Johnson (1975). In this model, data is gathered by the students who then use group discussion to interpret the information and incorporate each individual's efforts into a group product. In contrast to the Slavin model, this paradigm is used to train higher level skills, including problem solving, interpretation of data, and decision making.

Studies in Special Education. Several early studies used cooperative activity as an intervention strategy to increase social acceptance for handicapped children. Chennault (1967) formed groups consisting of EMR children identified as accepted or rejected on sociometric measures. Those students then worked together to plan, rehearse, and present a skit. Although Chennault found that the rejected students were accepted as a result of the intervention, the global nature of the intervention package made effects due specifically to the cooperative aspect of the strategy ambiguous.

Ballard, Corman, Gottlieb, and Kaufman (1977) extended research on use of cooperative learning activities to a mainstream setting. Because treatment gains had not been maintained in other intervention studies (Rucker & Vincenzo, 1970; Lilly, 1971) they instituted a longer and more intensive intervention program. Although improvements in acceptance were achieved and maintained for four weeks following the intervention, there were no concomitant improvements in the rejection of the handicapped children.

A more extensive program of research has been conducted on the effects of cooperative goal structuring by Johnson and Johnson and their colleagues (See Chapter 13 of this volume for an extensive review). One series of studies examined recreational activities (i.e., bowling or swimming) with nonhandicapped and either learning disabled or severely handicapped (SH) youngsters. Outcome measures included the frequency of friendly interactions between the handicapped and nonhandicapped children. These were consistently greater in the cooperative learning conditions than in either the competitive or individualistic conditions.

In related research carried out in a classroom setting, handicapped and nonhandicapped children were randomly assigned to groups stratified by ability (Cooper, Johnson, Johnson, & Wilderson, 1980). Teachers taught under each of three experimental conditions: cooperative, competitive, and individualistic. A sociometric instrument and an attitude scale were used to measure social outcomes. Results for the cooperative condition indicated that nonhandicapped children perceived themselves as giving more help, and all students perceived themselves as receiving more support from their peers. In both the cooperative and competitive conditions the nonhandicapped children chose the learning handicapped children as their friends.

Although the primary rationale for cooperative learning arrangements has emphasized potential social benefits, there have been a limited number of studies that have employed a cooperative learning strategy to affect academic outcomes for handicapped learners (e.g., Smith, Johnson, & Johnson, 1982). Other studies have concomitantly monitored both academic and social outcomes for handicapped learners. Madden and Slavin (1983) used the STAD model with learning handicapped and nonhandicapped children randomly assigned to STAD groups or to control groups for mathematics instruction. Social outcomes indicated that although there was less rejection of learning handicapped children taught with the cooperative learning strategy, there was no difference in the number of friendships identified between handicapped and nonhandicapped pupils. For academic outcomes, there was improvement in mathematics achievement for the whole group of STAD children, but not for the subsample of learning handicapped children.

Summary: Effects of Instructional Design on Social Outcomes.

Cooperative goal structuring represents an instructional design that appears effective in improving social outcomes for handicapped children. It is clear, however, that a cooperative strategy cannot be used as a short-term intervention with the expectation of long-lasting effects (Ballard et al., 1977). There is more limited evidence that academic outcomes are affected, although relatively few studies have focused on these effects.

There are characteristics of cooperative strategies that may limit their effectiveness in mainstreamed settings. The social nature of the cooperative task itself may require children to be at an appropriate developmental level to function in a group, as well as to take responsibility for their own learning. In addition, the evidence from the direct instruction literature indicates that handicapped children may take longer to grasp information, and that they need more intensified instruction. Group functioning may be difficult under these circumstances.

ANALYSIS OF EDUCATIONAL ENVIRONMENTS

The foregoing empirical studies related to the effects of two major variables in instructional design make it clear that learning time and goal structure constitute pedagogically important aspects of classroom environments. Although these variables have been central components of cohesive program models (Becker & Engelmann, 1976; Johnson & Johnson, 1975), they have typically been conceptualized and operationalized as discrete intervention components or independent variables for comparative research. Development of scaling methodologies for assessing natural distributions in these environmental characteristics across special education setings will be necessary for the advancement of analysis of environments research related to these variables. Methodological work in other fields, notably personality and social psychology (e.g., Endler & Hunt, 1968; Forgas, 1979) and environmental psychology (e.g., Barker, 1968; Moos, 1979) have provided guidance for development of several specific instruments and related lines of research in education settings that has relevance to present methodological needs in special education.

Theoretical Antecedents

The empirical work reviewed subsequently reflects theoretical orientations derived from early work in social psychology by Murray (1938) and Lewin (1951). Both developed theoretical models that focused on interrelationships between environmental characteristics and human behavior. Murray's model differentiated between the personal *needs* of individuals, and the *press* exerted by the environment. Needs refer to consistencies in the behavior of an individual that appear to be organized toward achieving a specific goal. Press variables refer to those environmental characteristics (e.g., rules, social expectations, behavioral contingencies) that facilitate or inhibit meeting specific needs. For example, certain classroom environments might be characterized as having a high press for academic achievement. Conversely, individual children in a given classroom might exhibit a high need for academic achievement.

The differentiation of these dimensions of the social environment organizes innumerable questions for research on the interrelationships between need and press variables, on differences between various social environments, and on differences between individuals. Many of the questions related to differences in the press dimensions of school environments, as well as questions related to degrees of "fit" between personal and environmental characteristics (Pervin,

1968), have been the subject of research that is highly related to conceptual and empirical issues regarding handicapped children and the identification of environments that are appropriate to meeting their needs.

The second major theoretical work that has stimulated research on analysis of environments has been Lewinian Field Theory (Lewin, 1951). Field theory represents a complex and highly unified model for mapping the interrelationships between personal and environmental factors affecting behavior. The theory emphasizes the importance of both the social and physical aspects of a situation in determing behavior. It assumes that accurate characterization of a field requires analysis of its specific features (e.g., stimuli, goals, needs) as well as its general atmosphere (e.g. friendly, hostile, tense). Thus, the characteristics of the field as a *whole* are just as important as its specific features. Both the Murray and Lewin conceptualizations have been reflected in many subsequent research efforts aimed at describing, classifying, and comparing social environments.

Describing Educational Environments

Efforts to systematically analyze characteristics of classroom environments have been underway for several decades. Early research focused on observation and description of aspects of teacher–student interaction. For example, Flanders' Interaction Analysis System (Amidon & Flanders, 1963) was developed as an observation instrument for assessment of classroom social climate. This widely used tool probed both teacher and student behavior in an attempt to describe relationships between "direct" and "indirect" aspects of teacher influence and student behavior.

Another influential approach to analysis of environments through direct observation was developed by Barker and his associates (Barker, 1968; Barker & Gump, 1964). Utilizing an ethnographic-type naturalistic observation methodology, Barker attempted to identify distinct "behavior-settings" in various social environments, based on theoretical principles from Lewinian Field Theory.

Direct observation techniques have a high degree of face validity as a method of describing environments due to the relatively low level of inference required for interpreting the data. However, the high costs of direct observation have precluded its use in many studies. Additionally, some researchers have argued that it is the *subjective* reality experienced by learners that is of primary interest in the analysis of classroom environments (Fraser, 1981).

Utilization of questionnaires has allowed researchers to collect information describing large numbers of social environments at relatively low cost. Two widely used instruments developed to characterize classroom environments are the Learning Environment Inventory (Anderson & Walberg, 1968) and the Classroom Environment Scale (Moos & Trickett, 1974).

The Classroom Environment Scale was based on the Murray Needs–Press theory. Items were generated from observation, interview, and related theoretical and empirical research and then subjected to psychometric analysis before final inclusion in the tool. Nine subscales, which measure psychosocial aspects of the environment such as involvement, affiliation, competition, and teacher control, are included. The CES consists of three forms that can be answered either by the teacher or by the students relating to: 1) the actual classroom, 2) the preferred or ideal classroom, and 3) the expected environment in a new class.

Based on work across a number of social settings (see Moos, 1974, 1979 for comprehensive reviews), Moos has identified three underlying dimensions along which even very different environments may be characterized. *Relationship* dimensions reflect the quality and quantity of interpersonal interaction, involvement, and support among participants in a social setting. *Personal growth* dimensions reflect the extent to which achievement of personal goals, academic accomplishment, and competition are characteristic of the social environment. *System maintenance and change* dimensions are related to environmental characteristics of orderliness, teacher-control, organization, rule clarity, and innovation (both teacher and student designed variations in classroom activities).

Anderson and Walberg (1968) developed the Learning Environment Inventory (LEI) in the context of a curriculum development and evaluation study in secondary schools—The Harvard Project Physics. This instrument describes classroom environments in terms of 15 scales, which can be reduced to areas similar to those of Moos (Fraser, 1981). The relationship area is captured in the LEI scales of cohesiveness, friction, favoritism, cliqueness, satisfaction, and apathy. The personal development scales include speed, difficulty, and competitiveness. The system change and maintenance area is measured by diversity, formality, environment, goal direction, disorganization, and democracy scales. While the CES describes both the teacher's and the students' perceptions of the classroom, the LEI is limited to students' perceptions. Walberg and Anderson have developed a form of the LEI—My Class Inventory—which is designed for elementary students, however, there is little reliability or validity data available on this measure (Fraser, 1981).

Classifications of Educational Environments

A number of investigations have been carried out that have sought to classify educational environments according to types of social-emotional climate. In one study Moos (1978) analyzed a representative sample of 200 junior high and high school classes drawn from across the United States. Using cluster analysis of CES scores, Moos was able to classify 196 of the 200 classrooms into nine types of environments. The conceptual similarity of several of the clusters resulted in reduction to six clusters of classroom environments.

Moos (1979) described these clusters both in terms of relative scores on subscales of the CES, and in terms of how performance on the subscales aggregated into the relationship, personal growth, and system maintenance dimensions. Two of the clusters emphasized the relationship dimension. *Innovation*-oriented classrooms reflected high scores on the innovation subscale of the CES, and an above-average emphasis on all three scales related to the relationship dimensions. These characteristics were contrasted with relatively less emphasis on organization, procedural clarity, and teacher control. *Structured relationship*-oriented classrooms were characterized by emphasis on student interaction, participation, and teacher support. Concomitant emphasis was evident on organizational aspects of the environment in these classrooms. Two other clusters emphasized different aspects of classroom goal orientation within a cohesive framework with a focus on teacher support. *Supportive task*-oriented classrooms were typified by relatively high scores on teacher support and task orientation subscales, as well as the order and organization indices of the CES. Relatively little emphasis on rule clarity and teacher control was found in these classrooms. *Supportive competition*-oriented classrooms emphasized competition in a context where students felt friendly toward each other, helped with homework, and enjoyed working together. There was an emphasis on organization and clarity and a de-emphasis on teacher control. The last two clusters represented uncombined clusters that Moos named *unstructured competition-oriented* and *control-oriented*. The former occurred infrequently, with an emphasis on goal orientation and a lack of emphasis in any other area. The final cluster of classrooms emphasized high teacher control and relatively low emphasis on anything else except competition (rated about average). This cluster constituted the most frequently occurring type of classroom environment identified, comprising over 23% of the classes sampled. Moos (1979) noted that these classes appeared to emphasize teacher control of student behavior to the exclusion of other aspects of learning environment, and may thus constitute a high priority population for further investigation and change.

In addition to delineating the main effects for specific types of environments, Moos (1979) noted the relevance of studying typologies of classroom environments as a means of identifying contextual factors that may interact with specific intervention programs. This suggests that the replicability of specific programs may be affected by aspects of the social-psychological environment that are not usually assessed. For example, although programs emphasizing student competition may have negative social side-effects in some types of classroom environments (Johnson & Johnson, 1980), the same competitive goal arrangements may be perceived more positively in environments characterized by a concomitant emphasis on positive student–teacher and student–student relationships. Compare, for example, the supportive competition and unstructured competition-oriented classrooms previously described.

Comparisons of Educational Environments

A third general purpose for an analysis of educational environments consists of the comparison of various environmental types and related effects. For example, Moos and Moos (1978) compared 19 high school classroom environments on dimensions of the CES. Outcome differences related to various subscales included higher absenteeism for classrooms rated as high in teacher control and low in teacher support. Higher grades were obtained by students in classrooms rated as high in involvement and low in teacher control.

Studies in Special Education. Forness, Guthrie, and MacMillan (1982) examined the relationship of teacher evaluations of classroom climate and observable behavior of students in special day classes. Twenty-eight teachers evaluated their classrooms using the CES. Students in those classes were then observed on measures of positive verbal behavior, on-task behavior, off-task behavior, and disruptive behavior. On the basis of these data, the authors were able to separate the classrooms into four clusters.

The first cluster was labeled *supportive* and represented the largest group. In this cluster the relationship dimension was emphasized most, with a moderately high emphasis on classroom organization and clarity of expectations. The behavior of children in these classrooms was high in attention and low in nonattention. These classes also had the lowest disruptive behavior, although these differences did not reach statistical significance. The second cluster of classrooms was termed *businesslike*. Teachers characterized these environments as more controlling, less supportive and less flexible in class routines. Children in these classrooms also exhibited high attending behavior. A third cluster, labeled *problematic*, constituted classrooms that were low in involvement, and that had moderately low teacher control, order, and organization. Students in these classes were inattentive and disruptive. The authors were unable to clearly characterize the final cluster of classrooms. Although the children in these environments demonstrated attending behaviors similar to those children in the supportive and businesslike classrooms, they showed more peer interaction.

Project PRIME. By far, the most ambitious attempt to conduct a thorough analysis of special education classroom environments is represented by Project PRIME (Kaufman, Agard & Semmel, 1978). This major federally sponsored project was unique in the scope of its underlying conceptualization, as well as in the extensiveness of the data collected.

Central to the design of the PRIME investigation was an explicit model for considering child plus environment interaction effects within special education settings. A taxonomic model based on relevant theoretical and empirical research, which identified likely sources of variance for outcomes related to both child and setting characteristics, was developed. Project PRIME attempted to derive empirical weightings for these variables within a regression equation predicting child outcomes.

The Project PRIME model parsed environmental variables into three components. First, the *participant composition* of the classroom was considered important. Thus, peer characteristics, such as school attitudes, intellectual performance, social-ethnographic background, and others were assessed. Teacher characteristics were also viewed as important, including training and experience, attitudes toward mainstreaming, attitudes toward educational issues, socio-ethnographic background, and others.

The second category of environmental characteristics identified in PRIME was *socio-emotional climate*. Related variables were designated as teacher leadership style and peer cohesiveness. Peer-cohesiveness characteristics were related to the degree of peer harmony and liking or disliking patterns observed in the classroom. Teacher leadership style was a composite of the teachers' techniques of influence, warmth, and the amount of directiveness.

The third cluster of environmental variables hypothesized to be related to learner outcomes was termed *instructional conditions*. These included the physical setting, curricular content, and special instructional materials used, and also behavioral dimensions, such as teacher strategies, peer instructional activity, cognitive discourse in the classroom, teacher feedback, and others.

Although more comprehensive data were reported, the present discussion focuses on learner outcomes in terms of academic and social competence. Academic outcomes were substantially related to environmental variables for all groups studied, but these effects were stronger for handicapped than nonhandicapped learners. Participant composition factors appeared most important in predicting academic outcomes, with teacher characteristics accounting for the largest portion of variance. Specifically, results indicated that teachers who had positive attitudes toward mainstreaming, and black teachers, were associated with positive academic outcomes for handicapped learners. Instructional conditions were related to academic status and academic behavior outcomes, but not to academic attitudes. Specifically, small-group instruction formats were associated with lower academic status outcomes for EMR learners. This finding is important given that instructional differentiation, i.e., individualization, has been generally assumed to have positive effects on learning outcomes. Socio-emotional climate variables were associated only with academic behaviors, specifically attention to task.

Social competence outcomes were more powerfully related to environmental factors. Participant composition variables affected both acceptance and social behavior outcomes. Particularly, teacher attitudes toward education, peer attitudes toward school, and percentage of peers with reading problems predicted higher social acceptance for EMR children in regular classes. Additionally, higher acceptance of EMR children was found in urban schools and in classrooms with high percentages of non Anglo students. Antisocial behavior was associated with classrooms with Anglo teachers, highly verbal teachers, and inexperienced teachers.

Findings for other environmental variables were also important. Instructional conditions associated with differential outcomes included teacher directiveness and grouping strategies. Specifically, high teacher directiveness was associated with relatively less variance in social behavior (i.e., less positive and negative behavior). Large-group instruction was associated with more acceptance and less rejection of EMR children.

The clearest findings related to social outcomes were obtained on socio-emotional climate variables. Here it was found that the cohesiveness of the classroom social environment was consistently associated with higher levels of peer acceptance. Specifically, peer harmony was related to positive social outcomes for all groups, while peer disliking was negatively related to these outcomes. Disliking was also related to higher levels of antisocial behavior.

Summary of Research on Educational Environments

Recent research on analysis of educational environments has demonstrated that reliable and "wholistic" descriptions of classroom ecologies may be obtained through questionnaire and observation methods (Barker & Gump, 1964; Kaufman et al., 1978; Moos, 1979). Further, it is apparent that typologies may be developed that organize the characteristics of classroom environments in a psychologically and educationally meaningful way (Moos, 1976; 1979). Finally, the validity and utility of directly assessing variables related to the social-psychological characteristics of classroom environments is supported by research showing relationships between these environmental characteristics and important student outcomes (Forness et al., 1982; Kaufman et al., 1978; Moos & Moos, 1978).

REVITALIZATION OF RESEARCH ON SPECIAL EDUCATION ENVIRONMENTS

The central argument advanced in this chapter has been that policy issues related to the effects of mainstreaming, identifying least restrictive environments, and other problems concerned with the effects of specific types of educational environments on child outcomes, will not be successfully resolved without a shift in conceptual and methodological approaches to analysis of special education environments. It appears that research on the effects of educational environments must be broadened in both concept and method if data that are useful for complex policy decisions, as well as individual program planning, are to be generated. Several characteristics of such research may be summarized on the basis of the literature reviewed.

First, research on effects of special education environments is likely to be more productive to the extent that it is multivariate in concept, design, and analysis. Clearly, the monothetic conceptualizations of differences between classroom environments, which have typified most special education research to date, represent a serious oversimplification of the characteristics of these environments. For example, although there exists substantial empirical evidence to support the proposition that differences in child outcomes are related to some specific instructional models (i.e., the direct instructional and cooperative learning models), no existing model appears to produce superior learning across all curriculum domains. Multiple attribute or polythetic conceptualizations (Sokal, 1974) will undoubtedly yield more reliable and valid strategies for identifying pedagogically important differences among classrooms. The most widely used instruments developed for the analysis of regular education environments, Moos and Trickett's CES and Anderson and Walberg's LEI, both exemplify polythetic models of the classroom environment. The usefulness of such instruments in explaining variance in child performance related to environmental factors (Moos, 1979) suggests that similar strategies might well be attempted in special education research.

A second characteristic of a revised approach to the analysis of special education environments should be an increased empirical focus on variables of more direct pedagogical significance than those categorized under administrative arrangements. Instructional design variables related to goal structure and engaged time clearly merit inclusion in any strategy for measuring pedagogically relevant dimensions of special education classroom environments. However, there has been relatively little work aimed at scaling either qualitative or quantitative aspects of these variables in classrooms. Assessing the extent to which classroom environments reflect use of one or another of these instructional models will be important if researchers are to be able to accurately describe natural variation in environmental characteristics. That is, dichotomous categorization of classrooms into, for example, individualistic versus cooperative comparison groups will not lead to accurate and externally valid information about what is likely to be a somewhat continuous distribution of these characteristics across classrooms. These issues are analogous to general problems with the use of laboratory research results in formulating social policy (Brofenbrenner, 1977; Brunswik, 1956).

A third characteristic of a revised approach to analysis of special education environments should be an increased consideration of contextual factors, and interrelationships among these, in evaluating the impact of specific environmental characteristics on child learning and performance. We assume the use of multivariate approaches to the measurement and categorization of environments, as discussed above. Moos (1979) has provided an example of the importance of considering contextual factors in interpreting the meaning of specific environmental phenomena. He noted that classrooms rated as high in competition were perceived more positively by students, depending on the extent to which those classrooms were also characterized by warm and supportive teacher–student and student–student relationships. What is suggested here is that the meaning of a given environmental characteristic can only be defined in context; that meaning is derived from the *interrelationships* between environmental characteristics—not those characteristics in isolation (Bateson, 1979; Mishler, 1979). The notion that classroom environments should be viewed more wholistically is consistent with shifts toward more organismic conceptual frameworks for understanding phneomena in other fields of scientific endeavor (Dennenberg, 1979; Miller, 1978; Whitehead, 1925).

A Research Agenda

Development of research methodologies consistent with the criteria identified here will allow several important types of questions related to the effects of special education environments to be pursued. These may be organized in terms of several general and somewhat overlapping goals (Moos, 1979): (a) description of natural variation in environmental characteristcs; (b) development of empirically-based classification and taxonomic models for environments; (c) comparison of specific environments or types of environments; (d) intervention toward improvement of environments. Each of these research goals has importance to the field of special education.

An important objective for research aimed at analysis of special education environments will be the accumulation of a data base describing normal variations in classroom characteristics of theoretically or empirically identified importance. Although experimental manipulation of variables hypothesized to have effects on child outcomes may demonstrate the *possibility* of effects due to these variables, the extent to which such variables actually impact children in natural settings can only be assessed through direct verification of their existence and operation in representative samples of special education classroom environments (Brofenbrenner, 1977). For example, while it is clear that various goal structures can have important effects on child performance, the extent to which competitive, individualistic, or cooperative goal structuring actually characterize special education classrooms remains unknown. Descriptive research will also provide important normative data on which further taxonomic, comparative, and intervention research may be based.

A second goal of research on special education environments should be the development of empirically-based classification or taxonomic models for classroom environments. Identification of classroom types constructed around pedagogically important variables would represent an important step toward describing interactions between environments and specific child outcomes. This achievement would, of course, provide a more meaningful way of identifying a "least restrictive environment" fit to defined child needs than have traditional administrative distinctions between environments. An important advantage to developing a polythetic typology of special education environments would be the organization of the plethora of variables of potential educational importance into naturally covarying classes (i.e., setting types). The reduction of data achieved through this process promises to facilitate use of the classroom as a unit of analysis for comparative and intervention research.

A third general goal of specific education research consists of obtaining comparative data on characteristics of various classroom environments. Numerous questions for comparative research on environments are suggested from the traditional special education literature. These include comparisons of classroom environmental differences due to: (a) class size (Walberg, 1969; (b) instructional or curriculum models (Stallings, 1975); (c) peer and teacher characteristics (Brophy & Good, 1974). Clearly comparative research must also be carried out to assess differences in child outcomes associated with various *types* of classroom environments defined through taxonomic studies as suggested above. To the extent that these differences in outcomes due to classroom type are found to be reliable, an important comparative research question involves whether classroom environment types are distributed normally within administratively defined categories of special education service settings. This strategy may produce some of the long sought empirical evidence regarding differences between mainstream and self-contained special education environments, because within category variance in classroom environment characteristics would be systematically analyzed rather than designated as error. This research could, of course, provide an empirical meaning to the notion of "least restrictive environment" when considered in context of priorities for specific child outcomes (Peck & Semmel, 1982).

A fourth goal of research on special education environments is the development of replicable interventions aimed at improving the characteristics of those environments. Priorities for environmental intervention may be identified from either the descriptive, taxonomic, or comparative research described above. For example, descriptive research may identify characteristics of specific classroom environments, such as high rates of teacher-or-peer mediated criticism or punishment, which may warrant intervention. Taxonomic research may identify types of special education settings, Moos' "control-oriented" type, for example, which suggest specific intervention programs for these classrooms. Comparative research may show that specific environmental characteristics (e.g., peer cohesiveness) may be associated with desirable outcomes—suggesting the need for interventions to improve this aspect of some classroom environments.

CONCLUSION

The evolution of the field of special education over the past 10 years serves as an interesting exemplar of the complex relationship between science and public policy (Semmel, 1984). Current research and practice in the field of special education has been shaped by major socio-legal factors. Legislation has imposed a set of requirements designed to protect the rights of handicapped children in the schools. These mandates have focused educational delivery systems on "compliance" issues related to assuring these rights. Hence, educational environments have been constructed and maintained following the criteria of adherence to law, but not necessarily following criteria related to the effectiveness of special education environments. In fact, the overwhelming influence of law has resulted in the adoption of a legal lexicon and conceptualizations of the field that correspond to the compliance objective.

This state of affairs is reflected in a confusion among researchers relative to distinctions between promising environmental research variables and ideological constructs. Most researchers, in designing empirical studies of the influence of special education environments on handicapped pupils, have uncritically adopted the administrative variables (i.e., special class, resource room, regular mainstream class) that generally reflect legal conceptions of LRE. Although critics of constrastive, between-group designs have repeatedly pointed to the wide variation that exists within administrative arrangements, and have underscored the overlap between such distributions, they have not generally offered alternative educationally relevant conceptualizations and research strategies.

The great danger in our current social context lies in a propensity to invoke law and ideology as the sources of verification for the effects of educational environments on handicapped pupils. These sources can only aspire to verify that educational environments are in compliance with the mandated rights of handicapped students, and to appropriately reflect a superordinate social value system. In constrast, only empirical research results, acceptable to both science and the law, can verify the educationally relevant effects of special education environments.

Certainly the final worth of any empirical approach to the analysis of educational environments must be evaluated on the basis of the effectiveness of the interventions it produces. We suggest that the prospects for improving the ability of special education researchers to effectively identify and alter characteristics of classroom environments toward maximizing the growth and adjustment of handicapped children rests with the ability to more broadly and flexibly conceptualize and measure the nature of those environments. The issues and promising directions in research reviewed here imply that this is an achievable goal.

REFERENCES

Amidon, E. J., & Flanders, N. A. (1963). *The role of the teacher in the classroom*. Minneapolis: Amidon.

Anderson, G. J., & Walberg, H. J. (1968). Classroom climate and group learning. *International Journal of Educational Sciences, 2*, 175–180.

Anderson, L. (1981). Instruction and time-on-task. A review. *Curriculum Studies, 13*(4), 289–303.

Aronson, E., Bridgeman, D. L., & Geffner, R. (1978). Interdependent interactions and prosocial behavior. *Journal of Research and Development in Education, 104*, 16–27.

Baer, D. M., Wolf, M. M., & Risley, T. (1968). Some current dimensions of applied behavior analysis. *Journal of Applied Behavior Analysis, 1*, 91–97.

Ballard, M., Corman, L., Gottlieb, J., & Kaufman, M. J. (1977). Improving the social status of mainstreamed retarded children. *Journal of Educational Psychology, 69*, 605–611.

Bandura, A. (1977). *Social learning theory*. Englewood Cliffs, NJ: Prentice Hall.

Barker, R. (1968). *Ecological psychology*. Stanford: Stanford University Press.

Barker, R. G., & Gump, P. (1964). *Big school, small school*. Stanford: Stanford University Press.

Bateson, G. (1979). *Mind and nature: A necessary unity*. New York: Bantam.

Becker, W. C., & Englemann, S. (1976). Analysis of achievement data on six cohorts of low-income children from 20 school districts in the University of Oregon Direct Instruction Follow Through Model (Follow Through Project, Technical Report #76–1). Unpublished manuscript, University of Oregon.

Bennett, A. (1932). A comparative study of subnormal children in the elementay grades. New York: Teacher's College Columbia University.

Bloom, B. S. (1964). *Stability and change in human characteristics*. New York: Wiley.

Bloom, B. S. (1976). *Human characteristics and school learning*. New York: McGraw-Hill.

Brofenbrenner, U. (1977). Toward an experimental ecology of human development. *American Psychologist, 32*, 513–531.

Brody, E. B., & Brody, N. (1976). *Intelligence: Nature, determinants, and consequences*. New York: Academic Press.

Brophy, J. E. & Good, T. L. (1974). *Teacher-student relationship: Causes and consequences*. New York: Holt, Rinehart & Winston.

Brunswik, E. (1956). *Perception and the representative design of psychological experiments*. Berkeley, CA: University of California Press.

Campbell, D. T., & Stanley, J. C. (1963). *Experimental and quasi-experimental designs for research*. Boston: Houghton Mifflin.

Carlberg, C., & Kavale, K. (1980). The efficacy of special versus regular class placement for exceptional children: A meta-analysis. *Journal of Special Education, 14*, 295–309.

Carroll, J. (1963). A model for school learning. *Teachers' College Record, 64*, 723–733.

Chennault, M. (1967). Improving the social acceptance of unpopular educable mentally retarded pupils in special classes. *American Journal of Mental Deficiency, 72*, 455–458.

Chow, S. H. (1981, July). A study of academic learning time of mainstreamed learning disabled students (Final report, Grant No. G007902007). San Francisco, CA: Far West Laboratory for Educational Research and Development.

Cook, T. D., & Campbell, D. T. (1979). *Quasi-experimentation*. Boston: Houghton Mifflin.

Cooper, L., Johnson, D. W., Johnson, R., & Wilderson, F. (1980). The effects of cooperative, competitive, and individualistic experiences on interpersonal attraction among heterogeneous peers. *Journal of Social Psychology, 111*, 243–252.

Denneberg, V. H. (1979). Paradigms and paradoxes in the study of behavioral development. In E. B. Thoman (Ed.)., *Origins of the infant's social responsiveness* (pp. 251–290). Hillsdale, NJ: Lawrence Erlbaum Associates.

Deno, E. (1970). Special education as developmental capital. *Exceptional Children, 37*, 229–237.

Doyle, W. (1977). Paradigms for research on teacher effectiveness. In L. S. Shulman (Ed.). *Review of research in education* (pp. 163–198) (Vol. 5). Itasca, IL: F. E. Peacock.

Dunn, L. M. (1968). Special education for the mildly retarded–Is much of it justifiable? *Exceptional Children, 35*, 5–22.

Endler, N. S. & Hunt, J. McV. (1968). S–R inventories of hostility and comparisons of the proportions of variance from persons, responses and situations for hostility and anxiousness. *Journal of Personality and Social Psychology, 9*, 309–315.

Englert, C. S., & Thomas, C. C. (1982). Management of task involvement in special education classrooms. *Teacher Education and Special Education, 5*, 3–10.

Fisher, C., Berliner, D., Filby, N., Marliave, R., Cahen, L., & Dishaw, M. (1980). Teaching behaviors, academic learning time, and student achievement: An overview. In C. Denham & A. Lieberman (Eds.). *Time to learn* (pp. 7–32). Washington, DC: National Institute of Education.

Forgas, J. P. (1979). Multidimensional scaling: A discovery method in social psychology. In G. P. Ginsburg (Ed.)., *Emerging strategies in social psychological research* (pp. 253–288). Chichester: Wiley.

Forness, S., Guthrie, D., & MacMillan, D. (1982). Classroom environments a they relate to mentally retarded children's observable behavior. *American Journal of Mental Deficiency, 87*, 259–265.

Fraser, B. J. (1981). Learning environment in curriculum evaluation: A review. *International Progress series*. London: Pergamon.

Gerber, M. M., & Semmel, M. I. (in press). Microeconomics of referral and reintegration: A paradigm for evaluation of special education. *Studies in Educational Evaluation*.

Goldstein, H., Moss, J., & Jordan, J (1965). *The efficacy of special class training on the development of mentally retarded children* (Cooperative Research Project No. 619). Washington, DC: U. S. Office of Education.

Guskin, S. L., & Spicker, H. H. (1968). Educational research in mental retardation. *International review in mental retardation, 3*, 217–279.

Hartup, W. W. (1970). Peer interaction and social organization. In P. H. Mussen (Ed.). *Carmichael's manual of child psychology* (pp. 361–465). (Vol. II). New York: Wiley.

Hunt, J. (1961). *Intelligence and experience*. New York: The Ronald Press.

Jensen, A. R. (1969). How much can we boost IQ and scholastic achievement? *Harvard Educational Review, 33*, 1–123.

Johnson, D. W., & Johnson, R. T. (1975). *Learning together and alone: Cooperation, competition, and individualization*. Englewood Cliffs, NJ: Prentice-Hall.

Johnson, D. W., & Johnson, R. T. (1980). Integrating handicapped students into the mainstream. *Exceptional Children, 47*, 90–98.

Kaufman, M., Agard, J., & Semmel, M. I. (1978). *Mainstreaming: Learners and their environments*. Research Report. Washington, DC: Bureau of Education for the Handicapped.

Kaufman, M. J., Gottlieb, J., Agard, J. A., & Kukic, M. B. (1975). Mainstreaming: Toward an explication of the construct. *Focus on Exceptional Children, 7*.

Kirk, R. E. (1968). *Experimental design*. Belmont, CA: Brooks/Cole.

Kirk, S. A. (1964). Research in education. In H. A. Stevens & R. Heber (Eds.). *Mental retardation* (pp. 57–99). Chicago: University of Chicago Press.

Kounin, J. S. (1970). *Discipline and group management in classrooms*. New York: Holt.

Leinhardt, G., & Pallay, A. (1982). Restrictive education settings: Exile or haven? *Review of Educational Research, 52*, 557–578.

Leinhardt, G., Zigmond, N., & Cooley, E. (1981). Reading instruction and its effects. *American Educational Research Journal, 18*, 343–361.

Lewin, K. (1951). *Field theory in social science*. New York: Harper & Row.

Lilly, M. S. (1971). Improving social acceptance of low sociometric status, low-achieving students. *Exceptional Children, 37*, 341–347.

Lovitt, T. (1984). *Teaching tactics*. Columbus, OH: Charles Merrill.

MacMillan, D. L., Meyers, C. E., & Morrison, G. M. (1980). System-identification of mildy mentally retarded children: Implications for interpreting and conducting research. *American Journal of Mental Deficiency, 85*, 108–115.

MacMillan, D. L., & Morrison, G. M. (1980). Evolution of behaviorism from the laboratory to special education settings. In B. Keogh (Ed.). *Advances in special education: Perspectives on applications* (pp. 1–28), *Vol. 2*. Greenwich, CT: JAI Press.

MacMillan, D. L., & Semmel, M. I. (1977). Evaluation of mainstreaming programs. *Focus on Exceptional Children, 9*.

Madden, N. A., & Slavin, R. E. (1983). Effects of cooperative learning on the social acceptance of mainstreamed academically handicapped students. *The Journal of Special Education, 17*, 171–182.

Maier, A. S. (1980). The effect of focusing on the cognitive processes of learning disabled children. *Journal of Learning Disabilities, 13*, 143–147.

Meyers, C. E., MacMillan, D. L., & Yoshida, R. K. (1980). Regular class education of EMR students, from efficacy to mainstreaming: A review of issues and research. In J. Gottlieb (Ed.).

Educating mentally retarded persons in the mainstream (pp. 176–206). Baltimore: University Park Press.

Miller, J. G. (1978). *Living systems*. New York: McGraw-Hill.

Mishler, E. G. (1979). Meaning in context: Is there any other kind? *Harvard Educational Review, 49*, 1–19.

Moos, R. H. (1974). *Evaluating treatment environments: A social ecological approach*. New York: Wiley.

Moos, R. H. (1976). *The human context: Environmental determinants of behavior*. New York: Wiley.

Moos, R. H. (1978). A typology of junior high and high school classrooms. *American Educational Research Journal, 15*, 53–66.

Moos, R. H. (1979). *Evaluating educational environments*. San Francisco: Jossey-Bass.

Moos, R. H. & Moos, B. S. (1978). Classroom social climate and student absences and grades. *Journal of Educational Psychology, 70*, 263–269.

Moos, R. H., & Trickett, E. J. (1974). *Classroom environment scale manual*. Palo Alto, CA: Consulting Psychologists Press.

Murray, H. (1938). *Explorations in personality*. New York: Oxford University Press.

Pany, D., Jenkins, J. R., & Schreck, J. (1982). Vocabulary instruction: Effects on word knowledge and reading comprehension. *Learning Disability Quarterly, 5*, 202–215.

Peck, C. A., & Cooke, T. P. (1983). Benefits of mainstreaming at the early childhood level: How much can we expect? *Analysis and Intervention in Developmental Disabilities, 3*, 9–22.

Peck, C. A., & Semmel, M. I. (1982). Identifying the least restrictive environment for children with severe handicaps: Toward an empirical analysis. *Journal of the Association for the Severely Handicapped, 7*, 56–63.

Pervin, L. A. (1968). Performance and satisfaction of individual-environment fit. *Psychological Bulletin, 69*, 56–68.

Rosenshine, B. V. (1979). Content, time and direct instruction. In P. L. Peterson & H. J. Walberg (Eds.). *Research on teaching* (pp. 28–56). Berkeley: McCutchan.

Rosenshine, B. V., & Furst, N. F. (1973). The use of direct observation to study teaching. In R. M. W. Travers (Ed.). *Second handbook of research on teaching* (pp. 122–183). Chicago: Rand McNally.

Rucker, C. N., & Vincenzo, F. M. (1970). Maintaining social acceptance gains made by mentally retarded children. *Exceptional Children, 36*, 679–680.

Semmel, M. I. (1984). Handbook of mental retardation: A critical review. *Contemporary Education Review, 3*, 289–296.

Semmel, M. I., Gottlieb, J., & Robinson, N. M. (1979). Mainstreaming: Perspectives on educating handicapped children in the public school. *Review of Research in Eduation, 7*, 223–279.

Skeels, H. M., & Dye, H. B. (1939). A study of the effects of differential stimulation on mentally retarded children. *Proceedings of the American Association on Mental Deficiency, 44*, 114–136.

Slavin, R. E. (1978). Student teams and achievement divisions. *Journal of Research and Development in Education, 12*, 39–49.

Slavin, R. E. (1980). Cooperative learning. *Review of Educational Research. 50*, 315–342.

Smith, K., Johnson, D. W., & Johnson, R. (1982). Effects of cooperative and individualistic instruction on the achievement of handicapped, regular and gifted students. *Journal of Social Psychology, 116*, 277–283.

Snell, M. E. (Ed.). (1983). *Systematic instruction of the moderately and severely handicapped*. (2nd Ed.). Columbus: Charles E. Merrill.

Sokal, R. R. (1974). Classification: Purposes, principles, progress, prospects. *Science, 185*, 1115–1123.

Stallings, J. (1975). Implementation and child effects of teaching practices in Follow-Through classrooms. *Monographs of the Society of Research in Child Development, 40*. (Serial No. 163).

Strain, P. S. (1981). Modification of sociometric status and social interactions with mainstreamed developmentally disabled children. *Analysis and Intervention in Developmental Disabilities, 1*, 157–169.

Strain, P. S., & Kerr, M. M. (1981). *Mainstreaming of children in schools*. New York: Academic Press.

Sulzer-Azaroff, B., & Mayer, G. R. (1977). *Applying behavior-analysis procedures with children and youth*. New York: Holt, Rinehart & Winston.

Tawney, J., & Gast, D. (1984). *Single-subject research in special education*. Columbus: Charles E. Merrill.

Walberg, H. (1969). Class size and the social environment of learning. *Human Relations, 22*, 465–475.

Whitehead, A. N. (1925). *Science and the modern world*. New York: Basic.

Wolfensberger, W. (1972). *Normalization: The principle of normalization in human services*. Toronto, Canada: National Institute on Mental Retardation.

12 Strategies for Enhancing the Social Outcomes of Mainstreaming: A Necessary Ingredient for Success

Frank M. Gresham
Louisiana State University

The field of special education thrives on and is reinforced by personal incompetence in children. Children found to be physically incompetent are placed into categories reflecting these deficiencies if their condition adversely affects educational functioning (e.g., health impaired, orthopedically handicapped, or sensory impaired). Similarly, children who are intellectually and adaptively incompetent are placed into the category of mental retardation. Membership into the remaining special education categories is based on the same process of identifying specific incompetencies in children. The label one receives depends on the type and number of incompetencies schools identify for children.

The assessment of the incompetencies is supposedly carried out to provide these children with appropriate education and related services in least restrictive environments with the hope of remediating their identified problems. Thus, one way to view special education is as a system designed to identify incompetence in children, place them into "appropriate" educational programs that are "least restrictive" with the goal of having them emerge as competent individuals. The relative success with which the special education enterprise accomplishes this goal is open to debate and depends on what criteria one uses to operationally define success. There are little data to support the notion that special education effectively remediates the academic, physical, and/or social incompetencies of handicapped children. Using a norm-referenced criterion, few handicapped children ever become "nonhandicapped" as a function of special education (other than by administrative declassification or fiat).

The purpose of this chapter is to present an argument for increased emphasis and consideration of *social competence* in handicapped children, particularly as this relates to the mainstreaming process. A central thesis is that the social outcomes of mainstreaming have been disappointing and that mainstreaming per se has done little to enhance the social competencies of handicapped children (Asher & Taylor, 1981; Gottlieb, 1981; Gresham, 1981a, 1983a; Levine, Hummel & Salzer, 1982).

Potential reasons for the negative social outcomes of mainstreaming are discussed. These reasons include: (a) the faulty assumptions underlying mainstreaming; (b) the values and priorities of the schools; (c) motivational deficits of handicapped children; (d) the social behavior standards held by regular educators. A conceptualization of academic and social competence is presented and various types of social skill deficiencies are explained. Social skills training strategies are also discussed in relation to the social behavior standards that exist in the regular classroom. Finally, the *social validity* of the mainstreaming concept is discussed in terms of the social significance of mainstreaming goals; the social acceptability of mainstreaming procedures; and the social importance of the effects produced by education of handicapped children in the regular classroom.

DEFINITIONS OF MAINSTREAMING

There are at least three distinct definitions of mainstreaming than can be gleaned from the special education literature. These are discussed in the following sections to elucidate the intent, practice, and outcomes of mainstreaming, respectively.

Philosophical Definition

The first definition of mainstreaming can be termed the philosophical definition because it embodies the ideals of the mainstreaming process. The definition by Kaufman, Gottlieb, Agard, and Kukic (1975) best represents the philosophical ideals of mainstreaming: "Mainstreaming refers to the temporal, instructional, and social integration of eligible exceptional children with normal peers" (p. 40). Note in this definition that handicapped children must not only be integrated physically with peers, but they must also be integrated instructionally and socially as well.

The criteria by which the success of a philosophical definition of mainstreaming would be judged are apparent in the definition itself. That is, one could say that mainstreaming is successful when a handicapped child is physically placed in a regular classroom for a portion of the school day, is instructed academically with nonhandicapped students, and is socially integrated and accepted by nonhandicapped peers. As we shall see later, the empirical data regarding the above criteria do not suggest that the philosophical goals of mainstreaming have been attained.

Practical Definition

The second definition can be called the practical or pragmatic definition because it is the one most easily accomplished and hence, the most frequently practiced in the schools. This definition is extracted from the review by Semmel, Gottlieb, and Robinson (1979) and defines mainstreaming as the placement of handicapped children into regular classrooms for a portion of the school day. "Portion" is typically defined by a handicapped child spending at least 50% of his/her time in a regular classroom (Semmel, Gottlieb, and Robinson, 1979).

It is important to note the distinction between integration and placement implicit in the philosophical and practical definitions of mainstreaming. That is, one can be placed into a setting without being integrated (either instructionally or socially), but one cannot be integrated into a setting without having also been placed. The philosophical definition stresses integration of handicapped children whereas the practical definition emphasizes the placement of handicapped children.

Empirical Outcomes Definition (Social Competence)

The final definition of mainstreaming can be termed the empirical outcomes definition because it is based on a large number of studies regarding the social competence outcomes of mainstreaming handicapped children. According to this definition, mainstreaming refers to the physical placement of handicapped children into regular classrooms for a portion of the school day. As it is typically practiced, mainstreaming results in handicapped children being poorly accepted and/or socially rejected by nonhandicapped peers (Ballard, Corman, Gottlieb, & Kaufman, 1977; Bryan, 1974, 1978; Gottlieb, 1975; Morgan, 1977), in low or negative rates of social interaction between handicapped and nonhandicapped children (Allen, Benning, & Drummond, 1972; Bryan, 1976; Ray, 1974), and little, if any, beneficial modeling effects for mainstreamed handicapped children (Apolloni & Cooke, 1978; Cooke, Apolloni, & Cooke, 1977; Marburg, Houston, & Holmes, 1976).

Handicapped children remaining in self-contained classrooms tend to be better accepted and less often rejected by nonhandicapped peers than handicapped children who have been mainstreamed into regular classrooms (Goodman, Gottlieb, & Harrison, 1972; Gottlieb & Budoff,1973; Iano, Ayers, Heller, McGettigan, & Walker, 1974). That is, handicapped children remaining in special (segregated) classes are rated by their peers as being more socially accepted and less often rejected than handicapped children in mainstreamed (integrated) classrooms.

The aforementioned empirical outcomes have been repeatedly demonstrated in the literature and are relatively clearcut. Reviews of the literature over the past six years consistently support the social competence outcomes discussed in the foregoing paragraphs (Asher & Taylor, 1981; Gottlieb, 1981; Gottlieb &

Leyser, 1981; Gresham, 1981a, 1982a, 1983a, in press a; Levine, Hummel & Salzer, 1982; Madden & Slavin, 1983; Semmel, Gottlieb & Robinson, 1979).

Given the empirical outcomes of mainstreaming in terms of social competence, specific interventions are needed to teach social skills to handicapped children to improve peer-to-peer as well as teacher-to-handicapped child social interactions in the regular classroom. The reader at this point is probably asking; What is social competence? How is it differentiated from academic competence? Are there different types of social skill deficiencies? The following section provides answers to these questions.

CONCEPTUALIZATION AND DEFINITION OF SOCIAL SKILLS

Social competence and social skills represent two distinct constructs. McFall (1982) states that social skills are the specific behaviors that an individual exhibits in order to perform competently on a task. In contrast, social competence is an evaluative term based on judgments (given certain criteria) that a person has performed a task adequately. These judgments can be based on opinions of significant others (e.g., parents, teachers, or peers), comparisons to explicit criteria (e.g., number of social tasks performed correctly in relation to a pre-established criterion, or comparisons to a normative sample).

Competence does not imply exceptional performance; it merely indicates that a given performance was adequate. By analogy, scoring at the 50th percentile on an intelligence test does not imply exceptionality, it only indicates that the intellectual performance was adequate in comparison to a normative sample.

The issue of social competence can be recast in terms of social validity: the determination of the clinical, applied, and/or social importance of exhibiting certain social behaviors in particular situations (Kazdin, 1977; Van Houten, 1979; Wolf, 1978). In other words, behavior can be considered socially competent if it predicts important social outcomes for individuals (Gresham, 1983b).

Reschly and Gresham (1981) have provided a conceptualization of academic and social competence for school-age children, which is helpful in illuminating these constructs. As Fig. 12.1 suggests, academic competence is comprised of intellectual skills, academic achievement, language skills, perceptual-motor skills, and so forth. Social competence is comprised of adaptive behavior competencies and social skills. Both academic and social competence make up the superordinate construct of personal competence (Greenspan, 1981).

It is important to distinguish between adaptive behavior and social skills within the domain of social competence. Adaptive behavior for children and youth includes independent functioning skills, physical development, self-direction, personal responsibility, and the like. That is, adaptive behavior represents an

PERSONAL COMPETENCE

ACADEMIC COMPETENCE	SOCIAL COMPETENCE
• General Intelligence	• Adaptive Behavior
• Academic Achievement	• Social Skills
• Perceptual-Motor Skills	
• Language Skills	

Fig. 12.1 Domains and subdomains of personal competence

SOCIAL COMPETENCE

ADAPTIVE BEHAVIOR	SOCIAL SKILLS
• Independent Functioning	• Interpersonal Behaviors
• Physical Development	• Self-Related Behaviors
• Self-Direction	• Academic-Related Skills
• Personal Responsibility	• Assertion
• Economic-Vocational Activity	• Peer Acceptance
• Functional Academic Skills	• Communication Skills

Fig. 12.2 Domains and subdomains of social competence

individual's ability to meet the standards of self-sufficiency and personal responsibility set forth by society (Grossman, 1973). Social skills, on the other hand, include interpersonal behaviors, self-related behaviors, academic-related behaviors, assertion, and so forth.

Fig. 12.2 provides a distinction between adaptive behavior and social skills within the social competence domain. More detailed discussions of adaptive behavior and social skills can be found in several recent publications (Gresham, 1981a, 1981b, 1982a, 1982b; Leland, 1978; Reschly, 1979, 1982).

Definitions of Social Skill

At least three general definitions can be distilled from the accumulated literature on children's social skills. One definition can be termed the peer acceptance definition in that researchers use indices of peer acceptance or popularity (e.g., peer sociometrics) to define social skill. Using a peer acceptance definition, children and adolescents who are accepted by or who are popular with their peers in school and/or community settings, can be considered socially skilled. This definition has been implicit in the work of many prominent researchers in the social skills area (Asher & Hymel, 1981; Asher, Oden, & Gottman, 1977; Gottman, 1977; Ladd, 1981; Oden & Asher, 1977).

In spite of its relative objectivity, the major drawback of a peer acceptance definition is that it cannot identify what specific behaviors lead to peer acceptance or popularity. As such, we can identify poorly accepted or unpopular children, but we have no knowledge of the specific behaviors (or lack thereof) that resulted in poor acceptance or unpopularity.

This being the case, some researchers have opted for a behavioral definition of social skills. This approach defines social skills as those situation-specific responses that maximize the probability of securing or maintaining reinforcement or decreasing the likelihood of punishment or extinction contingent on one's social behavior. Measures used to define social skills in this manner typically consist of observations of behavior in naturalistic or role-play situations and settings. Many well-known investigators adopt a behavioral definition of children's social skills (Bellack & Hersen, 1979; Combs & Slaby, 1977; Foster & Ritchey, 1979; Greenwood, Todd, Hops, & Walker, 1982; Greenwood, Walker, & Hops, 1977; Greenwood, Walker, Todd, & Hops, 1979; Strain, 1977; Strain, Cooke, & Apolloni, 1976).

The behavioral definition has the advantage over the peer acceptance definition in that antecedents and consequences of particular social behaviors can be identified, specified, and operationalized for assessment and remedial purposes. However, this definition does not ensure that the particular social behaviors targeted for change are in fact socially skilled, socially significant, or socially important. Merely increasing the frequency of certain behaviors that are defined a priori as social skills may not impact on goals or outcomes valued by society at large.

A final and less frequently discussed definition of social skills may be termed the social validity definition. According to this definition, social skills are those behaviors which, within given situations, predict important social outcomes for children and youth. These important social outcomes may be: (a) peer acceptance or popularity; (b) significant others' judgments of social skill (e.g., parents or teachers) and/or (c) other social behaviors known to consistently correlate with a and b above.

This definition uses naturalistic observations of behavior, sociometric measures, and behavioral ratings by significant others to assess and define social skill. It has the advantage of not only specifying behaviors in which a child is deficient, but also can define these behaviors as socially skilled based on their relationship to socially important outcomes (e.g., peer acceptance, teacher acceptance, parental acceptance, academic achievement, etc.). The social validity definition has received recent empirical support (Green, Forehand, Beck, & Vosk, 1980; Gresham, 1981c; 1982c; 1983a) as well as past indications of validity (Hartup, Glazer, & Charlesworth, 1967; Marshall & McCandless, 1957; McCandless & Marshall, 1957; McGuire, 1973; Moore & Updegraff, 1964; Singleton & Asher, 1977).

Classification of Social Skill Problems

Gresham (1981a, 1981b, 1982c, 1984) categorized social skill problems into four general areas: (1) skill deficits, (2) performance deficits, (3) self-control skill deficits, and (4) self-control performance deficits. The basis for making distinctions among these four categories rests on whether or not a child knows how to perform the skill in question and the presence of an emotional arousal response (e.g., anxiety, anger, impulsivity, etc.). This four-category conceptualization of social skill difficulties is depicted in Fig. 12.3 and will be elaborated briefly in order to provide a heuristic framework for assessment, classification, and remediation of children's social skill problems.

Skill Deficits. Children with social skill deficits either do not have the requisite social skills in their behavioral repertoires to interact appropriately with peers or they do not know a critical step in the performance of the skill. A social skills deficit is similar to what Bandura (1977a) refers to as an acquisition or learning deficit. For example, a child may not know how to initiate positive interactions with peers, how to maintain or terminate conversations with adults, or how to appropriately ask to be recognized in class. The child's knowledge or past performance of the skill is the important criterion for determining the existence of a social skill deficit. Most social deficits are remediated primarily through modeling, behavioral rehearsal, and/or coaching (Gresham, 1981b; Gresham & Lemanek, 1983).

Performance Deficits. A social performance deficit describes children who have the social skills in their repertoires, but do not perform them at acceptable levels. Performance deficits can be conceptualized as a deficiency in the number of times a social behavior is emitted and thus, may be related to a lack of motivation (i.e., reinforcement contingencies) or an absence of opportunity to perform the behavior (i.e., stimulus control problem). The key in identifying a performance deficit is determining whether or not the child can perform the

	Learning Deficit	Performance Deficit
Emotional Arousal Response Absent	Social Skills Deficit	Social Performance Deficit
Emotional Arousal Response Present	Self-Control Skills Deficit	Self-Control Performance Deficit

[1]Emotional arousal responses are internal responses such as anxiety, impulsivity, anger, etc. that prevent either the acquisition or performance of appropriate social behaviors.

Fig. 12.3 Classification of social skills problems[1]

behavior. For example, if a child does not perform a given social behavior in a classroom situation, but can perform the behavior in a role-play situation, it is indicative of a social performance deficit. Strategies for remediating social performance deficits include peer initiations (Strain, Shores, & Timm, 1977), sociodramatic activities (Strain, 1975), contingent social reinforcement (Allen, Hart, Buell, Harris, & Wolf, 1964), and group contingencies (Gamble & Strain, 1979).

Self-control Skill Deficits. This type of social skill problem describes a child who has not learned a particular social skill because some type of emotional arousal response has prevented the acquisition of the skill. Anxiety is an example of such a response. Anxiety has been shown to impede the acquisition of appropriate coping responses, particularly with respect to fear and phobias (Bandura, 1969; 1977a, 1977b, 1982). Hence, a child may not learn to interact with peers because social anxiety prevents social approach behavior. In turn, avoidance of or escape from, social situations reduces anxiety thereby negatively reinforcing social isolation behaviors.

Determination of a self-control skill deficit rests upon two criteria: (a) the presence of an emotional arousal response and (b) the target child either not knowing or never having performed the social behavior in question. Remediation strategies typically involve anxiety-reduction techniques (e.g., flooding, desensitization, etc.) paired with modeling/coaching and self-control strategies (e.g., self-talk, self-monitoring, etc.) (Kendall & Braswell, 1982; Meichenbaum, 1977).

Self-control Performance Deficits. Children with self-control performance deficits have a specific social skill in their repertoires, but do not perform the skill at desired levels because of an emotional arousal response and problems in antecedent and/or consequent control. That is, a child knows how to perform a desired behavior, but does so infrequently or inconsistently. The critical difference between self-control skill and self-control performance deficits is whether or not the child has the social skill in his or her behavioral repertoire. The two major criteria used to determine a self-control performance deficit are: (a) the presence of an emotional arousal response and (b) the inconsistent performance of the skill in question. Interventions with children experiencing social skill difficulties where a self-control performance deficit is present typically focus on strategies that teach inhibition of inappropriate behavior (e.g., due to impulsivity) and reinforcement contingencies for appropriate social behaviors (Bolstad & Johnson, 1972; O'Leary & Dubey, 1979; Rosenbaum & Drabman, 1979).

Handicapped children are deficient in a variety of social skills due to various combinations of skill, performance, and self-control deficits. Delineation of these various types of social skill deficits requires an adequate assessment utilizing multiple assessment techniques. A discussion of the advantages and disadvantages of these assessment strategies is beyond the scope of the present chapter, but can be found in recent publications on this topic (Greenwood, Walker & Hops, 1977; Gresham, 1981b, 1981c, 1983b; Gresham & Elliott, in press; Stumme, Gresham & Scott, 1982, 1983).

POTENTIAL REASONS FOR OUTCOMES OF MAINSTREAMING

The empirical outcomes of mainstreaming with respect to the social competencies of handicapped children can be related to several phenomena. Four possible reasons for these disappointing outcomes of mainstreaming are presented here. These are: (a) faulty assumptions underlying mainstreaming; (b) values and priorities held by schools; (c) motivational deficits of handicapped children; and (d) the social behavior standards held by regular educators.

Faulty Assumptions

Gresham (1981a, 1982a) asserts that part of the reason for the relative lack of success of mainstreaming (in terms of social competence outcomes) is the faulty assumptions on which the concept of mainstreaming was based. One faulty assumption made by the proponents of mainstreaming was that physical placement of handicapped children in regular classrooms would result in increased social interaction between handicapped and nonhandicapped children. A second faulty assumption was that placement of handicapped children in regular classrooms would result in increased social acceptance of handicapped children by handicapped peers. A third faulty assumption was that mainstreamed handicapped children would model or imitate the appropriate behaviors of their nonhandicapped peers as a result of increased exposure to them.

Gresham's (1982a) review of 40 studies demonstrated that, for the most part, mainstreamed handicapped children do *not* become better accepted, less rejected, interact more positively, nor derive beneficial modeling effects as a result of physical placement in regular education classrooms. Thus mainstreaming has not lived up to the original expectations of many because of the faulty assumptions on which it was based regarding social competence benefits.

Values and Priorities of Schools

Part of the reason for the outcomes of mainstreaming may also be due to the values and priorities schools hold regarding academic achievement (Levine, Hummel & Salzer,1982). That is, mainstreaming as a social policy creates conditions that may be antithetical to the predominant value schools place on the academic attainment of all children.

The current Zeitgeist of accountability, minimal academic competence for all students, and fiscal containment does not bode well for mainstreamed handicapped children (Timar & Gutherie, 1980). Add to this the Reagan administration's recommendations to repeal critical sections of Public Law 94–142 as well as their preference for block grants, and we see a threat to the equality of educational opportunity for all handicapped children.

Given that schools and government will likely continue to place top priority on academic attainment for all students and given that the majority of mainstreamed handicapped children will almost always fail to achieve at grade level, mainstreaming efforts as currently practiced will most likely fail. An increased emphasis on social skills for handicapped children, as called for by several authors (Cartledge & Milburn, 1978; Gresham, 1981a, 1982a, 1983a; Stephens, 1978), has the potential of improving the poor social competence outcomes of mainstreaming. A discussion of how this might be accomplished in light of the values and priorities of the public schools it provided in a subsequent section.

Motivational Deficits

Another possible reason for mainstreaming's lack of success can be related to a variety of motivational deficits that are characteristic of handicapped children (Cromwell, 1963; Harter, 1978; Zigler, 1971). In particular, it has been demonstrated that many handicapped children have a high need for social reinforcement, exhibit anxiety in mastery situations, are motivated more by failure-avoidance than by success striving, and have a low expectancy for success (Harter, 1978). These motivational deficits obviously interfere with those social behavior standards held by regular education teachers and, hence, detract from the philosophical goals of mainstreaming (i.e., the physical, instructional, and social integration of handicapped children in regular classrooms).

Several psychological theories of human motivation stress the importance of perceived competence or mastery over one's environment. For example, White (1959) has suggested that a primary motivator of behavior is an individual's striving to be competent or effective in their interactions with the environment (i.e., effectance motivation). Harter (1978) has reconceptualized and expanded White's (1959) theory specifying three components of effectance motivation: cognitive, social, and physical. In the expanded theory, it is possible for an individual to feel competent or effective in one domain (e.g., physical), but not the other domains (e.g., cognitive and social).

Seligman's (1975) theory of learned helplessness represents another view of human motivation based on an individual's perception of the relationship between their own behavior and its consequences. An individual is said to be in a state of learned helplessness when he or she perceives that behavior and its outcomes are independent. Hence, persons learn on the basis of past response-outcome interactions that their behavior is not effective in mastering the environment.

Many mainstream classrooms represent settings in which handicapped children learn to perceive that there is no relationship between their behavior and successful outcomes (i.e., they can be said to be in a state of learned helplessness). These individuals learn over a series of failure-based experiences that there is no relation between effort (behavior) and changes in surroundings or the attainment of a goal (outcomes). Thomas (1979) has recently provided extensive documentation of this in learning disabled children.

Bandura (1977b, 1982) has amended and reconceptualized the aforementioned ideas of effectance and helplessness into a theory known as self-efficacy. The basic phenomenon in self-efficacy focuses on an individual's perception that one can produce and regulate events in one's life. In self-efficacy theory, efficacy expectations are differentiated from outcome expectations. That is, an outcome expectation represents a person's estimate that a given behavior will result in a certain outcome. In contrast, an efficacy expectation represents a person's belief that he or she can perform the behavior or behaviors to produce a certain outcome. Outcome and efficacy expectations are differentiated because a person can believe that behaviors will produce certain outcomes, but they may not believe that they can execute the behaviors that will produce those outcomes. Mainstream classrooms often present situations in which handicapped children feel they cannot perform certain behaviors to produce desired outcomes.

The preceding three theories of effectance motivation, learned helplessness, and self-efficacy provide an interesting framework from which to view the behavior of handicapped children in regular classrooms. Handicapped children are frequently placed or remain in regular classrooms where they have experienced academic and/or social failure. They have not learned to be effective or competent in mastering the behaviors required by this environment to produce desired outcomes.

Mainstreaming, as currently practiced, does not appear to consider the previously discussed motivational deficits in that handicapped children are either reintegrated into regular classrooms where they have experienced academic and/or social failure, or they are placed for the first time into an environment where they have little basis for mastery experiences (i.e., they have no learning history in the regular classroom). The likely result of these two cases is that handicapped children will experience failure, a low sense of self-efficacy, learned helplessness, and exhibit behaviors to avoid demands placed on them in the regular classroom (e.g., social withdrawal or acting out).

The expectations that individuals hold about their ability to master certain tasks affect both the initiation and persistence of coping behavior. Moreover, the strength of these expectations predicts whether or not a person will even try to cope within given situations. This perceived self-efficacy also influences choices of behavior settings in that persons avoid settings or situations that they believe exceed their coping skills and approach those settings and situations in which they believe they can successfully cope.

Handicapped children have no choice of the setting in which they will be placed. Schools in general, and special education placement committees in particular, who adhere to the philosophy of mainstreaming often place handicapped children into mainstreamed environments ostensibly for the children's own good or to comply with the strictures of the least restrictive environment. As a result, handicapped children are often forced into settings and situations in which failure experiences are probable. The net result of many mainstreamed placements is that handicapped children fail to develop a sense of effectance because they come to believe that they cannot perform the behaviors that result in preferred outcomes (e.g., adequate academic achievement).

In summary, I believe that a major reason for the present and past outcomes of mainstreaming has been the failure to consider the effects of motivational variables that impact on the handicapped child. Clearly, we must address the issue of motivational deficits in the regular classroom to change it from a primarily failure-based to a success-oriented setting, which will enhance the social competencies of handicapped children.

Social Behavior Standards

The standards, expectations,and tolerance levels that teachers hold for children's social behavior function in such a way as to influence teaching behavior as well as peer interaction in the classroom (Hersh & Walker, 1983). For example, students perceived to be brighter or more competent receive more teacher attention, are given greater opportunities to respond, are praised more, and are given more verbal cues during teaching interactions (Brophy, 1981; Brophy & Good, 1974; Good & Brophy, 1978).

Teachers also hold certain expectations, standards, and tolerance levels for children's social behavior in the classroom in addition to academic achievement. Most teachers would consider a behavioral repertoire to be indicative of successful adjustment if it: (a) facilitated academic performance (e.g., listening to the teacher, completing tasks, complying with teacher requests, etc.) and (b) is marked by the absence of disruptive or unusual behaviors that challenge the teacher's author and disrupt the classroom environment (Hersh & Walker, 1983). These standards for classroom behavior were most likely established on the basis of past interactions in the classroom that resulted in positively reinforcing (i.e., a quiet and compliant group of children) and punishing (i.e., defiant and disruptive children) consequences. Hence, teachers probably adopt those social behavior standards that lead to reinforcing outcomes and that avoid aversive consequences. For most teachers, a class that is quiet, still, and docile is reinforcing (Winnett & Winkler, 1972) whereas a class that is noisy, active, and assertive is punishing.

In light of the aforementioned social behavior standards held by most teachers, one can derive a model behavioral profile for students in classroom settings. The model behavioral profile for a given student would most likely be a child who: stays in his/her seat; attends to instruction; completes tasks independently (i.e., does not ask for teacher assistance); complies with teacher commands, instructions, or directions; follows classroom rules (which probably include all of the above); and who does not: defy the teacher; behave in an aggressive or disruptive manner; make loud or obscene gestures; steal; and vandalize or otherwise damage school property (Hersh & Walker, 1983; Walker, in press).

Obviously, many handicapped children who are mainstreamed into regular classrooms do not fit this model behavior profile. In fact, their divergence from this model profile is most likely the reason many of them were referred to and placed in special education. To expect that mainstreaming alone (i.e. physical placement) will somehow magically produce a model behavioral profile in a handicapped child is ludicrous. However, the majority of our mainstreaming efforts have been based on this assumption (Gresham, 1981a, 1982a, 1983a).

This model behavioral profile does in fact contribute to successful school adjustment (as judged by teachers) and does in fact facilitate academic achievement. It also serves the convenience needs of classroom teachers for discipline and control in the classroom (Hersh & Walker, 1983). It has little to do with the development of interpersonal skills, social competence, and the ability to cope effectively with peers. We know how to teach "social skills," but these skills do not fit into the model behavioral profile expected by teachers.

SOCIAL SKILLS TRAINING PROCEDURES

The previous section discussed four potential reasons for the disappointing outcomes of mainstreaming to date. The faulty assumptions of mainstreaming, emphasis on academic achievement, motivational deficits of handicapped children, and the social behavior standards held by regular educators all probably interact to mitigate against the realization of the philosophical goals of education in least restrictive environments. It is obvious that schools are simply not ready to target social behaviors as primary skills to be taught in the curriculum.

Given the assumption that social skills are vitally important for the psychological and social development of handicapped children, how do we prompt educators to teach these skills in mainstream settings? I have identified at least three plausible strategies that may be successful in teaching important social skills to handicapped children while at the same time adhering to the emphasis on academics and maintaining teachers' social behavior standards. These strategies should also serve to correct the previously described motivational deficits of handicapped children (i.e., effectance, helplessness, and self-efficacy).

Recruiting Natural Communities of Reinforcement

Stokes and Baer (1977) talk about introducing subjects to natural maintaining communities of reinforcement as a technique for programming generalization. The logic is simple. If the natural environment functions to maintain target behaviors in a way similar to the experimental conditions, then the natural environment should operate on the target behaviors in the absence of experimental intervention, thus promoting generalization.

The natural environment, however, cannot always be trusted to maintain new behaviors. Natural communities of reinforcement need to be functioning and identified before they can be used to maintain behavior (Stokes, Fowler, & Baer, 1978). The data presented regarding the social behavior standards of teachers suggest that a natural community of reinforcement for peer-to-peer social skills is not likely in the typical classroom.

Some researchers have advocated an active approach to establishing natural communities of reinforcement called recruiting or cueing (Cantor & Gelfand,1977; Graubard, Rosenberg, & Miller, 1971; Seymour & Stokes, 1976; Stokes & Baer, 1977; Stokes, Fowler, & Baer, 1978). For example, Seymour and Stokes (1976) taught delinquent females to prompt or cue staff members for evaluations of their work when it was of high quality. Similarly, Cantor and Gelfand (1977) taught elementary school children to smile at adults, talk politely, and ask for feedback after completion of tasks.

The preceeding studies have all taught children to recruit reinforcement for academic or vocational task completion. It seems logical to assume that this same strategy would be effective in the area of social behavior. Rogers-Warren and Baer (1976) have demonstrated this with preschoolers' social behavior in their study of the correspondence between "saying" and "doing." It seems reasonable that the research in this area could be greatly expanded in order to develop a technology for teaching children to recruit reinforcement from teachers for social skills. Although it is purely conjecture at this point, recruiting natural communities of reinforcement for social behavior might change the social behavior standards of teachers such that social skills would be more highly valued by teachers.

Peer Initiation Strategies

Strain and his colleagues (Strain, 1977; Strain & Fox, 1981; Strain, Shores, & Timm, 1977) have conducted excellent research on the use of what might be termed an antecedent control technique for teaching social skills called peer social initiations. In this procedure, children in the target child's peer group or class are taught to persist in directing certain social approach behaviors toward the target child. This research has demonstrated that peer social initiations can dramatically increase reciprocal social exchanges in classroom settings. The peer initiation strategy is conducted without the teacher having to prompt or reinforce target behaviors. In fact, teacher intrusion into an ongoing social exchange between children often terminates the exchange (Strain & Fox, 1981).

Peer social initiation strategies may be another way to affect the social behavior standards for teachers. However, these strategies make the assumption that teachers will let certain children leave their classes to be trained as peer confederates and that positive social exchanges in the classroom will not be punished on their return. In spite of these potential drawbacks, peer initiation strategies hold great promise for social skills training in mainstream settings.

Cooperative Learning Strategies

The past 30 years has seen an abundance of research in the applied social psychology literature concerning the effects of cooperative, competitive, and individualistic structures on individual and group productivity. More recently, the field of educational psychology has begun to study the effects of cooperative learning strategies (CLS) on the academic achievement of elementary and secondary school children.

According to Slavin (1983), a cooperative incentive structure is one in which two or more individuals are rewarded, based on their performance as a group. A competitive incentive structure indicates that two or more individuals are compared with one another, and those performing best are rewarded. An individualistic incentive structure is one in which individuals are rewarded, based own their own performance, regardless of others' performance.

Analogous strategies have been used in the behavior analysis literature under various names such as interdependent, dependent, and independent group contingencies to control disruptive behavior and to enhance academic performance (Gresham & Gresham, 1982; Litow & Pumroy, 1975; Zwald & Gresham, 1983). The "Good Behavior Game" of Barrish, Sauders,and Wolf (1969) was an example of a combination of an interdependent group contingency (cooperative incentive structure) and a competitive incentive system (i.e., the team with the least disruptive behavior earned reinforcement).

The 46 studies reviewed by Slavin (1983) indicate that cooperative learning strategies that used group rewards and individual accountability lead to higher academic achievement gains than competitive or individual incentive systems. Although cooperative learning strategies have focused on school achievement, many researchers and practitioners would hold academic achievement to be secondary to the social interaction benefits of cooperative learning. These procedures have been shown to increase a variety of prosocial behaviors such as helping, sharing, cooperating, and generalization of cooperation to other settings (Johnson & Johnson, 1983; Slavin, 1983).

It would appear that CLS could be used to indirectly teach social skills to children in classroom settings because the contingencies of reinforcement require cooperating, helping, and sharing from all group members. This strategy would most likely be acceptable to teachers because the salient effects of CLS are a quieter classroom (model behavioral profile), in which students produce more academic tasks that are accurate.

SOCIAL VALIDITY OF THE MAINSTREAMING CONCEPT

The present concept of mainstreaming and the resulting emphasis on education in so-called least restrictive environments has been in existence for about 16 years. Dunn's (1968) classic article condemning special class placements for the majority of mildly handicapped learners heightened awareness of special educators regarding the disappointing effects of special education.

Mainstreaming was born from a larger sociopolitical-legalistic philosophy, which viewed racially segregated education as inherently unequal, and hence, in violation of the civil rights of racial minorities. Extension of this same reasoning to the rights of handicapped children further involved the courts, state legislatures, and Congress in providing appropriate education for handicapped children (Gottlieb, 1981).

Mainstreaming, or, more accurately, education in the LRE, is a social policy that springs from the judicial and legislative governmental arena rather than from empirical social science or from the values and priorities of the majority of our population. As such, the decision to impose the LRE requirement on the schools was not made on the basis of whether this is desirable, beneficial, important, or even potentially damaging to handicapped and nonhandicapped children. In short, the social validity of the concept of mainstreaming was never considered before, during, or after its implementation as a social policy.

Social validity is an important concept that stresses the importance of considering the social context for deciding the goals of intervention procedures, the appropriateness or acceptability of these interventions, and evaluating the outcomes produced by interventions (Kazdin & Matson, 1981). Wolf (1978), perhaps most clearly, articulated the concept of social validation by stating that it occurs on three levels: the social significance of the goals of an intervention; the social acceptability of the intervention procedures used to accomplish these goals; and the social importance of the effects or outcomes produced by interventions. These dimensions of social validity are discussed in relation to the mainstreaming concept.

Social Significance

Determining the social significance of any intervention procedure forces one to ask the following question: Are the specific behavioral goals of the intervention really what society wants? It is important to recognize that the social significance of behavioral goals are typically based on subjective evaluation (Kazdin, 1977; Wolf, 1978; Van Houten, 1979). Subjective evaluations are judgments made by persons who are in a special position to judge behavioral goals, given their involvement in, and/or vested interest in, the goals of interventions.

It is obvious from the polemics, discussions, and documentation surrounding mainstreaming that no one seems to have asked the question regarding the social significance of mainstreaming goals. Worse still, we are certainly nowhere near an answer to this unposed question, other than a series of faulty assumptions (previously discussed) and a plethora of personal opinions.

What are the behavioral goals of mainstreaming? Are these goals what society wants? Perhaps a place to start answering this question would be to look into the special education literature for a hint as to the goals of mainstreaming. Fig. 2.4 depicts the goals of mainstreaming mentioned in the literature. (See reviews by Asher & Taylor, 1981; Gottlieb, 1981; Gottlieb & Leyser, 1981; Gresham, 1981a, 1982a, 1983b; Levine, Hummel, & Salzer, 1982; Madden & Slavin, 1983; Semmel, Gottlieb,& Robinson, 1979).

One can see that these goals are not well operationalized or specified. As such, we have a list of amorphous goals that can take on a variety of different meanings. Most important, we have no idea as to the social significance of these goals as judged by society.

Some detractors may say that the judicial and legislative bases for the LRE mandate, by definition, makes the goals in Fig. 12.4 socially valid. One must remember, however, that these goals have never been clearly specified by social policy makers nor has their relative significance for handicapped children been judged. Mandated education in LREs has little to do with the social significance of the goals of this policy. It perhaps has even less to with the educational and psychological benefits of these goals.

It is now time to clearly specify and operationalize the goals of mainstreaming. After such specification, we will be in a position to judge the social significance of these goals using social validation procedures. Mainstreaming will never be

---

1) Normalization of handicapped children
2) Education of all handicapped children in the least restrictive environment
3) Placement of handicapped children in regular classrooms for a portion of the school day
4) Instructional integration of handicapped children with non-handicapped children
5) Social integration of handicapped children with non-handicapped children
6) Peer acceptance of handicapped children by nonhandicapped children
7) Academic achievement
8) Positive social interaction between handicapped children and nonhandicapped children
9) Improved self-concept or enhanced self-esteem of handicapped children
10) Reduction of stigma and bias against handicapped children
11) Acceptance of handicapped children by regular educators
12) Better psychological and social adjustment of handicapped children
13) Opportunities to learn from age-appropriate role models in regular classrooms

---

Fig. 12.4 Goals of mainstreaming derived from the literature

an effective social policy intervention unless we clearly specify and prioritize its goals.

Social Acceptability

The social acceptability of an intervention procedure forces one to ask the following questions: Do the ends justify the means? Do the participants, caregivers, and consumers consider the intervention procedure acceptable? Acceptability is a broad term and encompasses whether an intervention is appropriate for a given problem, whether it is fair, reasonable, or intrusive, and whether the intervention is consistent with conventional notions of what an intervention should be (Kazdin, 1980). In short, acceptability consists of judgments from intervention consumers pertaining to whether or not they like the intervention procedure (Witt & Elliott, in press).

How acceptable are the procedures used to implement mainstreaming in the schools? Again, we have no clearcut answers to this question and must rely on research that has only tangentially addressed this issue.

Ringlaben and Price (1981) presented a study in which regular educators were asked their opinions regarding the effects of mainstreaming. Results of this study showed that 26% of the sample felt that mainstreaming had a *negative effect* on nonhandicapped children and 54% felt that regular students had no beneficial effect on mainstreamed handicapped students. Moreover, 70% of the sample felt that mainstreaming was not working in their classrooms. These data would suggest that regular educators view mainstreaming as a relatively unacceptable intervention in their classrooms. Thus, the mere *physical placement* or physical presence of a handicapped child in some teachers' regular classrooms without the teacher having to alter the curriculum or teaching style, appears to be unacceptable.

In their review, Madden and Slavin (1983) cite two well-designed and well-controlled studies that showed superior academic gains for mildly handicapped students in regular classes over their special class counterparts (Calhoun & Elliott, 1977; Leinhardt, 1980). The curriculum in both settings was identical and consisted of individualized instruction for all handicapped students. One must ask the question: How much regular class teachers would find it acceptable to individualize instruction for one or two handicapped children in their classrooms? Given that many teachers view mainstreaming negatively and that the mere physical presence of handicapped children in their classes is sometimes viewed as detrimental to nonhandicapped children, how can individualized instruction (which requires teacher time, effort, etc.) by viewed as acceptable? Although there are no specific data to answer this question conclusively, a reasonable hypothesis would be that regular class teachers would view individualized instruction for mainstreamed handicapped children as an unacceptable practice.

Social skills training has been promulgated by many to enhance the social competence outcomes of handicapped children in mainstream classrooms (Gresham, 1981b, 1982a, 1983a; Madden & Slavin, 1983; Stephens, 1978; Walker in press). Teaching appropriate interpersonal behaviors directly in regular classrooms is a potentially powerful means of promoting the social acceptance of handicapped children and in facilitating the overall social development of handicapped children. However, teachers view social skills, such as cooperation, appropriate peer interaction, sharing, and the like, as being relatively unimportant in their classrooms (Hersh & Walker, 1983). That is, social skills training would probably be perceived as being a relatively unacceptable intervention in regular classrooms. Although social skills training with handicapped children in regular classrooms would in all liklihood be effective, it presently is not being implemented on any kind of large-scale basis, probably because of the unimportance regular teachers assign to these behaviors in their classrooms.

It seems relatively clear that, generally speaking, teachers harbor somewhat negative attitudes toward mainstreaming. As a result of these attitudes, teachers would probably find individualized instruction and social skills training as being unacceptable interventions in their classrooms in spite of the potential efficacy of these procedures. Previous research has demonstrated that the acceptability of interventions is strongly related to the amount of time, effort, resources, and expertise needed to implement a given intervention. (See Witt & Elliott, 1985 for a review.) Thus, individualized instruction and social skills training are perhaps viewed as unacceptable to teachers because of the time required, the resources needed (e.g., curricula, materials, etc.), and the expertise that is essential for effective implementation of these procedures.

Social Importance

Evaluating the social importance of the effects produced by a given intervention requires one to ask the following question: Does the quantity and quality of behavior change make a difference in terms of an individual's functioning in society? In other words, do changes in targeted behaviors predict an individual's standing on important social outcomes (Gresham, 1983b)?

Two methods have been discussed as means of establishing the social importance of effects produced by interventions: (a) subjective evaluation and (b) social comparison (Kazdin, 1977; Kazdin & Matson, 1981; Van Houten, 1979; Wolf, 1978). Subjective evaluation involves asking persons who are in a special position to judge the importance of the effects produced by a given intervention. Social comparison consists of comparing the level of behavior of children after intervention with the behavior of normal peers (i.e., a norm-referenced comparison).

Are the effects produced by mainstreaming socially important? Again, we have to rely on related data because no studies have formally addressed this issue. The desired outcomes of mainstreaming have previously been discussed in the section concerning the social significance of the goals of mainstreaming. Briefly, these can be classified into the following categories: (a) peer acceptance; (b) positive peer interaction; (c) negative peer interaction; (d) self-concept of handicapped children; (e) academic achievement of mainstreamed handicapped children.

Using social comparison criteria, has mainstreaming produced socially important effects in terms of moving mainstreamed handicapped children into normal ranges of functioning? The answer to this question, using currently available studies must be a resounding no. There are no data to suggest that mainstreaming, as currently practiced, results in handicapped children being moved into normative ranges of functioning in the areas of peer interaction, peer acceptance, self-concept, or academic achievement. At least 10 major reviews of the mainstreaming literature since 1975 have offered little evidence for the social importance of the effects produced by mainstreaming using social comparison procedures (Asher & Taylor, 1981; Gottlieb, 1981; Gottlieb & Leyser, 1981; Gresham, 1981a, 1982a, in press a; Kaufman et al., 1975; Levine, Hummel, & Salzar, 1982; Madden & Slavin, 1983; Semmel, Gottlieb, & Robinson, 1979).

The foregoing discussion of social validity suggests that the goals of mainstreaming may be considered socially insignificant by many; that the social acceptability of mainstreaming as an intervention is relative low; and that mainstreaming does not produce socially important effects for the majority of handicapped children. As such, it appears that the social validity of the mainstreaming concept is, at best, questionable using currently available data.

CONCLUSIONS AND FUTURE DIRECTIONS

Philosophically, mainstreaming calls for the temporal, instructional, and social integration of handicapped children with nonhandicapped children. Pragmatically, mainstreaming involves the physical placement of handicapped children in regular classrooms for a portion of the school day. Empirically, the social outcomes of mainstreaming are: poor social acceptance of handicapped children by nonhandicapped peers; low and often negative rates of social interaction between handicapped and nonhandicapped children; poor self-concepts of many mainstreamed handicapped children; and a general negative attitude towards mainstreaming held by regular educators.

Four potential reasons for the social outcomes of mainstreaming were identified in this chapter. These were: (a) the faulty assumptions underlying mainstreaming; (b) the values and priorities schools hold regarding academic achievement; (c) the motivational deficits of handicapped children; and (d) the social behavior standards held by regular educators. These four phenomena all interact to produce the disappointing social outcomes of mainstreaming. Moreover, there is little evidence to support the social validity of the mainstreaming concept on the dimensions of the social significance of its goals, the social acceptability of its procedures by teachers, or the social importance of the effects produced by it.

Social skills training was identified as a potentially viable means of improving the social outcomes of mainstreaming. It was demonstrated, however, that social skills do not fit the model behavioral profile expected by teachers in the regular classroom. Several procedures were identified as a possible means of indirectly teaching social skills in regular classrooms. Teaching handicapped children to recruit natural communities of reinforcement; using peer initiation strategies to promote recriprocal social exchanges between handicapped and nonhandicapped children; and cooperative learning, all hold great promise for improving the social outcomes of mainstreaming.

Education of handicapped children in the least restrictive environment represents a social policy decision based on a legalistic rather than a scientific philosophy. A close, hard look at the empirical social outcomes of mainstreaming as an intervention in the schools suggests that is has not produced the desired effects (i.e., the instructional and social integration of handicapped children with nonhandicapped children). It is time to empirically establish the social significance of mainstreaming goals, the social acceptability of intervention procedures to accomplish these goals, and to evaluate the social importance of the effects produced by education in least restrictive environments. To do less would deny handicapped children their more basic right to an appropriate education.

REFERENCES

Allen, K. E., Benning, P. M., & Drummond, T. W. (1972). Integration of normal and handicapped children in a behavior modification preschool: A case study. In G. Semb (Ed)., *Behavior analysis and education*. Lawrence, Kansas: University of Kansas Press.

Allen, K. E., Hart, B. M., Buell, J. S., Harris, F. R., & Wolf, M. M. (1964). Effects of social reinforcement on isolate behavior of a nursery school child. *Child Development, 35*, 511–518.

Apolloni, T., & Cooke, T. P. (1978). Integrated programming at the infant, toddler, and preschool levels. In J. J. Guralnick (Ed.), *Early intervention and the integration of handicapped and nonhandicapped children*. Baltimore: University Park Press.

Asher, S. R., & Hymel, S. (1981). Children's social competence in peer relations: Sociometric and behavioral assessment. In J. D. Wine & M. D. Smye (Eds.), *Social competence*. New York: Guilford.

Asher, S. R., Oden, S. L., & Gottman, J. M. (1977). Children's friendships in school settings. In L. G. Katz (Ed.), *Current topics in early childhood education* (Vol. 1). Norwood, NJ: Ablex.

Asher, S. R., & Taylor, A. R. (1981). The social outcomes of mainstreaming: Sociometric assessment and beyond. *Exceptional Education Quarterly, 1,* 13–30.

Ballard, M., Corman, L., Gottlieb, J., & Kaufman, M. J. (1977). Improving the social status of mainstreamed retarded children. *Journal of Educational Psychology, 69,* 605–611.

Bandura, A. (1969). *Principles of behavior modification*. New York: Holt, Rinehart, & Winston.

Bandura, A. (1977a). *Social learning theory*. Englewood Cliffs, NJ: Prentice-Hall.

Bandura, A. (1977b). Self-efficacy: Toward a unifying theory of behavior change. *Psychological Review, 84,* 191–215.

Bandura, A. (1982). Self-efficacy mechanism in human agency. *American Psychologist, 37,* 122–147.

Barrish, H. H., Saunders, M., & Wolf, M. M. (1969). Good behavior game: Effects of individual contingencies for group consequences on disruptive behavior in a classroom. *Journal of Applied Behavior Analysis, 2,* 119–124.

Bellack, A. S., & Hersen, M. (Eds.). (1979). *Research and practice in social skills training.* New York: Plenum.

Bolstad, O. D., & Johnson, S. M. (1972). Self-regulation in the modification of disruptive classroom behavior. *Journal of Applied Behavior Analysis, 5,* 443–454.

Brophy, J. (1981). Teacher praise: A functional analysis. *Review of Educational Research, 51,* 5–32.

Brophy, J., & Good, T. (1974). *Teacher-student relationships: Causes and consequences.* New York: Holt, Rinehart, & Winston.

Bryan, T. S. (1974). Peer popularity of learning disabled children. *Journal of Learning Disabilities, 7,* 621–625.

Bryan, T. S. (1976). Peer popularity of learning disabled children: A replication. *Journal of Learning Disabilities, 9,* 307–311.

Bryan, T. S. (1978). Social relationships and verbal interactions of learning disabled children. *Journal of Learning Disabilities, 11,* 107–115.

Calhoun, G., & Elliott, R. (1977). Self-concept and academic achievement of educable retarded and emotionally disturbed pupils. *Exceptional Children, 44,* 379–380.

Cantor, N. L., & Gelfand, D. M. (1977). Effects of responsiveness and sex of children on adults' behavior. *Child Development, 48,* 232–238

Cartledge, G., & Milburn, J. (1978). The case for teaching social skills in the classroom: A review. *Review of Educational Research, 48,* 133–156.

Combs, M. L., & Slaby, D. A. (1977). Social skills training with children. In B. B. Lahey & A. E. Kazdin (Eds.), *Advances in child clinical psychology* (Vol. 1). New York: Plenum.

Cooke, T. P., Apolloni, T., & Cooke, S. A. (1977). Normal preschool children as behavior models for retarded peers. *Exceptional Children, 43,* 531–532.

Cromwell, R. L. (1963). A social learning approach to mental retardation. In N. R. Ellis (Ed.), *Handbook of mental deficiency.* New York: McGraw-Hill.

Dunn, L. M. (1968). Special education for the mildly retarded: Is much of it justifiable? *Exceptional Children, 35,* 5–22.

Foster, S. L., & Ritchey, W. L. (1979). Issues in the assessment of social competence in children. *Journal of Applied Behavior Analysis, 12,* 625–638.

Gamble, R., & Strain, R. S. (1979). The effects of dependent and interdependent group contingencies on socially appropriate responses in classes for emotionally handicapped children. *Psychology in the Schools, 16,* 253–260.

Good, T., & Brophy, J. (1978). *Looking in classrooms.* New York: Harper & Row.

Goodman, H., Gottlieb, J., & Harrison, R. N. (1972). Social acceptance of EMRs integrated into a nongraded elementary school. *American Journal of Mental Deficiency, 76,* 412–417.

Gottlieb, J. (1975). Attitudes toward retarded children: Effects of labeling and behavioral aggressiveness. *Journal of Educational Psychology, 67,* 581–585.

Gottlieb, J. (1981). Mainstreaming: Fulfilling the promise. *American Journal of Mental Deficiency, 86,* 115–126.

Gottlieb, J., & Budoff, M. (1973). Social acceptability of retarded children in nongraded schools differing in architecture. *American Journal of Mental Deficiency, 78,* 15–19.

Gottlieb, J., & Leyser, Y. (1981). Facilitating the social mainstreaming of retarded children. *Exceptional Education Quarterly, 1,* 57–70.

Gottman, J. M. (1977). The effects of a modeling film on social isolation in preschool children: A methodological investigation. *Journal of Abnormal Child Psychology, 5,* 69–78.

Graubard, P. S., Rosenberg, H., & Miller, M. B. (1971). Student applications of behavior modification to teachers and environments or ecological approaches to social deviancy. In E. A. Ramp and B. L. Hopkins (Eds.), *A new direction for education: Behavior analysis.* Lawrence, Kansas: Support and Development Center for Follow Through.

Green, K. D., Forehand, R., Beck, S. J., & Vosk, B. (1980). An assessment of the relationship among measures of children's social competence and children's academic achievement. *Child Development, 51,* 1149–1156.

Greenspan, S. (1981). Social competence and handicapped individuals: Practical implications and a proposed model. *Advances in Special Education, 3,* 41–82.

Greenwood, C., Todd, N., Hops, H., & Walker, H. (1982). Behavior change targets in the assessment and treatment of socially withdrawn preschool children. *Behavioral Assessment, 4,* 237–297.

Greenwood, C. R., Walker, H. M., & Hops, H. (1977). Issues in social interaction/withdrawal assessment. *Exceptional Children, 43,* 490–499.

Greenwood, C. R., Walker, H. M., Todd, N., & Hops, H. (1979). Selecting a cost-effective screening measure for the assessment of preschool social withdrawal. *Journal of Applied Behavior Analysis, 12,* 639–652.

Gresham, F. M. (1981a). Social skills training with handicapped children: A review. *Review of Educational Research, 51,* 139–176.

Gresham, F. M. (1981b). Assessment of children's social skills. *Journal of School Psychology, 19,* 120–133.

Gresham, F. M. (1981c). Validity of social skills measures for assessing the social competence in low-status children. A multivariate investigation. *Developmental Psychology, 17,* 390–398.

Gresham, F. M. (1982a). Misguided mainstreaming: The case for social skills training with handicapped children. *Exceptional Children, 48,* 422–433.

Gresham, F. M. (1982b). Social skills instruction for exceptional children. *Theory into Practice,* 129–133.

Gresham, F. M. (1982c). *Social skills: Principles, practices, and procedures.* Des Moines, Iowa: Iowa Department of Public Instruction.

Gresham, F. M. (1983a). Social skills assessment as a component of mainstreaming placement decisions. *Exceptional Children, 49,* 331–336.

Gresham, F. M. (1983b). Social validity in the assessment of children's social skills: Establishing standards for social competency. *Journal of Psychoeducational Assessment, 1,* 297–307.

Gresham, F. M. (in press a). Conceptual issues in the assessment of social competence in children. In P. Strain, M. Guralnick, & H. Walker (Eds.), *Children's social behavior: Development, assessment, and modification.* New York: Academic Press.

Gresham, F. M. (1984). Social skills and self-efficacy for exceptional children: A refocusing of the mainstreaming process. *Exceptional Children, 51,* 253–261.

Gresham, F. M., & Elliott, S. N. (1984). Advances in the assessment of children's social skills. *School Psychology Review, 13,* 292–301.

Gresham, F. M., & Gresham, G. N. (1982). Interdependent, dependent, and independent group contingencies for controlling disruptive behavior. *Journal of Special Education, 16,* 101–110.

Gresham, F. M., & Lemanek, K. L. (1983). Social skills: A review of cognitive-behavioral training procedures with children. *Journal of Applied Developmental Psychology, 4,* 439–461.

Grossman, H. J. (1973). *Manual on terminology and classification in mental retardation.* Washington, D.C.: American Association on Mental Deficiency.

Harter, S. (1978). Effectance motivation reconsidered: Toward a developmental model. *Human Development, 21,* 34–64.

Hartup, W. W., Glazer, J. A., & Charlesworth, R. (1967). Peer reinforcement and sociometric status. *Child Development, 38,* 1017–1024.

Hersh, R. H., & Walker, H. M. (1983). Great expectations: Making schools effective for all students. *Policy Studies Review, 2,* 147–188.

Iano, R. P., Ayers, D., Heller, H. B., McGettigan, J. F., & Walker, V. S. (1974). Sociometric status of retarded children in an integrative program. *Exceptional Children, 40,* 267–271.

Johnson, R., & Johnson, D. W. (1983). Effects of cooperative, competitive, and individualistic learning experiences on cross-handicap relationships and social development. *Exceptional Children, 49,* 323–329.

Kaufman, M., Gottlieb, J., Agard, J., & Kukic, M. (1975). Mainstreaming: Toward an explication of the construct. In E. L. Meyer, G. A. Vergason, & R. J. Whelan (Eds.), *Alternatives for teaching exceptional children.* Denver: Love.

Kazdin, A. E. (1977). Assessing the clinical or applied importance of behavior change through social validation. *Behavior Modification, 1,* 427–451.

Kazdin, A. E. (1980). Acceptability of alternative treatments for deviant child behavior. *Journal of Applied Behavior Analysis, 13,* 259–273.

Kazdin, A. E., & Matson, J. L. (1981). Social validation in mental retardation. *Applied Research in Mental Retardation, 2,* 39–53.

Kendall, P. C., & Braswell, L. (1982). Assessment for cognitive behavioral interventions in the schools. *School Psychology Review, 11,* 21–31.

Ladd, G. W. (1981). Effectiveness of a social learning method for enhancing children's social interaction and peer acceptance. *Child Development, 52,* 171–178.

Leinhardt, G. (1980). Transition rooms: Promoting maturation or reducing education? *Journal of Educational Psychology, 72,* 55–61.

Leland, H. W. (1978). Theoretical considerations of adaptive behavior. In A. Coulter & H. Morrow (Eds.), *Adaptive behavior: Concepts and measurements.* New York: Grune & Stratton.

Levine M., Hummel, J. W., & Salzer, R. T. (1982). Mainstreaming requires something more: The person-environment fit. *Clinical Psychology Review, 2,* 1–25.

Litow, L. & Pumroy, D. (1975). A brief review of classroom group-oriented contingencies. *Journal of Applied Behavior Analysis, 8,* 341–347.

Madden, N. A., & Slavin, R. E. (1983). Mainstreaming students with mild handicaps: Academic and social outcomes. *Review of Educational Research, 53,* 519–569.

Marburg, C. C., Houston, B. K., & Holmes, D. S. (1976). Influence of multiple models on the behavior of institutionalized retarded children: Increased generalization to other models and other behaviors. *Journal of Consulting and Clinical Psychology, 44,* 541–519.

Marshall, H. R., & McCandless, B. R. (1957). A study in the prediction of social behavior of preschool children. *Child Development, 28,* 149–159.

McCandless, B. R., & Marshall, H. R. (1957). Sex differences in social acceptance and participation of preschool children. *Child Development, 28,* 421–425.

McFall, R. M. (1982). A review and reformulation of the concept of social skills. *Behavioral Assessment, 4,* 1–33.

McGuire, J. M. (1973). Aggression and Sociometric status with preschool children. *Sociometry, 36,* 542–549.

Meichenbaum, D. (1977). Cognitive behavior modification. New York: Plenum.

Moore, S. G., & Updegraff, R. (1964). Sociometric status of preschool children related to age, sex, nurturance giving, and dependency. *Child Development, 35,* 519–524.

Morgan, S. R. (1977). A descriptive analysis of maladjusted behavior in socially rejected children. *Behavioral Disorders, 3,* 23–30.

Oden, S. L., & Asher, S. R. (1977). Coaching children in social skills for friendship making. *Child Development, 48,* 496–506.

O'Leary, S. G., & Dubey, D. R. (1979). Applications of self-control procedures by children: A review. *Journal of Applied Behavior Analysis, 12,* 449–465.

Ray, J. S. (1974). *Behavior of developmentally delayed and non-delayed toddler-age children:* An ethological study. Unpublished doctoral dissertation. George Peabody College.

Reschly, D. J. (1979). Nonbiased assessment. In G. Phye, & D. Reschly (Eds.), *School psychology: Perspectives and issues*. New York: Academic Press.

Reschly, D. J. (1982). Assessing mild mental retardation: The influence of adaptive behavior, sociocultural status, and prospects for nonbiased assessment. In C. R. Reynolds & T. B. Gutkin (Eds.), *The handbook of school psychology*. New York: Wiley.

Reschly, D. J., & Gresham, F. M. (1981). *Use of social competence measures to facilitate parent and teacher involvement and nonbiased assessment*. Unpublished manuscript. Iowa State University.

Ringlaben, R., & Price, J. (1981). Regular classroom teachers' perceptions of mainstreaming effect. *Exceptional Children, 47*, 302–304.

Rogers-Warren, A., & Baer, D. M. (1976). Saying and doing: The verbal mediation of social behaviors. *Journal of Applied Behavior Analysis, 9*, 335–354.

Rosenbaum, M. S., & Drabman, R. S. (1979). Self-control training in the classroom: A review and critique. *Journal of Applied Behavior Analysis, 12*, 467–485.

Seligman, M. (1975). *Helplessness: On depression, development, and death*. San Francisco: Freeman.

Semmel, M. I., Gottlieb, J., & Robinson, N. M. (1979). Mainstreaming: Perspectives on educating handicapped children in the public schools. In D. Berliner (Ed.), *Review of research in education* (pp. 223–279). (Vol. 7). Washington, D.C.: American Educational Research Association.

Seymour, F. W., & Stokes, T. F. (1976). Self-recording in training girls to increase work and evoke staff praise in an institution for offenders. *Journal of Applied Behavior Analysis, 9*, 41–54.

Singleton, L. C., & Asher, S. R. (1977). Peer preferences and social interaction among third-grade children in an integrated school district. *Journal of Educational Psychology, 69*, 330–336.

Slavin, R. E. (1983). When does cooperative learning increase student achievement? *Psychological Bulletin, 94*, 429–445.

Stephens, T. M. (1978). *Social skills in the classroom*. Columbus, OH: Cedars Press.

Stokes, T. F., & Baer, D. M. (1977). An implicit technology of generalization. *Journal of Applied Behavior Analysis, 10*, 349–367.

Stokes, T. F., Fowler, S. A., & Baer, D. M. (1978). Training preschool children to recruit natural communities of reinforcement. *Journal of Applied Behavior Analysis, 11*, 285–303.

Strain, P. S. (1975). Increasing social play of severely retarded preschoolers with sociodramatic activities. *Mental Retardation, 13*, 7–9.

Strain, P. S. (1977). An experimental analysis of peer social initiations on the behavior of withdrawn preschool children: Some training and generalization effects. *Journal of Abnormal Child Psychology, 5*, 445–455.

Strain, P. S., Cooke, R. P., & Apolloni, T. (1976). *Teaching exceptional children: Assessing and modifying social behavior*. New York: Academic Press.

Strain, P. S., & Fox, J. E. (1981). Peers as behavior change agents for withdrawn classmates. In A. E. Kazdin & B. Lahey (Eds.), *Advances in clinical child psychology*. (Vol. 4). New York: Plenum.

Strain, P. S., Shores, R. E., & Timm, M. A. (1977). Effects of peer social initiations on the behavior of withdrawn preschool children. *Journal of Applied Behavior Analysis, 10*, 289–298.

Stumme, V. S., Gresham, F. M., & Scott, N. A. (1982). Validity of *Social Behavior Assessment* in discriminating emotionally disabled from nonhandicapped students. *Journal of Behavioral Assessment, 4*, 327–342.

Stumme, V. S., Gresham, F. M., & Scott, N. A. (1983). Dimensions of children's classroom social behavior. *Journal of Behavioral Assessment, 5*, 161–177.

Thomas, A. (1979). Learned helplessness and expectancy factors: Implications for research in learning disabilities. *Review of Educational Research, 49*, 208–221.

Timar, T. B., & Gutherie, J. W. (1980). Public values and public school policy in the 1980s. *Educational Leader, 81*, 112–115.

Van Houten, R. (1979). Social validation: The evolution of standards of competency for target behaviors. *Journal of Applied Behavior Analysis, 12*, 581–591.

Walker, H. M. (in press). The SBS Program (Social Behavior Survival): A systematic approach to the integration of handicapped children into less restrictive settings. *Education and Treatment of Children.*

White, R. W. (1959). Motivation reconsidered: The concept of competence. *Psychological Review, 66,* 287–333.

Winnett, R. A., & Winkler, R. C. (1972). Current behavior modification in the classroom: Be still, be quiet, be docile. *Journal of Applied Behavior Analysis, 5,* 499–504.

Witt, J. C., & Elliott, S. N. (1985). Acceptability of classroom management strategies. In T. R. Kratochwill (Ed.), *Advances in school psychology* (Vol. IV, pp. 251–288). Hillsdale, NJ: Lawrence Erlbaum Associates.

Wolf, M. M. (1978). Social validity: The case for subjective measurement or how applied behavior analysis is finding its heart. *Journal of Applied Behavior Analysis, 11,* 203–214.

Zigler, E. (1971). The retarded child as a whole person. In P. Adams, & D. Boardman (Eds.), *Advances in experimental clinical psychology* New York: Pergamon.

Zwald, L., & Gresham, F. M. (1983). Behavioral consultation in a secondary class: Using DRL to decrease negative verbal interactions. *School Psychology Review, 11,* 428–432.

13 Impact of Classroom Organization and Instructional Methods on the Effectiveness of Mainstreaming

David W. Johnson
Roger T. Johnson
University of Minnesota

Mainstreaming is based on the assumption that placing heterogenous students (in terms of handicapping conditions) in the same school and classroom will facilitate positive relationships and attitudes among the students. Yet there is considerable disagreement among social scientists as to whether there are conditions under which physical proximity between handicapped and nonhandicapped students will lead to constructive relationships. The lack of theoretical models and apparently inconsistent research findings have left the impression that mainstreaming may not be working and may not be constructive. Selective reviews that have contained only a subset of studies and seemingly partisan research efforts have added confusion about what conclusions may be valid. Perhaps the key factor identified by the research as determining whether mainstreaming promotes positive or negative relationships among heterogenous students is whether the students cooperate, compete, or work independently on their academic assignments. By structuring positive, negative, or no goal interdependence among heterogeneous students during academic learning situations, teachers can influence the pattern of interaction among students and the interpersonal attraction that results (Deutsch, 1962; Johnson & Johnson, 1975; Johnson Johnson Holubec, & Roy, 1984).

Lewin's theory of motivation postulates that a state of tension within an individual motivates movement toward the accomplishment of desired goals and that it is a drive for goal accomplishment that motivates cooperative, competitive, or individualistic behavior. Deutsch (1949, 1962), in formalizing a theory of how the tension systems of different people are interrelated, conceptualized three types of goal structures that organize interpersonal behavior: cooperative, competitive, and individualistic. In a *cooperative* goal structure, the goals of the separate individuals are so linked together that there is a positive correlation among their goal attainments. Under purely cooperative conditions, individuals can attain their goals. Thus, a person seeks an outcome that is beneficial to all those with whom he or she is cooperatively linked. In a *competitive* social situation, the goals of the separate participants are so linked that there is a negative correlation among their goal attainments. An individual can attain his or her goal if and only if the other participants cannot attain their goals. Thus, a person seeks an outcome that is personally beneficial, but is detrimental to the others with whom he or she is competitively linked. Finally, in an *individualistic* situation there is no correlation among the goal attainments of the participants. Whether an individual accomplishes his or her goal has no influence on whether other individuals achieve their goals. Thus, a person seeks an outcome that is personally beneficial, ignoring as irrelevant the efforts of goal achievement of other participants in the situation.

OUR RESEARCH PROGRAM

For the past eight years, we have been conducting a program of research on the relative impact of cooperative, competitive, and individualistic experiences on mainstreaming. The pattern of activities has been to develop a theoretical model, conduct a series of studies to validate the theory, conduct large-scale meta-analyses of all the relevant studies, operationalize the results for teachers, and work with numerous school districts throughout North America to implement cooperative learning procedures in mainstream classrooms. Our implementation efforts lead to new issues, which we explore in research studies. The material reviewed in this chapter is based on the interaction between theory, research, and practice.

Basically, we chose to conduct highly controlled field-experimental studies in actual classrooms and schools. The typical study lasted 3 weeks, compared cooperative learning situations with individualistic and/or competitive learning situations, and involved students from different ethnic groups and ability levels. We obtained the help of three classroom teachers who agreed to assist us in conducting the study. In order to ensure that there were no differences among students in each condition, students were randomly assigned making sure that there were an equal number of males and females, majority and minority, and high-, medium-, and low-ability students in each condition. To ensure that the high quality teaching occurred in each condition, the teachers received a minimum of 90 hours of training on how to implement cooperative, competitive, and individualistic learning situations and were given a daily script to follow. Any differences among conditions we found were not due to differences in teaching ability. The teachers were rotated across conditions, so that each teacher taught each condition for one week. The ways we implemented cooperative, competitive, and individualistic learning were carefully structured to be unambiguous so that the study did in fact test our theory. The students studied the identical curriculum. To verify that the teachers were teaching the conditions appropriately, we observed them daily. Finally, observations of how students interacted with each other were collected. We were determined to conduct our research in as highly controlled and careful a way as possible so we could be confident about the results. What follows is a summary of our theory and research and a brief description of the meta-analysis we conducted to help test the theory.

Much of the research conducted in intergroup relations between 1930 and 1970 indicated that cooperative interdependence was a key aspect in structuring interaction among heterogeneous individuals in a way that promoted positive relationships. However, very little theorizing about the processes through which cooperative experiences promoted interpersonal attraction accompanied this research. Consequently, the research on mainstreaming has lacked an appropriate theoretical framework within which to organize the existing research and to direct future research.

In response to this need for a theoretical framework, Johnson and Johnson (1980) proposed a model (see Fig. 13.1), which posits:

1. There are preinteraction negative attitudes existing between handicapped and nonhandicapped students.
2. Physical proximity is a necessary, but not sufficient, condition for a reduction of this negativity.
3. Depending on whether instruction is organized cooperatively, competitively, or individualistically, attitudes become more positive or more negative. A cooperative, compared with a competitive or individualistic, context promotes greater interpersonal attraction among heterogeneous individuals.
4. Part of the relationship between cooperative experiences and interpersonal attraction may be explained by the more constructive interaction patterns, the greater feelings of support and acceptance, the more accurate perspective taking, the more differentiated view of others, the higher self-esteem, and the greater success promoted by cooperation.

Preinteraction Attitudes

The first proposition states that both handicapped and nonhandicapped students have negative attitudes toward each other, even before they interact. There can be little doubt that in the United States handicapped students are viewed by nonhandicapped peers in negative and prejudiced ways, whether or not the handicapped children and adolescents are in the same or separate classrooms (Bruininks,1978; Bruininks, Rynders, & Gross, 1974; Bryan, 1974, 1978; Goodman, Gottlieb, & Harrison, 1972; Gottlieb & Budoff, 1973; Gottlieb & Davis, 1973: Gottlieb, Semmel, & Veldman, 1978; Heber & Heber, 1957; Iano, Ayers,

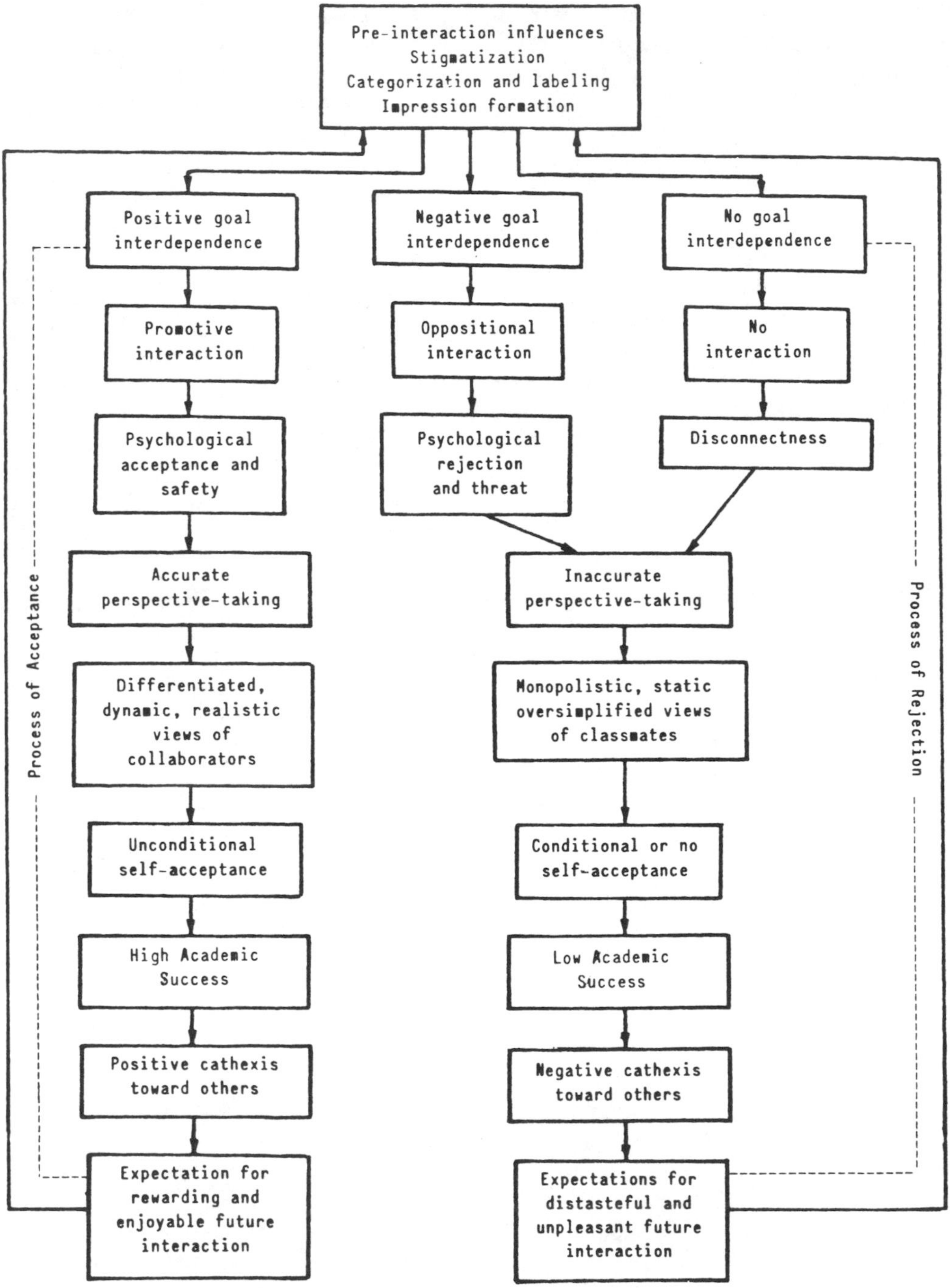

Fig. 13.1 Social judgment process.

Heller, McGettigan, & Walker, 1974; Jaffe, 1966; Johnson, 1950; Johnson & Kirk, 1950, Miller, 1956; Novak, 1975; Rucker, Howe, & Snider, 1969; Scranton & Ryckman, 1979; Siperstein, Bopp, & Bak, 1978, Vacc, 1972). Many teachers and nonhandicapped students have negative evaluations of handicapped students and low expectations for their performance (Combs & Harper, 1967; Guerin & Szatlocky, 1974; Jones, 1972; Kelley, 1973), regardless of the amount of time spent in physical proximity (Gottlieb, Semmel, & Veldman, 1978), the fact that the behavior of handicapped students has often been documented to be no different from the behavior of nonhandicapped students (Semmel, Gottlieb, & Robinson, 1979), and the observation that the presence of students with a history of engaging in inappropriate behavior (i.e., emotionally disturbed) does not necessarily create a disrupting effect on the regular class (Saunders, 1971). There is some evidence, furthermore, that the stigmas attached to handicaps transfer across settings. Even when learning-disabled children attend new schools with new classmates, they continue to be rejected (Bryan, 1974; Siperstein, Bopp, & Bak, 1978). Thus, stigmatization of each other by nonhandicapped and handicapped students takes place even before direct contact begins. Any categorization rule that provides a basis for classifying an individual as belonging to one social grouping as distinct from another can be sufficient to produce differentiation of attitudes toward the two groups in and of itself (Hamilton, 1976; Hensley & Duval, 1976; Tajfel, 1969, 1970).

When initial contact is made between handicapped and nonhandicapped students, first impressions are formed on the basis of "primary potency" characteristics that overshadow much observed behavior. Such first impressions may become monopolistic (taking into account only a few characteristics); static (remaining unchanged from situation to situation); and stereotyped; or they may become differentiated (taking into account many different characteristics); dynamic (in a constant state of change); and realistic, depending on the nature of the interaction that subsequently takes place between nonhandicapped and handicapped students. For many nonhandicapped students and teachers, the perception of a student as being handicapped results in a monopolistic, static, and stereotyped impression that leads to a negative evaluation and low expectations for performance. Once labeled as being handicapped, the strong possibility exists that the student will be rejected by nonhandicapped classmates. The same is true for nonhandicapped students being labeled by handicapped students.

Physical Proximity

Physical proximity among nonhandicapped and handicapped students is the beginning of an opportunity, but like all opportunities, it carries a risk of making things worse as well as the possibility of making things better. Physical proximity does not mean that nonhandicapped and handicapped students will like and accept each other.

Several studies indicate that placing handicapped and nonhandicapped students in physical proximity (e.g., the same classroom) may increase nonhandicapped students' prejudice toward and stereotyping and rejection of their handicapped peers (Goodman, Gottlieb, & Harrison, 1972; Gottlieb & Budoff, 1973; Gottlieb, Cohen, & Goldstein, 1974; Iano et al., 1974; Panda & Bartel, 1972; Porter, Ramsey, Trembly, Iaccobo, & Crawley, 1978). On the other hand, there is also evidence that placing handicapped and nonhandicapped students in the same classroom may result in more positive attitudes of nonhandicapped students toward their handicapped peers (Ballard, Corman, Gottlieb, & Kaufman, 1977; Higgs, 1975; Jaffe, 1966; Lapp, 1957; Sheare, 1975; Wechsler, Suarez, & McFadden, 1975).

During the initial interaction between handicapped and nonhandicapped classmates, furthermore, the nonhandicapped students may feel discomfort and show "interaction strain." Davis (1961), Jones (1970), Siller and Chipman (1967), and Whiteman and Lukoff (1964) found that physically nonhandicapped persons reported discomfort and uncertainty in interaction with physically handicapped peers. Nonhandicapped individuals interacting with a physically handicapped (as opposed to physically nonhandicapped) person have been found to exhibit greater motoric inhibition (Kleck, 1968); greater physiological arousal (Kleck, 1966); less variability in their behavior; a greater tendency to terminate interaction soon; more expressions of opinion not representative of their actual beliefs; fewer gestures; more reported discomfort in the interaction (Kleck, Ono, & Hastorf, 1966); and in the case of a person said to have epilepsy, greater maintenance of physical distance (Kleck, Buck, Goller, London, Pfeiffer, & Vukcevic, 1968). Jones (1970), furthermore, found that nonhandicapped college students who performed a learning task in the presence of a blind confederate (as opposed to a sighted confederate) reported stronger beliefs that they would have performed better on the task if the blind person had not been present, even when the actual performance data indicated that the presence of a blind or sighted person had no significant effects on the college students' achievement.

The nonhandicapped students may not be the only ones experiencing interaction strain in the mainstreaming situation. Comer and Piliavin (1972) found that handicapped students feel tension and discomfort when interacting with nonhandicapped peers. Farina, Glina, Boudreau, Allen, and Shermen (1971) found that when mental patients believed that another person knew of their psychiatric history (as opposed to believing that another person did not know) they felt less appreciated, found the task more difficult, and performed at a lower level. Moreover, objective observers perceived them to be more tense, anxious, and poorly adjusted than the patients who believed that their partners did not know their psychiatric status. In a previous study, Farina, Allen, and Saul (1968) demonstrated that merely believing another person views one in a stigmatized way creates expectations of being viewed negatively by others and rejected by them.

Another aspect of interaction between nonhandicapped and handicapped students is that the norm to be kind to the handicapped may result in over-friendliness by nonhandicapped students in initial encounters, which usually decreases with further interaction (Kleck, 1966). Handicapped students tend not to receive accurate feedback concerning the appropriateness of their own behavior and tend not to experience the normal behavior of nonhandicapped peers (Hastorf, Northcraft, & Picciotto, 1979) and may, as a result, become socially handicapped and believe that other people like them less the better those others get to know them.

Finally, there seems to be considerable ambivalence on the part of the nonhandicapped when interacting with the handicapped. In their review of the relevant research, Barker, Wright, Meyerson, and Gonick (1953) concluded that public, verbalized attitudes toward the handicapped are favorable on the average, whereas deeper, unverbalized feelings are frequently rejectant, a conclusion that is also made by Wright (1960). Doob and Ecker (1970) reported that nonhandicapped subjects were more willing to help a person with an eyepatch than a person without an eyepatch, but only when the helping did not entail sustained social contact. Gergan and Jones (1963) conducted an experiment in which nonhandicapped subjects displayed amplified positive or negative reactions to stimulus persons described as mental patients when the patients' behavior had had either favorable or unfavorable consequences for the subjects. Presumably, the stimulus person's behavior "split" the subject's ambivalent attitude so that one component was suppressed and the other component was enhanced. Dienstbier (1970) found a similar amplification of either positive or negative responses when white students interacted with black peers.

Goal Interdependence and Interpersonal Attraction

The third proposition is that the type of goal interdependence used to structure classroom learning determines whether the attitudes of heterogeneous students toward each other become more negative or more positive. Recently we conducted a meta-analysis of research comparing the relative impact of cooperative, competitive, and individualistic situations on interpersonal attraction between handicapped and nonhandicapped individuals (Johnson, Johnson, & Maruyama, 1983). Given the disagreement among social scientists as to whether mainstreaming can produce constructive cross-handicap relationships and the limitations of the summary-impression methodology used in previous reviews, there was a need for a comprehensive review of the existing research that examined the magnitude of any differences among the three goal structures as well as the probability of finding such differences. We reviewed 26 studies that yielded 105 relevant findings. Three types of meta-analysis were used: voting method, effect-size method, and *z*-score method. When cooperation was compared with interpersonal competition, the results (Table 13.1) favored cooperation with a voting method score of 14 to 0 with 9 no differences; an effect size of .86, indicating

Table 13.1
Meta-Analyses of Mainstreaming Findings

	Voting			Effect Size			z-score		
	N	*ND*	*P*	*M*	*SD*	*N*	*z*	*N*	*Fail-safe n*
Cooperative vs. group competitive	0	0	0	—	—	—	—	—	—
Cooperative vs. competitive	0	9	14	.86	.54	16	7.88	17	373
Group competitive vs. competitive	0	5	3	.41	.55	2	1.97	2	1
Cooperative vs. individualistic	0	6	48	.96	.55	30	15.39	33	2,856
Group competitive vs. individualistic	0	1	3	.82	.15	3	5.87	4	47
Competitive vs. individualistic	0	5	1	.27	.63	5	2.41	5	6

that the cross-handicap liking at the 50th percentile in the cooperative condition was comparable to the cross-handicap liking at the 81st percentile in the competitive condition; and a *z*-score of 7.88 ($p < .001$). When cooperative and individualistic conditions were compared, the results favored cooperation by a voting method score of 48 to 0 with 6 no differences; an effect size of .96, indicating that the average cross-handicap liking in the cooperative condition was equivalent to the cross-handicap liking at the 83rd percentile in the individualistic condition; and a *z*-score of 15.39 ($p < .0001$). There is, therefore, strong evidence that cooperative learning experiences promote more positive cross-handicap relationships than do competitive and individualistic ones. Our own studies, some of which have been completed since the previous review, may be described as follows (see Table 13.2):

1. Johnson, Rynders, Johnson, Schmidt, and Haider (1979) mainstreamed trainable mentally retarded students from a special station school into a junior high school bowling class with nonhandicapped students from public and private schools. Students were randomly assigned to cooperative, individualistic,and laissez-faire conditions, stratifying so that six nonhandicapped students and four trainable retarded students were in each condition. Teachers were randomly assigned to and rotated across conditions. Behavioral observations were conducted by trained observers who rotated among conditions. Average interrater reliability was 80–90%. A significantly greater number of positive cross-handicap interactions was found in the cooperative than in the other two conditions, with far more encouraging and accepting cross-handicap remarks being made.

2. The cooperative/individualistic design was also used by Martino and Johnson (1979) in the study of 12 second- and third-grade boys enrolled in a summer

beginning-swimming program that consisted of 11 sessions. A pretest measure asking students who they would like to work with if they learned to swim in pairs found that nonhandicapped students selected a learning-disabled peer; only one learning-disabled student chose a learning-disabled peer for a partner. Six nonhandicapped and six learning-disabled students were then randomly assigned to each condition and, in the cooperative condition, the nonhandicapped and learning-disabled students were randomly paired. Students received 45 minutes of instruction and then were given 15 minutes of free time to swim for fun. Over the nine days of instruction, only one friendly cross-handicap interaction was observed in the individualistic condition. In the cooperative condition, there were up to 20 friendly cross-handicap interactions with an average of 10 per free-time period. An average of three hostile cross-handicap interactions occurred each day in the individualistic condition, whereas in the cooperative condition there was an average of one per day. The learning-disabled students in the individualistic condition spent far more time alone than did their counterparts in the cooperative condition.

3. Cooper, Johnson, Johnson, and Wilderson (1980) compared the effects of cooperative, competitive, and individualistic learning situations on the cross-handicap interaction and relationships of 60 randomly selected junior high school students. Students were randomly assigned to conditions stratifying for sex and handicapped condition. Twelve of the students were either learning disabled or emotionally disturbed. The students studied together for 3 hours a day in English, science, and geography classes for 15 instructional days. On a sociometric nominations measure, students indicated more reciprocal cross-handicap helping in the cooperative than in the other two conditions and more cross-handicap friendships in the cooperative than the individualistic condition.

4. Rynders, Johnson, Johnson, and Schmidt (1980) conducted a subsequent study integrating severely handicapped Down's Syndrome students into a junior high school bowling class. Students were randomly assigned to cooperative, competitive, and individualistic conditions so that six nonhandicapped and four handicapped students were included in each condition. Working in pairs, instructors were rotated across conditions. Six trained observers collected behavioral data, obtaining an interrater agreement of 90%. On the average, each Down's Syndrome student interacted positively with nonhandicapped peers 29 times per hour in the cooperative condition as compared with two positive interactions per hour in the competitive condition and four positive interactions per hour in the individualistic condition.

5. In a study by Armstrong, Johnson and Balow (1981), 40 fifth- and sixth-grade students were randomly assigned to conditions, stratifying for achievement level (learning disabled or normal progress) and sex. The students participated in either cooperative or individualistic learning experiences. Certified, trained teachers were randomly assigned to each condition. The results indicate that greater interpersonal attraction between the learning-disabled and nonhandicapped students was evident in the cooperative condition.

Table 13.2
Mainstreaming Research Summary: Characteristics of Studies

	Johnson, Rynders, Johnson, Schmidt & Haider 1979	*Martino & Johnson 1979*	*Cooper, Johnson, Johnson & Wilderson 1980*	*Rynders, Johnson, Johnson & Schmidt 1980*
Length of Study	6 days	9 days	15 days	9 days
Grade Level	Jr. High	2 & 3	7	Jr. High
Subject Area	Bowling	Swimming	Science; English; Geography	Bowling
Group Size	10 (4)	2 (1)	4 (1)	10 (4)
Type of Heterogeneity	Trainable Retarded	Learning Disabled	Learning Disabled, Emotionally Disturbed	Trainable Retarded
Length of Instructional Session	60 min.	45 min.	180 min.	60 min.
Sample Size	30 (12)	12 (6)	60 (12)	30 (12)
Free-time	None	Daily: 15 min.	None	None
Comparison Conditions	Individ., Laissez-Faire	Individid.	Competi., Individ.	Competit., Individ.

	Nevin, Johnson & Johnson, 1982		*R. Johnson & Johnson 1982*	*Smith, Johnson, & Johnson 1982*
	Study 3	*Study 4*		
Length of Study	17 days	9 months	15 days	5 days
Grade Level	9	1	4	6
Subject Area	Math	All	Science, Social Studies	Social Studies, Science
Group Size	3 (1)	3 (1)	4 (1)	4 (1)
Type of Heterogeneity	Learning Disabled, Emotionally Disturbed	Emotionally Disturbed	Learning Disabled, Emotionally Disturbed	Learning Disabled, Gifted
Length of Instructional Session	45 min.	120 min.	45 min.	65 min.
Sample Size	16 (5)	22 (5)	51 (10)	55 (7)(12)
Free-Time	None	None	Daily: 10 min.	None
Comparison Conditions	Individ.	Individ.	Competit.	Individ.

Table 13.2 (*cont.*)

Armstrong, Johnson & Balow 1981	*Johnson & Johnson 1981a*	*R. Johnson & Johnson 1981*	*Nevin, Johnson & Johnson, 1982*	
			Study 1	*Study 2*
17 days	16 days	16 days	30 days	10 days
5 & 6	4	3	1	7
Language Arts	Social Studies	Math	Reading	Math
4 (1)	4 (1)	4 (1)	3 (1)	3
Learning Disabled	Learning Disabled, Emotionally Disturbed	Learning Disabled, Emotionally Disturbed	Learning Disabled	Learning Disabled, Emotionally Disturbed
90 min.	45 min.	25 min.	30 min.	60 min.
40 (10)	51 (12)	40 (8)	12 (4)	11 (11)
None	Daily: 10 min.	Two: 30 min.	None	None
Individ.	Individ.	Individ.	Individ.	Individ.

Johnson & Johnson 1982a	*R. Johnson & Johnson 1983*	*Johnson, Johnson, DeWeerdt, Lyons & Zaidman 1983*	*Johnson & Johnson 1984a*	*Johnson & Johnson 1985*
16 days	15 days	10 days	15 days	15 days
11	4	7	4	3
Math	Science, Social Studies	Science	Social Science	Math
4 (1)	4 (1)	4 (1)	4 (1)	4(1)
E.M.R., Learning, Disabled	Learning Disabled, Emotion. Disturbed	Mentally Retarded	Learning Disabled	Hearing Impaired
55 min.	50 min.	40 min.	55 min.	55 min.
31 (6)	59 (12)	48 (9)	48 (12)	30 (10)
None	Daily: 10 min.	Two: 30 min.	Two: 30 min.	None
Individ.	Competit., Individ.	Individ.	Individ.	Individ.

Table 13.2 (*cont.*)

	Johnson & Johnson in press	*Yager, Johnson, Johnson & Snider 1985*	*Johnson & Johnson 1984b*	*Johnson, Johnson, Scott & Ramolae 1985*
Length of Study	11 days	54 days	10 days	21 days
Grade Level	6th	4th	4	5 & 6
Subject Area	Social Studies	Social Studies; Science	Science	Science
Group Size	4	4, 3	4, 5	4
Type of Heterogeneity	Severe Learning & Behavior Problems	Learning Disabled	Learning Disabled & Emotionally Disturbed	Learning Disabled
Length of Instructional Session	55 min.	45 min.	55 min.	45 min.
Sample Size	72 (27)	59 (15)	51 (15)	154
Free Time	Two: 30 min.	None	None	None
Comparison Conditions	Controversy; Debate; Individualistic	Cooperative/ Individualistic; Individualistic	Intergroup Cooperation; Intergroup Competition	Single-Sex Coop; Mixed-Sex Coop; Individualistic

	Mesch, Lew, Johnson, & Johnson 1985	*Johnson, Johnson, Warring & Maruyama 1985*	
		Study 1	*Study 2*
Length of study	125 days	11	10
Grade Level	8	6	6
Subject Area	Foreign Language, Math	Social Studies	Science
Group Size	4	4 (1)	4 (1)
Type of Heterogeneity	Learning Disabled	Learning Disabled & Emotionally Disturbed	Learning Disabled & Emotionally Disturbed
Length of Instructional Session	50 min.	55 min.	55 min.
Sample Size	66	72 (27)	51 (15)
Free-Time	None	None	None
Comparison Conditions	Baseline; Grp. Academic Contingency; Grp. Academic Contingency with Social Skills	Controversy; Debate; Individualistic	Intergroup Cooperation; Intergroup Competition

6. Johnson and Johnson (1981a) studied the impact of cooperative and individualistic learning experiences on relationships between handicapped (learning disabled and emotionally disturbed) and nonbhandicapped fourth-grade students. Fifty-one students were assigned to conditions on a stratified random basis controlling for handicap, ability, and sex. Students participated in one instructional unit for 45 minutes a day for 16 instructional days. Teachers were trained, randomly assigned, and then rotated across conditions. Behavioral measures were taken for cross-handicap interaction within the instructional situation, during daily free-time periods, and during a postexperimental problem-solving situation with new peers. A number of attitude measures were also given. There was more cross-handicap interaction during both instructional and free-time situations and more interpersonal attraction between handicapped and nonhandicapped students in the cooperative than in the competitive condition.

7. Johnson and Johnson (1981) studied the effects of cooperative and individualistic learning experiences on interpersonal attraction between handicapped (learning disabled and emotionally disturbed) and nonhandicapped third-grade students. Forty students (eight handicapped) were randomly assigned to conditions stratifying for sex, ability, handicap, and peer status. Students participated in a math unit for 25 minutes a day for 16 instructional days. Teachers were trained, randomly assigned, and rotated across conditions. The results indicate that cooperative learning experiences compared with individualistic ones, promote more cross-handicap interaction during instruction. The interaction was characterized by involving handicapped students in the learning activities, giving them assistance, and encouraging them to achieve. Cooperative learning experiences also resulted in more cross-handicap friendships.

8–11. Nevin, Johnson, and Johnson (1982) reported three studies conducted in three different rural Vermont school districts. The studies focused on mainstreaming low-achieving, special-needs, first-, seventh-, and ninth-grade students who had also been referred by several teachers and the guidance counselor because of disruptive behavior. Students were placed on an individual contingency program and then switched to a group contingency program. Variations of A-B-A designs were used in the studies. The results consistently indicated that group contingencies (compared with individual and no contingencies) promoted greater social acceptance of handicapped students by nonhandicapped peers.

12. Johnson and Johnson (1982) compared the effects of cooperative and competitive learning experiences on interpersonal attraction between handicapped (learning disabled and emotionally disturbed) and nonhandicapped fourth-grade students. Fifty-one students were assigned to conditions on a stratified random basis controlling for handicap, ability, and sex. They participated in two instructional units for 45 minutes a day for 15 instructional days. Specially trained teachers were randomly assigned to conditions and then rotated so that each teacher taught each condition the same number of days. Cross-handicap interaction during daily free-time periods and a number of attitudes were measured.

The results indicated that cooperative learning experiences, compared with competitive ones, promoted more interpersonal attraction between handicapped and nonhandicapped students.

13. Smith, Johnson, and Johnson (1982) compared the effects of cooperative and individualistic instruction on the relationships among learning disabled, normal progress, and gifted sixth-grade students. Fifty-five students were assigned to conditions randomly stratifying for ability and sex. They participated in one instructional unit for 65 minutes a day for five instructional days. Teachers were trained, randomly assigned, and rotated across conditions. The results indicated that cooperative learning experiences promoted more positive relationships among the three types of students than did individualistic learning experiences.

14. Johnson and Johnson (1982a) compared the impact of cooperative and individualistic learning experiences on interpersonal attraction between handicapped (educable mentally retarded and learning disabled) and nonhandicapped eleventh-grade students. Thirty-one students were assigned to conditions randomly stratifying for handicap, ability, and sex. They participated in a math unit for 55 minutes a day for 16 instructional days. Teachers were trained, randomly assigned, and rotated across conditions. The results indicate that cooperative learning experiences promoted more cross-handicapped interaction during instruction and greater interpersonal attraction between handicapped and nonhandicapped students than did individualistic learning experiences.

15. R. Johnson and Johnson (1983) compared the effects of cooperative, competitive, and individualistic learning situations on the mainstreaming of fourth-grade students with severe learning and behavioral problems. All 59 students (of whom 12 were handicapped) were randomly assigned to conditions, stratifying for ability, sex, and handicap. One regular teacher and one certified teacher trained for the study were randomly assigned to each condition and then rotated across conditions. The study lasted for 15 instructional days. Six research assistants observed the cross-handicap interaction in each condition. The results indicated that cooperative learning experiences promoted more interpersonal attraction between handicapped and nonhandicapped students than did competitive or individualistic ones.

16. Johnson, Johnson, DeWeerdt, Lyons, and Zaidman (1983) studied the effects of cooperative and individualistic learning experiences on relationships between nonhandicapped and severely functionally handicapped students who normally spent their entire day in a self-contained special education classroom (IQs from untestable low to 80). Forty-eight seventh-grade students (nine handicapped) were randomly assigned to conditions stratifying for ability, sex, and handicap. They participated in a science unit for 40 minutes a day for 10 instructional days. Teachers were trained, randomly assigned, and rotated across conditions. In the cooperative (compared with the individualistic) condition, the mentally retarded students participated more in the learning activities, interacted

more frequently with their nonhandicapped classmates, perceived greater peer support and acceptance, and were better liked and accepted by the nonhandicapped students. Nonhandicapped students in the cooperative condition indicated a greater motivation to seek out and interact with their mentally retarded classmates during free time.

17. Johnson and Johnson (1984a) compared the impact of cooperative and individualistic learning on interpersonal attraction between handicapped (learning disabled and emotionally disturbed) and nonhandicapped students. Forty-eight fourth-grade students (12 of whom were handicapped) were randomly assigned to conditions stratifying for ability, sex, social class, and handicap. Teachers were trained, randomly assigned, and rotated across conditions. Students participated in a social studies unit for 55 minutes a day for 15 instructional days. The results indicated that cooperative learning experiences, compared with individualistic ones, promoted greater interpersonal attraction between handicapped and nonhandicapped students as well as more cross-handicap interaction focused on supporting and regulating efforts to learn and ensure active involvement of all students in the learning tasks.

18. Johnson and Johnson (1985) compared the impact of cooperative and individualistic learning experiences on relationships between nonhandicapped and hearing-impaired students. Thirty third grade students (10 of whom were hearing impaired) were randomly assigned to conditions stratifying for ability, sex, and handicap. They participated in a math unit for 55 minutes a day for 15 instructional days. Teachers were trained and rotated across conditions. In the cooperative (compared with the individualistic) condition, there was more interaction between hearing and hearing-impaired students and the hearing students indicated more acceptance and liking for hearing-impaired classmates, greater motivation to seek out and interact with the hearing-impaired students during free-time, and greater willingness to academically support and encourage their hearing-impaired peers.

19. Johnson and Johnson (in press) compared the effects of cooperative controversy, cooperative debate, and individualistic learning on interpersonal attraction between nonhandicapped and students with severe learning and behavioral problems. Seventy-two sixth-grade students were assigned to conditions on a stratified random basis controlling for sex, reading ability, and handicap. They participated in a science unit for 55 minutes a day for 11 days. Teachers were trained, randomly assigned, and rotated across conditions. The results indicated that cooperative controversy promoted the most positive relationships between handicapped and nonhandicapped students, cooperative debate the next most positive, and individualistic learning the least.

20. Yager, Johnson, Johnson, and Snider (1985) compared the effects of cooperative, cooperative followed by individualistic, and individualistic learning situations on the interpersonal attraction between nonhandicapped and learning

disabled fourth-grade students. Sixty-nine students were assigned to conditions on a stratified random basis controlling for sex, age, and handicap. They participated in a science class for 45 minutes a day for 54 instructional days. Nonhandicapped peer ratings of the social acceptability of each handicapped student were obtained four separate times at 18-day intervals. The results indicate that cooperative learning promoted more positive growth in interpersonal attraction, social acceptability, and self-esteem between handicapped and nonhandicapped students than did individualistic learning. When cooperation was replaced by individualistic learning, decay in the relationships between handicapped and nonhandicapped students occurred.

21. Johnson and Johnson (1984b) compared the impact of intergroup cooperation and intergroup competition on interpersonal attraction between nonhandicapped and learning-disabled and emotionally disturbed students. Fifty-one fourth-grade students were assigned to conditions on a stratified random basis controlling for the handicap status and sex. They participated in a science unit for 55 minutes a day for 10 instructional days. Two teachers were trained, randomly assigned, and rotated across conditions. The results indicated that intergroup cooperation promoted more inclusion of handicapped students and more positive cross-handicap relationships than did intergroup competition.

22. Johnson, Johnson, Scott, and Ramolae (1985) compared the effects of single-sex cooperative, mixed-sex cooperative, and individualistic learning situations on relationships between nonhandicapped and learning disabled fifth- and sixth-grade students. One hundred fifty-four fifth- and sixth-grade students were assigned to conditions on a stratified random basis controlling for ability, sex, grade level, homerooms, and handicap. They participated in a study for 45 minutes a day for 21 days in science class. Teachers were trained, randomly assigned, and rotated across conditions. The results indicated that cooperative learning situations, compared with individualistic ones, promoted more positive cross-handicap relationships.

23. Mesch, Lew, Johnson, and Johnson (1985) compared the effects of working alone or in a group with no academic contingency, working in cooperative learning groups with a group academic contingency, working in cooperative learning groups with social skills training, and working in cooperative learning groups with both academic and social skills contingencies. Socially withdrawn and isolated students were targeted. The results indicated that the combined use of academic and social skills contingencies significantly increased the frequency of appropriate social interaction with peers, acceptance and liking by peers, positive attitudes toward the subject area, and achievement of socially isolated and withdrawn students.

24–25. Johnson, Johnson, Warring, and Maruyama (1985) compared different levels of cooperation on cross-handicap interaction in two studies. In the first study, 74 6th-grade students were randomly assigned to three conditions (cooperative controversy, cooperative debate, and individualistic) stratifying for sex, ability level, and handicap. They participated in the study for 55 minutes a day for 11 instructional days. In the second study 51 fourth-grade students were randomly assigned to two conditions (intergroup cooperation and intergroup competition) stratifying for sex, ability level, and handicap. They participated in the study for 55 minutes a day for 10 instructional days. An Activity Report Scale was given to students to determine who they interacted with in structured class activities, unstructured class activities, school activities outside of class, and activities in the home. The results indicated that pure cooperation promoted more frequent cross-handicap interaction than did a mixture of cooperation and competition. The interaction patterns formed within cooperative learning situations generalized into unstructured class and school activities.

Processes of Acceptance and Rejection

The meta-analysis and the results of our studies validate the proposition that cooperative learning experiences promote greater interpersonal attraction between handicapped and nonhandicapped peers than do competitive or individualistic learning experiences. The theoretical model presented in Fig. 13.1 posits that there are any number of variables that partially explain these results. It is proposed that cooperative experiences, compared with competitive and individualistic experiences, result in more promotive and less oppositional interaction, greater perceived peer encouragement and acceptance, more accurate perspective-taking, greater differentiation of views of others, higher self-esteem based on unconditional self-acceptance, greater academic success, and greater expectations for rewarding future interaction. Each of these variables, in turn, is posited to increase the positive cathexis (or interpersonal attraction) among students. That is:

1. The more promotive the pattern of interaction among students, and the more students faciliate each other's goal achievement, the greater the resulting interpersonal attraction.
2. The greater one's conviction that others are encouraging, supporting, and accepting of one's efforts to achieve, the greater the interpersonal attraction.
3. The more accurate one's perspective-taking, the greater one's empathy with, understanding of, and altruism for others, which results in greater interpersonal attraction.
4. The more realistic, dynamic, and differentiated one's perceptions of others, the more one likes and identifies with them.
5. The higher one's self-esteem, the less one's prejudices against, and the higher one's liking for others.
6. The greater one's academic success, the more one likes those who have contributed to and facilitated that success.

7. The more one expects future interaction to be positive and productive, the more one likes others.

The more cooperative experiences tend to promote the occurrence of these variables, the greater the resulting interpersonal attraction among students regardless of their heterogenity.

Promotive versus oppositional or no interaction

One reason why cooperative experiences may promote more interpersonal attraction among heterogeneous individuals than do competitive or individualistic experiences is that within cooperative situations participants benefit from facilitating each other's efforts to achieve, whereas in competitive situations participants benefit from obstructing each other's efforts to achieve, and in individualistic situations the success of others is irrelevant. There are two approaches to research in this area. One has focused on students' perceptions of helping during learning situations; the second has focused on observing actual interaction among students.

There is more helping between handicapped and nonhandicapped students in cooperative than in competitive or individualistic learning situations (Armstrong, Johnson, & Balow, 1981; Cooper, Johnson, Johnson, & Wilderson, 1980; Johnson & Johnson, 1981b, 1982a, 1982b, 1984a). A number of studies with homogeneous samples have found more peer helping and tutoring in cooperative than in competitive or individualistic learning situations (Buckholdt, Ferritor, & Tucker, 1974; DeVries & Edwards, 1974; Devries, Edwards & Wells, 1974; DeVries & Mescon, 1975; Hamblin, Hathaway & Wordarski, 1971; Hamblin, Buckholdt, Ferritor, Kozloff, & Blackwell, 1971).

Volunteered help of the sort that characterizes cooperative learning situations has been found to elicit more liking of the helper than does involuntary helping (Broll, Gross, & Piliavin, 1974; Gross & Latane, 1974). Help from an ally (as in the case of another group member) leads to a positive shift in feelings for the helper, whereas help from an opponent does not (Nadler, Fisher, & Streufert, 1974). Somewhat contrary to this finding, when aid is expected in advance, as it is from an ally, its arrival does not increase favorable perceptions of the donor (Morse, 1972; Morse & Gergen, 1971).

Most of the research on helping has used paper-and-pencil nomination measure of who helped whom. One of the problems with the research on mainstreaming is that there is little evidence concerning the actual interaction among heterogeneous students during instruction. Johnson and Johnson (1982) found that cooperative learning experiences promoted more cross-handicapped helping than did competitive learning experiences, as well as the perception that the class was more cohesive. R. Johnson and Johnson (1983) found that there was more positive cross-handicapped interaction during instruction in the cooperative than in the competitive and individualistic conditions. Nevin, Johnson, and Johnson (1982) found that there was less negative interaction between handicapped and nonhandicapped students in the cooperative than in the individualistic condition. Johnson and Johnson (1982a) found more positive interaction between handicapped and nonhandicapped students in the cooperative than than in the individualistic condition. Johnson, Rynders, Johnson, Schmidt, and Haider (1979) and Rynders, Johnson, Johnson, and Schmidt (1980) found more positive interaction between handicapped and nonhandicapped students during instruction in the cooperative than in competitive and individualistic conditions. Finally, Johnson and Johnson (1981) and Johnson and Johnson (1984a) used an observation instrument that would differentiate more precisely the nature of the interaction between handicapped and nonhandicapped students. They found more questions, directions and suggestions, helping and assisting, and encouraging and praising comments in the cooperative than in the individualistic condition, while hostile and rejecting comments were more frequency in the individualistic condition.

The documentation that cooperative learning situations are characterized by more facilitation of classmates' achievement than are competitive and individualistic learning situations is important, as there is evidence that individuals like those who facilitate their goal accomplishment and dislike those who obstruct their goal accomplishment (Ashmore, 1970; Berkowitz & Daniels, 1963; Burnstein & McRae, 1962; Deutsch, 1949; Goranson & Berkowitz, 1966; Johnson & Johnson, 1972; Secord & Backman, 1964; Zajonc & Marin, 1967). Expectations that another person will facilitate one's goal accomplishment (Johnson & Johnson, 1972) and perceptions that another person is exerting effort to facilitate one's goal accomplishment (Tjosvold, Johnson, & Johnson, 1981) are enough to induce liking.

Perceived peer support and acceptance

Cooperative learning experiences, compared with competitive and individualistic experiences, have been found to result in stronger beliefs that one is personally liked, supported, and accepted by other students; that other students care about how much one learns; and that other students want to help one learn (Cooper et al., 1980; Gunderson & Johnson, 1980; Johnson & Johnson, 1981a, 1981b, 1983, 1984a; Johnson, Johnson Johnson & Anderson, 1976; Johnson, Johnson, Roy, & Zaidman, 1985; Johnson, Johnson, Tiffany, & Zaidman, 1983; Johnson, Johnson, Warring, & Maruyama, in press; Johnson, Skon, Johnson, 1980; Johnson, Bjorkland, & Krotee, 1984; Johnson, Johnson, DeWeerdt, Lyons, & Zaidman, 1983; Lew, Mesch, Johnson, & Johnson, 1985a, 1985b; Mesch, Lew, Johnson & Johnson, 1985; Skon, Johnson, & Johnson 1981; Smith, Johnson, & Johnson, 1981; Tjosvold, Marino, & Johnson, 1977). Attitudes toward cooperation, furthermore, are significantly related to believing that one is liked by other students and to wanting to listen to, help, and do schoolwork with other students. Johnson & Ahlgren, 1976; Johnson, Johnson, & Anderson, 1978). Many of these same studies found evidence that students within cooperative learning situtions or with cooperative attitudes perceive teachers as being more supportive and accepting, both academically and personally, than do students in competitive or individualistic learning situations. Finally, there is some evidence that cooperation promotes a lower fear of failure and higher psychological safety than do the other two goal structures (Johnson & Johnson, 1975).

Accuracy of perspective-taking

A potentially important influence on the building of constructive relationships among heterogenous students is the ability to take each other's perspectives. Social perspective-taking is the ability to understand how a situation appears to another person and how that person is reacting cognitively and emotionally to the situation. The opposite of perspective-taking is egocentrism, the embeddedness in one's own viewpoint to the extent that one is unaware of other points of view and of the limitations of one's perspective. Several studies have found that cooperativeness is positively related to the ability to take the emotional perspective of others (Johnson, 1975a, 1975b; Murphy, 1937). Contrarily, Levine and Hoffman (1975) found no relationship. Competitiveness, on the other hand, has been found to be related to egocentrism (Barnett, Matthews, & Howard, 1979). Cooperative learning experiences, furthermore, have been found to promote greater cognitive and emotional perspective-taking abilities than either competitive or individualistic learning experiences (Bridgeman, 1977; Johnson & Johnson, 1984a; Johnson, Johnson, Johnson, & Anderson, 1976; Johnson, Johnson, Pierson, & Lyons, in press; Johnson & Johnson, 1981, 1982b; Smith, Johnson, & Johnson, 1981; Tjosvold & Johnson, 1978; Tjosvold & Johnson, & Johnson, 1984).

Differentiation of view of others

It may be posited that negative stereotypes and labels lose their primary potency when a view of a person becomes highly differentiated, dynamic, and realistic. A differentiated, dynamic, and realistic impression includes many different categories. Each category is assigned a weight as to its importance according to the demands of any specific situation, and the weight or salience of each category changes as the requirements of the situation change. New information concerning the person is admitted to one's impression as it becomes relevant. The conceptualization of a stigmatized peer stays in a dynamic state of change, open to modification with new information and takes into account situational factors. Worchel (1979) suggests that one of the principal mechanisms by which cooperative experiences influence intergroup relations is through reducing the salience of intergroup distinctions. The "we" feeling developed within cooperative groups may outweigh the "they" perceptions between majority and minority students. Katz (1976) states that getting to know members of other ethnic groups may reduce the tendency to generalize negative characteristics to all members of the ethnic group. Stephan and Rosenfield (1980) state that varied experiences with different members of other ethnic groups should increase the complexity of one's perceptions of the ethnic view and undermine any belief that most members of the ethnic group fit one's stereotype. Armstrong, Johnson & Balow (1981) found a more differentiated view of handicapped peers resulting from a cooperative, compared with an individualistic, learning experience. Ames (1981) found that within a cooperative situation, participants seemed to have a differentiated view of collaborators and tended to minimize perceived differences in ability and view all collaborators as being equally worthwhile, regardless of their performance level or ability. Johnson, Johnson, and Scott (1978) found that when given a choice of future collaborators, low achievers were picked by classmates just as frequently as high achievers.

The ease with which monopolistic, static, and oversimplified views of members of other ethnic groups develop led Allport (1954) to state that humans operate under the "principle of least effort," which means that monopolistic impressions are easier to form and maintain than are differentiated impressions. Monopolistic impressions, by their very nature, are static and oversimplified due to their rigid weighting of a few characteristics of primary potency, regardless of the demands of the current situation. Competitive and individualistic experiences probably tend to reinforce the importance of status characteristics (such as reading and math abililty) in the process of relationship formation. This tends to strengthen the power and prestige of high-achieving white students at the expense of less advantaged, minority, and handicapped students. Cohen (1975, 1980), Gerard and Miller (1975), Hoffman (1973), Stulac (1975), Rosenholtz (1980), and Stephan and Rosenfield (1979) indicate that white students are usually from higher socioeconomic status backgrounds, have higher academic achievement scores, read better, and are accorded more status and respect by the school staff. These status differentials may tend to reinforce negative stereotypes of minority and handicapped students. Ames (1981) found that students in competitive situations tended to focus primarily on differences in ability in their evaluations of each other, and they tended to perceive the nonwinners as being less deserving of reward. Finally, both competitive and individualistic learning activities (with their emphasis on rows-by-columns seating arrangement, strict rules against movement and talking, and individual seatwork) provide little or no information about student's different ethnic groups and handicapping conditions, thus allowing initial stereotypes to continue. What little information that is available is likely to confirm existing stereotypes and the boundaries of ethnic membership and handicapping conditions tend not to be clarified. Unrealistic and oversimplified views of handicapped peers and members of other ethnic groups tend to be promoted in competitive and individualistic learning situations.

Self-esteem

There is evidence that self-esteem and prejudice are positively related (Stephan & Rosenfield, 1978b, 1979; Trent, 1957), and increases in self-esteem are associated with decreases in prejudice (Stephan & Rosenfield, 1978a). It may be, therefore, that self-esteem explains some of the relationship between cooperation and interpersonal attraction among heterogenous individuals. There is some evidence that cooperative learning situations, compared with competitive and individualistic situations, promote higher levels of self-esteem and healthier processes for deriving conclusions about one's self-worth (Blaney, Stephan, Rosenfield, Aronson, & Sikes, 1977: DeVries, Lucasse, & Shackman, 1979; Geffner, 1978; Gunderson & Johnson, 1980; Johnson & Ahlgren 1976; Johnson & Johnson, 1984a; Johnson, Johnson, & Anderson, 1978; Johnson, Johnson, & Scott, 1978; Johnson, Johnson, Tiffany, & Zaidman, 1983; Johnson & Norem-Hebeisen, 1977; Johnson & Johnson, 1981; Johnson, Bjorkland & Krotee, 1984; Johnson, Johnson, DeWeerdt, Lyons, & Zaidman, 1983; Johnson, Johnson, & Rynders, 1981; Nevin, Johnson, & Johnson, 1982; Norem-Hebeisen & Johnson, 1981; Slavin & Karweit, 1979; Smith, Johnson & Johnson, 1981; Yager, Johnson, Johnson, & Snider, 1985). Norem-Hebeisen and Johnson (1981) found that attitudes toward cooperation tended to be related to basic self-acceptance and positive self-evaluation compared to peers; competitiveness tended to be related to conditional self-acceptance; and positive attitudes toward individualistic situations tended to be related to basic self-rejection. Ames (1981) found that winning in a competitive situation produced self-aggrandizement, whereas losing lowered students' self-perceptions of their ability and satisfaction. Ames, Ames, and Felker (1977) found that failure in competitive situations promotes increased self-derogation. Finally, the impact of positive peer evaluations (frequently found in cooperative situations) may be especially powerful for individuals who have a history of failure (Turnure & Zigler, 1958).

Academic success

There is considerable evidence that cooperative, compared with competitive or individualistic, learning situations promote higher achievement (Johnson, Maruyama, Johnson, Nelson, & Skon, 1981). More interpersonal attraction should occur among heterogenous students when learning situations are structured cooperatively.

Expectations toward future interaction

The final aspect of the process of acceptance is that it promotes expectations toward rewarding and enjoyable future interaction between minority and majority students. The final aspect of the process of rejection is that it promotes expectations toward negative, frustrating, and unpleasant future interaction between majority and minority students.

Generalizations of interaction to free-time situations

Even though students express liking for peers from other ethnic groups or with handicapping conditions, and in fact interact with them in constructive ways during instructional situations, there is a need to determine whether these relationships and interaction patterns will generalize to postinstructional, free-choice situations in which students can interact with whomever they wish. Several recent studies have demonstrated that when students were placed in postinstructional, free-choice situations, there was more cross-ethnic interaction (Johnson & Johnson, 1981a, 1982b; Johnson, Johnson, Pierson & Lyons, in press; Johnson, Johnson, Tiffany, & Zaidman, 1983) and more cross-handicap interaction (Johnson & Johnson 1981b, 1984a; Johnson, Johnson, DeWeerdt, Lyons, & Zaidman, 1983, R. Johnson & Johnson, 1981, 1982; Martino & Johnson, 1979) when students had been in a cooperative rather than a competitive or individualistic learning situation. In other words, the relationships formed within cooperative learning groups among heterogeneous peers do seem to generalize to postinstructional situations.

IMPLEMENTATION IN THE SCHOOLS

Social psychology has often been criticized for generating extensive but trivial knowledge. It has been noted that although social psychological theorizing and research has generated much information, it has not provided the concise answers required to solve even the simplest social problems. As can be seen from this chapter, one of the areas of inquiry where social psychology is least deserving of such criticism is the study of cooperative, competitive, and individualistic situations. For not only have theory development, the validation of theory, and the summarization of existing knowledge been addressed, but the specific bridges to practice have also been built. The practical procedures for implementing cooperative learning procedures in the classroom and school have been specified, and considerable training of teachers has taken place (Chasnoff, 1979; Johnson & Johnson, 1975; Lyons, 1980; Roy, 1982). The productivity of this area is largely due to the interaction between theory, research, and application.

Over the past 10 years, we have field tested our operationalizations of cooperative learning in a wide variety of preschool, elementary, secondary, college, and adult education settings throughout the United States, Canada, and several other countries. A conservative estimate is that we and our colleagues have trained over 20,000 teachers. We have built an international network of school districts involved in long-term efforts to implement cooperation learning. Teachers who wish to use cooperative learning procedures to promote effective mainstreaming can rest assured that the procedures have been field tested in a variety of settings.

Both mainstreaming and desegregation are required by law and are being implemented through North America. In many classrooms, however, mainstreaming and desegregation are being conducted in a highly individualistic way. Students work on their own, on individualized materials, and with a minimum of interaction with their classmates. This chapter provides some basis for recommending that cooperative learning procedures should be utilized in mainstreamed and desegregated classrooms if the goal of improved intergroup acceptance is to be achieved.

REFERENCES

Allport, G. (1954). *The nature of prejudice*. Cambridge, MA: Addison-Wesley.

Ames, C. (1981). Effects of group reward structures on children's attributions and affect. *American Educational Research Journal, 18*, 273–288.

Ames, C., Ames, R., & Felker, D. (1977). Informational and dispositional determinants of children's achievement attributions. *Journal of Educational Psychology, 68*, 63–69.

Armstrong, B., Johnson, D. W., & Balow, B. (1981). Effects of cooperative versus individualistic learning experiences on interpersonal attraction between learning-disabled and normal-progress elementary school students. *Contemporary Educational Psychology, 6*, 102–109.

Ashmore, R. (1970). Solving the problem of prejudice. In B. Collins (Ed.), *Social psychology: Social influence, attitude change, group processes, and prejudice* (pp. 298–337). Reading, MA: Addison-Wesley.

Ballard, M., Corman, L., Gottlieb, J., & Kaufman, M. (1977). Improving the social status of mainstreamed retarded children. *Journal of Educational Psychology, 69*, 605–611.

Barker, R., Wright, B., Meyerson, L., & Gonick, M. (1953). *Adjustment to physical illness: A survey of the social psychology of physique and disability*. New York: Social Science Research Council.

Barnett, M., Matthew, K., & Howard, J. (1979). Relationship between competitiveness and empathy in 6- and 7-year-olds. *Developmental Psychology, 15*, 221–222.

Berkowitz, L., & Daniels, L. (1963). Responsibility and dependency. *Journal of Personality and Social Psychology, 66*, 429–436.

Blaney, N., Stephan, C., Rosenfield, D., Aronson, E., & Sikes, J. (1977). Interdependence in the classroom: A field study. *Journal of Educational Psychology, 69*, 139–146.

Bridgeman, D. (1977). *The influence of cooperative, interdependent learning on role taking and moral reasoning: A theoretical and empirical field study with fifth-grade students*. Unpublished doctoral dissertation, University of California, Santa Cruz.

Broll, L., Gross, A., & Piliavin, I. (1974). Effects of offered and requested help on help seeking and reactions to being helped. *Journal of Applied Social Psychology, 4*, 244–258.

Bruininks, V. (1978). Peer status and personality characteristics of learning disabled and nondisabled students. *Journal of Learning Disabilities, 11*, 29–34.

Bruininks, V., Rynders, J., & Gross, J. (1974). Social acceptance of mildly retarded pupils in resource rooms and regular classes. *American Journal of Mental Deficiency, 78*, 377–383.

Bryan, T. (1974). Peer popularity of learning disabled students. *Journal of Learning Disabilities, 9*, 307–311.

Bryan, T. (1978). Social relationships and verbal interactions of learning disabled children. *Journal of Learning Disabilities, 11*, 56–66.

Buckholdt, D., Ferritor, D., & Tucker, S. (1974, April). *Effects of training in tutoring of shared group consequences on reading and performance and tutoring behaviors*. Paper presented at the annual meeting of the American Educational Research Association, Chicago.

Burnstein, E., & McRae, A. (1962). Some effects of shared threat and prejudice in racially mixed groups. *Journal of Abnormal and Social Psychology, 64*, 257–263.

Chasnoff, R. (1979). (Ed.) *Structuring cooperative learning experiences in the classroom: The 1979 handbook*. New Brighton, MN: Interaction Book Co.

Cohen, E. (1975). The effects of desegregation on race relations. *Law and Contemporary Problems, 39*, 271–299.
Cohen, E. (1980). Design and redesign of the desegregated school: Problem of status, power, and conflict, In W. Stephen & J. Fengin (Eds)., *Desegregation: Past, present, and future*. New York: Plenum.
Combs, R., & Harper, J. (1967). Effects of labels on attitudes of educators toward handicapped children. *Exceptional Children, 34*, 399–406.
Comer, R., & Piliavin, J. (1972). The effects of deviance upon face-to-face interaction: The other side. *Journal of Personality and Social Psychology, 55*, 33–39.
Cooper, L., Johnson, D. W., Johnson, R., & Wilderson, F. (1980). Effects of cooperative, competitive, and individualistic experiences on interpersonal attraction among heterogeneous peers. *Journal of Social Psychology, 111*, 243–252.
Davis, F. (1961). Deviance disavowal: The management of strained interaction by the visibly handicapped. *Social Problems, 9*, 120–132.
Deutsch, M. (1949). An experimental study of the effects of cooperation and competition upon group process. *Human Relations, 2*, 199–232.
Deutsch, M. (1962). Cooperation and trust: Some theoretical notes. In M. R. Jones (Ed.), *Nebraska Symposium on Motivation* (pp. 275–319). Lincoln: University of Nebraska Press.
DeVries, D., & Edwards, K. (1974, April). *Cooperation in the classroom: Towards a theory of alternative reward-task classroom structures*. Paper presented at the annual meeting of the American Educational Research Association, Chicago.
DeVries, D. L., Edwards, K. J., & Wells, E. H. (1974) *Teams-games-tournament in the social studies classroom: Effects on academic achievement, student attitudes, cognitive beliefs, and classroom climate* (Report #173) Balitmore, MD: Center for Social Organization of Schools, John Hopkins University.
DeVries, D. L., Lucasse, P., & Shackman, S. (1979, September). *Small group vs. individualized instruction: A field test of their relative effectiveness*. Paper presented at the annual convention of the American Psychological Association, New York.
DeVries, D. L., & Mescon, I. T. (1975). *Teams-games-tournament: An effective task and reward structure in the elementary grades* (Report #189) Baltimore, MD: Center for Social Organization of Schools, Johns Hopkins University.
Dienstbier, R. (1970). Positive and negative prejudice: Interactions of prejudice with race and social desirability. *Journal of Personality, 38*, 138–215.
Doob, A., & Ecker, B. (1970). Stigma and compliance. *Journal of Personality and Social Psychology, 14*, 302–304.
Farina, A., Allen, J., & Saul, B. (1968). The role of the stigmatized in affecting social relationships. *Journal of Personality, 36*, 176–182.
Farina, A., Gliha, K., Boudreau, L., Allen, J., & Sherman, M. (1971). Mental illness and the impact of believing others know about it. *Journal of Abnormal Psychology, 77*, 1–5.
Geffner, R. (1978). *The effects of interdependent learning on self-esteem, inter-ethnic relations, and intra-ethnic attitudes of elementary school children: A field experiment*. Unpublished doctoral dissertation, University of California, Santa Cruz.
Gerard, H., & Miller, N. (1975). *School desegregation*. New York: Plenum.
Gergan, K., & Jones, E. (1963). Mental illness, predictability, and affective consequences as stimulus factors in person perception. *Journal of Abnormal and Social Psychology, 67*, 94–104.
Goodman, H., Gottlieb, J., & Harrison, R. (1972). Social acceptance of EMRs integrated into a nongraded elementary school. *American Journal of Mental Deficiency, 76*, 412–417.
Goranson, R., and Berkowitz, L. (1966). Reciprocity and responsibility reactions to prior help. *Journal of Personality and Social Psychology, 3*, 277–232.
Gottlieb, J., & Budoff, A. (1973). Social acceptability of retarded children in nongraded schools differing in architecture. *American Journal of Mental Deficiency, 78*, 15–19.

Gottlieb, J., Cohen, L., & Goldstein, L. (1974). Social contact and personal adjustment as variables relating to attitudes toward educable mentally retarded children. *Training School Bulletin, 71,* 9–16.

Gottlieb, J., & Davis, J. (1973). Social acceptance of EMR children during overt behavioral interactions. *American Journal of Mental Deficiency, 78,* 141–143.

Gottlieb, J., Semmel, M., & Veldman, A. (1978). Correlates of social status among mainstreamed mentally retarded children. *Journal of Educational Psychology, 70,* 396–405.

Gross, A., & Latane, J. (1974). Some effects of giving and receiving help. *Journal of Applied Social Psychology, 3,* 210–223.

Guerin, G., & Szatlocky, K. (1974). Integration programs for the mildly retarded. *Exceptional Children, 41,* 173–179.

Gunderson, G., & Johnson, D.W. (1980). Building positive attitudes by using cooperative learning groups. *Foreign Language Annals, 13,* 39–46.

Hamblin, R., Buckholdt, D., Ferritor, D., Kozloff, M., & Blackwell, L. (1971). *The humanization processes.* New York: Wiley.

Hamblin, R., Hathaway, C., & Wordarski, J. (1971). Group contingencies, peer tutoring, and accelerating academic achievement. In E. Ramp & B. Hopkins (Eds.), *A new direction for education: Behavior analysis.* Lawrence: University of Kansas.

Hamilton, D. (1976). Cognitive bases in the perception of social groups. In J. Carroll & J. Payne (Eds.), *Cognition and social behavior.* Hillsdale, NJ: Lawrence Erlbaum Associates.

Hastorf, A., Northcraft, G., Picciotto, S. (1979). Helping the handicapped: How realistic is the performance feedback? *Personality and Social Psychology Bulletin, 5,* 373–376.

Heber, R., & Heber, M. (1957). The effect of group failure and success on social status. *Journal of Educational Psychology, 48,* 129–134.

Hensley, V., & Duval, S. (1976). Some perceptual determinants of perceived similarity, liking, and correctness. *Journal of Personality and Social Psychology, 34,* 830–836.

Higgs, R. (1975). Attitude formation–contact or information? *Exceptional Children, 41,* 496–497.

Hoffman, D. (1973). *Students' expectations and performance in a simulation game.* Unpublished doctoral dissertation, Stanford University.

Iano, R., Ayers, D., Heller, H., McGettigan, J., & Walker, V. (1974). Sociometric status of retarded children in an integrated program. *Exceptional Children, 40,* 267–271.

Jaffe, J. (1966). Attitudes of adolescents toward the mentally retarded. *American Journal of Mental Deficiency, 70,* 907–912.

Johnson, D. W. (1975a). Affective perspective taking and cooperative predisposition. *Developmental Psychology, 11,* 869–870.

Johnson, D. W. (1975b). Cooperativeness and social perspective taking. *Journal of Personality and Social Psychology, 31,* 241–244.

Johnson, D. W., & Ahlgren, A. (1976). Relationship between students' attitudes about cooperation and competition and attitudes toward schooling. *Journal of Educational Psychology, 68,* 92–102.

Johnson, D. W., & Johnson, R. (1975). *Learning together and alone: Cooperation, competition, and individualization.* Englewood Cliffs, NJ: Prentice-Hall.

Johnson, D. W., & Johnson, R. (1980). Integrating handicapped students into the mainstream. *Exceptional Children, 46,* 89–98.

Johnson, D. W., & Johnson, R. (1981a). The integration of the handicapped into the regular classroom: Effects of cooperative and individualistic instruction. *Contemporary Educational Psychology, 6,* 344–353.

Johnson, D. W., & Johnson, R. (1981b). Effects of cooperative and individualistic learning experiences on interethnic interaction. *Journal of Educational Psychology, 73,* 454–459.

Johnson, D. W., & Johnson, R. (1982a). Effects of cooperative and individualistic instruction on handicapped and nonhandicapped students. *Journal of Social Psychology, 118,* 257–268.

Johnson, D. W. & Johnson, R. (1982b). Effects of cooperative, competitive, and individualistic learning experiences on cross-ethnic interaction and friendships. *Journal of Social Psychology, 118,* 47–58.

Johnson, D. W., & Johnson, R. (1983). Social interdependence and perceived academic and personal support in the classroom. *Journal of Social Psychology, 120,* 77–82.

Johnson, D. W., & Johnson, R. (1984a). Building acceptance of differences between handicapped and nonhandicapped students: The effects of cooperative and individualistic instruction. *The Journal of Social Psychology, 122,* 257–267.

Johnson, D. W., & Johnson, R. (1984b). The effects of intergroup cooperation and intergroup competition on in group and out group cross-handicap relationships. *Journal of Social Psychology, 124,* 84–94.

Johnson, D. W., & Johnson, R. (1985). Mainstreaming hearing-impaired students: The effect of effort in communicating on cooperation. *Journal of Psychology, 119*(1), 31–44.

Johnson, D. W., & Johnson, R. (in press). Classroom conflict: Controversy versus debate in learning groups. *American Educational Research Journal.*

Johnson, D. W., Johnson, R., & Anderson, D. (1978). Relationships between student cooperative, competitive, and individualistic attitudes and attitudes toward schooling. *Journal of Psychology, 100,* 183–199.

Johnson, D. W., Johnson, R., Johnson, J., & Anderson, D. (1976). The effects of cooperative vs. individualized instruction on student prosocial behavior, attitudes toward learning, and achievement. *Journal of Educational Psychology, 68,* 446–452.

Johnson, D. W., Johnson, R., Holubec, E., & Roy, P. (1984). *Circles of learning.* Alexandria, VA: Association for Supervision and Curriculum Development.

Johnson, D. W., Johnson, R., & Maruyama, G. (1983). Interdependence and interpersonal attraction among heterogeneous and homogeneous individuals: A theoretical formulation and a meta-analysis of the research. *Review of Educational Research, 53,* 5–54.

Johnson, D. W., Johnson, R., Pierson, W., & Lyons, V. (in press). Controversy vs. concurrence seeking in multigrade and single-grade learning groups. *Journal of Research in Science Teaching.*

Johnson, D. W., Johnson, R., Roy, P., & Zaidman, B. (1985). *Oral interaction in cooperative learning groups: Speaking, listening, and the nature of statements made by high-, medium-, and low-achieving students.* Manuscript submitted for publication.

Johnson, D. W., Johnson, R., & Scott, L. (1978). The effects of cooperative and individualized instruction on student attitudes and achievement. *Journal of Social Psychology, 104,* 207–216.

Johnson, D. W., Johnson, R., Tiffany, M., & Zaidman, B. (1983). Are low-achievers disliked in a cooperative situation? A test of rival theories in a mixed ethnic situation. *Contemporary Educational Psychology, 8,* 189–200.

Johnson, D. W., Johnson, R., Warring, D., & Maruyama, G. (in press). Different cooperative learning procedures and cross-handicap relationships. *Exceptional Children.*

Johnson, D. W., Maruyama, G., Johnson, R., Nelson, D., & Skon, L. (1981). The effects of cooperative, competitive, and individualistic goal structures on achievement: A meta-analysis. *Psychological Bulletin, 89,* 47–62.

Johnson, D. W., Norem-Hebeisen, A. (1977). Attitudes toward interdependence among persons and psychological health. *Psychological Reports, 40,* 834–850.

Johnson, D. W., Skon, L., & Johnson, R. (1980). Effects of cooperative, competitive and individualistic conditions on children's problem-solving performance. *American Educational Research Journal, 17,* 83–94.

Johnson, G. (1950). A study of the social position of mentally handicapped children in the regular grades. *American Journal of Mental Deficiency, 55,* 60–89.

Johnson, G., & Kirk, S. (1950). Are mentally handicapped children segregated in the regular grades? *Exceptional Children, 55,* 60–89.

Johnson, R., Bjorkland, R., & Krotee, M. (1984). The effects of cooperative, competitive, and individualistic student interaction patterns on achievement and attitudes of the golf skill of putting. *The Research Quarterly for Exercise and Sport, 55,* 49–54.

Johnson, R., & Johnson, D. W. (1981). Building friendships between handicapped and nonhandicapped students: Effects of cooperative and individualistic instruction. *American Educational Research Journal, 18,* 415–424.

Johnson, R., & Johnson, D. W. (1982). Effects of cooperative and competitive learning experiences on interpersonal attraction between handicapped and nonhandicapped students. *Journal of Social Psychology, 116,* 211–219.

Johnson, R., & Johnson, D. W. (1983). Effects of cooperative, competitive, and individualistic learning experiences on cross-handicap relationships and social development. *Exceptional Children, 49,* 323–328.

Johnson, R., & Johnson, D. W., DeWeerdt, N., Lyons, V., & Zaidman, B. (1983). Integrating severely adaptively handicapped seventh-grade students into constructive relationships with nonhandicapped peers in science class. *American Journal of Mental Deficiency, 87,* 611–618.

Johnson, R., Johnson, D. W., & Rynders, J. R. (1981). Effect of cooperative, competitive, and individualistic experiences on self-esteem of handicapped and nonhandicapped students. *Journal of Psychology, 108,* 31–34.

Johnson, R., Johnson, D. W., Scott, L., & Ramolae, B. (1985). Effects of single-sex and mixed-sex cooperative interaction on science achievement and attitudes and cross-handicap and cross-sex relationship. *Journal of Research in Science Teaching, 22,* 207–220.

Johnson, R., Rynders, R., Johnson, D. W., Schmidt, B., & Haider, S. (1979). Producing positive interaction between handicapped and nonhandicapped teenagers through cooperative goal structuring: Implications for mainstreaming. *American Educational Research Journal, 16,* 161–168.

Johnson, S., & Johnson, D. W. (1972). The effects of other's actions, attitude similarity, and race on attraction towards the other. *Human Relations, 25,* 121–130.

Jones, R. (1970). Learning and association in the presence of the blind. *The New Outlook,* 317–329.

Jones, R. (1972). Labels and stigma in special education. *Exceptional Children, 38,* 553–564.

Katz, P. (1976). The acquisition of racial attitudes of children. In P. Katz (Ed.), *Toward the elimination of racism.* New York: Pergamon.

Kelley, H. (1973). The processes of causal attribution. *American Psychologist, 28,* 107–128.

Kleck, R. (1966). Emotional arousal in interaction with stigmatized persons. *Psychological Reports, 19,* 1226.

Kleck, R. (1968). Physical stigma and nonverbal cues emitted in face-to-face interaction. *Human Relations, 21,* 19–28.

Kleck, R., Buck, P., Goller, W., London, R., Pfeiffer, J., & Vukcevic, D. (1968). Effect of stigmatizing conditions on the use of personal space. *Psychological Reports, 23,* 111–118.

Kleck, R., Ono, H., & Hastorf, A. (1966). The effects of physical deviance upon face-to-face interaction. *Human Relations, 19,* 425–436.

Lapp, E. (1957). A study of the social adjustment of slow learning children who were assigned parttime to regular classes. *American Journal of Mental Deficiency, 62,* 254–262.

Levine, L., & Hoffman, M. (1975). Empathy and cooperation in four-year-olds. *Developmental Psychology, 11,* 533–534.

Lyons, V. (1980). (Ed.) *Structuring cooperative learning experiences in the classroom: The 1980 handbook.* New Brighton, MN: Interaction Book Company.

Martino, L., & Johnson, D. W. (1979). Cooperative and individualistic experiences among disabled and normal children. *The Journal of Social Psychology, 107,* 177–183.

Mesch, D., Lew, M., Johnson, D. W., & Johnson, R. (1985). *Isolated teenagers, cooperative learning, and social skills training.* Manuscript submitted for publication.

Miller, G. (1956). The magical number seven, plus or minus two: Some limits on our capacity for processing information. *Psychological Review, 63,* 81–97.

Morse, S. (1972). Help, likability, and social influence. *Journal of Applied Social Psychology, 2,* 124–146.

Morse, S., & Gergen, K. (1971). Material aid and social attraction. *Journal of Applied Social Psychology, 1,* 150–212.

Murphy, L. (1937). *Social behavior and child personality.* New York: Columbia University Press.

Nadler, A., Fisher, J., & Streufert, S. (1974). The donor's dilemma: Recipient's reactions to aid from friend or foe. *Journal of Applied Social Psychology, 4,* 275–285.

Nevin, A., Johnson, D. W., & Johnson, R. (1982). Effects of group and individual contingencies on academic performance and social relations of special needs students. *Journal of Social Psychology, 116,* 41–59.

Norem-Hebeisen, A., & Johnson, D. W. (1981). Relationship between cooperative, competitive, and individualistic attitudes and differentiated aspects of self-esteem. *Journal of Personality, 49,* 415–425.

Novak, D. (1975). Children's responses to imaginary peers labeled as emotionally disturbed. *Psychology in the Schools, 12,* 103–106.

Panda, K., & Bartel, N. (1972). Teacher perception of exceptional children. *Journal of Special Education, 6,* 261–266.

Porter, R., Ramsey, B., Trembly, A., Iaccobo, M., & Crawley, S. (1978). Social interactions in heterogeneous groups of retarded and normally developing children: An observational study. In B. Sackett (Ed.), *Observing behavior: Theory and applications in mental retardation.* Baltimore, MD: University Park Press.

Rosenholtz, S. (1980). Treating problems of academic status. In J. Berger & M. Zelditch (Eds.), *Status attributions and justice.* New York: Elsevier.

Roy, P. (Ed.). (1982). *Structuring cooperative learning experiences in the classroom: The 1982 handbook.* New Brighton, MN: Interaction Book Company.

Rucker, C., Howe, C., & Snider, B. (1969). The acceptance of retarded children in junior high academic and nonacademic regular classes. *Exceptional Children, 35,* 617–623.

Rynders, J., Johnson, R., Johnson, D. W., & Schmidt, B. (1980). Effects of cooperative goal structuring in producting positive interaction between Down's Syndrome and nonhandicapped teenagers: Implications for mainstreaming. *American Journal of Mental Deficiencies, 85,* 268–273.

Saunders, B. (1971). The effect of the emotionally disturbed child in the public school classroom. *Psychology in the Schools, 8,* 23–26.

Scranton, T., & Ryckman, D. (1979). Sociometric status of learning disabled children in an integrative program. *Journal of Learning Disabilities, 12,* 49–54.

Secord, R., & Backman, C. (1964). Interpersonal congruency, perceived similarity, and friendship. *Sociometry, 27,* 115–127.

Semmel, M., Gottlieb, J., & Robinson, N. (1979). Mainstreaming: Perspectives on educating handicapped children in the public school. In D. Berliner (Ed.), *Review of research in education* (pp. 223–279) (*Vol. 7*). Washington, DC: American Educational Research Association.

Sheare, J. (1975). *The relationship between peer acceptance and self-concept of children in grades 3 through 6.* Doctoral dissertation, Pennsylvania State University. (University Microfilms No. 76–10, 783).

Siller, J., & Chipman, A. (1967). *Attitudes of the nondisabled toward the physically disabled.* New York: New York University.

Siperstein, F., Bopp, M., & Bak, J. (1978). Social status of learning disabled students. *Journal of Learning Disabilities, 11,* 49–53.

Skon, L., Johnson, D. W., & Johnson, R. (1981). Cooperative peer interaction versus individual competition and individualistic efforts: Effects on the acquisition of cognitive reasoning strategies. *Journal of Educational Psychology, 73,* 83–92.

Slavin, R., & Karweit, N. (1979). *An extended cooperative learning experience in the elementary school.* Paper presented at the annual convention of the American Psychological Association, New York.

Smith, K., Johnson, D. W., & Johnson, R. (1981). Can conflict be constructive? Controversy versus concurrence seeking in learning groups. *Journal of Educational Psychology, 73,* 651–663.

Smith, K., Johnson, D. W., & Johnson, R. (1982). Effects of cooperative and individualistic instruction on the achievement of handicapped, regular, and gifted students. *Journal of Social Psychology, 116,* 277–283.

Stephan, W., & Rosenfield, D. (1978a). Effects of desegregation on racial attitudes. *Journal of Personality and Social Psychology, 36,* 795–804.

Stephan, W., & Rosenfield, D. (1978b). The effects of desegregation on racial relations and self-esteem. *Journal of Educational Psychology, 70,* 670–679.

Stephan, W., & Rosenfield, D. (1979). Black self-rejection: Another look. *Journal of Educational Psychology, 71,* 706–716.

Stephan, W., & Rosenfield, D. (1980). Racial and ethnic stereotypes. In A. Miller (Ed.), *In the eye of the beholder: Contemporary issues in stereotyping.* New York: Holt, Rinehart & Winston.

Stulac, J. (1975). *The self-fulfilling prophecy: Modifying the effects of a unidimensional perception of academic competence in task-oriented groups.* Unpublished doctoral dissertation, Stanford University.

Tajfel, H. (1969). Cognitive aspects of prejudice. *Journal of Social Issues, 25,* 79–97.

Tajfel, H. (1970). Experiments in intergroup discrimination. *Scientific American, 223(2),* 96–102.

Tjosvold, D., & Johnson, D. W. (1978). Controversy within a cooperative or competitive context and cognitive perspective-taking. *Contemporary Educational Psychology, 3,* 376–386.

Tjosvold, D., Johnson, D. W., & Johnson, R. (1981). Effect of partner's effort and ability on liking for partner after failure on a cooperative task. *The Journal of Psychology, 109,* 147–152.

Tjosvold, D., Johnson, D. W., & Johnson, R. (1984). Influence strategy, perspective-taking, and relationships between high and low power individuals in cooperative and competitive contexts. *The Journal of Psychology, 116,* 187–202.

Tjosvold, D., Marino, P., & Johnson, S. (1977). The effects of cooperation and competition on student reactions to inquiry and didactic learning. *Journal of Research in Science Teaching, 14,* 281–288.

Trent, R. (1957). The relation between expressed self-acceptance and expressed attitudes toward Negroes and whites among Negro children. *Journal of Genetic Psychology, 91,* 25–31.

Turnure, J., & Zigler, E. (1958). Outer-directedness in the problem solving of normal and retarded students. *Journal of Abnormal and Social Psychology, 57,* 379–388.

Vacc, N. (1972). Long-term effects of special class intervention for emotionally disturbed children. *Exceptional Children, 39,* 15–22.

Wechsler, H., Suarez, A., & McFadden, M. (1975). Teachers' attitudes toward the education of physically handicapped children: Implications for implementation of Massachusetts Chapter 766. *Journal of Education, 157,* 17–24.

Whiteman, M., & Lukoff, I. (1964). A factorial study of sighted people's attitudes toward blindness. *Journal of Social Psychology, 64,* 339–353.

Worchel, S. (1979). Cooperation and the reduction of intergroup conflict: Some determining factors. In W. Austin & S. Worchel (Eds.), *The social psychology of intergroup relations.* (pp. 262–273). Monterey, CA: Brooks/Cole.

Wright, B. (1960). *Physical disability—a psychological approach.* New York: Harper & Row.

Yager, S., Johnson, D. W., Johnson, R., & Snider, B. (1985). The effects of cooperative and individualistic learning experiences on positive and negative cross-handicap relationships. *Contemporary Educational Psychology, 10,* 127–138.

Zajonc, R., & Marin, I. (1967). Cooperation, competition, and interpersonal attitudes in small groups. *Psychonomic Science, 7,* 271–272.

BIBLIOGRAPHY

STUDY 1: Johnson, R., Rynders, J., Johnson, D. W., Schmidt, B., & Haider, S. (1979). Interaction between handicapped and nonhandicapped teenagers as a function of situational goal structuring: Implications for mainstreaming. *American Educational Research Journal, 16*(2), 161–167.

STUDY 2: Martino, L., & Johnson, D. W. (1979). Cooperative and individualistic experiences among disabled and normal children. *Journal of Social Psychology, 107,* 177–183.

STUDY 3: Cooper, L., Johnson, D. W., Johnson, R., & Wilderson, F. (1980). The effects of cooperative, competitive, and individualistic experiences on interpersonal attraction among heterogeneous peers. *Journal of Social Psychology, 111,* 243–252.

STUDY 4: Rynders, J., Johnson, R., Johnson, D. W., & Schmidt, B. (1980). Producing positive interaction among Down's Syndrome and nonhandicapped teenagers through cooperative goal structuring. *American Journal of Mental Deficiency, 85,* 268–273.

STUDY 5: Armstrong, B., Johnson, D. W., & Balow, B. (1981). Effects of cooperative vs. individualistic learning experiences on interpersonal attraction between learning-disabled and normal-progress elementary school students. *Contemporary Educational Psychology, 6,* 102–109.

STUDY 6: Johnson, D. W., & Johnson, R. (1981a). The integration of the handicapped into the regular classroom: Effects of cooperative and individualistic instruction. *Contemporary Educational Psychology, 6,* 344–353.

STUDY 7: Johnson, R., & Johnson, D. W. (1981). Building friendships between handicapped and nonhandicapped students: Effects of cooperative and individualistic instruction. *American Educational Research Journal, 18,* 415–423.

STUDY 8–11: Nevin, A., Johnson, D. W., & Johnson, R. (1982). Effects of group and individual contingencies on academic performance and social relations of special needs students. *Journal of Social Psychology, 116,* 41–59.

STUDY 12: Johnson, R., & Johnson, D. W. (1982). Effects of cooperative and competitive learning experiences on interpersonal attraction between handicapped and nonhandicapped students. *Journal of Social Psychology, 116,* 211–219.

STUDY 13: Smith, K., Johnson, D. W., & Johnson, R. (1982). Effects of cooperative and individualistic instruction on the achievement of handicapped, regular, and gifted students. *Journal of Social Psychology, 116,* 277–283.

STUDY 14: Johnson, D. W., & Johnson, R. (1982a). Effects of cooperative and individualistic instruction on handicapped and nonhandicapped students. *Journal of Social Psychology, 118*, 257–268.

STUDY 15: Johnson, R., & Johnson, D. W. (1983). Effects of cooperative, competitive and individualistic learning experiences on social development. *Exceptional Children, 49*, 323–329.

STUDY 16: Johnson, R., Johnson, D. W., DeWeerdt, N., Lyons, V., & Zaidman, B. (1983). Integrating severely adaptively handicapped seventh-grade students into constructive relationships with nonhandicapped peers in science class. *American Journal of Mental Deficiency, 87*, 611–618.

STUDY 17: Johnson, D. W., & Johnson, R. (1984a). Building acceptance of differences between handicapped and nonhandicapped students: The effects of cooperative and individualistic problems. *Journal of Social Psychology, 122*, 257–267.

STUDY 18: Johnson, D. W., & Johnson, R. (1985). Mainstreaming hearing-impaired students: The effect of effort in communicating on cooperation and interpersonal attraction. *Journal of Psychology, 119*(1), 31–44.

STUDY 19: Johnson, D. W., & Johnson, R. (in press). Classroom conflict: Controversy versus debate in learning groups. *American Educational Research Journal.*

STUDY 20: Yager, S., Johnson, R., Johnson, D. W., & Snider, B. (1985). The effects of cooperative and individualistic learning experiences on positive and negative cross-handicap relationships. *Contemporary Educational Psychology, 10*, 127–138.

STUDY 21: Johnson, D. W., & Johnson, R. (1984b). The effects of intergroup cooperation and intergroup competition on ingroup and outgroup cross-handicap relationships. *Journal of Social Psychology, 124*, 85–94.

STUDY 22: Johnson, R., Johnson, D. W., Scott, L., & Ramolae, B. (1985). Effects of single-sex and mixed sex cooperative interaction on science achievement and attitudes and cross-handicap and cross-sex relationships. *Journal of Research in Science Teaching, 22*, 207–220.

STUDY 23: Mesch, D., Lew, M., Johnson, D. W., & Johnson, R. (1985). Isolated teenagers, cooperative learning, and social skills training. Manuscript submitted for publication.

STUDY 24–25: Johnson, D. W., Johnson, R., Warring, D., & Maruyama, G. (in press). Different cooperative learning procedures and cross-handicap relationships. *Exceptional Children.*

14 Learning Experiences. . . . An Alternative Program for Preschoolers and Parents: A Comprehensive Service System for the Mainstreaming of Autistic-Like Preschoolers

Phillip S. Strain
Bonnie Jamieson
Marilyn Hoyson
University of Pittsburgh

Though a number of sound educational models have been developed to serve school-age autistic children in developmentally homogeneous environments, few models exist for the systematic integration and education of autistic children with normally developing peers. Integrated models for preschool-age children are even more scarce (Nordquist, 1978).

Where attempts have been made to establish integrated preschool programs with less handicapped children, social and instructional interactions between normally developing and disabled youngsters have often been left to chance (Strain & Kerr, 1979). With autistic children, who by definition exhibit profound social isolation, such a laissez-faire approach to social integration cannot be justified.

The systematic efforts to enhance the social behavior repertoire of autistic children have been focused mainly on the manipulation of reinforcement contingencies administered by teachers or other adults (Hingtgen, Sanders, & DeMyer, 1965; Lovaas & Koegel, 1973). For the vast majority of cases, these efforts have produced transient effects (Strain & Fox, 1981). More recently, normal peers have been taught to act as trainers to improve the social repertoires of young autistic children (Ragland, Kerr, & Strain, 1978; Strain, Kerr, & Ragland,

1979). In contrast to outcomes produced with adults, peer interventionists have been successful in building skills in their peers that better generalize to new settings and maintain across time (Hendrickson, Strain, Tremblay, & Shores, 1982). The peer-mediated interventions that have been used are particularly attractive from an efficiency standpoint. Specifically, nonhandicapped or less handicapped children can provide one-to-one instruction to disabled peers that would not be possible with an adults-only model of intervention.

Although various peer-mediated models of intervention have been used in brief treatment outcome studies, no attempts have been made to incorporate a peer-based model of child treatment into a total preschool program. In the treatment program described herein, Learning Experiences. . .An Alternative Program for Preschoolers and Parents (LEAP), normally developing children, age 3 to 5 years were taught systematically to aide in the instruction of their autistic-like classmates. The specific curriculum content of that instruction was individualized with the aide of a unique model for lesson design and implementation.

In this chapter, the essential elements of peer involvement and the curriculum planning process are described. For evaluative studies on program components, the reader is referred to Hoyson, Jamieson, and Strain (1984) and Odom, Hoyson, Jamieson, and Strain (1984). Briefly, these studies show that:

1. On areas targeted for intervention, the normally developing children in our experimental intervention program make two-months of developmental gain for each month they are in the program.
2. When compared to a group of similar age, normally developing children, the nonhandicapped children in our program engage in similar levels of appropriate language, social interaction, and disruptive behavior.
3. On developmental outcomes, LEAP handicapped children are making approximately twice the rate of progress when compared to comparison subjects.
4. Levels of deviant, disruptive behaviors by LEAP children show significant improvement in 1 to 3 months of treatment, whereas similar behaviors by comparison children have not changed appreciably.

Prior to offering a description of peer-involvement and the curricular process, a few preparatory remarks regarding the overall conceptual model of LEAP are in order. The LEAP model is designed to match, as closely as possible, three primary learning characteristics of autistic-like children.

First, because these severely handicapped children often do not show evidencc of generalized behavior change across instructional stimuli or settings, it is necessary to develop curriculum targets that represent functional skills in the settings in which the children will be served following program participation. Therefore, the development of the curricula began with an empirically-based assessment of those competencies exhibited by similarly handicapped children and normally developing children judged to be making a satisfactory adjustment by significant social agents in schools, day care facilities, and other community agencies. The descriptive data may be found in McConnell, Strain, Kerr, Stagg, Lenkner, and Lambert (in press) and Strain (1983; 1984).

Second, because children with autistic-like behaviors tend not to maintain behavioral gains after leaving treatment programs, it is essential that indigenous treatment agents, including parents, teachers from future placement settings, and peers, be actively involved in educational programming. In the LEAP model, extensive parent involvement is offered. Because of the close ties between the targets of instruction for peer- *and* parent-mediated instruction, the parent component is also reviewed in this chapter. Also, the training/liaison efforts of the program are aimed specifically at training receiving teachers and other relevant personnel in educational procedures that have demonstrated effectiveness with individual children. Finally, carefully programmed use of peers as instructional agents is a major program emphasis.

Third, because children who exhibit autistic-like behaviors often display learning characteristics (i.e., stimulus overselectivity, unpredictable responsiveness to traditional reinforcing events, and seemingly unexplainable loss of previously acquired discriminations and skills) that result in dramatic day-to-day variations in observed levels of appropriate responding during instructional sessions, it is essential that each period of intervention be precisely planned, implemented, and evaluated. Only in this way can those setting conditions and consequent events responsible for erratic responding be identified and altered. Moreover, daily monitoring of child behavior (and, on occasion, teacher behavior) is necessary to implement educational technologies (e.g., trend analysis) that offer teachers hypotheses about the immediate temporal causes of behavior.

ESSENTIAL ELEMENTS OF PEER INVOLVEMENT

The specific utilization of peers as instructional resources takes three forms in the LEAP model: (a) peers as indirect mediators of behavior change; (b) peers as behavioral models; and, (c) peers as direct agents of training. Each of these procedures is described here.

Peers as Indirect Mediators of Behavior Change

Group-oriented contingencies represent one of the most thoroughly researched procedures for managing children's behavior in classroom settings (Litow & Pumroy, 1975). Not only have these procedures been shown to be as effective as individually based contingencies, but they also have the advantage of being cost-effective vis-a-vis effort required to implement, likelihood of being used again, and potential positive side effects.

Of the various group-oriented strategies, interdependent reinforcement contingencies seem to be most efficient. As utilized by Gamble and Strain (1979), interdependent conditions are said to exist when all members of a group must perform to a minimum standard before any member of the group can achieve some positive consequence. Of course, the procedure makes for easy individualization in that performance standards and behaviors can be selected on a child-by-child basis.

Putting this information into practice, the following procedures are implemented:

1. Normally functioning age-peers and handicapped children participate in a classroom behavior management program based on interdependent contingencies. For example, during a 15-minute group instructional period, each of the nonhandicapped children may have a behavioral goal of answering 100% of teacher questions correctly. During this same time period, one of the handicapped children may have the goal of remaining in the assigned seat for 80% of the time; another handicapped child may have the goal of looking at the teacher when spoken to on 80% of the opportunities; still another handicapped child may have the goal of not body-rocking more than 10% of the time interval. For any of the children to receive a positive consequence, each must meet their own goal.

2. Prior to beginning each instructional period in which the group interdependent contingency is in effect (those situations in which children have the opportunity to influence each other's performance), the teacher announces each child's goal for that time period.

3. At the end of designated instructional periods, the teacher will announce each child's goal attainment, where appropriate. Then, the handicapped children are prompted to distribute reinforcers to class peers.

Peers as Behavioral Models

One of the more often-voiced arguments for the integration of handicapped and nonhandicapped children is that the normally developing children will model appropriate behaviors for handicapped youngsters (Bricker, 1978; Guralnick, 1976; Peck, Cooke, & Apolloni, 1981). There is little doubt that normal peers indeed provide (at least on an informal basis) appropriate behavioral models. However, the mere availability of appropriate models in no way sets the occasion for handicapped children to *imitate* these behaviors. With autistic-like children who display severe behavioral handicaps, this situation is further complicated by the general lack of observational learning skills exhibited by these youngsters. To realistically hope to utilize the influence of appropriate behavioral models, a number of preconditions must be established:

1. First, each of the handicapped children participate in a Peer Imitation Training (PIT) program as outlined by Peck et al. (1981). Briefly, in this procedure, a handicapped and nonhandicapped child are paired together for training. The nonhandicapped child is trained initially to model specific appropriate behaviors by an accompanying teacher. The teacher then prompts the handicapped child to imitate the modeled behavior and subsequently reinforces correct responding. Daily PIT sessions typically include 20–30 opportunities for children to imitate appropriate behaviors. After predesignated criteria have been met on specific behaviors, the teacher begins a response-dependent fading procedure so that prompts and reinforcement events are systematically reduced. This response-dependent fading procedure has been validated with severely handicapped preschool children by Timm, Strain and Eller (1979).

2. In addition to the PIT procedures, which are designed to develop basic prerequisite skills in order for these severely handicapped children to profit from exposure to appropriate behavioral models, all daily group activities (e.g., free play, worktable time, snack time) are structured so as to enhance the likelihood of positive, appropriate behaviors being imitated by target children. The later description here of a prototypic worktable time will serve to illustrate how grouping, curriculum planning, and instructional components are arranged to facilitate the modeling of appropriate behavior.

Obviously, if children do not have the opportunity to observe repeated examples of appropriate behaviors, then no observational learning effects will be obtained (Strain, Shores, & Kerr, 1976). Therefore, an initial consideration is the grouping and physical placement of children that set the occasion for opportunities to observe competent behavior. In free-play periods, our research on autistic-like children suggests that dyad grouping and a limited number of cooperative-use toys are important elements of successful social behavior programming (Strain & Kerr, 1979). We also suspect that dyad groupings and a limited number of preselected behaviors to be imitated will lead to optimum effects in the worktable setting. Specifically, children are seated next to one another with a supervising adult stationed behind both children.

In terms of curriculum planning issues, it is most important that modeled behaviors be those that the handicapped child already exhibits, but at an inconsistent or unacceptable level. In the group worktable setting, behaviors likely to be selected for imitation include: inseat behavior, requesting help, functional object use.

Probably the most consistent finding regarding the implementation of the observational learning paradigm is that the model child's behavior must be obviously reinforced by events that are also reinforcing to handicapped children (Strain & Hill, 1979; Strain & Kerr, 1979). Accordingly, teachers implement the following instructional procedures: (a) provide direct verbal, and where necessary, physical prompts for handicapped children to observe their peers (in the worktable example, "Jonathan, watch Tim hammer"); (b) provide direct reinforcers (any which are effective with *both* children) to the nonhandicapped child while specifying the desired behavior(s) ("Tim, I like the way you hit the peg with the hammer, you earned a piece of pretzel"); (c) provide direct verbal and, where necessary, physical prompts to the handicapped child to initiate imitative behavior ("Jonathan, use your hammer like Tim"); (d) provide direct positive consequences to the handicapped child for approximations toward accurate imitation.

The outlined procedures do not represent an instructional departure from PIT; rather, they reflect an attempt to program for the generalization of observational learning skills across settings, model children, and target behaviors.

Peers as Direct Agents of Training

The successful use of young nonhandicapped age-peers as intervention agents for socially withdrawn children requires attention to: (a) the selection of peer trainers; and, (b) training of peer trainers.

Selection of Peer Trainers. An analysis of the literature that reports on the use of peers as training agents suggests a few distinct criteria for selection of peer helpers. The following criteria are used in the LEAP program:

1. The student must attend school regularly, to insure uninterrupted training.
2. The student must display positive, unprompted social initiations toward peers during free-play periods.
3. The student must respond positively to social initiations from peers.
4. The student must follow adult directions reliably.

Unlike many job descriptions, this one does not include minimum age (peer helpers as young as 36 months have been trained successfully), previous experience (only one had prior training as a peer helper), or a certain type of education (several peer helpers themselves have been enrolled in classes for behaviorally disordered or mentally retarded children, e.g., Ragland, Kerr, & Strain, 1978).

In prior training efforts, we have found that teacher nominations based on the above listed criteria provide a reliable and cost-effective selection procedure (Strain & Kerr, 1979).

Training of Peer Trainers. Teaching a student to modify the isolate behavior of peers seems like a major undertaking. Yet, the previous studies have relied on a rather simple training procedure, which took place before any actual play sessions. The following two-part strategy was used at LEAP:

1. The children are given an explanation of the task, such as, "Try hard to get the others to play with you."

2. "Training to expect rejection" is accomplished through a roleplay in which the adult ignores every other initiation by the peer helper, explains this behavior, and, finally, encourages the peer helper: "Keep trying, even when children don't play at first" (Strain, Shores, & Timm, 1977).

These training steps are repeated in 20-minute daily sessions (usually four), until the peer helper can reliably make social bids to the occasionally reluctant adult.

Peer helpers rehearse in the actual play setting and use toys that are selected for the isolate children. The teacher will occasionally praise the peer helper's effort during actual treatment sessions.

The successful involvement of peers in the LEAP program, or in any other program, is not just dependent on well-structured interventions to shape good teaching skills. Equally important is the "what" of instruction, or the curriculum content to which children are exposed via peer-mediation.

ESSENTIAL CURRICULAR ELEMENTS

The descriptive material here highlights: (a) assessment/curricular linkage in LEAP; (b) planning lessons that include objectives for handicapped and nonhandicapped children; and (c) systematic data collection procedures.

Assessment/Curricular Linkage

The initial component of the LEAP curriculum model involves frequent child assessment; the results of which dictate the scope and sequence (curriculum) of instruction on a child-by-child basis. As children (handicapped and nonhandicapped) enter the intervention program, the *Learning Accomplishment Profile* (LAP) (LeMay, Griffin, & Sanford, 1977) is administered; and, the LAP is repeated at 3-month intervals.

The results of assessment in each skill area are reported as a basal level (age-level at which items are easy for the child) and a ceiling level (age-level at which items are difficult for the child). The basal and ceiling level are expressed as developmental ages in months.

Once developmental levels for the basal and ceiling are identified, the "functioning range" is established. Objectives are chosen for each child that fall within the functioning range in each skill area. For example, a child who is functioning in fine motor writing (FMW) between the 30–42 month level may have an objective such as copying a circle, which is a 36-month level skill. The functioning ranges in each area, and a list of all the objectives chosen for the child are listed on a TRIIC Objective Sheet (Fig. 14.1). This sheet is updated after every three-month diagnostic assessment.

For normally developing children, four functional skill objectives are initially chosen in four different skill areas: fine motor, gross motor, cognitive, and language. Behavioral objectives are then written for each skill and entered on the TRIIC Objective Listing. (See Fig. 14.2). Mastery of these skills is assessed after two weeks of classroom training. At the end of two weeks, all nonhandicapped children are assessed to determine if they have met the criteria as stated for each objective. If they have met criteria, four new objectives are chosen for the following two weeks. This test–teach–test procedure is continued throughout the normally developing children's stay in the program.

For the handicapped children, objectives are based on individual need. Some children may have three language objectives, one gross motor, one fine motor, two behavioral, and one independent functioning objective targeted at the same time. The objectives are task analyzed and written on the TRIIC Goal Plan Form (Fig. 14.3). Unlike for normally developing children, data is collected daily until the child meets the stated criterion. When an objective is completed, a new one is selected. Additional objectives are selected at any time depending on the needs of the child.

In sum, the Assessment/Curriculum Linkage at LEAP permits: An individualized curriculum for handicapped and nonhandicapped children; Frequent assessment of intervention impact; and Opportunities to revise curricular objectives as children progress.

Developing individualized goals for handicapped and nonhandicapped children is a necessary, but not sufficient, step to achieve highly functional instruction. After individual goals are established, a system must be available whereby those goals can be taught in a peer-mediated group context.

Planning Lessons that Include Objectives for All the Children in the Group

Individual objectives selected for each child (both handicapped and nonhandicapped) are listed with a corresponding curriculum code (Fig. 14.4). In order to plan a lesson that meets the needs of all of the children in the group, a series of planning steps must be followed:

1. List the objectives for each child in each skill area (e.g., language, motor, and cognitive. (A sample listing in language for a class of children at different functioning levels is included in Fig. 14.4.).

2. Locate the curriculum code (Fig.14.5) corresponding to the objectives in the *TRIIC INDEX* (The *TRIIC INDEX* contains a listing of the number of lessons for each skill or objective in the *Bag of TRIICS* (card file of lessons). Fig. 14.5 displays a list of the lessons developed for Language-Receptive.

NAME JOHN Birthdate: 8-12-79

Age Range: FMM: 30–42 LN: 24–36 CM: 30–42 GMOM: 42–54 SH: ______

FMW: 30–42 LC: 36–42 CC: — GMB: 36–48

OBJECTIVE STATEMENT	AGE	CODE	DATE BEGAN	DATE ACHIEVED
Cuts paper with scissors	36	FM20		
Copies a circle from a model	36	FM16	10-28-83	11-21-83
Begins to climb ladder or jungle gym	36	GM21		
Stands on one foot for 8 seconds	36	GM24		
Catches thrown playground ball with arms and body	48	GM27a		
Throws ball to specific target	48	GM36		
Names primary colors when asked	36	CRR2	11-2-83	
Labels objects based on verbal information given	36	CRR5		
Points to correct size when named	36	CMR2		
Counts three objects	36	CMR4		
Indicates which object was removed from a few others	36	CVM4	10-14-83	
Groups objects that vary only in color	36	CCG3	10-14-83	
Uses three word sentences	33	LE13		
Names objects by use	36	LE18		
Uses Please and Thank you	36	LE24	10-14-83	
Points to unfamiliar pictures	36	LR13		

Fig. 14.1 TRIIC objective sheet.

SETTING: 1. 1–1 2. Groups 3. Workjobs 4. Other

OBJECTIVE	SETTING	DATE ACCOMPLISHED
When presented with three colors, red, blue, and yellow, the child will name each color when asked. Two times per color, 100% each time.	Lesson Group	
When playground ball is thrown underhand, child will catch with arms and body. Three out of three times.	Gross Motor	
When asked questions such as, what do we sit on?, child will name object. Answer 5 different questions correct.	Language Group	

Fig. 14.2 TRIIC objective listing.

TITLE: Responds to name | RELATED OBJECTIVES: Socialization | MATERIALS: None

STUDENT: Rick | CURRICULUM AREA: Language | PRESENT GROUP: Large

OBJECTIVE: When the name "Rick" is spoken by a teacher or child, Rick will turn toward the person that said the name and maintain eye contact for 3 seconds, 3 trials for 3 consecutive days.

PROCEDURE: Do procedure during every group activity. Record data for 3 activities per day.

STEPS:	CORRECTION PROCEDURE:	CRITERION	REINFORCEMENT	SCHEDULE OF REINFORCEMENT
1. The teacher will say "Rick" and physically prompt the child to turn his head toward her.		3 trials for 3 consecutive days.	Give child a favorite toy and praise.	Continuous
2. The teacher will say "Rick" and will turn his head toward the teacher.	Teacher will physically prompt child by touching the top of his head.	" "	" "	" "
3. The teacher will say "Rick" and child will turn his head toward the teacher.	" " "	" "	Give child any toy and verbal praise.	" "
4. " " "	" " "	" "	Verbal praise	" "
5. Child will say "Rick" and the child will turn his head toward the child who called his name.	" " "	" "	" "	" "
6. Objective as stated above.				

PROGRAM CHANGE CRITERION: 5 days not meeting criterion unless upward trend.

GENERALIZATION: Throughout the day

MAINTENANCE: 2 weeks after criterion is met

Fig. 14.3 TRIIC goal plan form.

3. Choose a lesson from the listing and decide whether to: (a) use it; or (b) select another lesson from the listing. (Any of the other curriculum codes corresponding to the objectives for the class of children may be used in the same manner to select a lesson.) Lesson #009 (Fig. 14.6) is appropriate for children with the needs or objectives displayed in Fig. 14.4. It has skills corresponding to the objectives of the children. (Each lesson card included in the *Bag of TRIIC's* has the skills contained in that lesson on the reverse of the card.)

NAME	OBJECTIVE	CURRICULUM CODE
Rick	Responds to name	LR1
John	Points to colors	CRR1
Joey	Points to color word	CRR16
Sally	Matches colors	CVD2
Nancy	Names colors	CRR9
Phil	Responds to in and on	LR9
Jill	Recognizes color words	CRR16
Marcia	Follows simple commands	LR3
Michelle	Identifies children in class	S5
Scott	Reads simple sentences	CRR24

Fig. 14.4 Sample objective listing.

Curriculum Codes	*Lesson Numbers*
LR1-24m:	005, 340, 293, 009
LR2-24m:	008, 190, 215, 225, 227, 228, 263, 268, 269, 340, 342, 395, 303, 494, 495
LR3-24m:	004, 016, 028, 038, 081, 082, 100, 129, 139, 184, 185, 213, 215, 263, 342, 294, 479, 516
LR4-24m:	188, 263, 268, 269, 340, 395, 477, 490, 497, 516, 517
LR5-24m:	017, 064, 065, 067, 068, 077, 078, 089, 115, 186, 198, 207, 221, 284, 342, 343, 245, 303, 465, 466, 467 476, 477, 464, 511
LR6-24m:	043, 044, 078, 114, 165, 186, 207, 216, 263, 395, 472, 517
LR7-24m:	017, 043, 089, 119, 187, 231, 232, 291, 292, 303, 515
LR8-24m:	263, 009
LR9-30m:	063, 067, 068, 077, 078, 143, 191, 192, 197, 198, 206, 342, 517
LR10-33m:	263, 340, 249, 250, 291, 518
LR11-33m:	128, 277, 340, 518
LR12-24m:	027, 165, 237, 280, 281, 283, 284, 274, 343, 518
LR13-36m:	010, 027, 237, 284, 343, 518
LR13a-36m:	291, 292, 511
LR14-36m:	009, 006, 197, 016
LR15-36m:	008, 040, 186, 187, 192, 198, 215, 303, 472, 479, 487, 510, 517
LR16-48m:	010, 477, 491, 516, 517, 518
LR17-48m:	130, 274, 491, 518
LR18-48m:	064, 065, 066, 067, 186, 342, 303, 517
LR19-48m:	291, 292, 511

Fig. 14.5 Triic, index, language receptive.

Materials: 5 rubber ducks 2′ high, each a different color, 5 bowls of water, the color of the bowls will match the ducks. Word printed: red, green, orange, yellow, blue; and sentences: The duck is in the water; The duck is on the grass; The duck is on the road; The red duck is in the water. An easel and a table.

Procedure: Children will sit in a semi-circle around the table where the ducks and the bowls of water are setting. The children will be told that they are going to "play with the ducks"; The teacher will call each child up to the front of the room for his or her turn. Using the list of needs, the teacher will ask questions such as: "Find the yellow duck"; Find the word "Red"; "Give the red duck to Joey"; "Put the blue duck in the blue pond." Each child must have a turn to play with the ducks.

Fig. 14.6 Sample lesson.

Systematic Data Collection.

In order to maintain up-to-date Individual Program Plans (IPPs), data is collected daily on the individual objectives of all handicapped children. In the sample list of objectives and children (Fig. 14.4), the handicapped children and their Language Objective or need are:

Rick	Responds to name ______
Sally	Matches colors ______
Marcia	Follows simple commands ______
Michelle	Identifies children in the class ______
Phil	Responds to in and on ______

All objectives chosen for handicapped children are written on the *TRIIC Goal Plan Sheet* and task analyzed as appropriate. A sample completed goal plan can be seen in Fig. 14.3. A goal plan such as this must be assessed daily to meet the requirements of the Criteria section. In this goal plan, the child must perform each step three times correctly during a lesson for 3 consecutive days. Daily review of the data is necessary to appropriately move the child from one step to the next of the goal plan. In the sample lesson, the child is on Step 3: When the teacher says, "Rick," Rick will turn and look at the teacher for 3 seconds. Then the teacher (or peer) will reinforce him verbally and give him a toy. This must be done three times during the lesson. Also, in this lesson there are four other children who must have the data on their goal plans assessed daily. In order to keep this information efficiently, the TRIIC for Mainstreaming utilizes a *TRIIC Goal Plan Data Collection Sheet* (see Fig. 14.7). This sheet is placed on a clipboard that is available during the lesson to tally the correct and incorrect responses of each handicapped child in the lesson group.

Period of Day	Child Name	OBJECTIVE	Week of M	T	W	Th	F
	Rick Marsha Phil Michele	Matches simple objects (5 objects) Points to primary colors (red, blue, green, 3 times each) Matches letters and numerals (5 of each) Points to 1–5 when named (2 for each number)					
	Rick Marsha Phil Michele	Copy vertical line from a model (3 with verbal and physical cues) Discriminates like and different pictures on a worksheet Matches letters and numerals in worksheet format Copies shapes (triangle, square, circle, rectangle)					
	Rick	Imitates word “cookie” and “juice” given verbal cue “What do you want,” (and provide model) give two cues if necessary					
	Rick Sally Marsha Phil	Responds to name for 3/3 trials Matches colors (4 of 5 colors) Follows simple command (3 commands) Responds to in and on					
	Rick Marsha Phil Michele	Push a ball given verbal cue (3 trials) Catch ball with hands and body (3 trials) Skip alternating feet (for 6 foot distance) Jump over three inch rope (3 trials)					
	Rick Phil	Complete or carry through 3 tasks in each free play area (physically take child through, fade prompts till independent) At beginning of each area tell him to “talk nicely to your friends” reinforce intermittently					
	Michele	Identify children in the class (for 10 children)					

Fig. 14.7 TRIIC goal data collection sheet.

In sum, Systematic Data Collection in TRIIC permits: (a) Daily review of each handicapped child's goal plans; and (b) A method to record the data in an efficient manner.

Parent-Family Involvement

As indicated earlier, parents of handicapped preschoolers at LEAP are intimately involved in their child's treatment. Because the parent-as-therapist component is so central to peer involvement and the entire intervention package, it is not appropriate to evaluate or present one intervention component without the other.

Parents or guardians of target children in the program are involved in the model center at several levels: (a) Representation on the Advisory Council; (b) In-school training; and (c) In-home/community training.

Representation on Advisory Council. The growth and maintenance of the LEAP program is based on feedback from its primary consumers: children, their parents/guardians, and cooperating community agencies. Thus, the majority of the advisory council is composed of parents/guardians who have handicapped and nonhandicapped children enrolled in the program. Via this supervisory and advisory mechanism, parents have direct input into determining the structure and functioning of the program.

In-School Training. A continuum of in-school training and service options are available to parents/guardians. Services to children are, in fact, contingent on a prespecified level of parental involvement necessary to establish a sound treatment program. In-school training opportunities available to parents include the following *Orientation Modules:*

1. *Educational Intervention with Severely Disturbed, Autistic-like Children*—This module is composed of three one-hour lecture/discussions (supplemented with videotape) in which the efficacy of various interventions with the client group is reviewed, along with an introduction to how the techniques are applied in this program. Parents take an objective pre–post test over the material covered.
2. *Important Behavior Repertoires for Children Under Six*—This module is comprised of three one-hour lecture/discussions (supplemented with videotape) in which the importance of and course of development for the following competencies are presented: (a) social responsiveness; (b) verbal and gestural communication; (c) imitation of adults and peers; (d) appropriate toy use; (e) preacademic skill acquisition; (f) certain cognitive discriminations (e.g., self–others, today–yesterday–tomorrow, physical attributes of stimuli). Parents take an objective, pre–post test over a videotape to assess vocabulary and basic concept acquisition.

3. *Managing Difficult Behavior*—This module is composed of three one-hour lecture/discussions (supplemented with videotape) in which the following difficult behaviors and their treatment are reviewed: (a) opposition to requests; (b) stereotypic behavior; (c) echolalia and mutism; (d) tantruming. Parents take an objective pre–post test covering a videotape to assess basic vocabulary and concept acquisition.

The three *Orientation Modules* are offered continuously throughout the year. The goal here is not to teach techniques but to provide parents with a conceptual understanding of treatment procedures and a basic, common vocabulary so that they can function as well-informed advocates for their children and this program.

Several weeks prior to leaving the program, parents are offered the following *Exit Modules:*

1. *Monitoring IEP's*—This module is composed of three one-hour lectures/discussions regarding necessary IEP components and how to tell when the IEP is or is not being faithfully implemented. Parents are provided with needed checklists and a step-by-step procedure for IEP monitoring. Skill acquisition is assessed via rehearsals on mock IEPs and videotaped educational sequences.
2. *Evaluating and Selecting Community Services*—This module is composed of three one-hour group discussions/lectures in which parents and program staff develop specific plans for acquiring appropriate community resources for themselves and their children. Individualized plans include a delineation of resources for the following needs: (a) child medical care; (b) child dental care; (c) child day care; (d) family social service support; (e) child educational services; (f) family psychological support.

In addition to outlining a plan for resource development, parents are provided with a decision-making strategy for selecting appropriate agencies and evaluating their performance. The evaluation of this module is by permanent produce, namely, the community resource plan.

Skill training for parents during in-school activities begins immediately on entry into the program. The instruction includes both didactic and directly supervised tutoring of their own children. Each parent has a specifically-tailored skill training program in that the "field work" portion of training takes place with their own child, using the IEP objectives as instructional targets. All parents begin instruction by targeting for change their child's behavior(s) that is most difficult for them. Although parents are necessarily taught different skills to meet the educational needs of their children, all participants are provided with a core curriculum which addresses the following areas: (1) Identifying and Defining Behavior; (2) Analyzing Behavior; (3) Observing and Measuring Behavior; (4) Introduction to Positive Reinforcement; (5) How and When to Use Positive Reinforcement; (6) Preventing Misbehavior (How to set up environments to prevent misbehavior); (7) How to Weaken Misbehavior; (8) Teaching New

Behaviors I: Task Analysis, Shaping, and Chaining; (9) Teaching New Behaviors II: Assistance, Correction, and Fading; and (10) Developing and Evaluating Behavior Change Programs.

In-Home/Community Training. This component involves three levels of parent-implemented instruction for their children. First, specific child skills that are taught in school are assessed, and where necessary, also taught in home and community settings. Example competencies that have across-setting utility, and which are subject to extra-school training include: (a) appropriate social interaction skills with adults and age-peers; (b) use of communicative gestures or speech; (c) imitation of appropriate behaviors; (d) compliance to requests; (e) discriminative responding to potential danger; (f) demonstration of cognitive skills such as matching; following sequential, multiple directions; classification of objects; and basic numerosity (i.e., as many as, same number).

For these school- and home-taught skills, parents are directly replicating instructional procedures that they themselves or project teachers have demonstrated to be effective with a particular child.

In addition to the extra-school training on skills originally taught in the program, there are a number of specific behaviors that can be most logically and efficiently taught in the home and community setting. In many cases, these skills are exhibited *only* in extra-school environments. Examples of such skills include: (a) exhibiting age-appropriate behavior at the department store, grocery store or playground; (b) putting away toys, materials at the end of an activity; (c) getting food, water for self at appropriate times; (d) negotiating traffic safely with adult supervision; (e) following general rules of family; (f) performing simple, age-appropriate chores.

The final level of *In-Home/Community Training* centers on Generic Parenting Skills necessary to prevent and deal effectively with difficult behaviors (e.g., noncompliance, tantruming, physical aggression). Specific skills taught include: (a) establishing a predictable routine; (b) giving brief, clear requests (only once); (c) catching children being good; (d) using exclusionary time-out and mild aversive procedures for severe problem behaviors; and (e) giving positive feedback and support to husband/wife. These generic skills are taught during weekly home visits (1 hour in the evening). Each of the skill areas are evaluated during meeting rehearsals, practice in home, and observations in the home. Simultaneously, parents evaluate the efficacy of specific intervention procedures via their child's performance data.

SUMMARY

As emphasized by Guralnick (this volume), positive social outcomes of preschool mainstreaming are far from secured by simply providing handicapped children increased access to normally developing peers. We would add that simply providing intervention on social skills is not sufficient either. Rather, it is our view that nothing short of a comprehensive service delivery system, aimed at social and *academic* integration, will yield the true potential of preschool mainstreaming.

REFERENCES

Bricker, D. (1978). A rationale for the integration of handicapped and nonhandicapped preschool children. In M. J. Guralnick (Ed.), *Early intervention and the integration of handicapped and nonhandicapped children.* Baltimore: University Park Press.

Gamble, A., & Strain, P. S. (1979). The effects of dependent and interdependent group contingencies on socially appropriate responses in classes for emotionally handicapped children. *Psychology in the Schools, 16,* 312–318.

Guralnick, M. J. (1976). The value of integrating handicapped and nonhandicapped preschool children. *American Journal of Orthopsychiatry, 46,* 236–245.

Hendrickson, M. J., Strain, P. S., Tremblay, A., & Shores, R. E. (1982). Functional effects of peer social initiations on the interactions of behaviorally handicapped children. *Behavior Modification, 6,* 323–353.

Hingtgen, J. N., Sanders, B. J., & DeMyer, M. K. (1965). Shaping cooperative responses in early childhood schizophrenics. In L. Ullmann & L. Krasner (Eds)., *Case studies in behavior modification.* New York: Holt, Rinehart, & Winston.

Hoyson, M. H., Jamieson, B., & Strain, P. S. (1984). Individualized group instruction of normally developing and autistic-like children: A description and evaluation of the LEAP curriculum model. *Journal of the Division of Early Childhood, 8,* 157–172.

Lemay, D., Griffin, P., & Sanford, A. (1977). *Learning Accomplishment Profile—Diagnostic Edition.* Chapel Hill, NC: Chapel Hill Training-Outreach Project.

Litow, L., & Pumroy, D. K. (1975). A review of classroom group-oriented contingencies. *Journal of Applied Behavior Analysis, 8,* 341–347.

Lovaas, O. I., & Koegel, R. L. (1973). Behavior modification with autistic children. In C. Thoresen (Ed.), *Behavior modification in education.* Chicago: University of Chicago Press.

McConnell, S. R., Strain, P. S., Kerr, M. M., Stagg, V., Lenkner, D. A., & Lambert, D. L. (in press). An empirical definition of elementary school adjustment: Selection of target behaviors for a comprehensive treatment program. *Behavior Modification.*

Nordquist, V. M. (1978). A behavioral approach to the analysis of peer interactions. In M. J. Guralnick (Ed.), *Early intervention and the integration of handicapped and nonhandicapped children* Baltimore: University Park Press.

Odom, S. L., Hoyson, M. H., Jamieson, B., & Strain, P. S. (in press). Effects of peer social initiations on handicapped preschooler's social interaction: Cross-setting and component analysis. *Journal of Applied Behavior Analysis.*

Peck, C. A., Cooke, T. P., & Apolloni. T. (1981). Utilization of peer imitation in therapeutic and instructional contexts. In P. S. Strain (Ed.), *Peers as classroom change agents.* New York: Plenum.

Ragland, E.U., Kerr, M. M., & Strain, P. S. (1978). Effects of peer social initiations on the behavior of withdrawn autistic children. *Behavior Modification, 2,* 565–578.

Strain, P. S., & Fox, J. E. (1981). Peers as behavior change agents for withdrawn classmates. In A. E. Kazdin, & B. Lahey (Eds.), *Advances in child clinical psychology.* New York: Plenum.

Strain, P. S., & Hill, A. D. (1979). Social interaction. In P. Wehman (Ed.), *Leisure time skills for the severely handicapped.* Baltimore: University Park Press.

Strain, P. S., & Kerr, M. M. (1979). Treatment issues in the remediation of preschool children's social isolation. *Education and Treatment of Children, 2,* 197–208.

Strain, P. S., Kerr, M. M., & Ragland, E. U. (1979). Effects of peer-mediated social initiations and prompting reinforcement procedures on the social behavior of autistic children. *Journal of Autism and Developmental Disorders, 9,* 41–54.

Strain, P. S., Shores, R. E., & Kerr, M. M. (1976). An experimental analysis of "spill-over" effects on social interaction among behaviorally handicapped preschool children. *Journal of Applied Behavior Analysis, 9,* 31–40.

Strain, P. S., Shores, R. E., & Timm, M. A. (1977). Effects of peer initiations on the social behavior of withdrawn preschool children. *Journal of Applied Behavior Analysis, 10,* 289–298.

Strain, P. S. (1983). Identification of social skill curriculum targets for severely handicapped children in mainstream preschools. *Applied Research in Mental Retardation, 4,* 369–382.

Strain, P. S. (1984). Social behavior patterns on nonhandicapped and developmentally disabled friend pairs in mainstream preschools. *Analysis and Intervention in Developmental Disabilities, 4,* 15–28.

Timm, M. A., Strain, P. S., & Eller, P. H. (1979). Effects of systematic, response-dependent fading and thinning procedures on the maintenance of child–child interaction. *Journal of Applied Behavior Analysis, 12,* 308.

Author Index

C

H

R

S

Subject Index